Global Urbanization

The City in the Twenty-First Century

Eugenie L. Birch and Susan M. Wachter, Series Editors

A complete list of books in the series is available from the publisher.

GLOBAL URBANIZATION

Edited by

Eugenie L. Birch and Susan M. Wachter

UNIVERSITY OF PENNSYLVANIA PRESS

PHILADELPHIA

Published by
University of Pennsylvania Press
Philadelphia, Pennsylvania 19104-4112

Printed in the United States of America on acid-free paper
10 9 8 7 6 5 4 3 2 1

Cataloging-in-Publication Data is available from the Library of Congress.
ISBN 978-0-8122-4284-3

Contents

PART I

Twenty-First-Century Population Prospect

Emerging Needs

Chapter 1

World Urbanization:
The Critical Issue of the Twenty-First Century

Eugenie L. Birch and Susan M. Wachter

In 2010, a majority of the world's population lived in cities, an important milestone actually reached in 2008; by 2050, this proportion will approach 70 percent. These simple facts point in two directions: looking back, they confirm the intensity with which the world has urbanized over the past fifty years and, moving forward, they mark the world's cities as the central terrain on which the critical issues of human development will play out over the course of the twenty-first century. This chapter explores the implications of these facts and frames them within broad societal goals of achieving socially inclusive economic growth, environmental sustainability and disaster-resistant resilience in the world's cities and metropolitan regions. Further, it lays a foundation for probing urbanization more deeply through emerging research methods that uncover better understandings of urban growth and development, the subject of this book.

According to UN demographers, past and future world urban growth rates are higher than those for the overall population. They estimate that between 2009 and 2050, the global urban population rate (100 percent) will dwarf the total population rate (44 percent). This prediction generally holds for individual regions, regardless of the level of development. However, the Global South (121 percent urban, 54 percent overall) will surpass the Global North (22 percent urban, 8 percent overall) with Africa showing the greatest change (167 percent urban, 122 percent overall) followed by Asia (119 percent urban, 33 percent overall).

Rates of urbanization vary not only between more and less developed countries but among regions of the Global South due to wide differences in the current size and distribution of population. Latin America and the Caribbean, for instance, have much smaller populations than

Asia or Africa and are already far more urbanized; in fact, at 79 percent urban, Latin American and the Caribbean are more urbanized even than Europe (73 percent). Accordingly, the UN predicts that in the next decades Latin America and the Caribbean will urbanize at rates (about .34 percent annually between 2009 and 2025 and .23 between 2025 and 2050) much closer to those of North America (whose projected rates are .28 and .20 percent annually for the same periods) and Europe (.36 and .37 percent annually). By contrast, Africa and Asia—at 1.10 percent for 2009–2025 and 1.07 thereafter and 1.13 and 1.03 percent annually—should see urbanization rates three to four times those of North America, Europe, or the Caribbean. By midcentury, Asia and Africa will be home to most of the world's urban population, with Asia having 54 percent and Africa having 20 percent of the total (UN 2010).

In share and sheer number, the Asian urban population overshadows all others today and will do so in the future. In 2009, it held 50 percent of the total urban population (and 60 percent of the world's population); by 2050 its 3.4 billion urban inhabitants will constitute 54 percent of all urbanites—notably, as this rise occurs, its relative share of the world's total population will decline slightly (table 1.1).

This rise of *urban* populations, with their associated development issues, calls into question the tendency of many social scientists to measure and analyze national-level data and to ignore internal spatial variation (Krugman 1991, 1998). Their reliance on such broad statistical measures as GDP and GDP-per-capita, inflation, and unemployment does not measure the right things; it misses the progress of society (Brugmann 2010). In 2008, French President Nicolas Sarkozy realized the extent of this problem when he appointed the Commission on the Measurement of Economic Performance and Social Progress (or Stiglitz Commission), calling on it to review global statistical measurements and recommend improvements. In its fall 2009 report, the commission concluded that "what we measure affects what we do; and if our measurements are flawed, decisions can be distorted"; it acknowledged that global metrics are flawed and suggested better measures, including those to assess "well-being" (economic and noneconomic aspects of people's lives) and "sustainability" (stocks of capital—natural, physical, human, and social—that can be passed on to future generations) as well as improved economic indicators (Stiglitz, Sen, and Fitoussi 2009, 4, 11). Yet the commission, in its list of recommended metrics, lacked an important dimension: the level of urbanization. This oversight misses an important indictor because high levels of urbanization are positively correlated with high levels of economic development (see Malpezzi in this volume).

Further, cities are critical players in their nations' economies. All

Table 1.1: Distribution of World Population: Total, Urban and Rural, 1975–2050 (in millions)

					Total Population						
	1975	2009	2025	2050	% change 1975–2009 (annual change)	% change 2009–2025 (annual change)	% change 2025–2050 (annual change)	% of total 1975	% of total 2009	% of total 2025	% of total 2050
WORLD	**4.1**	**6.8**	**8.0**	**9.2**	**68 (1.5)**	**17 (1.0)**	**14 (.5)**	**100**	**100**	**100**	**100**
Global North	**1**	**1.2**	**1.3**	**1.3**	**17 (0.5)**	**4 (0.2)**	**0 (−0.01)**	**26**	**18**	**16**	**14**
Global South	**3**	**5.6**	**6.7**	**7.9**	**86 (2)**	**20 (1.2)**	**17 (0.6)**	**74**	**82**	**84**	**86**
Africa	0.4	1	1.4	1.9	153 (2.6)	39 (2) 36	(1.4)	10	15	84	21
Asia	2.4	4.1	4.8	5.2	71 (1.6)	17 (0.9)	8 (0.4)	59	60	60	57
Latin America/ Caribbean	0.3	0.6	0.7	0.7	100 (1.7)	17 (0.9)	0 (0.3)	7	9	9	8
Europe	0.6	0.7	0.7	0.7	9 (0.2)	0 (−0.03)	−5 (−0.22)	17	11	9	8
North America	0.2	0.3	0.4	0.5	42 (1.1)	12 (0.8)	32 (0.5)	6	5	5	5
Oceania	0.02	0.04	0.04	0.05	(1.5)	(1.2)	(0.8)	0.5	0.5	0.5	0.6

Table 1.1: (Continued)

	Urban Population										
	1975	2009	2025	2050	% change 1975–2009 (annual change)	% change 2009–2025 (annual change)	% change 2025–2050 (annual change)	% of total 1975	% of total 2009	% of total 2025	% of total 2050
WORLD	**1.5**	**3.4**	**4.6**	**6.3**	**(2.4)**	**(1.7)**	**(1.3)**	**100**	**100**	**100**	**100**
Global North	**0.7**	**0.9**	**1**	**1.1**	**31 (0.8)**	**10 (0.6)**	**9 (0.3)**	**46**	**27**	**22**	**18**
Global South	**0.8**	**2.5**	**3.5**	**5.2**	**209 (3.3)**	**41 (2.2)**	**47 (1.6)**	**54**	**73**	**78**	**83**
Africa	0.1	0.4	0.7	1.2	269 (3.9)	66 (3.1)	86 (2.5)	7	12	15	20
Asia	0.6	1.8	2.4	3.4	201 (3.2)	39 (2)	42 (1.4)	38	50	53	54
Latin America/ Caribbean	0.2	0.5	0.6	0.7	136 (2.5)	21 (1.2)	16 (0.6)	13	14	12	10
Europe	0.4	.5	.6	.6	20 (0.6)	6 (0.3)	4 (0.2)	29	16	12	9
North America	0.2	0.3	0.3	0.4	59 (1.4)	19 (1.1)	19 (0.7)	12	8	7	6
Oceania	0.02	0.03	0.03	0.04	67 (1.4)	20 (1.2)	27 (0.1)	1	0.7	0.7	0.6

Rural Population

WORLD	**2.6**	**3.4**	**3.5**	**2.9**	**(0.9)**	**(0.12)**	**(−0.8)**	**100**	**100**	**100**	**100**	**100**
Global North	**0.4**	**0.3**	**0.3**	**0.2**	**−11**	**−16**	**−31**	**14**	**9**	**9**	**7**	**6**
Global South	**2.2**	**3.1**	**3.2**	**2.7**	**(−0.4) 41 (1)**	**(−1) 4 (0.2)**	**(−1.6) −16 (−0.7)**	**86**	**91**	**91**	**92**	**94**
Africa	0.3	0.6	0.7	0.8	96 (2)	21 (1.2)	4 (0.2)	12	18	18	21	27
Asia	1.8	2.4	2.4	1.9	33 (.8)	−1 (−0.03)	−23 (−1)	71	70	70	69	65
Latin America/ Caribbean	0.2	0.1	0.1	0.08	−5 (−0.2)	−10 (−0.7)	−25 (−1.2)	5	4	4	3	3
Europe	0.24	0.2	0.17	0.11	−14 (−0.2)	−16 (−1.1)	−36 (−1.2)	9	6	6	5	4
North America	0.6	0.6	0.57	0.4	0 (−0.5)	−10 (−1.1)	−23 (−1.8)	2	2	2	2	2
Oceania	0.06	0.11	0.12	0.13	83 (1.6)	9 (1)	8 (0.2)	0.2	0.3	0.3	0.3	0.5

Source: United Nations. 2010. *World Urbanization Prospects: The 2009 Revision.* Department of Economic and Social Affairs/Population Division: New York.

together, they produce 70 percent of the world's GDP, with individual cities or small groups of cities responsible for high percentages of their national GDPs. São Paolo, for example, accounts for 40 percent of Brazil's GDP; the hundred most populous U.S. metropolitan areas contribute 75 percent of America's GDP (Peirce and Johnson 2008). Yet the commission did not move beyond recommending national-level indicators. When challenged, a commission member dismissed the necessity of considering a spatial dimension, claiming that as a "horizontal" and not "vertical" measure, it was not useful for decision-makers.[1]

However, the aspatial approach is becoming increasingly outdated. The World Bank, for example, is now asserting that "place matters," observing that people living in highly urbanized countries with well-connected urban agglomerations integrated into the global economy have higher per capita income and life expectancies than others who do not live in these conditions. Its *World Development Report 2009: Reshaping Economic Geography* asserted: "A child born in a village far from Zambia's capital Lusaka will live half as long as a child born in New York City—and during that short life, will earn just $0.01 for every $2 a New Yorker earns" (World Bank 2009, 1).

Unquestionably, world leaders have increasing capacity to add an urban lens to their assessments should they so choose. Today's researchers have improved survey techniques, can handle massive databases, have developed mapping based on remote sensing and geographic information systems (GIS), and have crafted predictive growth models based on these data sources. While different places have varied abilities to collect data, new technologies mentioned above effectively fill gaps in information and facilitate the fine-grained approaches needed to assess urbanization and urban conditions in places throughout the world (see Sheppard and Ottichilo essays in this volume). The result would be a greater ability to tailor public and private policy and programs to address local variations. For example, supplying shelter or water to a densely settled slum is far different from servicing a rural village.

To craft research, shape analysis, and direct policy recommendations that recognize emerging spatial-demographic patterns, the World Bank, United Nations, Brookings Institution (Wolfsohn Center), Lincoln Institute of Land Policy, Rockefeller Foundation, and many others are redirecting their approaches to take into account the different characteristics and needs of urban places. They are now linking individual nations' prosperity to policies differentiated by level of urbanization and scale (e.g., national transportation infrastructure, regional water supply, local [city versus village] housing). For the World Bank, the issues are assuring the coordination of density, connectivity, and integration; for the UN, the issue is pursuit of the Millennium Development Goals with their potential for dramatically improving the lives of poor city-dwellers; for Brookings, it is eliminating urban poverty through internal and external program delivery; and for Lincoln, it is activating urban land markets and urban infrastructure provision and finance. Further, while recognizing that all parts of the world have urban concerns, these groups focus on key, fast-changing regions in Africa and Asia that will experience the highest rates of urbanization in the next forty years.

Demographers are delineating the basic outlines of contemporary and future urban arrangements, but there is ample room for more detailed research, as the essays in this volume reveal. And in fact, the twenty-first century urban research agenda encompasses growth (mapping and prediction), delivery of critical services (water, health, education, personal safety), basic support (housing, transportation, employment, food security), and municipal capacity and finance. The United Nations Department of Economic and Social Affairs/Population Division, which has monitored urban growth since 1950, annually offers broad estimates of total urban growth to 2050 and narrower estimates of urban growth by size of cities to 2025 (United Nations 2010).

The UN data offer four important insights into current and future patterns of urban development, especially with regard to the distribution of cities and their populations by city size. First, today, 1.8 billion (or 52 percent) of the world's urban population live in minor cities (under 500,000 in population). Second, of the remaining 1.7 billion (48 percent) of urbanites, slightly more than a billion (or 67 percent) live in small (500,000 to 1 million) or medium-sized (1 million to 5 million) cities (figure 1.1a). Third, the number of small cities makes up more than half (54 percent) and the medium cities another 40 percent of the world's cities with over 500,000 inhabitants; *together they are 94 percent of the total* (figure 1.1b). Despite their prominence in the popular mind, the megacity (over 10 million, or only 2 percent of the total) and the large city (5 to 10 million, or only 3 percent) are not so significant numerically as the smaller cities, yet together, the megacity and large city hold 33 percent of the urban population in cities with populations over 500,000.

Fourth, in the next two decades, the number of cities, regardless of size, will grow. By 2025 there will be a third more cities with populations over half a million—total of 1,248. Megacities and large cities will have the highest growth rates (38 and 44 percent, respectively). But even small cities will increase by about a third. And together, *small and medium-sized cities will continue to constitute 94 percent of the total* (table 1.2a). In terms of the number of people living in cities over 500,000 population, more than 40 percent will live in medium-sized cities, a fifth in megacities and another fifth in small cities in 2025 (table 1.2b).

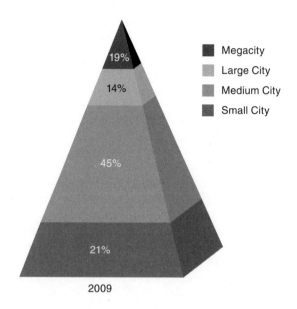

Figure 1.1a. Share of Population by City Size, 2009

This figure illustrates the distribution of population in cities over 500,000, revealing that 66 percent of the total lives in small or medium-sized cities.
Source: United Nations Department of Economic and Social Affairs/Population Division, *World Urbanization Prospects 2009* (New York, 2010).

Notably, in this picture of global urbanization and the distribution of urban population and of cities by size-category, national profiles vary. For example, 67 percent of Europeans live in places under 500,000 people and only 8 percent live in cities of five million or more. Africa has a similar profile. In contrast, Asia, Latin America/Caribbean, and North America each has about a fifth of its population living in large cities (UN 2009, 9).

With regard to overall urbanization Asia is dominant. In all size categories, it has and will continue to house 50 percent or more of total city dwellers. Furthermore, today it is home to the five fastest-growing megacities of the past quarter-century—Dhaka, Delhi, Karachi, Istanbul, and Mumbai; and in the next twenty-five years it will still be home to the five fastest-growing cities—Dhaka, Karachi, Kolkata, Mumbai, and Manila (UN 2007). In fact, it contains 55 percent of all megacities today, and by 2025, this portion will rise to 59 percent.

Globally, the continued numeric and population prominence of small- and medium-sized cities (500,000 to 5 million population), how-

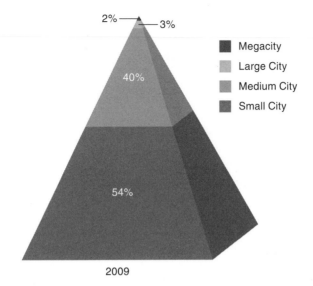

2% ———▲——— 3%

■ Megacity

□ Large City

■ Medium City

■ Small City

40%

54%

2009

Figure 1.1b. Distribution of Cities of 500,000 to 10 Million +, 2009

This figure emphasizes the importance of small and medium-sizes cities, which represent 94 percent of all cities over 500,000.
Source: United Nations Department of Economic and Social Affairs/Population Division, *World Urbanization Prospects 2009* (New York, 2010).

ever, offers both hope and reason for concern, since their size both moderates and exacerbates their difficulties. Smaller size does allow for greater flexibility in decision-making and more direct feedback between policy formulation and conditions on the ground. Yet such cities frequently lack effective local government, which results in their populations being underserved in such basic services as waste disposal, water purification, housing, and transportation (UNFPA 2007). It remains to be seen how processes of globalization will affect these smaller urban areas going forward. The growing tendency toward fiscal decentralization and governmental devolution (see Smoke in this volume) may help these cities meet their challenges more efficiently, and the increasing ability, at least in theory, of the global economy to disperse its functions may help them become more economically viable. At the same time, the world's attention will also be drawn to the plight of megacities and large cities that are challenged by the scale of their service-delivery demands. At the moment, however, these UN data serve as a reminder of both the diversity of urban form that continues to exist across the Global South and the questions and challenges cities of all sizes face in trying to shel-

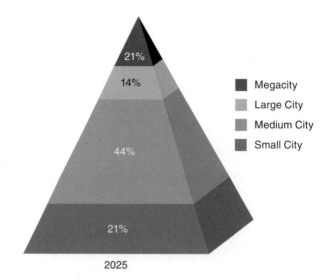

Figure 1.1c. Share of Population by City Size, 2025

This figure shows a slight shift in population shares, with megacities and large cities gaining at the expense of the small cities, though small and medium-sized cities still hold the largest share (65 percent together).
Source: United Nations Department of Economic and Social Affairs/Population Division, *World Urbanization Prospects 2009* (New York, 2010).

ter, feed, and provide services to their populations. How the Global South meets these challenges is a central question facing researchers and decision-makers alike. They will need to facilitate and promote three developmental objectives:

- socially inclusive economic growth;
- environmental sustainability;
- resilient infrastructure in the face of disaster.

Socially Inclusive Economic Growth

Questions of spatial distribution are importantly linked to questions of economic distribution. Economic development, urbanization, and spatial concentration appear to be nearly universally correlated (Masahisa, Krugman, and Venables 1999). This connection between spatial density and the concentration of economic activity is a phenomenon visible in both developed and developing countries: the coastal regions of China

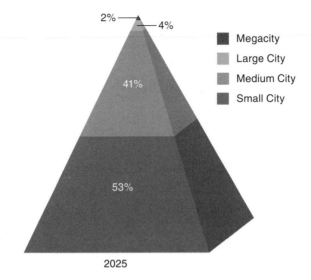

Figure 1.1d. Distribution of Cities of 500,000 to 10 Million +, 2025

This figure shows small and medium-sized cities are still dominant.
Source: United Nations Department of Economic and Social Affairs/Population Division,
World Urbanization Prospects 2009 (New York, 2010).

produce more than half the country's GDP on less than one-fifth of its land area; Greater Tokyo accounts for 40 percent of Japan's national output on only 4 percent of its land area (World Bank 2009). As many have argued, economic and spatial concentration are yoked together by economies of scale (Krugman 1991; Kanbur and Venables 2005; Malpezzi in this volume).

   Much of the foundational research on the disparities that these economies of scale create focuses on rural versus urban disparities. Some studies look at urban bias in development efforts (Lipton 1977, Agarwala 1983; Malpezzi 1990). More recently, however, finer-grained approaches that focus on the increasing inequalities within cities, or between one urban region and another, have evolved. These spatial-economic disparities present analytical hurdles since they can be obscured by national and even state- or provincial-level data (Kanbur and Venables 2005), and accurate assessment has been historically increasingly difficult at the smaller scales, particularly given the growing and shifting populations of cities in the developing world. Nonetheless, recent advances in spatial-analysis technologies are resulting in substantial progress in this area (Muvenc 2010; International Federation of Surveyors 2010; Sheppard, Seto, and Ottichilo essays in this volume).

Table 1.2a: Number of Urban Places with Population over 500,000, 1975–2025

TYPE (Population)	1975 number (% share)	2009 number (% share)	2025 number (% share)	1975–2009 percent change	1975–2025 percent change	2009–2025 percent change
Megacity (10 million +)	3 (1%)	21 (2%)	29 (2%)	600%	867%	38%
Large City (5–10 million)	15 (4%)	32 (3%)	46 (4%)	113%	207%	44%
Medium City (1–5 million)	163 (39%)	374 (40%)	506 (41%)	129%	210%	35%
Small City (500,000 to 1 million)	237 (57%)	509 (54%)	667 (53%)	115%	181%	31%
Total	418 (100%)	936 (100%)	1,248 (100%)	124%	199%	33%

Source: United Nations. 2010. *World Urbanization Prospects: The 2009 Revision*. New York: Department of Economic and Social Affairs/Population Division; United Nations 2008. *World Urbanization Prospects: 2007 Revision*. New York: Department of Economic and Social Affairs/Population Division.

Table 1.2b: Population in Urban Places with Population over 500,000, 1975–2025 (in millions)

TYPE (Population)	1975 population (% share)	2009 population (% share)	2025 population (% share)	1975–2009 % change	1975–2025 % change	2009–2025 % change
Megacity (10 million +)	53 (9%)	320 (19%)	469 (21%)	504%	785%	47%
Large City (5–10 million)	110 (18%)	225 (14%)	321 (14%)	105%	192%	43%
Medium City (1–5 million)	292 (48%)	748 (45%)	1,004 (44%)	156%	244%	34%
Small City (500,000 to 1 million)	156 (26%)	352 (21%)	466 (21%)	126%	199%	32%
Total	611 (100%)	1,645 (100%)	2,260 (100%)	169%	270%	37%

Source: United Nations. 2010. *World Urbanization Prospects: The 2009 Revision.* New York: Department of Economic and Social Affairs/Population Division.

Moreover, despite difficulties these conditions pose for methods of assessment or data collection, as a matter of policy it is clear that the relationship between economic and urban development presents countries with two crucially related imperatives: to integrate growing populations into already industrialized economies and to develop policies that enhance the informal economies found in slums and peri-urban developments.

The first issue—ensuring the inclusiveness of a city's economy—is likely to present a continuing challenge. The arrival to urban areas of workers from elsewhere, and in some cases the financial descent of workers already employed within a city's industry, produce the vast squatter settlements that are a nearly universal feature of cities in the developing world. As shown in one study, some cities in Brazil have as much as a third of their population living in settlements that are "temporary" by definition if not in fact (see Pasternak in this volume).

The prevalence of these temporary conditions—their paradoxical permanence as features of cities in the developing world—is generally understood to be an effect of the mobility of global capital (Godfrey 1995), which compels workers to move from one place to another. While urbanization was primarily understood as the effect of rural workers moving to urban areas in search of better opportunities, research over the past decades has deepened our sense of both the multiple directions and the number of factors which can influence migration. Cities grow not just when rural workers move to urban areas, but when workers move from smaller to larger cities, from one city to another, or from a city in one country to a city in another; and the variables that determine migration direction include a complex interplay of "push" and "pull" factors—differences in regional development, caste or ethnic affiliations, transportation routes, and information flows (Chapman and Prothero 1985; Kasarda and Crenshaw 1991; Prothero and Chapman 2010).

To handle the constant flux of population flows, cities must be extremely absorptive systems in terms of both their physical and economic structure. The burdens that increased populations put on infrastructural systems are primarily associated with environmental problems (discussed below). But there is a significant economic dimension to this issue, as cities need to develop systems that will allow individuals fuller participation in the economic life of the city. Transportation networks—like the exemplary cable-car system developed in Medellín, Colombia, which provides mobility to workers in otherwise low-access mountainside settlements or the metro/tram/funicular arrangements in Istanbul, which enables better circulation in a city with an area of more than 2,000 square miles—are central to efforts to increase economic access. But even those improvements with a perhaps less directly apparent economic impact, like ensuring the health and safety of these growing populations, can have dramatic effects on their overall productivity. It has been shown, for example, that while poverty makes little contribution to pollution (indeed, efforts to quantitatively assess the environmental impacts of consumption make it clear that the poorest citizens are often the greenest [Stern et al. 1997]), pollution and other environmental hazards are major contributors to poverty (Satterthwaite 2003). The industrialization that comprises much of the economic activity in developing cities, this is to say, is a double-edged sword: the economic benefits it offers often come accompanied by costs that are no less economic for being environmental and which fall disproportionately on the poorest members, who lack the means to avoid them. The economic consequences of environmental characteristics underline the crucial roles governance and planning professions have to play. Policy and planning not only secure the physical connections that allow workers on the periphery to be integrated into the city's economic activity but also can minimize the vicious cycles to which the very engines of economic growth can subject those who need their benefits most.

Infrastructure, health, and safety resources are not the only components of what is required to integrate citizens more equally into the economic life of their cities—achieving more inclusive development will also require reconfiguring the activities central to that economy. The temporary settlements common to peri-urban areas in the developing world are the built equivalents of the informal economies that thrive in them. Over the past decades the informal economy has become an object of much analytical scrutiny (Gërxhani 2004). More than a decade ago, Kasarda and Crenshaw (1991) claimed that the urban informal sector was the most critical area of research in the study of urbanization of the Global South. More recently, the Rockefeller Foundation reinforced this idea with publication of Neal R. Peirce and Curtis W. Johnson's *Century of the City, No Time to Lose* (2008).

Despite the intensity of this scholarly focus, however, there appears to be little consensus about exactly what defines the informal economy (e.g., should illegal activities be included alongside merely sublegal business?), how to measure it (Vuletin 2008), and even whether economic activity should be divided into formal and informal in the first place (UN-HABITAT, 2010; Kannappan 1983, 1985; Kasarda and Crenshaw 1991). Opinion seems no less divided as to what ought to be done about it—some studies advocate for the economic benefits of its growth (Becker 2004) while others suggest that the informal economy saps governments of much-needed tax revenue and amounts to unfair competition against more productive, formal industries (Farrell 2004).

It is possible, however, that these apparently polarized research findings actually understate the amount of agreement among the researchers. Both those who advocate the growth of the informal economy and those who argue that its informality should be suppressed are taking pro-growth positions at the level of the national economy. There are those, moreover, who suggest not only the tenuous nature of the distinction between formal and informal economies, but see in certain characteristics of the informal economy—its fluidity, its decentralization, and its reliance on extensive information networks—lessons that could usefully inform more mainstream economic activities (Light 2004). Others point to the persistence of informal economies in cities like London or New York as proof that informal economies do not signal either a general lack of economic development or the absence of formal alternatives (Williams 2001; Snyder 2004). The common chord among all of these, though, is the agreement that these activities thrive in dense urban environments.

Likewise, it is clear that growing the informal economy will likely mean at least partially formalizing it in physical places with retooled financial instruments. Notions of collateral, title, and capital will have to be adjusted to fit situations where loans need to be made to groups of people (rather than individuals). Over the past decades, community-based organizations have developed microcredit programs as one strategy to tailor financial practices to the immediate needs of a population. Such approaches have often been praised for providing the credit structures on which economic development depends. Despite their popularity—and the amount of attention they received particularly after the 2006 Nobel Prize went to Muhammad Yunus and Grameen Bank, the microcredit institution (MCI) he created—reasons for the failure or success of such microfinance institutions remain incompletely understood (Woolcock 1999), insufficiently transparent, or still in a marginal relation to international financial markets (Nieto 2004). At the same time, the fuller integration of MCIs into mainstream financial markets raises its own set of concerns about whether the ascendance of the profit motive (as private investors, rather than nongovernmental lenders, become the primary risk-takers) or the centralization of funding will impede the socially sustainable development and local autonomy that have been central to the success of MCIs. The informal economy thus presents policymakers with a delicate balancing act as efforts are made to ensure these markets' regularity, predictability, and transparency on the one hand, without sacrificing their crucial flexibility and communitarian ethics on the other.

Environmental Sustainability

In addition to these economic challenges, acute environmental questions face rapidly growing cities. It is increasingly clear that the urbanization of the developing world and climate change are intricately interrelated questions at the level of both the effects of climate change and the causes of that change itself. Cities in the developing world are, for a variety of reasons, at much greater risk from the effects of climate change than are cities in the more developed world: they tend to be (1) geographically disadvantaged, being disproportionately located in warmer areas of the globe; (2) dependent on agriculture, the industry most susceptible to alterations in the climate; and (3) without the resources to adapt to a changing environment (Stern 2007). This vulnerability decreases as these cities develop, but this development typically means that they have become much greater contributors to the environmental problems themselves. Even though many countries are now taking efforts to disarticulate GDP growth and carbon dioxide (CO_2) production, the two have traditionally been directly correlated, and given the increasing energy demands in places like China and India, even aggressive policies to moderate GDP-CO_2 ratios may be dwarfed by the dramatic increase in the energy demands of these rapidly growing populations.

Cities of the developing world have thus become the focal point of a tension that has both ethical and empirical dimensions. In terms of ethics, developing cities focus a tension between the virtues of conservation and the virtues of equity—as the importance of minimizing environmental impact runs up against the injustice of vast inequalities in living standards. This ethical conflict maps onto an empirical debate about whether population growth or resource consumption is the most significant cause of environmental damage. These conflicts become particularly fraught when viewed through the lens of the more developed parts of the world—home to high levels of resource consumption—and less developed nations—which tend to be home to very large populations and comparatively minimal per capita resource consumption.

As Stern et al. (1997) observe, however, these ways of framing the problem may be inadequate, both because they rely on a false either-or dichotomy between population and consumption as the cause of environmental disruption (when the two, in fact, exist in many different relationships), and because such views are often supported by a general lack of accurate or appropriately detailed understandings of the environmental impacts associated with various forms of consumption. Responsible policy, therefore, requires more nuanced and detailed understandings of both what we are referring to when we talk about "environmental problems" and how these particular issues are related to the population growth and densification involved in urbanization.

Satterthwaite (1997), for example, divides the environmental transformations associated with urbanization into five categories: environmental hazards (chemical pollutants, biological pathogens, etc.); use of renewable resources that exceeds natural rate of replacement; use of nonrenewable resources; generation of nonbiodegradable wastes; and overuse of biodegradable sink capacity. Some of these problems—like the overuse of renewable resources—do worsen as population increases and urbanization progresses. Certain problems, though, have a more uneven relation to urbanization. Susceptibility to environmental hazards, for instance, typically decreases as cities develop more sophisticated systems; similarly, use of nonrenewable resources can be greatly influenced by policy and planning (McGranahan 2007).

Such facts point up two things. First, they provide a more precise understanding of the challenges cities in the developing world face. This detailed understanding is crucial especially if, as some have argued, today's rapidly developing cities present a historically unique situation, one that cannot simply be understood as a repetition of the rapid urbanization the developed world saw a hundred years ago. Marcotullio (2007) argues that the environmental challenges of today's cities are appearing sooner (at lower levels of income), increasing faster (relative to income level), and appearing in greater numbers and in more complex interrelation than in previous episodes of urbanization. If this is so, it has an important bearing on policy response since previous methods may be poorly suited for today's environmental problems. Research and data collection become indispensable policy tools.

Second, such attempts to arrive at a more detailed understanding of the nature of the environmental problems in today's developing cities and their relationship to population growth and expansion also make it possible to understand these environmental challenges as opportunities in the longer view. It is in the handling of such environmental questions that the Global South has one of its best opportunities to demonstrate how the efficient organization of cities can contribute to sustainability. These cities can take their environmental impact into account as they develop, rather than struggling, like some cities of the North are currently doing, to adapt or retrofit an infrastructure designed around cheap oil and indifferent pollution (Birch and Wachter 2008). Indeed, as cities in the North are coming to terms with the interrelation of urban systems in their effort to make changes to elaborate and established systems, the complex and integrated nature of environmental problems in developing cities already requires a holistic conception of urban environment (Pugh 1996).

In these ways, the intersection of the issue of climate change and of urbanization in the developing world comprises a complex set of opportunities and imperatives. If the developing world is to take advantage of an opportunity to urbanize sustainably, those issues need to be put front and center immediately. As one economist points out, because "power-stations, buildings, [and] industrial plants . . . last for decades," today's "overinvestment in long-lived, high-carbon infrastructure" not only has immediate environmental costs but will rigidly shape development strategies for years to come (Stern 2007). At the same time, it is increasingly clear that there is only so much national governments can do on their own; the systemic change and the technological innovation required for sustainable twenty-first-century cities require international cooperation to incentivize change. Even ambitious sustainability goals set by centralized governments, like China's commitment to reducing its energy-to-GDP ratio by 20 percent by 2020, have faltered due to lack of economic incentives for local governments on which much of the burden of these policies falls. China's discovery of the importance of market-driven incentives in effecting large-scale change provides a national version of what some economists have argued for at the international level. Although Nicholas Stern's monumental *Stern Review* (2007) continues to be criticized (by both those who feel it understates and those who feel it overstates the costs of climate change), its fundamental political insight—that carbon mitigation requires a coordinated strategy of international economic policy—is increasingly valid. Because these environmental questions are global issues and intricately tied to the world market, it is clear that not only are the economic and environmental development of the Global South linked but that the economic and environmental development of the Global South are not issues that can be confined to geographic borders. Urbanization is thus an issue of critical importance not just for the developing world, where it is primarily taking place, but for the planet as a whole.

Resilient Infrastructure and Disaster Response

For cities struggling to handle rapid growth with limited resources, the long-term planning perspective that can lead to truly resilient cities can be a particular challenge to develop. This planning is, however, all the more necessary for cities in the Global South, which are often situated in locations particularly vulnerable to natural disaster and rely on infrastructures that have trouble meeting demand even at the best of times. The rapid growth of these cities makes the solutions that careful urban planning and cooperatively developed social policy might provide both imperative and challenging. Seeing how cities in the Global North—which tend to have significantly more financial and organizational resources, established bureaucracies, and (comparatively) very stable populations—come up lacking in their responses to natural disasters makes clear how critical it is for cities in the Global South, where resources are more scarce and populations are growing much more rapidly, to develop systems of disaster preparedness (Birch and Wachter 2006).

Cities as populous and rapidly changing as those studied in this book require great informational resources if they are to nurture diverse economies, grow in ways attentive to long-term viability, and develop systems capable of responding to environmental and demographic instability. All nations require sufficient knowledge, data, and techniques in order to craft responsive policies, just as all nations require the financial resources and political will to implement those policies their growing populations require.

An inclusive, vibrant economy; environmentally responsible development; and an infrastructure resilient in the face of continued population growth and natural disaster: these are goals any city—regardless of its geographical location—would be proud to achieve. Because of the populations involved in the urbanization of the Global South, however, both the stakes of and challenges to this achievement are very steep. This is why urbanization, across the globe but especially in Asia and Africa, is *the* critical issue of the twenty-first century.

As great as these challenges are, however, the urban areas of the Global South are not without certain advantages in meeting them. Urban areas in the North are, of course, far more developed—possessed of more sophisticated legal and economic systems and more extensive resources for sustainable development. At the same time, though, these apparent advantages can pose their own obstacles. Greater wealth means a population less disposed to conservation and better able to maintain lifestyles that demand increasing supplies of energy. A developed infrastructure, most of it designed in the absence of significant concerns about energy and the environment, resists adaptation to a world with more people and fewer resources between them. And, as is particularly evident in the American context, neither a legal system that leaves land-use issues to local government nor an economic philosophy that relegates decision-making to individual actors is particularly well-suited to problems that demand systemic or regional approaches. Fragmented governmental structures have difficulty both in resolving the conflicts that arise between older cities, suburbs, and outlying areas, and in enabling the large-scale planning required as demographic and economic shifts lead individual cities to become participants in multistate, mega-urban regions.

Responding to this growth and its environmental and societal challenges requires better governance and economic solutions as well as an enhanced capacity to plan at all levels of government. Whether these solutions follow the "Washington Consensus" (market-driven) or the "Beijing Consensus" (government-driven) or some combination of the two will be one of the critical issues of the future (Wilson 2004, Halper 2010). Regardless, dealing with the most fundamental questions touched upon in the first part of this chapter (Who are these new urban dwellers? Where will they live? How can services for them best be financed and supplied?) requires a collaborative effort and demands contributions from a wide range of thinkers drawn from the social sciences and the fields of engineering, city planning, and urban design. With its multidisciplinary approach, this book provides an example of the breadth of expertise the challenge of twenty-first-century urbanism requires. Inquiries into methods of population measurement, the effects of demographic changes, the requirements of environmentally sustainable development, the trials (and necessity) of delivering health and education services, and the implications of policy initiatives and financial practices: all of these must be considered if we are to ensure the success of our urban areas over the next half-century. The practitioners collected in this volume undertake their work in the hopes of making the urban world a place of healthy, safe, and well-educated communities. Work like that collected here will be essential for improving our cities, both for the millions already living in them and for the millions more who are on the way.

Chapter 2

Human Population Grows Up

Joel E. Cohen

The decade ending in 2010 spanned three unique, important transitions in the history of humankind. Before 2000, young people always outnumbered old people. From 2000 forward, old people will outnumber young people. Until approximately 2007, rural people always outnumbered urban people. From approximately 2007 forward, urban people will outnumber rural people. From 2003 on, the worldwide *median* number of children per woman per lifetime at current fertility rates (the total fertility rate) was at or below the number required to replace the parents in the following generation, even though the declining *average* total fertility rate remained above the replacement level by as much as half a child per woman.

The century 1950–2050 marks three additional unique, important transitions in human history. First, no person who died before 1930 had lived through a doubling of the human population. Nor is any person born in 2050 or later likely to live through a doubling of the human population. In contrast, everyone 50 years old or older in 2010 has seen more than a doubling of human numbers, from 3 billion in 1960 to 6.8 billion in 2010. The peak population growth rate ever reached, about 2.1 percent a year, occurred between 1965 and 1970. Human population never grew with such speed before the twentieth century and is never again likely to grow with such speed. Our descendants will look back on the late-1960s peak as the most significant demographic event in the history of the human population, even though those of us who lived through it did not recognize it at the time.

Second, the dramatic fall since 1970 of the global population growth rate to 1.1 or 1.2 percent a year in 2010 resulted primarily from choices by billions of couples around the world to limit the number of children born. Global human population growth rates have probably risen and fallen numerous times in the past. The great plagues and wars of the fourteenth century, for example, reduced not only the growth rate but also the absolute size of global population, both largely involuntary changes. Never before the twentieth century has a fall in the global population growth rate been voluntary.

Finally, the past half a century saw, and the next half a century will see, an enormous shift in the demographic balance between the more developed regions of the world and the less developed ones. Whereas in 1950 the less developed regions had roughly twice the population of the more developed ones, by 2050 the ratio will exceed six to one.

These colossal changes in the composition and dynamics of the human population by and large escape public notice. Occasionally, one or another symptom of these profound shifts does attract political attention. Proposed Social Security reforms in the U.S., however, often fail to recognize the fundamental aging of the population, while debates in Europe and the U.S. over immigration policy often overlook the differences in population growth rates between these regions and their southern neighbors.

In this essay, I will focus on the four major underlying trends expected to dominate changes in the human population in the coming half-century and on some of their long-term implications. The population will grow bigger, more slowly, more urban, and older. Of course, precise projections remain highly uncertain. Small changes in assumed fertility rates have enormous effects on the projected total numbers of people, for example. Despite such caveats, the projections do suggest some of the problems that humanity will have to face over the next fifty years.

Rapid but Slowing Growth

Although the rate of population growth has fallen since the 1970s, the logic of compounding means that current levels of global population growth are still greater than any experienced prior to World War II. The first absolute increase in population by one billion people took from the beginning of time until the early nineteenth century. The increase from 6 billion people in 1999 to 7 billion people expected in 2011 will take twelve years. By 2050 the world's population is projected to reach 9.1 billion, plus or minus 2 billion people, depending on future birth and death rates. The anticipated increase from 6.1 billion in 2000 to 9.1 billion in 2050 equals the total population of the world in 1960, which was 3 billion people.

In short, rapid population growth has not ended. Human numbers increased from mid-2009 to mid-2010 by roughly 75 million people annually, the equivalent of adding another U.S. to the world every four years. But most of the increases are not occurring in countries with the wealth of the U.S. Between 2005 and 2050 population will at least triple in Afghanistan, Burkina Faso, Burundi, Chad, Congo, Democratic Republic of the Congo, East Timor, Guinea-Bissau, Liberia, Mali, Niger, and Uganda. These countries are among the poorest on earth.

Virtually all population growth in the next forty years is expected to happen in today's economically less developed regions. Despite higher death rates at every age, poor countries' populations grow faster than rich countries' populations because birth rates in poor countries are much higher. In 2009, the average woman bore nearly twice as many children (2.7) in the poor countries as in the rich countries (1.7 children per woman).

Half the global increase to 2050 will be accounted for by just nine nations. Listed in order of their anticipated contribution, they are India, Pakistan, Nigeria, Democratic Republic of the Congo, Bangladesh, Uganda, the U.S., Ethiopia, and China. The only rich country on the list is the U.S., where roughly one-third of population growth is driven by a high rate of immigration. In contrast, fifty-one countries or areas, most of them economically more developed, will lose population by 2050. Germany is expected to drop from 83 million to 79 million people, Italy from 58 million to 51 million, Japan from 128 million to 112 million and, most dramatically, the Russian Federation from 143 million to 112 million. Thereafter Russia's population is projected to be slightly smaller than Japan's.

Slowing population growth everywhere means that the twentieth century was probably the last in human history in which younger people outnumbered older ones. The proportion of all people who were children aged four years and younger peaked in 1955 at 14.6 percent and gradually declined to an estimated 9.3 percent by 2010, whereas the fraction of people aged sixty years and older increased from a low of 8.1 percent in 1960 to 11.0 percent in 2010. In around 2000 each group constituted about 10 percent of humanity. Now and henceforth the elderly have the numerical upper hand.

This crossover in the proportions of young and old reflects both improved survival and reduced fertility. The average life span grew from perhaps thirty years at the beginning of the twentieth century to about sixty-eight years in 2010. The more powerful influence, however, is reduced fertility, which adds smaller numbers to the younger age groups.

The graying of the population is not proceeding uniformly around the globe. In 2050 nearly one person in three will be sixty years or older in the more developed regions and one person in five in the less developed zones. But in eleven of the least developed countries—

Afghanistan, Angola, Burundi, Chad, Democratic Republic of the Congo, Equatorial Guinea, Guinea-Bissau, Liberia, Mali, Niger, and Uganda—half the population will be aged twenty-three years or younger.

If recent trends continue as projected to 2050, virtually all of the world's population growth will be in urban areas. In effect, the poor countries will have to build the equivalent of a city of more than one million people each week for the next forty years at least.

Although long-term demographic projections to 2050 and beyond are routine, economic models are not well developed for long-term projection. They are vulnerable to unpredictable changes in institutions and technology and to shifts in the dominance of regions and economic sectors. Most models do, however, predict that the world will become richer. In the brightest scenarios, the ratio of income per person in industrial nations to that in developing nations could drop from an estimated 16 to 1 in 1990 to between 6.6 to 1 and 2.8 to 1 in 2050. These gains are not assured. Other models predict stagnating poverty.

Projections of billions more people in developing countries and more elderly people everywhere, coupled with hopes of economic growth especially for the world's poor, raise concerns in some quarters about the sustainability of present and future populations.

Beyond Human Carrying Capacity

In the short term, our planet can provide room and food, at least at a subsistence level, for 50 percent more people than are alive now because humans are already growing enough cereal grains to feed 9 to 11 billion people a vegetarian diet. But as demographer-sociologist Kingsley Davis observed in 1991, "There is no country in the world in which people are satisfied with having barely enough to eat." The question is whether 2050's billions of people can live with freedom of choice and material prosperity, however freedom and prosperity may be defined by those alive in 2050, and whether their children and their children's offspring will be able to continue to live with freedom and prosperity, however they may define them in the future. That is the question of sustainability.

This worry is as old as recorded history. Cuneiform tablets from 1600 B.C. show that the Babylonians feared the world was already too full of people. In 1798, Thomas Malthus renewed these concerns, as did Donella Meadows in her 1972 book *The Limits to Growth.* While some people have fretted about too many people, optimists have offered reassurance that deities or technology will provide for humankind's well-being. Early efforts to calculate earth's human carrying capacity assumed that a necessary condition for a sustainable human society could be measured in units of land. In the first known quantitative reckoning, Anton van Leeuwenhoek estimated in 1679 that the inhabited area of earth was 13,385 times larger than Holland and that Holland's population then was about one million people. Assuming that "the inhabited part of the earth is as densely populated as Holland, though it cannot well be so inhabited," he wrote, "the inhabited earth being 13,385 times larger than Holland yields . . . 13,385,000,000 human beings on the earth," or an upper limit of roughly 13.4 billion.

Continuing this tradition, in 2002, Mathis Wackernagel, an author of the "ecological footprint" concept, and his colleagues sought to quantify the amount of land humans used to supply resources and to absorb wastes. Their preliminary assessment concluded that humanity used 70 percent of the global biosphere's capacity in 1961 and 120 percent in 1999. In other words, by 1999, people were exploiting the environment faster than it could regenerate itself, they claimed, a situation they considered clearly unsustainable.

This approach has many problems. Perhaps the most serious is its attempt to establish a necessary condition for the sustainability of human society in terms of the single dimension of biologically productive land area. For instance, to translate energy use into land units, Wackernagel and his colleagues calculated the area of forests that would be needed to absorb the carbon dioxide produced in generating the energy. This approach fails for energy generation technologies that do not emit carbon dioxide, such as solar panels, hydropower, or nuclear plants. Converting all energy production to nuclear energy would change the dilemma from too much carbon dioxide to too much spent nuclear fuel. The problem of sustainability remains, but biologically productive land area is not a useful indicator of it.

Other one-dimensional quantities that have been proposed as ceilings on human carrying capacity include water, energy, food, and various chemical elements required for food production. The difficulty with every single index of human carrying capacity is that its meaning depends on the value of other factors. If water is scarce and energy is abundant, for example, it is easy to desalinate and transport water; if energy is expensive, desalination and transport may be impractical. Attempts to quantify earth's human carrying capacity or a sustainable human population size face the challenge of understanding the constraints imposed by nature, the choices faced by people, and the interactions between them.

Some of the constraints imposed by nature are dealt with elsewhere in this volume. Here I will draw attention to the questions of human choice involved in assessing sustainability. What will humans desire and what will they accept as the average level and distribution of material well-being in 2050 and beyond? What technologies will be used? What domestic and international political institutions will be used to resolve conflicts? What economic arrangements will provide credit, regulate trade, set standards, and fund investments? What social and demographic arrangements will influence birth, health, education, marriage, migration, and death? What physical, chemical, and biological environments will people want to live in? What level of variability in population size and other demographic characteristics will people be willing to live with? (For example, if people do not mind seeing human population size drop by billions when the climate becomes unfavorable, they may regard a much larger population as sustainable when the climate is favorable.) What level of risk are people willing to live with? (Are mud slides, hurricanes, or floods acceptable risks or not? The answer will influence the area of land viewed as habitable.) What time horizon is assumed? Finally, and significantly, what will people's values and tastes be in the future? As anthropologist Donald L. Hardesty noted in 1977, "A plot of land may have a low carrying capacity, not because of low soil fertility but because it is sacred or inhabited by ghosts."

Most published estimates of earth's human carrying capacity uncritically assumed answers to one or more of these questions. In my book *How Many People Can the Earth Support?* I collected and analyzed more than five dozen of these estimates published from 1679 onward. Those made in just the past half a century ranged from less than 1 billion to more than 1,000 billion. These estimates are political numbers, intended to persuade people, one way or another: either that too many humans are already on earth or that there is no problem with continuing rapid population growth. Scientific numbers are intended to describe reality. Because no estimates of human carrying capacity have explicitly addressed the questions raised above and have taken into account the diversity of views about their answers in different societies and cultures, no scientific estimates of sustainable human population size can be said to exist. Too often attention to long-term sustainability is a diversion from the immediate problem of making tomorrow better than today, a task that does offer much room for science and constructive action. Let us therefore briefly consider two major demographic trends, urbanization and aging, and some of the choices they present.

Boom or Bomb?

Many major cities were established in regions of exceptional agricultural productivity, typically the floodplains of rivers, or in coastal zones and islands with favorable access to marine food resources and maritime commerce. If the world's urban population roughly doubles in the next half a century, from 3 billion to 6 billion, while the world's rural population remains roughly constant at 3 billion, and if many cities expand in area rather than increasing in density, fertile agricultural lands around those cities could be removed from production, and the waters around coastal or island cities could face a growing challenge from urban waste. Right now the most densely settled half of the planet's population lives on 2 to 3 percent of all ice-free land. If cities double in area as well as population by 2050, urban areas could grow to occupy 6 percent of land. Withdrawing that amount mostly from the 10 to 15 percent of land considered arable could have a notable impact on agricultural production. Planning cities so they avoid consuming arable land would greatly reduce the effect of their population growth on food production, a goal very much in the urbanites' interest because the cities will need to be provisioned.

Unless urban food gardening surges, on average each rural person will have to shift from feeding herself (most of the world's agricultural workers are women) and one city dweller today to feeding herself and two urbanites in less than half a century. If the intensity of rural agricultural production increases, the demand for food, along with the technology supplied by the growing cities to the rural regions, may ultimately lift the rural agrarian population from poverty, as happened in many rich countries. At the same time, if more chemical fertilizers and biocides are applied to raise yields, the rise in food production could put huge strains on the environment.

For city dwellers, urbanization threatens frightening hazards from infectious disease unless adequate sanitation measures supply clean water and remove wastes. Yet cities also concentrate opportunities for educational and cultural enrichment, access to health care, and diverse employment. Clearly, if half the urban infrastructure that will exist in the world of 2050 must be built in the next forty-five years, the opportunity to design, construct, operate, and maintain new cities better than old ones is enormous, exciting, and challenging.

Urbanization will interact with the transformation of human societies by aging. Cities raise the economic premium paid to younger, better-educated workers, whereas the mobility they promote often weakens traditional kin networks that provide familial support to elderly people. An older, uneducated woman who could have familial support and productive work in agriculture if she lived in a rural area might have difficulty finding both a livelihood and social support in a city.

After 2010, most countries will experience a sharp acceleration in the rate of increase of the elderly dependency ratio—the ratio of the number of people aged sixty-five and older to the number aged fifteen to sixty-four. The shift will come first and most acutely in the more developed countries, whereas the least developed countries will experience a slow increase in elderly dependency after 2020. By 2050 the elderly dependency ratio of the least developed countries is projected to approach that of the more developed countries in 1950.

Extrapolating directly from age to economic and social burdens is unreliable, however. The economic burden imposed by elderly people will depend on their health, on the economic institutions available to offer them work, and on the social institutions on hand to support their care.

Trends in the health of the elderly are positive overall, despite severe problems in some economies in transition and in regions afflicted by AIDS. The rate of chronic disability among elderly Americans, for example, declined rapidly between 1982 and 1999. As a result, by 1999, 25 percent fewer elderly Americans were chronically disabled than would have been expected if the U.S. disability rate had remained constant since 1982.

Because an older person relies first on his or her spouse in case of difficulty (if there is a spouse), marital status is also a key influence on living conditions among the elderly. Married elderly people are more likely to be maintained at home rather than institutionalized compared with single, widowed, or divorced persons.

The sustainability of the elderly population depends in complex ways not only on age, gender, and marital status but also on the availability of supportive offspring and on socioeconomic status—notably educational attainment. Better education in youth is associated with better health in old age. Consequently, one obvious strategy to improve the sustainability of the coming wave of older people is to invest in educating youth today, including education in those behaviors that preserve health and promote the stability of marriage. Another obvious strategy is to invest in the economic and social institutions that facilitate economic productivity and social engagement among elderly people.

No one knows the path to sustainability because no one knows the destination, if there is one. But we do know much that we could do today to make tomorrow better than it would be if we do not put our knowledge to work. As economist Robert Cassen remarked, "Virtually everything that needs doing from a population point of view needs doing anyway."

Chapter 3

Measuring and Coping with Urban Growth in Developing Countries

Nefise Bazoglu

It took the development community two decades, if not more, to come to terms with the unprecedented urban growth rates that occurred in the developing world between 1950 and 2005 (figure 3.1). The dramatic increase in the proportion of urban population—from 17 percent to 26 percent—that took place between 1950 and 1975 was the first sign that the new order in the Third World would be predominantly urban. Surprisingly, however, the initial response to the urban growth trend was indifference or denial (Chamie 2004).

When the development community began to take urbanization seriously in the late 1970s, two opposing opinions emerged. One side emphasized urbanization's positive aspects; the other, its negative features. Those in favor of urbanization pointed to the economic benefits of cities, such as economies of scale and large concentrations of production, consumption, and specialized services (UN Centre for Human Settlements 1996). Those against urbanization, a group originally in the majority, highlighted its ill effects: slums, traffic jams, air pollution, and crime. They saw urbanization as creating ecological footprints that jeopardized biodiversity and exacerbated deforestation. Cities, they believed, "exert enormous environmental impacts, far beyond their boundaries and face challenges in several areas" (Desai 1996, 233). They sought to curb urbanization either by direct, and sometimes forceful (e.g., slum evictions), interventions or by more indirect means such as pumping development funds to agricultural programs aimed at encouraging rural populations to remain in their villages (UN-HABITAT 2006; UN Development Program 2005; Sachs 2005). Against these claims, those favoring urbanization argued that the problems created by population pressure could be dealt with by good governance. They held that government

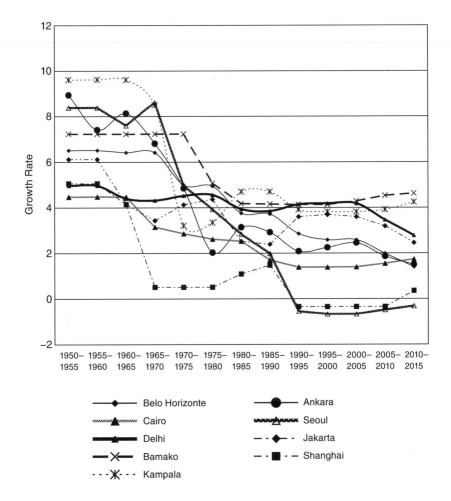

Figure 3.1. Selected Cities Reaching Highest Growth Rate, 1950–1960

Source: United Nations Department of Economic and Social Affairs 2003.

incapacity to tackle urban poverty, unemployment, service delivery, and other quality-of-life issues—not the size of the urban population—was the central issue (Cheema 1992; NRC 2003; Gilbert 1996; Rakodi 1997). United Nations publications—the UN-HABITAT's State of the World's Cities and Global Human Settlement Reports published continually since 2001 and the United Nations Population Fund's (UNFPA) State of the World's Population reports begun in the late 1980s, monitoring urban growth and conditions—reflect the shifting views. They originally focused on the negative aspects of urbanization but by the end of the first decade of the twenty-first century, they began to support the pro-urbanization view. Their subtitles tell the story: Whereas in 2003 the UN published a Global Human Settlement Report called *The Challenge of the Slums*, four years later the State of the World's Population report was subtitled *Unleashing the Potential of Urban Growth* (2007) and the State of the World's Cities was *Harmonious Cities* (2008). The later reports recognize that urbanization is here to stay and that world leaders should aim to ameliorate resulting negative conditions through improved governance.

This chapter explores the pro-urbanization line of thought. First, it analyzes four waves of growth from 1950 to 2005 in 119 cities drawn from the UN-HABITAT Global City Sample.[1] Second, it organizes a typology relating urban growth and governance for a fifty-two-city subset of the sample, places for which development indicators (access to piped water; connection to sewer, electricity, and communications; under-five mortality rates; and parity of female/male literacy) are available.[2] Third, it discusses best practices in governance for more developed cities.

Four Waves of Urban Population Growth

Three general findings emerge from the analysis of the historical growth of the sample cities shown in figure 3.2. First, high rates of urbanization date from the 1950s, but can be differentiated in four periods or waves: 1950–1960, 1960–1980, 1980–1990, and 1990–2005. Second, urban growth rates differ by region, with some dominant in one wave and others in another. Third, the sources of growth are variable, rooted in natural increase, migration, and geopolitical phenomena.

The First Wave (1950–1960)

In terms of overall, worldwide urban growth, the highest rates occurred in the first wave. Although many cities continued to grow in the succeeding waves, no other period matches the 1950s in terms of magnitude. Of the 119 sample cities, 50 percent experienced their highest growth rates at this time. In the second wave, 37 percent of cities had peak growth rates; in the third and fourth waves, the percentages of cities having their peaks are 8 and 5 percent, respectively.

In this first period, cities in many regions contributed to global urban growth, but those in Latin America, where one in four cities had its peak growth rate, took the lead. The Middle East and North Africa followed (one in five cities hit peak growth during these years) and sub-Saharan

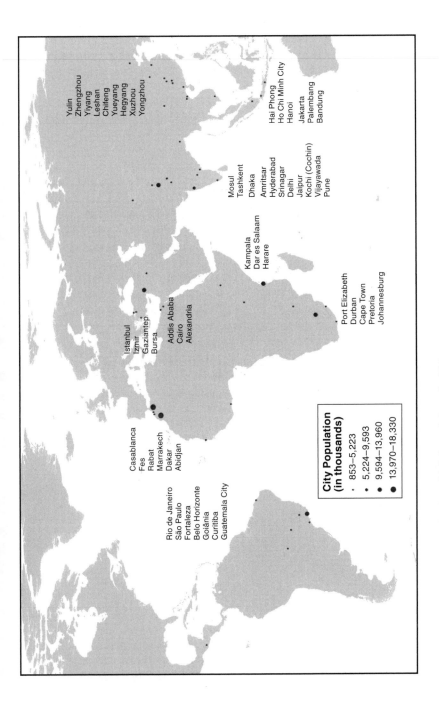

Figure 3.2. Population Distribution: 52 Selected Sample Cities

Source: UN-HABITAT 2007; United Nations Department of Economic and Social Affairs 2003 (for growth rate).

Africa was next (with about one in six or seven peaking). Among the fast-growing places were cities in Brazil, China, Egypt, India, Indonesia, Mexico, Nigeria, Syria, and Turkey. The genesis of new megacities (e.g., Lagos, Istanbul, São Paolo, and Dhaka) dates from the 1950s as these cities joined older megacities (e.g., Shanghai, Mexico City, Cairo) that were already over the 1 million mark. The transformation of small cities into big cities (e.g., Belo Horizonte, Kinshasha) also began to occur.

In 70 percent of the sample cities, the annual growth rate was moderate but steady, ranging from 4 to 7 percent. In 28 percent of the cities, the annual growth was very high, ranging from 7 to 10 percent. These trajectories had immense effects on urban places. Within a very short period, five years or so, many cities had to absorb between 30 and 80 percent (and sometimes as much as 100 percent) more people. Beijing and Shanghai, for example, added a million inhabitants while Delhi and Jakarta increased by half a million.

The growth had several sources: the completion of the demographic transition (lower fertility and mortality rates with births at replacement level [1.89 children/woman]) already experienced in the developed world; in-migration and/or geopolitical events, including independence from colonial rule; and internal political strife or national partition. Of these factors, natural increase, due to the universal reduction of mortality, was the most important. Breakthroughs had come from the enhancement of public health and successful campaigns to reduce or eradicate tuberculosis, malaria, and other diseases. In addition, the introduction and distribution of contraceptives reduced fertility rates, albeit more slowly than the drop in the death rate (Villa and Rodriques 1996). Rural-to-urban migration played a secondary role in urban growth at this time. One important factor in many countries was the success of postwar reconstruction efforts in transforming Third World agriculture from subsistence to commercial levels, thus mitigating some of the drive for migration-induced urbanization (Vining 1985).

The Second Wave (1960–1980)

The second wave of urban growth was much less intense than the first. Change occurred within a longer time frame (twenty years), and the proportion of cities reaching their peak growth rates was lower (37 percent). Notably, during the early years of this period, the growth rates in some cities were carryovers from the 1950s. Although peak growth rates of individual cities were still high, fewer peaked and those that did grew more slowly overall than in the 1950s. In contrast to the earlier period, only about half the sample grew at a moderate rate (4 to 7 percent);

one in three grew at very high rates (7 to 10 percent); and one in ten grew at extremely high rates (greater than 11 percent) annually.

The Middle East and North Africa were the locus of growth in this era (28 percent of their cities reached peak growth in the period). Sub-Saharan Africa, Latin America, and South Asia followed (growth peaked in 20 percent of their cities). Today's Dhaka, Manila, Bangkok, Istanbul, Rio de Janeiro, and São Paulo are all products of the high growth rates of the 1960s. These increases—like those of Mumbai, Calcutta, Karachi, Delhi, Bogotá, Mexico City, Jakarta, and Kuala Lumpur—were primarily due to in-migration (Vining 1985).

The sources of urban growth were also variable in the 1960s. Again, the most important component for most places was natural increase. (Exceptions to this included Turkey, Tunisia, Libya, Puerto Rico, Guyana, and the Republic of Korea, places where in-migration explains more than half the growth [Chen et al. 1996].) In the 1970s, the situation changed as migration rose in importance in Kenya, Tanzania, Cuba, Bangladesh, Indonesia, Malaysia, Thailand, and Turkey (Chen et al. 1996).

During the second wave, development policies also affected urbanization rates. The predominant strategy of encouraging import substitution and fostering local industries helped sustain large population concentrations and the manufacturing industries that offered incentives for rural-to-urban migration (Gilbert 1996; Vining 1985).

The Third (1980–1990) and Fourth Waves (1990–2005)

After the 1980s, dealing with the magnitude of urban populations—not the rate at which they were growing—became a critical issue for the development community. In general, urban populations were in place and growth slowed down. Two phenomena contributed to the deceleration. First, in many places child mortality rates rose as measured by the infant mortality rate (the number of deaths of infants under one year old per 1,000 live births in a given year) and the under-five mortality rate (the number of deaths of children under five per 1,000 live births in a given year, or U5MR). In São Paolo, for example, infant mortality increased from 50 to 55 in the five years between 1980 and 1985; in urban Ghana, it grew from 85 to 120 between the late 1970s and late 1980s (Macedo 1988; UNICEF, Accra 1998). The urban U5MR was also high. For example, in the mid-1990s, it was 97 in Bangladesh, 63 in India, 53 in Egypt, and 42 in Indonesia. A reduction of rural-to-urban migration also occurred; its overall contribution to urban growth fell to 39 percent in the 1980s, down from 43 percent in the 1970s (Chen et al. 1996).

A second cause of the decline in urban growth was the drop in the total fertility rates (the number of births per 1,000 women). This drop was most notable in urban areas. In Bangladesh, for example, the overall fertility rate decreased from 6.3 in 1970 to 3.3 in 1985, with the urban rate at 2.5 and rural at 3.5. This pattern also held for India, where the urban fertility rate was 2.3 and rural rate 3.1.

China offered a major exception to slowed urban growth. Its annual urban growth rate ranged from 5 percent between 1980 and 1990, 4 percent between 1990 and 2000, and 3 percent between 2000 and 2005. Its urban population expanded to 40 percent of the total in 2005, up from 20 percent in 1980 (UN Department of Economic and Social Affairs 2007, 91). This growth occurred for two reasons. First, while China still exerted strict controls on population movement, it moved from an economic strategy primarily occupied with rural areas to one that was increasingly urban focused: the goal was to increase manufacturing in its cities and allow the migration necessary to meet labor demand. Second, it revised its administrative classifications, counting formerly rural places as urban.

A Typology of Urban Growth and Governance for Fifty-Two Cities

High urban growth rates put pressure on municipal governments. Experience shows that annual growth rates above 2.5 percent affect service delivery in cities, especially in the areas of infrastructure, telecommunications, and education, all of which affect health, life expectancy, and quality of life for urban inhabitants. Using key indicators (access to piped water, sewer, electricity, and telephones, as well as rates of under-five mortality and gender literacy),[3] UN-HABITAT analysts created a typology of urban growth and governance for fifty-two cities of the sample for which these data are available.[4] The purpose is to reveal the association of governance and survival/quality-of-life issues. As shown in table 3.1, six categories of cities emerged:

1. high development and low population growth;
2. high development and high population growth;
3. medium development and low population growth;
4. medium development and high population growth;
5. low development and low population growth; and
6. low development and high population growth.

High-development/low-growth cities constitute 15 percent of the sample, range in size from 1.4 to 11 million, and are located in Brazil, Turkey, Vietnam, and Uzbekistan. In general, they experienced their highest

Table 3.1: City Clusters by Development Indicators and Population Growth Rate (1990–2003)

City	Country	Piped Water Connections 1990	Piped Water Connections 2003	Sewerage Connections 1990	Sewerage Connections 2003	Electricity 1990	Electricity 2003	Telephone 1990	Telephone 2003	Under-Five Mortality 1990	Under-Five Mortality 2003	Female-Male Ratio in Literacy 1990	Female-Male Ratio in Literacy 2003	Population Growth Rate 2000–2005	Population (thousands) 2005
High Development Level/Low Population Growth Rate															
Rio de Janeiro	Brazil		93.8		79.9	98.7	99.1	28.7	79.2	39.1	19.3	1.05	1.02	1.20	11,469
Bursa	Turkey	97.7	85.0	95.9	80.7	100.0	100.0	65.4	93.5	89.4	37.7	0.91	0.97	3.58	1,413
Istanbul	Turkey	99.2	99.2	86.6	86.6	91.4	98.7	100.0	100.0	55.0	39.1	95.9	99.4	2.20	9,760
Izmir	Turkey	98.2	94.4	93.4	99.2	100.0	100.0	62.4	97.5	37.4	29.2	0.95	1.00	2.41	2,500
Tashkent	Uzbekistan		98.7		79.4				64.5		39.0			0.11	2,160
Hanoi	Vietnam		78.8		95.1	100.0	100.0	16.8	79.2	77.4	39.0			2.01	4,147
Hai Phong	Vietnam		46.4	99.6	95.1	100.0	100.0	12.9	45.5	27.8	23.0			1.62	1,817
Ho Chi Minh City	Vietnam	90.3	88.7	83.9	95.6	99.6	99.8	12.3	81.5	14.2	19.0	1.00	1.02	1.7	5,030
High Development Level/High Population Growth Rate															
Belo Horizonte	Brazil		84.4		78.9	98.8	99.4	31.2	95.9	44.1	20.8	1.07	1.03	2.59	5,304
Curitiba	Brazil	55.4	82.0		84.2		55.4	97.3	99.8	37.4	16.1	97.3	99.3	2.81	2,871
Goiânia	Brazil		93.4		73.8	99.5	99.0	25.5	80.2	35.8	18.9	1.11	1.03	3.10	1,878
Cape Town	South Africa		95.7		93.8		92.0		45.2		13.0	1.00	1.00	2.67	3,103
Gaziantep	Turkey	96.8	90.9	79.1	95.4	100.0	100.0	48.0	88.8	72.2	32.9	1.00	1.00	3.47	1,004

Table 3.1: (Continued)

City	Country	Piped Water Connections		Sewerage Connections		Electricity		Telephone		Under-Five Mortality		Female-Male Ratio in Literacy		Population Growth Rate	Population (thousands)
		1990	2003	1990	2003	1990	2003	1990	2003	1990	2003	1990	2003	2000–2005	2005
Medium Development Level/Low Population Growth Rate																
São Paolo	Brazil		88.5		63.3	98.9	99.1	34.7	55.1	40.0	18.5	1.04	1.04	1.39	18,333
Hegyang	China			71.3		18.5						37.2	0.98	1.29	853
Xuzhou	China		34.6		12.4						32.5	0.97	1.00	1.42	1,662
Cairo	Egypt	93.0	99.6	47.1	71.9	98.7	99.8		73.4	78.1	33.3	0.72	0.85	1.39	11,146
Hyderabad	India	65.5	93.0	54.6	49.6	89.8	97.7		29.7	80.0		0.74	0.85	2.42	1,392
Casablanca	Morocco	78.2	83.1	48.6	87.6	56.4	96.1	28.5	68.9		36.0	0.64	0.81	2.25	3,743
Marrakech	Morocco		88.8		88.1		98.3				29.0	0.62	0.81	3.01	951
Rabat	Morocco	77.6	88.8	68.6	94.6	80.3	97.7	30.8	66.9		18.0	0.64	0.81	2.87	1,859
Harare	Zimbabwe	96.3	90.3	57.8	94.5	68.6	87.8	20.9	20.9		88.6	0.83	1.02	1.95	1,527
Medium Development Level/High Population Growth Rate																
Fortaleza	Brazil		76.8		19.8	95.4	99.1	20.6	65.1	73.7	28.2	1.25	1.07	2.52	3,261
Delhi	India	70.8	87.1	53.6	93.1	95.4	99.0		45.4	86.0	47.0	0.74	0.83	4.18	15,334
Srinagar	India	78.2	94.0	51.3	76.3	99.7	99.1		20.3	44.0	78.7	0.74	0.83	2.72	1,093
Bandung	Indonesia	53.5	41.3		71.2	97.6	98.5			45.0	38.0			3.30	4,020
Jakarta	Indonesia	94.9	96.7	27.2	35.6	44.4	59.5	99.1	99.9	46.2	39.0	91.9	95.0	3.60	13,194
Palembang	Indonesia	73.5	62.3	41.3	90.1	95.2	98.0				34.0	0.97	0.99	3.27	1,675
Mosul	Iraq		99.6		95.1								0.86	3.15	1,236

Low Development Level/Low Population Growth Rate

City	Country													Growth Rate	Population
Fes	Morocco	93.8	89.1	97.7	57.9						63.0	0.66	0.81	2.66	1,032
Johannesburg	South Africa	87.1	87.5	84.9	47.7						45.0	1.00	1.00	3.7	3,288
Pretoria	South Africa	87.1	87.5	84.9	47.7						45.0	1.00	1.00	3.36	1,282
Chifeng	China	33.4	10.3								50.3	0.97	0.99	0.96	1,140
Leshan	China		31.5	13.0							45.1	96.6	99.6	0.61	1,172
Yiyang	China	23.8	9.8								48.5	0.97	1.00	2.35	1,510
Yongzhou	China	20.4	6.7								63.7	0.97	1.00	1.49	1,182
Yueyang	China	30.5	16.5								64.6	0.97	1.00	1.18	1,286
Yulin	China	17.3	9.6								68.5	0.97	1.00	1.63	1,691
Zhengzhou	China	79.5	66.8	32.6							43.6	97.4	99.9	1.66	2,250
Alexandria	Egypt	92.8	94.5	98.5	59.9	79.7	98.6	99.7		61.2	38.4	72.2	83.6	1.4	3,760
Guatemala City	Guatemala	52.7	65.3	91.0					31.9	41.9	33.7	1.08	1.08	1.57	982
Kochi (Cochin)	India	28.2	27.1	86.1	27.5	82.4	90.3				35.3	0.81	0.96	1.72	1,461
Vijayawada	India	41.0	38.1	46.0	51.4	84.3	96.8	13.2			83.0	0.74	0.83	1.79	1,093
Durban	South Africa		37.9							24.5	50.0	1.00	1.00	2.18	2,643
Port Elizabeth	South Africa		28.4							17.6	42.0	1.00	1.00	0.82	998

Low Development Level/High Population Growth Rate

City	Country													Growth Rate	Population
Dhaka	Bangladesh	90.4	52.0	60.1				88.2		93.3	76.0	69.5	85.9	4.24	12,560
Abidjan	Cote d'Ivoire	76.3	57.9	79.2	76.7	19.2	41.2	59.8	94.1	112.6	120.4	44.2	82.8	2.80	3,516
Addis Ababa	Ethiopia	48.1	65.5	60.8	4.2			97.1			169.0	66.1	90.6	3.04	2,899
Amritsar	India	95.8	93.4	97.4	86.6	87.6	98.6	99.1	62.0		96.7	84.6	94.9	3.19	1,162
Jaipur	India	96.6	90.7	80.9	87.0	53.9	96.6	98.9			75.0	66.0	77.2	4.26	2,796
Pune (Poona)	India	79.0	73.1	52.7	46.5	15.0	91.0	93.1	51.5		75.3	63.9	74.7	4.09	4,485
Dakar	Senegal	59.0	80.5	89.2	40.0	62.3	95.6	91.4			75.8	58.6	81.2	3.22	2,313
Kampala	Uganda	55.0	61.8	15.1	13.6	2.0	44.5	57.1		191.0	81.0	90.9	90.4	3.81	1,345
Dar es Salaam	Tanzania	51.8	53.0	62.0	4.4	3.6	28.6	57.7		182.3	103.1	85.0	90.4	4.75	2,683

Source: UN-HABITAT, 2007; UNDESA 2003 (for growth rate).

growth rates before the 1980s. Their high levels of infrastructure coverage (excepting telephones) are associated with U5MRs low enough to be comparable to those in the developed world.

High-development/high-growth cities represent 10 percent of the sample, are generally smaller than those in the first group, range in size from 1 to 5.3 million, and are located in Brazil, South Africa, and Turkey. Their growth rates have been decelerating, dropping from 6 percent annually in previous decades to 2.6 to 3.5 percent year. Like their peers in the high-development/low-growth group, they are well connected to infrastructure (again the telephone is an exception), have low U5MR, and minimal or no gaps in gender literacy. With high- and low-growth variants taken together, the high-development group constitutes 25 percent of the total.

Medium-development/low-growth cities comprise 17 percent of the sample, range in size from under a million to 18 million, and are located in Brazil, China, Egypt, Morocco, and Zimbabwe. With the exception of those in China, these cities have high levels of basic infrastructure (water, sewer, and electricity) and slightly higher U5MR. (With a U5MR of 89, Harare, Zimbabwe, is an extreme outlier.)

Medium-development/high-growth cites make up 13 percent of the sample, range in size from 1 to 13 million, and are located in Brazil, India, Indonesia, and Iraq. Notwithstanding the enormous differences between these cities, they share two common features: low infrastructure coverage and high U5MR (excepting the Brazilian and Indonesian cities). The Indian cities have bigger gender literacy gaps than the others in the group. The patchy picture of development in this category indicates that not all aspects of local governance are functioning at their best. Altogether, the medium development cities represent 31 percent of the sample.

Low-development/low-growth cities are 31 percent of the sample, range in size from under a million to 3.7 million, and are located in six countries: China, South Africa, India, Egypt, Guatemala, and Morocco. The low infrastructure coverage and high U5MR are characteristic, especially among Chinese cities.

Low-development/high-population cities are 17 percent of the sample, range in size from 1.1 million to 13 million, and are located in Southeast Asia and Africa. As expected, low levels of infrastructure provision are associated with high U5MR. The low-development category constitutes 48 percent of the sample.

Urban Governance: Best Practices

Population pressure on cities, created by either past or present high growth rates, limits the capacity of government to supply infrastructure and deliver adequate poverty alleviation programs (UN Centre for Human Settlements 2001). As seen in the review above, some cities cope well with large and growing populations, while others do not. Highly developed cities tend to be able to adapt to high growth rates, as evidence from Latin America confirms (Gilbert 1996). In contrast, for the least developed cities, every increment of population increase, regardless of its source, is an additional burden.

If it is the development level of a city that shapes its capacity to cope with large or growing populations, then the same processes that have led to the success of highly developed cities in this area may also equip other places to buffer ongoing demographic pressures. While the sources of these developments vary depending on the role of the country in the global economy, certain elements of good governance have increasingly explained how cities cope with poverty and other issues (Friedman 1996; McCarney et al. 1995; Taylor 2004).

The experience of high- and medium-development/high-growth cities provides useful information about the relationship between good governance and the capacity to absorb population. Cities such as Belo Horizonte and Curitiba (Brazil), Gaziantep (Turkey), Jakarta and Bandung (Indonesia), and Delhi (India) vary greatly in population size (ranging from a million to 15 million) but share relatively high levels of infrastructure provision and low U5MR. And while most of them suffer from deeply embedded inequalities, visible in their economically segregated neighborhoods or vast differentials in access to health care and education, they have been relatively successful in absorbing new population.[5] Their shared characteristics of governance include political commitment to pro-urban development, responsible decentralization and empowerment of local government, performance monitoring with regard to infrastructure provision and poverty reduction programs, citizen participation, and an understanding of the importance of servicing urban corridors and/or metropolitan areas.

Development and Political Commitment That Help the Poor

While public investment that aims to improve conditions for the poor (or in UN parlance, "pro-poor public investment") is difficult to generalize about, and is a technical as well as political matter, crafting and implementing urban plans is one evaluation measure. The most recent Global Report on Human Settlements *Planning for Sustainable Cities* (2009) specified critical concerns in the cities of developing countries: informal settlements, peri-urban development, transport, environmental degradation and building capacity for planning and managing fast-growing cities. Regrettably, many cities have a troubling record in planning. Brazilian cities are an important exception. With its City Statute (2001), National Council of Cities, and Ministry of Cities, Brazil has been exemplary in tackling urbanization at all levels of government (Fernandes 2007). Nonetheless, as in other places, development policy in Brazil is subject to politics. A study of annual expenditures in the São Paolo metropolitan area between 1975 and 2000 reveals that infrastructure investment aimed at upgrading slums varied according to the views of the political parties in power, increasing when antipoverty parties dominated (Marques and Bichir 2003, 821). In contrast, Curitiba, a city that has been governed by the same political party for almost forty years, has been unwavering in its support of low-income groups (Macedo 2004).

There are other stand-outs. Turkey's political commitment to development that helps the poor has continued through several regimes—populist, elitist, and military—that shared a belief in modernization via investment in infrastructure and technology. Since 1983, the country's prime ministers (almost all of them engineers) have supported improvements in water, sewer, transportation, and communications infrastructure (Birch 2010; Gotuck, Soysal, and Tureli 2010). Autocratic societies, including Egypt, Morocco, and Tunis, have also supported urban development, albeit with limited citizen participation in the planning and decision-making processes. The 2006 and 2007 *State of the World's Cities* reports highlight progress in Egypt and Tunis.

Decentralization, Performance Monitoring, and Citizen Participation

Decentralization with mutually beneficial relationships between the central and local governments is imperative in order to render municipalities effective in providing infrastructure or alleviating poverty. More than two decades of experience in decentralization in the Third World reveals that cultivating strong links among (and coordination with) all levels of government pays high dividends.

Decentralization varies among countries, ranging from full (Brazil and Indonesia) to medium (Turkey) to limited autonomy (Vietnam) (Mello 2005; Usman 2001; Peterson and Muzzini 2005). In most cases, municipalities are responsible for urban planning, solid-waste management, transportation, and environmental protection. In some places like Brazil and Indonesia, local government is also in charge of education, health services, and social services (Mello 2005; Usman 2001).

The best results in infrastructure provision with decentralization have occurred when national governments have delegated authority *and* provided financial and technical assistance. In Brazil and Turkey, for example, local government can levy taxes on property and a variety of other things like infrastructure use, vehicles, and specified environmental services. They can also receive fund transfers from national budgets and external sources. Indonesian municipalities have all these privileges, and, in addition, have received technical assistance from the national government via the transfer of central government officials to local governments (Usman 2001).

Experience shows that either top-down or bottom-up performance monitoring is also essential for success. Such processes exist in Vietnam (top-down) and Brazil (bottom-up) (Peterson and Muzzini 2005, 212; UN-HABITAT 2005). Belo Horizonte provides an example of performance monitoring associated with citizen participation. Here, citizens are involved in planning and budgeting for housing, water, sanitation, education, and health. The local government uses client-satisfaction indicators, collected directly through surveys or indirectly through measuring participation rates in budgeting (Bretas 1996). Aided by the World Bank, Indonesia also uses surveys to understand citizens' attitudes towards municipal services.

Like performance monitoring, citizen participation is often facilitated by nongovernmental organizations (NGOs) and community-based organizations (CBOs). In Jakarta and Delhi, NGOs and CBOs partner with municipalities to develop housing and primary health care programs focusing on women and children. In the Jakarta metropolitan region, the Garda Emas effort reduced the number of poor families in Bogor from 33,000 to 16,000 between 1999 and 2003. Its programs include microfinance, management, and jobs training. Delhi's Asha (a CBO named for the Hindi word for hope), active in upgrading more than forty slums, works to secure water, solid waste disposal, and health care services, while engaging citizens, and especially women, in these community projects (UN-HABITAT 2007).

While decentralization associated with citizen engagement and community empowerment is of vital importance in development, the histories of Belo Horizonte and Jakarta indicate that this approach is not a panacea (IBAM 2003). It tends to exclude the poorest from participation, a flaw that requires government oversight to remedy (Roberts and Kanaley 2006). Providing access to local or central government support for all people is crucial.

Servicing Urban Corridors and/or Metropolitan Areas

The final shared characteristic among those cities that have successfully absorbed a growing population is the extension of infrastructure to peripheral areas or along urban corridors. The particulars of these investments vary according to whether the local approach is intended to be preventive or curative. Adopting the preventive approach, Curitiba, for example, invested in infrastructure to steer population toward its periphery before the situation was out of control (Rabinovitch 1996). In the 1970s, Gazientep, a Turkish city on the Syrian border, anticipated urban growth and oversaw controlled expansion at its periphery, so that today, despite ongoing waves of population growth from eastern Turkey, it has maintained its status as a livable city. Cairo, in a curative approach, built new towns in the desert after the population concentration had reached crisis proportions (Bazoglu 1998).

The mode by which local government directs population growth is important. Steering growth to wider zones and urban corridors does not always create livable metropolitan settlements, even if interventions are implemented at the right time (UN-HABITAT 2010; World Bank, 2010). Unless these geographic expansions are accompanied by economic development and access to transit, metropolitan regions can become hubs of urban poverty that lack economic vitality. The desert towns of Cairo, for example, fall under this category; people there are largely without employment opportunities and, without access to effective public transportation, are not able to seek jobs elsewhere (Sutton and Fahmi 2001; Bazoglu 1998).

Developing functional and equitable metropolitanization thus requires building the economic and residential infrastructure while simultaneously establishing the connectivity of these settlements to the core city, as well as to other peripheral settlements. One of the most remarkable examples of this approach is Curitiba, where deliberate land-use and transportation planning provided effective ways to direct urban growth (Rabinovitch 1996). Curitiba's mixed-use establishments foster an organic relationship among space, employment opportunities, and the population (Rabinovitch 1996), and minimize social segregation by creating the economic bases of a diverse social fabric.

The development of industry-driven settlement has also been implemented in Delhi by the New Okhla Industrial Development Authority (Potter and Kumar 2004), though success here has been more variable due to a possible misstep in the choice of location.

Conclusions

After differentiating the timing and magnitude of urban growth in the various places in the developing world, this chapter speculated about the reasons why some cities were more effective in accommodating new residents than others. In exploring places with measurable urban indicators, it presented preliminary results and argued that five characteristics seem to be present in those high- and medium-developed cities best able to handle expanding populations. In agreement with UN-HABITAT (2006), it held that political commitment to equitable development ranks highest on the list of characteristics of successfully growing cities. This commitment is associated with the decentralization of authority in ways that encourage local citizen involvement while making use of the extended financial and technical capacity of the national government. Finally, the physical directing or redirecting of development toward urban peripheries or along urban corridors, and the systematic investment in key infrastructural components that these efforts entail, are crucial enablers of the sustained, equitable development central to the success of these growing metropolitan areas.

Future studies are needed to confirm these findings. Today, such work is limited by the absence of reliable comparative data on most cities in the developing world. Addressing this gap will require the creation of additional information systems or modeling techniques.

Chapter 4

Urban Growth and Development at Six Scales: An Economist's View

Stephen Malpezzi

The world's population, roughly 6.7 billion people, spreads over about 13 billion hectares of land. (Of course, much of this land is arid or otherwise inhospitable to settlement, but more on that later.) Variously considered, people live in nations, regions, cities, and neighborhoods. The study of their urbanization is, more or less, the study of density as it occurs in these venues. This chapter classifies urbanization along six scales, ranging from the largest (conceptual) to the smallest (neighborhood) and outlines the specific issues of each. It employs urban economics to explore these scales and to suggest questions for prospective urban research.

Six Scales of Urbanization

The first scale, conceptual, crosses geographies and applies to many, if not all, the units of observation. The second scale, global, is self-explanatory and considers several worldwide patterns over time. The third scale, national, focuses on key patterns and drivers of urbanization in a country. The fourth scale, regional, looks at systems of cities. It is analytically problematic because different definitions of "region" make data collection difficult. Some definitions of region (e.g., regional labor markets) are actually closer to the fifth scale, city. For instance, "Chicago" can refer to both a metropolitan region and an area defined by political boundaries. The sixth scale, neighborhood, describes patterns of density and location within cities.

Scale One: Conceptual: Why and How Cities Exist

While a general definition of a "city" holds that it is a place where density (of people, jobs, firms, capital) is above average for a given country, to an economist a city is a place with higher value output than it would have if it were not dense. To understand this, consider two thought experiments. First, imagine that the roughly $24 trillion in capital stock of the U.S. and the country's 150 million workers randomly moved so that each of the nation's 10,000 zip codes had an equal share. GDP would drop substantially due to the loss of the benefits of economies of scale and agglomeration (discussed in some detail below); exactly how much is hard to pin down, but perhaps output would fall to a tenth of its current value. The fact that U.S. GDP is surely trillions of dollars more than it would be if there were no cities—and the same is broadly true for world GDP—is a measure of cities' value. Next, imagine that the entire capital stock of the U.S., or the world, moved to New York. GDP would again be reduced to a fraction of its previous value due to its concentration in one place. This is why there are systems of cities, or regions.

From an economic standpoint, cities exist because they offer opportunities for comparative advantage (increased trade), economies of scale (internal firm savings) and economies of agglomeration (external locational advantages). Several elements underpin these concepts. They include transaction costs (mixed but, on balance, lower), creativity and entrepreneurship (existence of and openness to innovation), variety and specialization (improved labor pooling; sharing of inputs; matching among labor, jobs and capital), and information (production, diffusion, and spillover effects).

Agglomeration economies, resulting from both public and private activities, are of two broad types: localization economies (external to the firm but internal to the industry) and urbanization economies (external to the firm and external to the industry). In the former, the kinds of firms (or other entities) and their locations matter; in the latter, the size of the urban area is important (Kahnert 1987; Segal 1976). Plentiful research debates the relative importance of each type of agglomeration; both forms seem to matter and the existence of one does not preclude the other (Carlino 1987; Henderson 1988; Rosenthal and Strange 2001).

Early examples of industrial agglomeration are legion and include Lancashire's textile industry (1770s), Glasgow's development of shipbuilding (1820s), Berlin's leadership in electrical engineering (1870s), and Detroit's innovation in automobile design and manufacturing (1900s) (Hall 1998). More recent examples of agglomeration identify such well-known high-tech locations as Silicon Valley, "Silicon Fen" (Cambridge), "Silicon Glen" (Glasgow), "Silicon Hills" (Austin), and

"Silicon Plateau" (Bangalore) (Saxenian 1996). Although Rosenthal and Strange's 2004 study of the software industry around Silicon Valley is notable among recent research focused on localization economies, the effects of localization do not appear to be confined to high-tech industries (Malpezzi, Seah, and Shilling 2001) and may extend beyond production to economies of scale in consumption (Benjamin, Boyle, and Sirmans 1990; Glaeser, Kolko, and Saiz 2001). Henderson (1988) and Moomaw (1988) find that U.S. cities produce relatively few kinds of goods and services (as measured by SIC code).

While urban economists view the city as an agglomeration of firms, they assume that the firms operate freely and that government acts to remove barriers to efficient functioning by addressing market failures, producing public goods, and regulating natural monopolies. Government intervention takes many forms and, depending on a country's legal structure, occurs at the national, regional, or local levels. In the case of urban market failure, government defines and enforces property rights through contract law (including sales, leases, operating agreements, and mortgages) and land-use regulation (including building and housing codes, zoning ordinances and environmental laws). Contract law is usually a national matter while land-use regulation is local. To produce public goods, defined as those from which consumers cannot be excluded, governments often directly provide them. Infrastructure is an example of this, typically with the central government providing goods like national defense and highways, and local government supplying water and sanitation. Public utilities, like electricity and telecommunications, are prime examples of natural monopoly regulation.

Scale Two: Global: Worldwide Patterns over Time

Figures 4.1 and 4.2, showing the actual and projected growth of rural and urban populations between 1970 and 2020, for developing and developed countries respectively, reveal several important patterns. About 1.5 billion of the world's 6.7 billion people—live in developed countries, which are roughly defined as Europe (east and west), North America, Australia, New Zealand, and Japan. The portion of the human population in developing countries has grown at about 1.8 percent per year, moving from under 3 billion to the current 5.2 billion. While the population in the developing world has been primarily rural, in the 1990s the number of city residents increased and, by 2010, the gap between the urban and rural population was closing. The United Nations anticipates that there will be more urban than rural people in the developing world by 2020. (For more on this claim, see chapters in the present volume by Cohen, Bazoglu, and Montgomery and Balk.)

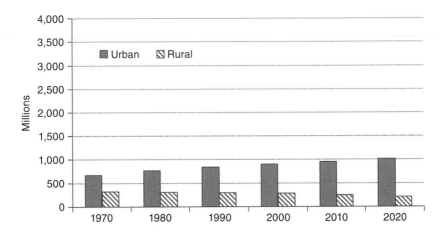

Figure 4.1. Population in Developed Countries

Source: United Nations World Urbanization Prospects: The 2006 Revision.

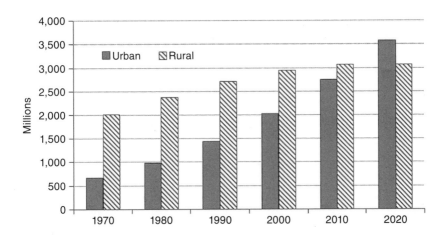

Figure 4.2. Population in Developing Countries

Source: United Nations World Urbanization Prospects: The 2006 Revision.

In developing countries, sources of urban growth are rural-to-urban migration and natural increase (with natural increase contributing slightly more than migration to the total), yielding annual growth rates ranging from 2 to 7 percent in many cities. These increases create high demand for investment in housing, infrastructure, and social services.

(In comparison, between 1980 and 1990 the median population growth rate of the twenty-five largest U.S. cities was less than .5 percent per year, with San Diego having the highest [2.4 percent]). While today's high growth rates in the cities of the developing world are not unprecedented (Chicago, for example, had an average annual growth rate of 8.4 percent between 1850 and 1900), what is unprecedented is the structure of today's urban growth. During the nineteenth century, most of the increase came from migration. Today, migration plus net births are the impetus for urban growth.

Modern urbanization has two other distinguishing characteristics. First, the absolute number of people in cities is higher and the size of the largest cities greater than in the past. Second, most of the world's really large cities are now in the developing world. The latter is not exactly unprecedented; historically, cities like Shanghai, Delhi, and Beijing were among the world's largest. But through the mid-twentieth century, most of the world's largest cities were in developed countries. In 1950, seven out of the top ten were in the developed world (New York, London, Tokyo, Paris, Shanghai, Moscow, Buenos Aires, Chicago, and the Ruhr agglomeration in Germany), but today most are in the developing world.

Scale Three: National: Drivers of Urbanization and Associated Patterns in Countries

For economists, cross-national comparisons of urbanization usually start with total and per capita income or its closely related variable, gross domestic product (GDP). In 2010, the five largest economies at official exchange rates were the United States, China, Japan, Germany, and France; together they produce about 46 percent of world output. Figure 4.3 confirms that there has been a wide range of growth rates over the past twenty years. In Figure 4.3, each country is represented by a circle with an area proportional to its population (for a similar analysis see Fischer [2003]). The two largest circles, to the left, represent China and India, with a little less than 40 percent of the world's population. China grew by 8.6 percent per annum over the period, and India by 3.6 percent. Real GDP per capita in 120 individual countries grew from an annual average of negative 7 percent per year to positive 8 percent per year—over twenty years. Such divergence in performance is astounding and stimulates such questions as do "the rich get richer and the poor get poorer"? Or do poor countries grow faster as they play "catch up"?

What is incontrovertible is that the variance in growth rates is much smaller for richer countries. Only one country with per capita income above $1,400 had a negative growth rate, while about twenty below

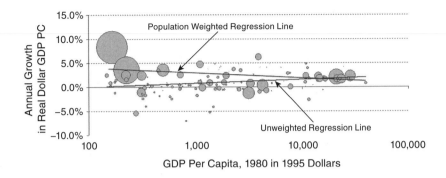

Figure 4.3. GDP Growth and Initial Conditions: Growth in Real US$, 1980–2000

Source: Malpezzi 2005.

$1,400 were negative. Only one country with per capita incomes over $2,200 had a growth rate much above 4 percent, while ten poorer countries had growth rates between 4 and 8 percent.

That there is mathematical correlation between level of urbanization and GDP per capita is unsurprising because the growth of cities has accompanied economic development for the last 5,000 years. In a naive interpretation, the equation suggests that urbanization "explains" about 55 percent of development—or vice versa. Among the richest countries, given their level of urbanization, are the city-states of Hong Kong and Singapore and the geographically small countries of Japan, Denmark, and Luxembourg. At the other extreme, highly urbanized Lebanon, Djibouti, Venezuela, and Jordan are poorer than their urbanization would suggest. Among developing countries that are richer than average given their urbanization are some small islands like St. Kitts, Nevis, and Antigua. Larger developing countries that are richer than their levels of urbanization imply include Thailand and Namibia. This fairly strong correlation between output and urbanization does not, however, imply a simple causal relationship. And rates of change in urbanization and of income over the past twenty years are uncorrelated (Malpezzi 1990, 2006).

Why are levels correlated while changes are not? This is a bit of a puzzle, since if every country started out undeveloped and un-urbanized (albeit a long time ago for developed countries), current correlation in levels implies some past correlation in changes. Perhaps the "initial conditions" are key factors. Running a multiple regression with both variables yields results that still do not offer sufficient reason to reject the null hypothesis that changes in percent urban are unrelated to growth in incomes per capita.

Here are some further clues to solving the puzzle. The urbanization rate is bounded (maximum 100 percent), but GDP is not. There is also some evidence that urbanization increases faster at lower levels and that the growth of urbanization slows down as cities develop. A study using a panel of 130 countries over thirty years shows that urban growth is a strong predictor of growth in per capita GDP, until a country is at about $4,000 per capita GDP and exceeds an urbanization rate of about 30 percent. After these markers, the contribution of urban growth tails off sharply (Malpezzi and Lin 2000). While this puzzle is not yet completely solved, it is nevertheless incontrovertible that, in the long run, economies urbanize as they develop.

Development comprises more than per capita GDP. Many other development indicators—life expectancy, literacy, the structure of production—are also strongly correlated with urbanization. In fact, a number of these alternative indicators, including the United Nations' Human Development Index, are actually more strongly correlated with urbanization than the initial development indicator, per capita GDP. Furthermore, urbanization's contribution is not due simply to some proxy effect of income. Simple regression models repeatedly show that, while per capita GDP explains much of the cross-country variation in development (indicated by things like access to sanitation and education outcomes), urbanization makes an additional and independent contribution to higher levels of development.

When urbanization peters out, efficiency of urbanization takes over as the driver. What is meant by efficiency? The answer lies at the regional and city levels discussed below.

Scale Four: Regions, Systems of Cities

At the regional scale, urban economists explain the existence of different-sized cities and explore questions related to optimal size, primacy, and appropriate levels of migration. They also look at whether national development policies have an urban bias.

The starting point for thinking about how cities of different sizes and specializations interact is "central place theory," devised by European geographers more than a century ago (Christaller 1933 [English trans. 1966] and Lösch 1940 [English trans. 1954]). Drawing on the concept of a firm's market area, the theory's key insight is the differentiation between lower-order goods, which have only modest economies of scale relative to per capita demand, and higher-order goods, which have large economies of scale relative to per capita demand. Pizza parlors are a good example of lower-order goods. Consumers eat pizza frequently, and there are few economies of scale involved in either its production or consumption. Jewelry stores are an example of higher-order goods. Consumers purchase jewelry infrequently, and agglomeration economies give rise to "jewelers' rows" in large cities and malls that facilitate comparison shopping. Central place theory suggests that a region supports a large number of small cities, producing lower-order goods, and a smaller number of large cities, producing both lower-order goods and higher-order goods.

That cities have negative qualities (congestion, pollution, crime) has given rise to the age-old question of whether they have an optimal size. Put in terms of urban economics, the question is whether, as a city grows, its negative agglomeration economies outweigh its positive. Some studies have tried to measure the marginal costs and benefits of population for a stylized city, typically claiming that there is some specific optimal size (usually of about 300,000). Other studies show that cities with populations of 2 million or above are more productive than those below that threshold (Segal 1979). Most current analysts are skeptical of these optimal-size theories, since while it may be that any particular city has some notional optimal size, there is no strong reason to believe that the optimal number of one city ought to apply for all cities (or for any particular city indefinitely). The existence of systems of cities of widely different sizes suggests that while there might be an optimal size for a certain city at a certain time, the search for the optimal size is fruitless.

Are some cities too large? Some argue that countries that are "too primate" (i.e., have some very large cities relative to the size of their total population) will find their growth adversely affected. However, the actual evidence for this assertion is fragmented and somewhat fragile. Figure 4.4 shows that the degree of primacy, measured by the share of a country's population in its largest city, is strongly related to the size of the country. The largest urban agglomerations in the world are currently on the order of 10 to 20 million people, depending in part on how one draws their boundaries. But national populations range from well over a billion to under a million. Thus, it is no surprise that very large countries like the U.S., India, and China have low values on the primacy index, even though they contain such very large cities as New York, Calcutta, Shanghai, and Beijing. In contrast, Singapore and Hong Kong are highly primate because 100 percent of each entity's population lives in one city. Overall, cities in Africa tend to be more primate than in Asia or Europe.

Figure 4.5 shows no obvious relationship between the primacy measure and per capita GDP growth rates in the succeeding period. However, estimating a preliminary regression that controls for other

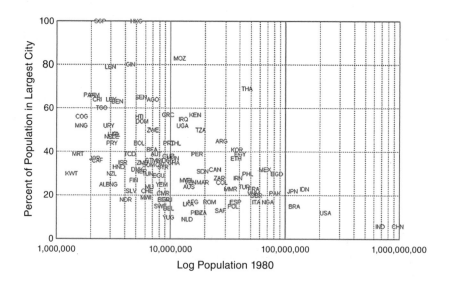

Figure 4.4. Primacy and Size of Country

Source: World Bank Development Indicators at http://data.worldbank.org/indicator.

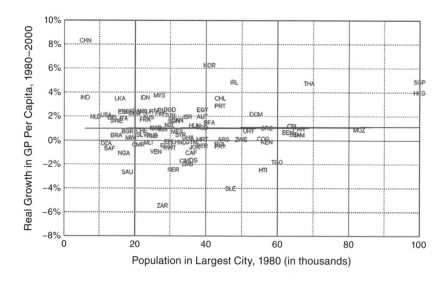

Figure 4.5. Growth and Primacy

Source: World Bank Development Indicators at http://data.worldbank.org/indicator.

determinants of primacy, including the size of the country and region, and then using the residual (the difference between the actual primacy and the primacy predicted from the regression equation) enables the measurement of how primate a country is after controlling for its size and region. This new variable shows that countries which, given their population and region, are more primate than would be expected, grow faster going forward. This analysis is too simple to prove that a more primate country will grow faster; but it does illustrate that the oft-cited concern with countries whose cities that have grown "too large" may well be overstated and not yet clearly demonstrated by careful research.

A question related to the issues of optimal size and primacy is whether rural-urban migration in developing countries can reach excessive levels, as influentially argued in the 1970s (Harris and Todaro 1970). Risk-neutral poor workers move to cities in hopes of obtaining high-paying jobs in the formal sector. But when urban labor markets cannot absorb them, an informal (or dual) labor market emerges, creating inefficiencies because "too many" migrants have come to the city. While the Harris-Todaro theory had a strong hold among the development community, it had little support theoretically or empirically (Williamson 1988; Scott 1981; Brueckner and Kim 2001; Brueckner and Zenou 1999). In the end, the Harris-Todaro model, despite its popularity, generated more heat than light.

Another issue regarding regional scale urbanization is the so-called urban bias. At issue is whether government policies favor the city relative to the countryside, and the effects of such discrimination if it exists. One measure of urban bias can be found in constructed indices of price distortion that serve as convenient measures of the public policy environment (Agarwala 1983; Malpezzi 1990). The Agawarla index, for example, reveals overvalued exchange rates, inappropriate agricultural and infrastructure prices, high tariffs, and so on, results that are demonstrably bad for a country's economy as a whole but can often benefit its urban dwellers. It hardly seems likely that such policies would be good for urban economies in the long run (even if in the short run some urban dwellers benefitted). Urban economists have generally joined with others in arguing against biased policies.

Scale Five: City: Local Land Markets, Capital Stock and Services

Despite the apparently intuitive nature of the city as a unit of observation, in reality, its use in economic analysis presents some problems. First, the labor and real estate markets that define a city conceptually rarely correspond to political boundaries. Second, city administrative definitions vary worldwide, often encompassing quite different geographies and jurisdictional units. Many cities around the world use the U.S. metropolitan designation (metro and micro statistical areas) to express city data, a practice which often causes a large number of cities, towns, villages, and unincorporated areas to be included. The "city" of Chongqing, China, comprises more than 80,000 square kilometers and 30 million people. The truly urbanized part of Chongqing—the functional city—has a population of only about 12 million and covers only a small fraction of the city's official area.

Nonetheless, the city scale illuminates important economic questions, especially those related to real estate markets and overall local development, such as how cities foster investment in, and efficient use of, real estate and housing, equipment, and infrastructure (water, sanitation, electricity); improve the scope and quality of education and training and react to changes in transport and communication; support important public and private services, including those related to health and personal safety; deal with "informality" with regard to land tenure and other issues; contribute to solving environmental challenges; and encourage not only allocative efficiency—the right mix of current activities—but "x-efficiency," a measure of firms' ability to combine inputs.

A large literature on urbanization and service delivery, the form of local governments, and federalism/decentralization reflects the scope and importance of these factors. Classic studies demonstrate the importance of a healthy local tax base and at least some linkage between local government spending and local resource mobilization (Dillinger 1988; Bahl and Linn 1992). Related studies discuss the effects of different forms of fiscal decentralization and federalism as well as which services should be provided by which level of government (Buckley 2005; Davoodi and Zou 1998; Peterson and Annez 2007; Kaufmann, Leautier, and Mastruzzi 2004). Local finance and governance are especially important as determinants of infrastructure availability and performance. Poorly designed infrastructure policies can be a serious drag on development (Lee and Anas 1989). For example, because of the poor performance of governments, the majority of Nigerian firms of any size must provide their own water supply, and virtually all provide private power.

A second order of local-government questions revolves around the scope and quality of education and training available within the economy. Studies show that cities and regions with higher levels of human capital have higher incomes, and many (though not all) studies have also found a positive relationship between human capital and growth rates. This latter correlation is not necessarily theoretically obvious; for example, it is easy to develop a simple model of growth in which there are diminishing returns to human capital. And there are difficulties in correctly estimating the true effects, since education is surely in turn affected by income, among other econometric issues (Moretti 2004; Rauch 1993).

That technical change affects urbanization (and vice versa) is well studied while much of the discussion of agglomeration is framed in terms of sharing ideas. Some studies look at the spatial dimension of knowledge production (Audretsch and Feldman 2004). They show that new communications technology, including the Internet, complements rather than substitutes for face-to-face contact in many (not all) production and consumption activities (Cairncross 1997; Gasper and Glaeser 1998; Kolko 2000).

Development is not only about such factors of production as capital, real estate, and labor but also about how those inputs are combined. The past century has seen a managerial revolution that has contributed to development and taken place largely in cities (Chandler 1977). In the jargon of economists, development describes not only sectoral shifts but improvements in x-efficiency or better ways of combining inputs (Leibenstein 1966). Business management is largely about sharing information and reducing transaction costs within firms, increasing total factor productivity.

Scale Six: Neighborhoods: Location Within the City and Urban Form

The economic analysis of neighborhoods is of interest to the urban economists who view issues of location within cities as dictated by the value of access to a particular, usually central, location. The increase in the value of a location is a function of the savings in transportation costs (Alonso 1964; Muth 1969; McMillen 2004). These studies contribute to the understanding of urban density.

Within cities, densities vary remarkably. Among large cities in the United States, for example, midtown Manhattan has a density approaching 200 people per hectare (pph) that falls off to 50 pph or less about twenty kilometers away. But because the central area of the city comprises a relatively small area, the average density of the New York metropolitan area is only about forty people per hectare. This density pattern corresponds to reality at least roughly (because rent and real estate prices deviate from the theoretical pattern more frequently and in greater amounts since prices can change faster than people can change density), not only in most U.S. cities but in most cities in market-oriented economies. It is sometimes referred to as a negative exponential pattern. In contrast, Moscow does not follow this pattern as its density increases with distance from the center. Why? Until the fall of the Soviet Union, decisions about the size, timing, and location of real estate investments, including housing, were made by central planners (Renaud

1995). There was no such thing as a land or housing or real estate market; the state allocated use rights to enterprises and individuals according to nonmarket criteria (Bertaud and Renaud 1997).

Not all recently communist cities were or are as strangely formed as Moscow. Chinese cities, for example, developed in ways much more recognizable to a market-oriented urban economist, even though they also lacked functioning land markets for many decades. In the late 20th century, Shanghai's core density of about 1,000 pph declined quickly as distance from the center increased. Certainly one reason large Chinese cities developed very differently from Russian cities was that when Shanghai was developing twenty to forty years ago, most commuters walked or bicycled; the distance one could walk in half an hour or so put a natural boundary on housing location relative to jobs in China.

Economic analyses of neighborhoods show that local neighborhood conditions affect both the structure of housing prices and urban form (Follain and Malpezzi 1981; Mills and Price 1984). New literature on neighborhoods extends and deepens the insights of pioneers by developing rigorous economic and psychological models of interdependent behavior (Wilson 1987; Durlauf 2004; Manski 1993; Topa 2001). A large number of recent studies looking at the spatial distribution of several factors (house value, employment, educational outcomes, criminal behavior, marriage and fertility, drug and alcohol use, IQ, mental health, and prenatal care) reveal that neighborhoods do matter. These findings are now informing the long debated "peoples versus place" question, that is whether public policies aimed at ameliorating poverty and other social problems should have some place-based elements or stay focused on individuals (see, for example, Ladd [1994]). While the design of policies remains complex, and while discovering neighborhood effects does not imply that all successful strategies will be place based, this research is clearly changing current thinking.

Still, despite the growing acceptance of the importance of neighborhood, its definitions remain difficult to specify. Most studies use a data-driven definition (zip code, census tract, block group, or county boundary) but none of these captures a neighborhood well. More servicable neighborhood definitions would include some measure of the spatial form of interactions, maximizing within-neighborhood context relative to across-neighborhood context. But many studies ignore these definitional issues.

A Research Agenda Categorized by the Six Scales of Urbanization

The six scales of urban development suggest a research agenda. Although many of the following issues can be studied across multiple scales, most seem to fit most naturally, if still provisionally, at one particular scale. This categorization is thus meant to be suggestive, rather than rigid or immutable.

Research at the Conceptual Level

There is much to be learned about the fundamental concept of agglomeration. One issue is whether recent studies of given industries or regions are idiosyncratic or applicable across a wide range of situations. Another frontier is learning more about neighborhood-level agglomeration. For urban economists, this has the promise of integrating two of the four or five "big ideas" of urban economics: namely, agglomeration and models of location within cities. To those with a policy bent, it has the potential to inform a host of important questions, since so many urban problems are much worse in particular locations. To give just one example, since the end of apartheid, blacks have been moving closer to historically white areas of Johannesburg, and, at the same time, more economic activity is taking place in the townships. But the process of adjustment is ongoing. Applying agglomeration and location models in this case can help determine the relative contributions of each of these developments and which (if either) might be the focus of public policy.

One of the most important unanswered questions about agglomeration is the strength of different kinds of location economies and their behavior at different levels of development (Quigley 2007). While some studies use cross-country data to study links between productivity and city size, few have offered explicit findings about the relative contributions of agglomeration in poor or transition countries compared to rich ones.

Research at the Country Level

One starting point for thinking about cross-country research is to reconsider the UN-HABITAT Housing and Urban Indicators project (see Angel 2000; Malpezzi and Mayo 1997). This was an effort to develop an equivalent for cities of the World Bank's well-known World Development Indicators (WDI). Using a varying sample of about 50 to 200 cities, researchers developed successive waves of the indicators that resulted in a somewhat irregular set of data on urban outcomes and policy measures. Housing outcomes are heavily represented (rents, house prices, vacancy rates, average floor space, etc.), but data on nonresidential real estate and other aspects of economic development are either limited or nonexistent. While information on the policy environment—land-use regulations, housing finance policies, and the like proved difficult to assemble or validate and were downplayed.

This scarcity of data is particularly unfortunate because understanding urban problems requires measuring, or at least categorizing, the environment in which they exist. This is not to minimize the difficulty of collecting data on policies which are by their nature very difficult to measure with precision. But the importance of these policies suggests the potential value of the substantial effort it would take to design and collect the appropriate indicators (Malpezzi and Mayo 1997). Such an effort would be an important contribution to the fulfillment of the promise of early research on urban indicators.

Many previous cross-country economic analyses of urban phenomena have revolved around so-called growth regressions, ordinary least-squares regressions, usually with a single cross-section of countries, that incorporate measures of urbanization, housing, or real estate investment and other relevant variables. This style of analysis has been around for some time (see Burns and Grebler 1977; Barro 1991, 1997). Recent advances in cross-country econometrics raise questions about the efficacy of the simple cross-country regression approach (Brock and Durlauf 2001; Sala-i-Martin 1997, 2001; Fernandez, Ley, and Steel 2001). The potential benefits of examining growth and development issues with a well-specified panel model are well understood and often put into practice. Less commonly implemented are gains from considering so-called convergence clubs and other fruitful stratifications, rather than simply plugging in some regional dummies in a simple cross-section of countries. The latter can yield a better understanding of some important puzzles. There is, for example, particular interest in learning whether African cities (and economies) are really "different" (Block 2001; Collier and Gunning 1999). There is, likewise, a need for approaches comparing and contrasting India's and China's responses to urbanization, given that these countries comprise roughly 38 percent of the world's population and each is at a point of inflection suggesting substantial urbanization over the next decade or two. Countries meriting special attention are in the Middle East and Central Asia, two regions whose cities and economies are exhibiting subpar performance.

Continued cross-country research on property rights remains fruitful. Comparative analysis would be greatly facilitated by a careful cross-market categorization and indexation of the specific "sticks" that make up the bundle of property rights. How to measure property rights, how to price them, and what their effects are on the housing market and on related markets (especially finance) all need further study. The developing and transition economy literature on tenure choice, tenure security, and mobility could profit from further application of models incorporating the relative user costs of owner-occupied and rental housing.

Regarding real estate, the first point to be noted is the amazing dearth of rigorous research on commercial real estate markets in most countries. Certainly housing is a larger fraction of the capital stock and almost certainly it generates more externalities and has deeper distributional implications. Nevertheless, commercial real estate has large social and public policy implications that are less well understood and addressed than they should be.

While economists know a lot about housing, especially income elasticity of demand and its remarkable stability across countries and markets, they know much less about the price elasticity of demand, given the difficulty of decomposing expenditure into price and quantity. New research on cross-country demand could have a high payoff. In this case, there is a reversal of the usual situation: most cross-country analysis of housing demand has focused primarily on developing countries, while developed and transition economies have been relatively neglected, leaving demand in middle- and even upper-income countries as yet unstudied (Malpezzi 1999). This is particularly important since many of the emerging markets in Eastern Europe and the former Soviet Union fit into the "omitted middle" of little-studied countries. Similarly, despite some progress, little empirical work has been done on housing supply and much of that only within the U.S. (Malpezzi 2007; Olsen 1987). Supply-focused studies can be extended and updated (Malpezzi and Mayo 1985; Johnson 1987; Ferchiou 1982).

Research on housing and the aggregate economy can be extended in several directions. For example, little is known about the relationship between housing and the business cycle in developing and former socialist countries. Davis and Ortalo-Magne (2007) present a model that could be applied in a range of countries to study how and whether housing market performance links to agglomeration and worker mobility.

Research on Regions and Systems of Cities

Despite years of writing on central place theory and a recent resurgence of work on the size and distribution of cities, little is known about exactly how cities are linked (Henderson 1998; Duranton and Puga 2000; Abdel-Rahman and Anas 2004). Current research focuses on connections between product and labor markets, leaving linkages between land/real estate and capital markets relatively neglected. There is a nascent literature on information spillovers. Border effects of state and national governments are also fruitful areas for future research.

Is there really anything to the simpler "primate city" hypotheses? If not, can a more sophisticated version tell us something about when larger cities are generally a good thing and when not? Is there an optimal-sized distribution of cities? Where and when are such optima observed? Because many public and private policies are undertaken in the name of (and even more often in violation of) principles enunciated by such research, it is essential to develop models to assess the costs and benefits of expanded urbanization.

Research on Cities

Cities are crucial providers of public goods. Without infrastructure and functioning schools, cities as well as the aggregate economies of their ecological setting will founder. However, some claim that city and other local governments, saddled with unfunded mandates and poorly matched resource bases, cannot perform properly, leading to several questions including how serious are the losses from suboptimally designed governmental structures? Is additional decentralization the answer for many countries, or simply an immediately appealing but flawed remedy? Under decentralization schemes, what, exactly, should be decentralized? What is the best mix of property taxes, intergovernmental transfers, and capital markets? Perhaps most important, is there a better system of incentives for local governments—how about for their state and national counterparts?

More work on which kinds of infrastructure work best—and under which conditions—is needed in order to design the most effective water, sanitation, and education programs for a given context. Transport issues are especially critical. How can China, for example, cope with increasing urban demand for cars in such dense cities and at such scale? How can urban schools deliver better education to higher enrollments? Generally, the incentives research on housing (the so-called Malaysia model of Malpezzi and Mayo [1997]) can be extended to study the bottlenecks in many urban services.

A large part of what is known about cities in developing countries stems, directly or indirectly, from a remarkable research project, the City Study, carried out by a group of Colombian and World Bank researchers some two decades ago. The City Study, which focused on Bogotá and Cali, Colombia, tackled the economics of transport, housing, land development, and local governance in an integrated fashion. The results of this study still inform ideas about these issues (Ingram 1998; Mohan 1994). Many follow-up studies, especially on housing and on local public finance, make use of data collection methods and analytic tools developed by the City Study. But much has changed in cities over the past three decades, including in other Latin American cities. It is time for a follow-up study, in Colombia or elsewhere.

Research on Neighborhoods

One of the most exciting research developments over the past decade has been the application of new spatial technology to questions of urban densities (Bertaud and Malpezzi 2003; Angel, Sheppard, and Civco 2005; and in Sheppard in this volume). There are a number of recent contributions to urban form that suggest research extensions to the city-based work discussed above, such as Liu's (2006) demonstration of how better to incorporate the effects of physical and regulatory barriers on such models. At another level, better integration of the analysis of density and the city's footprint would be a great advance. Density measures could be collected at different times and then analyzed dynamically.

Although recent years have yielded a lot of progress toward a more rigorous understanding of neighborhoods, few researchers have applied these advances in developing or transition economies, and there remains much to learn about the form of the city and its consequences. The first step would be finishing the basic measurements; then other questions could be pursued at the neighborhood level, such as these: What are the costs and benefits of urban form? How does form affect transport, energy use, and public finance? What are the "policy handles" on form?

Learning more about the politics of small areas, including slum settlements, would also be valuable for a range of reasons. For example, many in the development community have suggested community-based lending as a tool for urban development. This is an intriguing idea, but not without concerns. What does lending to a community, rather than an individual, really mean? How can community decisions—as opposed to those of an outside institution like a bank—about the allocation of funds maintain transparency? Of course, the benefits of lending further down-market might be well worth any such distributional concern. For community-based lending, researchers could extend Dahl's classic question, "Who governs?" to "Who gets loans?"

Data Needs Across the Six Scales

This chapter has organized potential research into six scales, but in practice data issues cross most, if not all, of them. There are, for example, potential gains to designing national Living Standard Measurement Surveys with a stratified cluster sampling strategy that permits more useful urban analysis and more urban-relevant questions (e.g., on housing, education, urban service levels). As discussed in several other contributions to this volume, including those by Bazoglu, Montgomery, Balk, Sheppard, Seto, Evans, and Pasternak, the data needs of urban analysis are consistently twofold: improved collection methods are needed at all scales, particularly in order to cope with rapidly changing settlement patterns in the developing world, and more effective distribution of data is needed across all scales in order to ensure integrated and efficient policy development. The scales into which this chapter has divided urbanization are necessary for determining the specificity of urban problems as well as particular gaps in our current understanding of them; solutions to the challenges of tomorrow's urbanization will require flexible, analytically rigorous cross-scale coordination.

Chapter 5

Urban Growth and Spatial Development: The China Case

Anthony Yeh

China has experienced rapid urban growth since the adoption of Economic Reform and Open Policy in 1978. Not only is more than one-third of the country's population now living in cities, but the remaining population is becoming increasingly dependent on cities and towns for its economic survival and livelihood. At the National People's Congress in March 2001, the central government clearly affirmed the coming reality of China as an urban nation and did so again when it made "urbanization" an important national strategy in the Tenth Five-Year Plan. At the Sixteenth National Congress of the Communist Party of China, held in November 2002, it reiterated its aim to build a moderately well-off society (*xiaokong shehue*), and a higher level of urbanization will be used to support this.

China has recently entered a period of very rapid urbanization. In 2003, the urbanization level topped 40 percent. Chinese experts predict that by 2050, the urban population is likely to reach 1.0 to 1.1 billion, with urbanization levels soaring upward of 75 percent and the urban sector contributing over 95 percent of the national economy (Li 2003). Accordingly, more than 600 million Chinese people will shift from rural areas to urban districts by 2050 (*People's Daily* 2002). Furthermore, projections show that by 2050, there are likely to be fifty ultra-large cities (with populations of more than 2 million), over 150 big cities, 500 medium-sized cities, and 1,500 small cities (*People's Daily* 2002). In addition to these demographic changes, other forces such as globalization and regional integration are expected to further accelerate the role of cities as centers of production, consumption, and social and political change.

Existing urban development in China reflects its transition from a

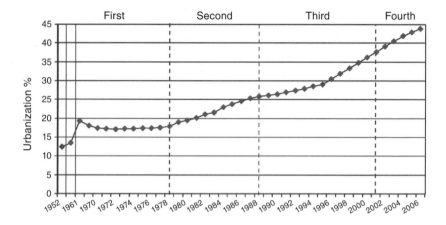

Figure 5.1. Four Waves of Urbanization in China

Source: China Population and Employment Statistical Yearbook 2007.

centrally planned economy to a more market-oriented economy, and because of this China has taken a different developmental path from those already market-oriented cities in the West and in other parts of Asia. China is also one of the few countries in the world that has an overt national urbanization policy. In order to understand the growth and spatial development of cities in China, we need to examine the changes in the urbanization trends since the establishment of the People's Republic of China in 1949.

Four Waves of Urbanization

Four main waves of urbanization can be identified in China since the establishment of the People's Republic of China in 1949 (figure 5.1) (Yeh, Xu, and Yi 2006). They have had different impacts on the urbanization level, city-size distribution, spatial distribution of cities, and internal structure of cities. The central government played an important role in urban system development in China up until the adoption of Economic Reform and Open Policy in 1978, after which this role has been increasingly reduced.

First Phase: Anti-Urbanization (1949–1978)

The first period of urbanization started in 1949 and ended in 1978. This period was characterized by low levels of urbanization and even anti-urbanization; during this period, the percentage of the population living in cities was never above 20 percent. Politics and public policy were the two most important factors in shaping urban development in China (Lo 1987). They exerted a strong control over the growth of urban population (Xu 1984a), urban system development (Chang 1976; Xu 1984b), and the provincial distribution of urban population (Yeh and Xu 1984). In the pre-1978 era, urban population growth was slow, maintaining an average annual growth rate of 2.8 percent (CSSB, 1999a). This was in sharp contrast to other countries in Asia, which were urbanizing at a rapid rate of over 5 percent per annum. Both the official policy of strictly controlling the size of large cities and the industrial policy of dispersing industries from the coast increased the urbanization level of cities in the interior provinces of northwest China and led to the development of small and medium-sized cities and a balanced urban system.

Economic policies during this period focused on harnessing the productive capacities of cities through massive socialist industrialization but did not attend to issues of infrastructure and service delivery. Cities, in short, were regarded as centers of production, not consumption, and development strategies sought to transform the capitalist consumption cities of the past into the socialist production cities of a new China. The government therefore developed overt policies to control the growth of large cities, such as Shanghai, which were regarded as oriented more toward consumption than toward production.

The Chinese government implemented its plans to control city growth mainly through population control and resource allocation. A household registration (*hukou*) system was established in 1954 to stop unauthorized migration from the countryside to the cities. The government divided the population into agricultural (*nongye renkou*) and nonagricultural (*fei nongye renkou*), a division which was used in conjunction with the food-rationing system to regulate the monthly quotas of foodstuffs, consumables, and consumer durables (Kirkby 1985). The household registration system required all neighborhood residents to register with their local police station. In collaboration with lower-level civilian officials, police ran late-night household registration checks to ensure that people did not move into the neighborhood without proper registration.

The household system, the widespread rationing of foods, and the state control of jobs and houses effectively controlled urban population until the late 1970s. Without a proper neighborhood registration, one had no access to jobs, education, and many highly subsidized and otherwise unavailable consumer necessities such as grain, cloth, oil, pork, bean curd, and soap. The predominantly public-owned housing was not available without registration, and the same was true for over 90 percent of all state- and collective-controlled jobs (Whyte and Parish 1983). The household system was further tightened by a migration law in 1958 that limited the entry of peasants into cities, except those who had obtained work permits from the labor bureau. The household registration system was effective during the Cultural Revolution (1966–1976) in sending youths to the countryside. The absolute population of the large cities declined, with a net decrease in the total population of the city system (Yeh and Xu 1990a, 1990b). Some of the extra-large and large cities were even sufficiently depopulated to classify as large and medium-sized cities.

Before the Economic Reform and Open Policy in 1978, the Chinese government was remarkably successful in using population control and resource allocation to shape the urban system according to their public policy and ideology. The growth of large cities was successfully curtailed, small towns were developing rapidly, and the balance of both cities and population was successfully shifted from the coast to interior and border locations. Because these were the results of a centrally controlled government, they are not available or applicable to many other countries. Without tremendous central control over human mobility and economic resources, it would not be possible to control the population and allocate resources so exactly. This control over jobs, housing, and the necessities of daily life made it possible to control immigration, and thus population growth, in the cities. The centralized ownership of industry made it possible to shift resources from larger, coastal cities to cities in the interior. All of this changed with the adoption of the Economic Reform and Open Policy in 1978.

Second Phase: Early Economic Reform and Open Policy (1978–1988)

The second phase of urbanization began with the economic reforms of the Economic Reform and Open Policy in 1978 and ended with land-use reform, which began in 1988. Soon after the economic reform of 1978, it was feared that the population in Chinese cities, especially the large cities, would grow too fast for the cities to handle. To prevent the urban problems that plagued the large cities in developing countries in the post–World War II period, the Urban Planning Conference held by the State Construction Commission in 1980 adopted a policy of "controlling the size of large cities, rationally developing medium cities and actively developing small cities." Rural industrialization, which allowed peasants to leave their farms without leaving their villages (*litu bu lixiang*), was proposed by Fei in 1984 and used to curtail the rapid massive migration of rural laborers to the cities (Fei 1984). The preferential policies and geographic location of the eastern coastal regions allowed them to attract a large amount of overseas investment during the freer markets of the Economic Reform and Open Policy.

Meanwhile, farmers in these regions gradually established a unique form of rural industrialization: developing township and village enterprises (TVEs). TVEs helped to absorb numerous surplus laborers in rural areas and thus facilitated the process of urbanization from below. Scholars have identified different models to understand the growth of TVEs. The South Jiangsu model highlights the role of prosperous collective industry in rural development (Ma and Fan 1994). The Wenzhou model stresses the importance of the private sector in the overall dynamics of urbanization (Liu 1992). The model which takes up "externally driven exo-urbanization" focuses on the significance of overseas capital from Hong Kong in facilitating rural industrialization in the Pearl River Delta (Eng 1997; Sit and Yang 1997). In all these models, the development of TVEs played a vital role in developing small cities and towns.

The result of rural industrialization was rural urbanization. Urban development in China's rural areas was phenomenal. There was a rapid increase in the number of towns,[1] from 2,176 in 1978 to 11,481 in 1988. Town population also increased rapidly, bringing the number of people living in towns nearly equal to the number living in cities. In some growing regions, such as the Pearl River Delta, small towns grew faster than cities, reversing the urbanization trend of most developing countries where cities grow faster than towns (Xu and Li 1990). Farmers were attracted to village and township industries. This caused a process of "urbanization from below" (Ma and Fan 1994; Cui and Ma 1999), in which farmers left the farmland but not their villages; they entered factories but not cities.

During this phase, land was still owned by the state and allocated free of charge to users. Cities still relied heavily on the state for their infrastructure development. This was drastically changed with land reform in 1988, after which cities could obtain revenue from leasing their land and use the revenue for developing their cities.

Third Phase: Urban Land Reform (1988–2001)

The third wave of urbanization (1988–2001) took place when a series of new reforms rapidly restructured urban space. In 2000, cities housed 36.22 percent of the national population, a 10 percent increase over 1990. This decade marked the growing strength of Chinese urban development in terms of both quantity and quality. It was strongly influenced by land reform in 1988, which generated revenue for city governments to improve their infrastructure and image to increase their competitiveness. There was further diversification of investment sources and increasing openness in the economic system; at the same time, this period also saw the declining importance of state enterprises; the declining importance of state-directed housing; and land reforms.

Further diversified finance environment. Before the economic reform, the state budget was the dominant source of Chinese investment in fixed assets. In 1957, the state budget accounted for 88.2 percent of the total investment. The percentage remained as high as 62.2 percent in 1978. However, it had decreased dramatically to only 6.8 percent by 1991. During the period from January to July 2007, the state budget represented only 4 percent of total fixed-asset investment (CSSB 1999b, 2008). Collectively raised funds, foreign investments, and loans became three major investment sources of increasing significance. Collectively raised funds are those raised by work units and developers through a variety of methods, including short-term liabilities, staff bonds (unlike shares that can be sold openly), stock markets, loans from financiers, and profits and funds that are obtained outside the control of economic plans, so-called "funds outside the planning system" (*jihua wai zijin*). Collectively raised funds can be used more flexibly than state investment.

The declining proportion of the state budget invested in fixed assets led to the decentralization of decision-making, both financially and spatially. The traditional means of controlling urban planning and urban development through centralized economic plans became less and less effective and continues to be deployed less and less frequently. Because a large amount of investment comes from collectively raised funds, industries and enterprises have much greater latitude and discretion. They can choose to locate in areas that they think are best for their operations.

The declining importance of state enterprises. Economic reform has changed the economic structure of China's cities. More people are working in the service sector and in non-state-owned enterprises. With a rising living standard and a need for a better network to sell the products of reformed enterprises, the service sector is growing rapidly. The service sector's contribution to the overall economy increased from 19.1 percent in 1978 to 39 percent in 2006; over the same period, the percentage of the population employed in the service sector increased from 24.2 percent to 31.4 percent (CSSB 2007).

The state was the dominant employer in cities in the 1980s and early 1990s, and the number of people employed in the state sector increased steadily between 1978 and 1995. The collective sector was another important area with a growing number of employees before 1992. Major changes occurred after the mid-1990s, when nonstate sectors in general, and private enterprises and self-employment in particular, began to play an increasingly important role in absorbing laborers. In 2005, among the total 273.31 million persons employed in urban areas, 64.88 million were employed by state-owned operations, 8.1 million by collectively owned operations, and 42.11 million by private ventures, overseas enterprises, and other nonstate actors. In 2003, there were 23.8 million self-employed individuals (SSB 2004). The manufacturing sector grew to be the most significant employer, hiring more than 33 percent of total employed persons in 2002. This sector is followed by education, culture, arts, broadcasting, film, and television (9.4 percent, combined); construction (8.87 percent); and wholesale and retail sale along with trades and catering services (7.49 percent) (SSB 2003).

Since the mid-1990s, the informal sector[2] has begun to play a greater role in the economy as a whole. First, it has helped to improve China's employment situation and alleviate poverty. In 2003, the private and self-employed sectors created more than 49 million jobs in urban areas, representing over 19 percent of the total number of employed persons. Second, the informal sector provides products and services that are often not available from the formal sector. Most of these are through low-profile jobs. The informal sector also involves a group of high-value-added freelancers, undertaking such jobs as software design and consultancy (Ministry of Labour and Social Security 2003). However, this group is only a very small part of the large informal workforce.

Not only is the proportion of state enterprises declining due to the emergence of multiple ownerships, but state-provided services and welfare are declining, too. Before economic reform, enterprises had to provide nearly all daily services to their staff: food service, barbershops, kindergartens, primary schools, clinics, high school, and transport. Now instead of providing these services themselves, state enterprises may lease out service facilities to individual enterprises to achieve efficiency or simply cut down these services and rely more heavily on the services provided by the city government.

Housing reform and the development of the housing market. Housing reform is a gradual process. In socialist systems, many theoretical controversies surround the issues of housing and housing subsidies: Is housing a commodity? Is private ownership of housing a breach of socialist ideology? Does leasing or renting involve some kind of exploitation? Housing reform started in the early 1980s as part of China's overall economic reform. Despite various experiments with rent adjustment and the sale of public housing in selected cities in the 1980s, the overall reform of housing was slow and piecemeal until 1998. Before the suspension of in-kind welfare allocation in 1998, China's housing system, like those in other socialist economies, was characterized by the dominance of public housing (Wu et al. 2007). Under the soft budget constraint, state work units used privatization to sell housing stock at extraordinarily low prices. Under this process of commercialization, these work units have withdrawn themselves from direct involvement in housing construction. However, on the consumption side, the low incomes of state employees have forced the work-unit system to remain an indispensable supplier of new housing. In fact, the state work units have played an increasing role in housing provision, because the large stock of housing built after the economic reform was in the form of work-unit housing (Wu 1996). The pivotal role of the state work unit in housing provision has been widely noted (Wu 1996; Zhou and Logan 1996; Huang and Clark 2002).

Land reform and development of the land market. Prior to the introduction of the paid land-use system, land uses were decided through a central planning process which involved negotiations and compromises among various government agencies, which were both land users and land-management organizations. Land-use approval came either from municipalities or the state. In the latter case, approval was registered in the municipalities. Once land was allocated to a particular user, it was difficult to alter land users or change land use. Although, in theory, land still belongs to the state, in practice, the state retains little control over the land, especially over its specific uses, once it has allocated land to a user such as a work unit. Despite this state control, land users effectively hold property rights, altering land uses according to their interests. The fact that land is categorized and managed according to the type of work unit to which it is allocated, not according to the actual use to which the land is put, enables this process. For example, land allocated to a manufacturing factory is referred to as industrial land even though, inside the land parcel, the factory may have subdivided it into manufacturing and residential areas. Land subdivision in the allocated land is outside the control of centralized urban planning.

Since adopting the paid land-use system, a land market has gradually formed. There are four basic types of paid land use systems, each with a different land pricing system (Yeh and Wu 1996). The first type is land requisition, in which the state acquires land collectively owned by farmers. Before economic reform, requisition of rural land was simply a process of administrative relocation, with the state typically compensating farmers for the crops they cultivated. Perhaps the most preferable method of compensation was for the state to arrange positions for the farmers as nonagricultural state workers and register their households in the city. After economic reform, the requisition of land became more complex. The government is unlikely to force farmers to surrender their land for nonstate projects. Compensation can be arranged between users and farmers. Accordingly, the standard set by the government becomes less and less effective as the price comes to be set by the market forces of supply and demand. Compensation paid to existing land users vary greatly. The municipality can expropriate 1 mu or 0.07 hectare of cultivated land at a compensation varying from a meager RMB 300 (US$36.20) in comparatively backward places to a rare RMB 5,000 (US$603.90) in more advanced regions such as Beijing (*China Daily* 2003). Numerous disputes arise from land expropriation because existing users are not satisfied with state compensation, which is set at a rate much lower than market value. This makes land expropriation a complicated and time-consuming process (Wu et al. 2007).

The second type of land allocation is administrative. This type of transaction applies to the development of nonprofitable urban projects, e.g., urban infrastructure, public utilities, and affordable housing. Land is primarily supplied to state work units or relevant departments. These developers are usually affiliated with municipal housing or construction bureaus and often have to pay land-acquisition fees and/or an initial land-development cost (i.e., the cost of changing raw land to serviced land) to the municipality. They are not allowed to transfer land-use rights without proper authorization.

The third type of paid land-use rights is land leasing, generally known as conveyance (*churang*), which is the state's granting of the right to use a piece of land. This is also known as the primary land market in China. There are six methods in land leasing, namely negotiation, tender, auction, quotation, short lease, and other flexible methods (Wu et al. 2007). Land conveyance through negotiation is not much different from traditional negotiation and compromise. Negotiation may be carried out only if there is only one developer showing interest in bidding on a piece of land, but it excludes land to be used for commerce, tourism, recreation, or commodity apartments. For tender, the conditions of a land plot and the development constraints are announced and tendering is invited. Land auction is an open competition in which the highest bidder will get land-use rights. Quotation (*gua pai*—literally, "hanging plate") is a relatively new practice and came into existence in 2002. It is a process whereby a city government publishes a notice disclosing the terms and conditions for granting land-use rights, and accepts quotations from bidders and updates prices in the notice accordingly. The winning bidder is the one who offers the highest price at the end of the notice period, which is set at least ten working days. Cities like Shenzhen have also invented innovative forms of land conveyance (Wu et al. 2007).

The fourth type of land transaction is generally known in China as the transfer of land-use right (*zhuanrang*), in which the right to use a piece of land is transferred from one user to another through payment. This is also known as the secondary land market in China. The market configuration in land trading between different developers has been reconfigured recently, as the effort to soften the landing for China's economy has led to a tighter monetary policy and a more controlled land supply. Higher land costs have bankrupted smaller developers, while larger ones, especially those with government backgrounds, have increased their land-development market share. Developers with previously obtained sites tend to bridge capital shortages by using land-use rights as collateral to obtain bank loans. This makes mortgages the most popular mode of land transaction in the secondary market (Wu et al. 2007).

As a result of the new system of paid transfer of land-use rights, a dual land market system has formed. On the one hand, land allocated before economic reform is charged a nominal land-use fee annually. On the other hand, new land is acquired through the market and can be quite expensive. Still, some land uses, such as administrative, cultural, military, and special uses, are allocated at a very low price. The present land system in China is different from that in Western societies, where there is only one land market with free transactions.

In addition to these four types of land transaction, the Chinese state has recently begun to experiment with a new type of rural land transaction. Previously, the state monopolized the primary land market and collectives were forbidden to sell or lease rural land-use rights to developers directly. Despite this, many collectives have circumvented this ban. Recognizing this reality, some places have been allowed to experiment with a new policy designed to legalize land transactions between collectives and developers. Like its urban counterpart, rural land can be traded by collectives or developers via conveyance, lease, transactions, or mortgage. This experiment has great implications for market configuration and land governance in China, since it means that the state no longer monopolizes land supply (Wu et al. 2007).

Impacts on urban growth and spatial development. With the further development of Economic Reform and Open Policy, there has been substantial growth of economic capacity, capital accumulation, and household income. Together with reforms to encourage the private ownership of housing, land reform in 1988 helped city governments generate revenue for improving their infrastructure and city images to increase their competitiveness. These economic changes generated significant urban growth.

The development of the land market has had great implications for the allocation of urban space. Land-use fees are now a significant factor in location decisions. In Guangzhou, for example, commercial land is divided into seven grades to reflect locational disparity within the city. A benchmark price provides a baseline for localities to determine the approximate average price of different land grades, based on such parameters as acquisition cost, location, availability of urban infrastructure, and allowed development density. Cities can thus make adjustment for other site-specific features when pricing individual sites (Li 1999). The introduction of land price triggers urban redevelopment since the land value of existing old housing is rather low compared with the land value of new housing or commercial building.

Urban redevelopment optimizes spatial structure by changing underused city centers into more intensively used and profitable areas. These city-center transformations have been actively pursued in two radically different ways: through "spontaneous" land conversions that deviate from government plans and through state-led renovations focused on central business district (CBD) formation and flagship redevelopment projects (Wu et al. 2007). The former often involve illegal land transactions or changes of land use without planning permission, while the latter frequently blend local governments and the private sector in an important partnership to create prestigious urban spaces through massive demolition and residential relocation.

Spontaneous land conversion was identified as a major factor causing disorder in the city centers in the 1990s (Yeh and Wu 1996), but there has been a major shift away from this view for two major reasons. First, state-initiated projects, while effectively exalting the urban image, have often been undertaken at a high cost to existing communities and, in many cases, simply resulted in the destruction of vibrant neighborhoods (e.g., courtyard houses in Beijing). To create financial feasibility for redevelopment, local states may link the renovation of old urban areas to the conspicuous consumption of land and the conversion of land uses, as evidenced by the case of Xitiandi in Shanghai (Wu et al. 2007). Second, while the possible drawbacks of state initiatives have become more clear, so too have the advantages of the illegal spontaneous land conversions taking place in Chinese cities. The redevelopment of the Huaqiang Road North in Shenzhen, from a dilapidated industrial area to a vibrant business district, offers a good example of the benefits these land conversions can have (Wang and Xu 2002). While illegal land conversions do not necessarily lead to spatial disorder, they do create some ungovernable features in the process of space commodification. For instance, they bring about a situation where the development of commercial space is not constrained by the supply of leased land (Wu et al. 2007).

Chinese cities used to be compact in comparison with sprawling North American cities. Rapid land development in recent years has created new city structures and new spaces of urban sprawl. Before land reform, most of the development was concentrated in the inner suburban fringe (five to eleven kilometers from the city center). After land reform, the central area experienced a sharp increase in land-use changes as a result of urban redevelopment spurred by the introduction of land values. Development in the inner suburban fringe, although still high, has decreased compared to the period before land reform, while development in the suburban area has increased. The distribution of land-use change after reform therefore reveals a strong bimodal tendency, i.e., more development in the central area and more near the subcenter (Wu et al. 2007). One result is the emergence of urban sprawl (the extension of the built-up area into suburbs in a discontinuous, low-density form), as development areas leapfrog and large peripheral residential communities combine to create new urban subcenters. Rapid urban expansion has transformed the compact Chinese city into a more dispersed and multicentered one (Yeh and Li 1999). For example, in 2003, the built-up area of Dongguan, the prosperous industrial town in the Pearl River Delta, reached 246 square kilometers, almost eighteen times the city's area in 1990 (Wu et al. 2007). In Guangzhou, the suburban node and ring has received an increasing proportion of land conversions. Changes in Guangzhou's administrative boundaries have continued to drive the urban structure into an increasingly dispersed and multicentered form (Wu et al. 2007) (figure 5.2).

The paid land-use system has provided the city government a new and substantial revenue source which was not available in the past when land was allocated free of charge. Lands are leased to foreign investors and local developers for industrial, residential, and commercial uses. In Hainan Province, money obtained from the property market was as high as one-fourth of the total revenue of the province (Zou 1992). The revenue obtained was used in turn to improve the urban infrastructure of cities. Many cities—Guangzhou, for example—are using the paid transfer of land-use rights to finance their underground railway system. Developers are allowed to develop residential and commercial properties on top of the underground stations, and the money obtained from such developments is used to finance part of the construction cost of the underground railway. As underground railway stations are convenient transport nodes, their land value is very high. And now that lands have value, the city government is willing to invest in infrastructure to improve its environment and accessibility so as to further increase those values. The main methods for developing special economic zones have been the so-called "five connections and one levelling" (*wutong yiping*): connecting roads, telecommunications, water service, electricity service, and port access; and levelling of sites (Yeh 1985). These initiatives are labor intensive. But because the cost of labor in China is relatively cheap and because better accessibility and service provision lead to significantly higher market values for land, their rate of return is very good.

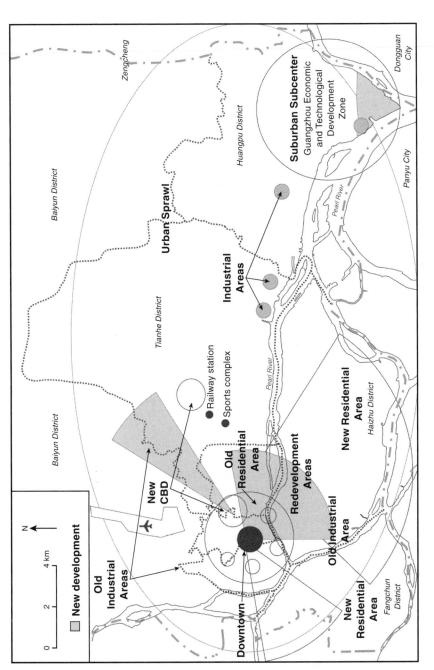

Figure 5.2. New Urban Spatial Structure: Guangzhou as an Example
Source: Wu and Yeh 1999.

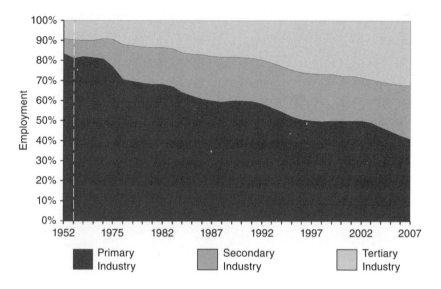

Figure 5.3. Economic Transition in China

Source: China Statistical Yearbook 2008.

These revenue returns can now be used to fund further infrastructure projects that would not have been possible before the introduction of the land market.

Current Wave: Growth of the Tertiary Industries (2001–Present)

Since 2000, several new trends have emerged in China's urbanization. Urban development continues to be affected by the further transition of a centrally planned economy to a more market-oriented economy and by the further advancement and refinement of land and housing reform. However, the most prominent factor now affecting urban development is the fast growth of the service industry.

Two major forces facilitate the growth of tertiary industries. The first is the economic transition, which has led to a growing share of tertiary industry in the nation's economic structure (figure 5.3). Reviewing the strategic difficulties faced by China, some scholars saw the poorly developed service industry, a result of the traditional prioritization of manufacturing over commerce, as a major structural problem. In 1978, for instance, the contribution of service industry to GDP was less than 30 percent. By 2003, the service industry had grown to account for 33 percent of GDP, while its share in the total employment was 29 percent.

Although this is a significant increase, these figures are still far behind those for developed countries and even for certain other developing countries.

The second force shaping the growth of the service sector is China's overall economic growth. World experience shows that GDP growth generates considerable demand for service industries. In 2003, China's per capita GDP was US$1,090, and this figure will soar to US$3,000 by 2020, according to President Hu Jintao. This increase in wealth will surely facilitate the development of a tertiary sector. The development of the service sector is an important indicator that urbanization in China is more than a simple quantitative issue brought on by rural-urban migration; rather, and more importantly, urbanization has to do with a qualitative transformation taking place along with the transition from a planned to a market-oriented economy. Enterprises are increasingly related to the international market and increasingly reliant on the service industry, and especially the producer service industry, to meet their needs.

China's producer service industry, especially professional services, is still at the fledgling stage, and its role in the entire national economy is very limited. Currently, China's urban development is facing both opportunities and challenges. The most daunting challenge comes from development pressures caused by the weakening of traditional comparative advantages and the intensified regional competition. The service industry can give cities a competitive edge and new growth impetuses. It can diversify the employment structure, open up new opportunities for low-threshold entrepreneurship, and ease the employment pressure. It is also an important way to improve living standards.

Under such conditions, the Chinese government proposed a strategy to facilitate the development of the tertiary industry in 1992. During the Tenth Five-Year Plan (2001–2005), the tertiary industry, especially the modern service industry, played a big part in ensuring the healthy development of the national economy, enhancing China's international competitiveness, easing employment pressure, and improving people's living standards. In recent years, the tertiary industry has experienced a rapid and comprehensive development. Predictably, the tertiary industry will continue to play an important role in the ongoing processes of urbanization. The proactive fiscal policy and the strategy to expand domestic demand will expedite the development of the tertiary industry, which will in turn transform urban spatial structure. The tertiary industry's demand for space, and particularly for space in CBDs, where professional services and corporate headquarters concentrate, will speed up the restructuring of urban inner space. This trend is already manifest in

Beijing, Shanghai, Guangzhou, and other big cities, where plans to develop CBDs and a "headquarter economy" are keenly under way.

The rapid growth of service-oriented cities will pose great challenges for the urban transport system. As incomes increase, more and more people are able to purchase private cars, putting enormous pressure on the existing urban transport system. Statistics show that it took only twenty years for the number of private cars in China to rise from 284,900 to 14,816,600, a fifty-two-fold growth. A similar increase occurred in Hong Kong in the early 1980s when the economy began to take off (Wang and Yeh 1993). According to the experiences of Hong Kong and other cities in the world, improved transport capacity (such as more roads and application of an intelligent transport system) alone is not an effective solution to increasingly severe traffic problems; instead, it may even encourage more people to purchase vehicles, leading to further deterioration of traffic conditions. Only measures from the demand side can reduce traffic congestion, such as levying a tax on motor vehicles, providing better public transportation, and improving the efficiency of the transit system to reduce the demand for cars (Wang and Yeh 1993).

Rapid urbanization also brings opportunities to reorganize the urban system. Unlike industrial enterprises, service enterprises tend to agglomerate. According to Christaller's (1966) central place theory, the thresholds of different services are different, with the more expensive ones having larger market areas. The higher and more diverse the functions of a place are, the higher it is ranked and vice versa. Therefore, the high-tech producer service industry should cluster around central cities so as to serve the surrounding areas. Some cities (such as New York, London, Tokyo, and Hong Kong) provide services for places far beyond their geographic locations, serving as regional and even global centers of commercial and producer services. In China, the service industry occupies a much larger proportion of the urban economy in big cities than in small and medium-sized cities, both of which are far behind their foreign counterparts. The modern service industry, including finance, insurance, and professional services, often concentrates in core cities. Those cities specializing in the service industry are closely connected and mutually supportive, forming a network that is both horizontally and vertically integrated and coordinated. These factors have a far-reaching impact on the structure of the urban system and set up new standards for urban system planning. How, for example, should the regional transport network be improved to link cities of different levels? How should infrastructure be arranged to avoid redundant construction and blind competition? How should the central city be determined—by political considerations or by regional status quo? Where ought central business districts be built?

Not only does the service sector's growing importance change the shape of individual cities, it also affects the conventional labor division between cities of different sizes. In China, because for a long time the major objective of urban development was to promote and support industrialization, there are currently no significant functional differences between big, medium-sized, and small cities. Usually, producer services will concentrate in larger cities due to the economies of agglomeration, which differentiate the roles of large cities from smaller ones. However, whether this also holds true for the Chinese urban system needs further investigation, because of China's unique urban and rural urbanization strategy.

Conclusion: Current Debates and Future Trends

Urban development in China has been phenomenally rapid. Although the Chinese government was dedicated as recently as the 1990s to controlling the population of large cities, it has increasingly realized that this strategy cannot be effectively implemented. In large cities like Beijing, Shanghai, Shenzhen, and Guangzhou, the size of population is still growing rapidly. Shenzhen, a booming city in southern China's Guangdong Province, now boasts a population of 12 million under its jurisdiction, more than thirty times its population twenty-five years ago, when it was designated as China's first Special Economic Zone. Among Shenzhen's population, only 1.65 million are registered permanent residents (*Yangcheng Evening News* 2007); others are immigrants who make their livings as workers in manufacturing and services industries (both long-term and temporary) or household helpers or babysitters in the city. According to statistics released by the central government, the number of rural migrant workers in China reached 99 million in 2004, an increase of 5 million over the previous year; and this number is still on the rise despite high unemployment in urban areas caused by redundancies from state-owned enterprises (*People's Daily* 2004). In addition, multipolarization and globalization have strongly encouraged and stimulated the growth of megacities in China. Successful international bids—the Olympics for Beijing and the World Expo for Shanghai—have triggered a wave of large-scale urban construction in big cities. All over China, the big cities are trying to optimize their economic structure and upgrade their infrastructure in an attempt to enhance their status in the urban system (Xu and Yeh 2005). These measures have greatly speeded up the process of urbanization.

Urbanization at this scale and speed has overwhelmed the ability of Chinese governments at various levels to manage urban areas. The flood of rural-urban migration has exacerbated the infrastructure burden of cities and led to tremendous growth of areas where millions of migrant workers lack adequate access to basic urban services. Laid-off workers, pensioners, suburban landless farmers, and other disadvantaged groups contribute to an increasing number of urban poor (Wang 2004). In 2003, the number of urban poor in China was around 30 million, about a tenth of the total urban population, and was still growing (CPIN 2003). At the same time, urban employment pressure is mounting. Township enterprises, which absorbed a large number of rural surplus laborers in the 1980s and 1990s, have had to adjust and can no longer employ so many people. At the same time, state workers are being laid off and facing reemployment difficulties. Concomitant with these processes is the widening income gap in urban areas and increasing rural-urban and regional disparities. Pseudo-urbanization, where urbanization is the result of population increase in the urban areas without concomitant increase in economic development and employment, has been a major cause of the housing and poverty problems in Third World cities in the postwar period (McGee 1971). China has been quite successful in curtailing rural-urban migration and population growth in the past. With rapid urbanization, growing regional disparity, and increasing difficulties for the rural areas to absorb surplus labor, it is questionable whether China can prevent pseudo-urbanization, regardless of its attempts to avoid it in the past.

In many cities, unemployment combined with inadequate social services and increasing income disparity has resulted in a high degree of social exclusion, leading to social unrest. In all cities there is a pressing need to address widespread misuse of land, urban sprawl, traffic congestion, and poor sanitation and living environments, though these needs are especially acute in cities threatened by rapid and often uncontrolled growth, inadequate and poorly maintained infrastructure, industrialization, and increasing vehicle ownership. While large cities receive a greater amount of investment, small cities and towns get too little to achieve what has been advocated by the "small cities, big issue" strategy. Some scholars, particularly economists, have argued that the strategy of developing small cities and towns may cause a lot of problems: diseconomies of scale, scattered distribution and duplication of production, and wasteful use of resources. These issues trigger heated debates about urbanization strategy in China.

To face these challenges, there has been a marked shift in China's urbanization strategy. The new strategy stresses the coordinated development of metropolises, medium-sized and small cities, and small towns. Small urban areas are allowed to grow as long as they can meet the required conditions. At the same time, there is a focus on developing large, clustered city-regions to replace rampant urban sprawl (China Mayor Association 2004). Taking this further, many cities have aggressively promoted economic restructuring and developed the tertiary sector by encouraging the participation of private and foreign investors as well as enlarging public spending.

China's fourth wave of urbanization is likely to be distinguished by four features: first, the service industry's demand for space will speed up center-city restructuring as more CBDs are created to meet the growing demand for professional services and corporate headquarter space; second, the rapid growth of service-oriented cities and the expected increases in personal income will exert pressure on existing urban transport systems; third, new opportunities for regional reorganization will appear, as high-end producer service industries cluster around central cities to serve the surrounding areas and in the process create new standards for regional planning and transport; and, fourth, the development of the service sector will alter the conventional labor division between cities of different sizes as producer services concentrate in larger cities.

Because of China's unique urban and rural urbanization strategies, more research and time are needed to see just how these trends will play out and how China will respond to the opportunities and challenges they present. The fourth wave of Chinese urbanization has gradually been emerging mainly in the coastal cities and is not widespread yet. It is observed that the fourth wave of Chinese urbanization did not take place in every region at the same time due to regional economic differences. It tends to happen sooner for the developed coastal areas and relatively later for inland regions. But despite these regional differences, the general contours of China's fourth wave of urbanization are beginning to become clear.

PART II

Urban Spatial Growth and Development

Chapter 6

The Urban Transition in Developing Countries:
Demography Meets Geography

Mark R. Montgomery and Deborah Balk

As urban populations continue to grow, poor countries and international aid agencies are likely to face mounting pressure to rethink their development strategies and set priorities with both rural and urban interests in mind. To engage effectively with the emerging trends, countries and agencies will need to base their decisions on demographic estimates that are scientifically sound. To plan for future growth, they will require informative forecasts of city size that are free from systematic bias. Unfortunately, demographic researchers are not yet in a position to deliver these scientific inputs.

In this chapter, we consider the current state of urban demographic research and argue that as the developing world continues to urbanize, and both local and national planners struggle to anticipate and adapt to city growth, they will increasingly need to draw upon spatially disaggregated demographic data. Although the urban transition has been in the making for decades, demographers are only belatedly coming to understand how much remains to be done to construct the kind of research infrastructure that will provide policymakers with scientific guidance (Panel on Urban Population Dynamics 2003; Bocquier 2005). As explained in the chapter's second and third sections, with the increasing availability of urban demographic and boundary data for small geographic units—including districts within cities—there are now good prospects for bringing spatial content to demographic research. The combination of spatial and population data will help to resolve some of the measurement issues that have long bedeviled demographers and will likely inject new energy into the field of city population estimation and forecasting.

Data Needs for the Urban Century Ahead

Needs for better urban data are especially pressing in Asia, which now contains the largest total number of urban dwellers among the major regions of developing countries, and will continue to do so. By 2025, Africa will likely have overtaken Latin America in terms of urban totals. Urban growth rates in developing countries in force before 2000 are substantially higher than the rates that were seen during comparable historical periods in the West, with the difference being due to lower urban mortality in present-day populations and stubbornly high urban fertility in some cases (Panel on Urban Population Dynamics 2003). Nevertheless, decade-to-decade changes in urban percentages—sometimes termed the pace of urbanization—in the developing world are not especially great by historical standards (Panel on Urban Population Dynamics 2003, table 3-5). The most prominent, indeed, unparalleled feature of today's urban transition is the emergence of hundreds of large cities. Yet this development is often misunderstood. Of all developing-country city dwellers in places of 100,000 population and above, only 12 percent live in megacities (those exceeding 10 million in size). More than half reside in cities smaller than 500,000 persons. In addition to their demographic importance, these smaller cities are relatively disadvantaged in terms of access to information and both technical and managerial expertise.

Much of what is known about urban populations of poor countries stems from the work of the United Nations Population Division (UNPD), which has been the sole source of internationally comparable city and urban estimates and projections. Much of its work has been carried out in-house, and the challenges that the UNPD faces are not well understood by the larger research and policy communities. In preparing its urban materials, the UN has had little alternative but to rely on data supplied by the national statistical offices of its member countries. The basic data are thus bound to the definitions of urban areas adopted by national authorities, which vary a great deal from one country to the next. Working with these disparate raw materials and refining them where possible to improve comparability, the UNPD develops estimates of both total urban and city-specific population sizes, compiling records from the 1950s to the present. For the city-specific population counts, the UN gives special attention to national capitals and to larger cities—those with 750,000 or more residents. Although entries for smaller cities are registered in the UN's city database, they have not generally been given the rigorous review that is routinely applied to larger cities. To accurately estimate city and urban populations is an enormous undertaking in itself, but the UN is also obliged to develop medium-term forecasts of city and urban growth and to monitor the performance of the forecasts. The results are issued on a biennial basis in the series *World Urbanization Prospects*, and upon publication, the UN's urban figures make their way into numerous international databases.

Related research by the UNPD, based on a sample of countries with two or more national censuses, has provided important insights into the demographic sources of urban population growth. As the UN has shown, urban population growth rates can be divided into a natural urban growth component—this is the difference between urban birth and death rates—and a residual that combines net migration with spatial expansion (Chen et al. 1998). The details are complicated—see Panel on Urban Population Dynamics (2003) for discussion of the method—and one could wish for a larger sample of countries in the analysis. Nevertheless, the results are strikingly at odds with the usual perception of the sources of urban growth. In developing countries, according to the UN findings, about 60 percent of the urban growth rate is due to natural growth; the remaining 40 percent is due to migration and spatial expansion (Chen et al. 1998). Recently, a very similar rule was established for India over the four decades from 1961 to 2001, with urban natural growth again accounting for about 60 percent of the total (Sivaramakrishnan et al. 2005). China, however, presents something of an exception to the rule. Given its low fertility levels, the tight bureaucratic controls that kept migration in check until the 1980s, and the subsequent unleashing of migration, the UN's estimate for China puts the contribution of natural urban growth at about 40 percent of the growth rate total, with migration and spatial expansion taking 60 percent. Even for China, however, natural growth is responsible for a large portion of urban growth overall.

As discussed in a recent *State of the World's Population* volume (UNFPA 2007), many policymakers in developing countries have been apprehensive about the rates of city growth in their countries, and they have not infrequently acted upon these concerns with aggressive interventions aiming to expel slum residents and repel rural-to-urban migrants. These policies have shown themselves to be ineffective as well as brutal. More enlightened regional development policies have the potential to redirect urban growth, but these policies seldom generate the rapid changes in its pace and spatial distribution that policymakers hope to achieve.

It is therefore surprising how little attention has been paid to an urban growth policy of a very different character: voluntary urban family planning programs. Over the past half-century, such programs have compiled an impressive record across the developing world in facilitating fertility declines and reducing unwanted fertility. As will be shown in the next section, an empirical analysis of developing-country city growth and fertility suggests that when national total fertility rates decline by one child, this is associated with a decline of nearly one percentage point in the city population growth rates for that country. There is good reason to believe that urban-specific family planning measures would be even more tightly linked to city growth rates. Hence, even if the health benefits of voluntary family planning programs are set to the side by policymakers fixated on the need to slow population growth, these programs clearly deserve more attention than they have received.

Repairing the Demographic Record

As urban scholars and demographers well know, the scientific basis for cross-country urban estimates and projections is generally adequate for identifying broad features and dominant trends. But an inspection of the detail that underlies the estimates shows that the state of the science is far from satisfactory. As urbanization proceeds, it is precisely the finer details of the process—that is, the spatially disaggregated estimates and forecasts—that become urgently needed by policymakers. In view of the wealth of new data for developing countries that has entered the public domain in recent years, there now exists considerable potential for improvement in city population estimates and projections. Two developments are especially notable. Urban data from a very large number of demographic surveys have greatly strengthened the basis for estimating the demographic components of urban growth and will continue to do so as these survey programs proceed. In addition, recent methodological advances have suggested new ways by which satellite imagery can be used to detect the spatial extent of urban areas, enabling the spatial dimensions of city growth to be quantified at relatively low cost (Angel et al. 2005; Balk et al. 2005; Small 2005).

Although, to date, its cities database has not incorporated a spatial component, and its forecasting methods have essentially ignored urban fertility and mortality rates, the UNPD is now considering whether to thoroughly rework its database and set it upon a firm spatial footing. In the discussion that follows, we first describe the nature of the problems that vex the current version of the cities database, and then evaluate the proposals for improving it and enhancing its spatial features.

The United Nations' Cities Database

The UN cities data take the form of a panel dataset, containing city population counts for individual cities over time, generally recorded at irregular intervals. (Occasionally, for countries that do not regularly conduct censuses, or that seldom tabulate population at the level of

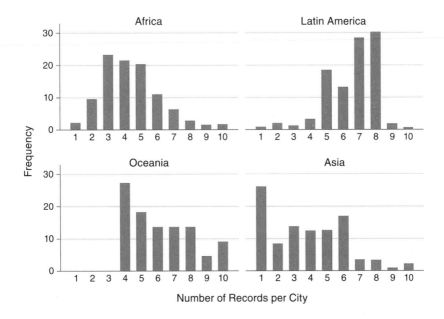

Figure 6.1. The UN Cities Database: Multiple Records on Some 3,300 Cities in Developing Countries

cities, the city population figures can refer to counts made more than a decade apart.) The UN monitors all cities with populations of 100,000 and above; when a given city crosses this threshold, the Population Division endeavors to reconstruct its history.

Figure 6.1 summarizes the number of observations available on a per-city basis for the cities of developing countries. As can be seen, outside Asia there are relatively few cities whose populations are recorded only once. Among cities in Africa, for example, over 20 percent are observed three times and over 70 percent of these cities appear anywhere from three to six times in the database. Likewise, in Latin America, almost 60 percent of cities contribute seven or eight records to the database.

Unfortunately, the units in which city populations are expressed can vary across all of the relevant dimensions: across countries, within countries, and over time for a given city. To organize its records, the UN has maintained three "statistical concepts" that serve to define city boundaries. The term *city proper* refers to the formal administrative boundaries of a city as set out by local authorities. The term *urban agglomeration* includes the city proper, but also incorporates contiguous areas lying outside that boundary that are populated at urban levels of density. A number of countries (especially, but not exclusively, in Latin America) have adopted a more spatially elastic definition, categorizing their populations in terms of *metropolitan regions*—the UN's third category—that include rural dwellers who fall within the sphere of influence of large urban places. Many countries have devised further variations on these boundary definitions, and the UN endeavors to fit them all within its three-category framework.

Member countries of the UN are asked by the UNPD to provide city population data for urban agglomeration boundaries; however, they may respond with data coded in terms of city proper or metropolitan region, or may provide population counts without any accompanying explanation of units. Where possible, these data are adjusted by UN staff to conform to the agglomeration concept—but of course this is not always possible. Indeed, in only a small percentage of cases recorded by the UN are all of the city's records expressed in terms of urban agglomerations. The city proper is by far the more common concept in these data (for 40 percent of cities); about one-third of cities report different units over time; and nearly one-quarter provide the UN with no clear account of the units.

The difficulties stemming from such mixed time series are illustrated by two cities. In the case of Luanda, Angola, the units in which the city's population was recorded are unknown for the 1950, 1960, and 1970 entries, whereas in 1982 population counts were provided for both the city proper and the urban agglomeration concepts. The next entry in the series is again of unknown type; it is followed by one report on the agglomeration and a final record whose defining concept is not specified. The series for Chittagong, Bangladesh, begins with two entries expressed in terms of the city proper, followed by one of unknown type and a final three records couched in terms of metropolitan region. In mixed cases such as these, it is certainly not obvious how to define a rate of population growth for spells of time that begin with one boundary concept but end with another. Neither is it obvious whether growth rates for agglomerations or metropolitan regions are strictly comparable with each other or with the rates for cities proper. In each new revision of *World Urbanization Prospects*, UN researchers succeed in eliminating some of the anomalous cases. Nevertheless, there is an irreducible minimum of boundary-related variation in these data, and far more heterogeneity remains in the city time-series than is commonly realized.

Forecasting City Growth

As part of the research summarized in *World Urbanization Prospects*, the UN Population Division provides medium-term forecasts of both total urban and city-specific population growth. These forecasts extrapolate the city population time series that we have been discussing, with all their attendant heterogeneity. Boundary variations alone would not be expected to inject any systematic bias into these forecasts, although the possibility deserves investigation. It seems more likely that "baseline errors" of this type would mainly reduce forecast precision and widen confidence bands without necessarily causing growth rates or projected populations to be either too high or too low on any consistent basis.

It is therefore disconcerting to realize that the UN urban and city forecasts have, in fact, exhibited considerable systematic bias: they have consistently projected growth rates (and thus population sizes) that are too high. The tendency to overproject is not evident in the UN's forecasts of total population at the national level, but it persists despite the insertion of an algorithm in the city forecasting model that is designed to slow projected growth rates as city size increases. The Panel on Urban Population Dynamics (2003) explains the forecasting method and provides a critical review of the issues, as does Bocquier (2005). The tendency for overprojection that is exhibited by the UN forecasts raises doubt about the scale and pace of urban change (if not the direction) that has been forecast for the twenty-first century. Understanding the sources of these forecast errors is a research priority of some urgency.

Given the uncertainties and measurement errors that plague the city population series, there are limits on how ambitious any forecast should strive to be. The UNPD has long couched its efforts in the most cautious of terms and has made plain its reservations about the proper scope of the forecasts. The United Nations (1980, 45) warned that "projection of city populations is fraught with hazards. . . . There are more than 1,600 cities in the data set, and it is obviously impossible to predict precisely the demographic future of most of them. . . . In most cases, national and local planners will have access to more detailed information about a particular place and could supply more reliable information about its prospects."

Referring to Mexico City, whose population was to rise to 31 million by the turn of the century according to the 1980 projection, the United Nations (1980, 57) cautioned: "Whether such size can actually be attained is, of course, questionable. It has been noted, for example, that population growth at Mexico City threatens to destroy tree cover that is necessary to prevent erosion and flooding. Water-supply also appears to be a potentially constraining factor in this case. Natural or social limits to growth could be encountered well before a size of 31 million is reached, or of 26 million for São Paulo, and so on down the line."

These concerns were not misplaced—the 2000 population of Mexico City was recorded at 18 million and that of São Paulo at 17 million, well below what was projected—and similar reservations would no doubt apply with much the same force today. Even so, to an extent that probably could not have been foreseen in the early 1980s, several streams of new data—on demographic behavior as well as land cover, water supply, and environment—have emerged over the past decades. These new materials may well support more informed and credible city population estimates and projections than the experts of 1980 could have envisioned.

Exploiting New Demographic Data

Although the United Nations operates a separate research program in which it estimates and projects fertility and mortality rates at the national level, its city and urban projection methods have not incorporated fertility or mortality in any direct way, despite the UN's own finding that 60 percent of urban growth is due to natural increase. The approach taken to city and urban projection thus ignores a large body of accumulated information on urban fertility and mortality rates, as well as some useful data on migration. Beginning with the World Fertility Surveys (WFS) fielded in the late 1970s, well over 200 nationally representative demographic surveys of developing countries have made their way into the public domain via the WFS and its two ongoing successor programs, the Demographic and Health Surveys (DHS) and the Multiple Indicator Cluster Surveys (MICS). Although the sample sizes of these surveys are too small to permit informative estimation of demographic rates at the city level, they are generally large enough to allow the rates to be estimated for the urban populations of the subnational geographic region within which a city is located. With the aid of statistical methods, it is possible to further refine the estimates to take some city-specific characteristics (e.g., coastal location) into account.

Because the cities database is a cross-section, time-series dataset, there is scope for including a great range of explanatory factors in city growth rate specifications. Urban total fertility rates and mortality rates would be of prime interest, as would migration rates; these demographic variables are linked to city population growth via basic demographic accounting identities. It is at least possible that the inclusion of urban fertility rates, in particular, would resolve the problem of overprojection that has plagued the UN forecasts, given the rapid declines in urban fertility that are underway in a number of developing countries. The growth rate specifications could be further enriched by the addition of multiple city-specific demographic and nondemographic variables. An additional benefit is that when forecasts are based on statistical models,

Table 6.1: Panel Data City Growth Regression Models, Developing Countries

	OLS	Random Effects	Fixed Effects
Total Fertility Rate	0.602	0.685	0.887
(Z Statistic)	(19.97)	(20.34)	(17.68)
Child Mortality Rate	−0.004	−0.005	−0.007
	(−5.53)	(−5.54)	(−4.49)
Constant	1.757	1.464	0.802
	(22.01)	(16.54)	(7.25)
Standard Deviation of City Effects σ_u		1.184	1.907
		(27.71)	
σ_{fit}	2.662	2.394	2.381
		(107.08)	
log-likelihood	−18624	−18446	−16568

Source: Montgomery and Kim 2006.

the results can be expressed in probabilistic terms with confidence bands indicating the uncertainty that surrounds a point forecast. Taken together, these considerations make for an inviting research agenda.

Table 6.1, based on data from the earlier (2003) revision of *World Urbanization Prospects*, may give an idea of the returns that can be secured from linking data on fertility and mortality rates to data on city growth. We use here the time series of national total fertility and child mortality rates (provided by the UN) rather than rates calculated from survey data for urban subnational regions, which would be preferred. Nevertheless, the regression results suggest a close connection. The most interesting results are those shown for the fixed-effects estimates (the third column of the table), which introduce the equivalent of a control for all influences on a given city's growth rate that are constant over time. Even having controlled for such important sources of variation, we see that (with a coefficient of 0.887 on the total fertility rate) a decline in national fertility of one child is associated with a decline of nearly one percentage point in city growth rates. In addition to being demographically important, this association is highly significant in statistical terms. Although they are also statistically significant, and point in the expected direction, the effects of child mortality are much weaker. The ordinary least squares (OLS) and random-effects (RE) fertility results are similarly significant, although the coefficients on fertility are somewhat smaller than the fixed-effects estimate. Taken as a whole, these results provide further confirmation, if any is still needed, of the important role that natural increase plays in city growth.

To pursue this line of inquiry and connect urban demographic data to city growth rates, we need to establish a direct link between the UN cities database and the demographic surveys. Surprisingly, this proves to be no easy task. The problem is that the WFS, DHS, and MICS contain very little information on the location of their respondents. The WFS somehow neglected to specify the city in which a sampling cluster was located (unless it happened to be the national capital or the only large city of an identified region), and for a number of years the DHS program did not rectify this error. (Since the late 1990s, however, the DHS has collected latitude and longitude coordinates for its sampling clusters in about half of its surveys. The MICS program, however, collects no spatially detailed data.) A further problem is that only the crudest summaries of migration histories are collected in these survey programs and the data available do not include the names (or even the regions) of former places of residence for migrants. This forecloses the possibility of making origin-to-destination estimates of migration rates. In short, the general neglect of space and geography in the major demographic survey programs makes it far more difficult than it should be to link survey data on urban fertility, mortality, and migration to city-specific and other geographically coded information. This is a longstanding and serious flaw in the urban demographic record—although it is a flaw that could be fixed at negligible cost in future survey efforts.

Constructing a Spatial Framework

In its current configuration, the UN's cities database provides a city's population but does not show how that population is distributed over space. When the first versions of the database were being assembled in the 1970s, this was a forgivable simplification. The UN experts of the time were well aware of boundary problems and recognized that cities evolve in their spatial extents over time, but simply lacked the data to engage with these issues in any comprehensive way. They were also aware that the practice of declaring some places to be definitively urban and others rural is simplistic and at times unhelpful—and this view is coming to predominate among urban researchers today, as evidence grows of the multiple linkages and flows across space of people, goods, and information. Although the conventional, binary, urban-rural distinction has not entirely lost its value, a consensus is emerging that to be most useful in the future, classification schemes will need to make a place for third categories, gray areas, indeterminacies, and degrees of urban-ness as well as the rural and urban ends of the spectrum (McGee 1991; Champion and Hugo 2004; Champion 2006).

A first step in this direction is to organize population data according to the smallest geographic units ("building blocks") that are available.

When population data are arrayed over space in reasonably fine detail, this enables a closer scrutiny of the areas lying on the peripheries of large cities where much urban population growth is believed to take place, and gives planners and policymakers a view of the communities situated between large cities that are likely to fuse with their neighbors. Geo-coded data also provide a window on the smaller cities and towns, where, as we have seen, a large percentage of urban residents live.

The case of Beijing shows what can be learned by coupling spatial data on administrative unit boundaries with population counts. Like other developing countries, China has made frequent changes in its administrative boundaries and accompanying urban definitions, a practice that has sown confusion among the experts struggling to understand this country's urban trends (Chan and Hu 2003). Even at one point in time, it can be difficult to grasp how boundaries are implicated in Chinese city definitions. To show how spatial data help to clarify matters, we present in table 6.2 the basic population counts for the administrative units that make up Beijing Province, and accompany these conventional tabular data with the maps shown in figure 6.2.

In 2000, according to the urban definitions most recently adopted by the Chinese government, the population of Beijing was reported to be 11.5 million persons. But to whom, precisely, does the label "Beijing resident" apply? The 11.5 million total (shown as subtotal B in table 6.2) was derived by adding the populations of the administrative districts in the city proper (the 8.5 million people of subtotal A, who live in the districts depicted with the darkest shading in panel 1 of figure 6.2) to the full populations of neighboring "city districts" (another 3 million persons, in the areas surrounding the city proper, whose outer boundaries are depicted in the black-and-white border). However, these city districts include a substantial number of rural residents. If we were to depart from the official definition and count only the urban residents of the city districts toward the total, this redefinition would reduce the population of Beijing from 11.5 million to about 9.9 million (subtotal C of the table). Going further afield, the entity of Beijing might be defined so as to take in those urban localities situated in the outlying counties of the province (counties are depicted in light shading in the figure), on the theory that the smaller cities participate in networks of transport, communication, and services that link them to Beijing proper and to other parts of the city. These adjustments would produce an estimated total population for Beijing of 10.5 million persons (subtotal E of the table). Clearly it would be difficult even to weigh the merits of these alternative definitions without reference to maps and other spatially coded data.

Table 6.2: Population Counts for the Administrative Districts of Beijing Province

Administrative Unit	*Population* Total	Urban	Urban %
City Proper			
Chaoyang Qu	2,289,756	2,289,756	100
Fengtai Qu	1,369,480	1,369,480	100
Shijinshan Qu	489,439	489,439	100
Handian Qu	2,240,124	2,240,124	100
Subtotal A	*8,503,385*	8,503,385	100
City Districts			
Mentougou Qu	266,591	187,616	70
Fangshan Qu	814,367	379,882	47
Tongzhou Qu	673,952	346,645	51
Shunyi Qu	636,479	207,341	33
Changping Qu	614,821	251,792	41
Subtotal B	*11,509,595*		
Subtotal C		*9,876,661*	
Beijing Counties			
Daxing Xian	671,444	188,109	28
Pinggu Xian	396,701	119,053	30
Huairou Xian	296,002	116,900	39
Miyun Xian	420,019	128,999	31
Yanqing Xian	275,433	92,742	34
Subtotal D	*13,569,194*		
Subtotal E		*10,522,464*	

Source: China 2000 County Population Census 2000.

It is not obvious from the tabular data alone where in Beijing's mainly rural counties the smaller cities are located—only the total number of urban dwellers in each county is reported in table 6.2. The cross-hatched areas seen in panel 2 of figure 6.2, derived from satellite imagery to be discussed below, depict the locations of a number of the urban concentrations in these counties. Here and in other parts of China, remote-sensing methods can detect new urban settlements that are not yet known to the country's statistical authorities, or whose growth has not been fully appreciated. In such cases, the satellite imagery could prompt further on-the-ground investigation and in this way bring about revisions in the urban population counts. For planners and policymakers grappling with the needs of smaller cities in the areas of water supply, transport, and the like, it will rarely be enough to know that the number of urban residents in a county is growing; they will usually need spatially explicit information on which small cities in the area require the most urgent attention.

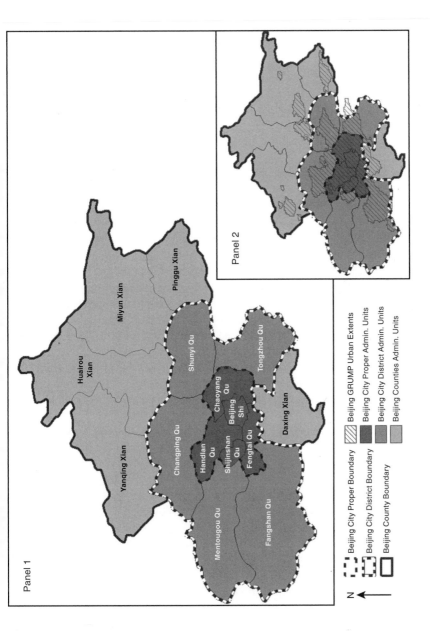

Figure 6.2. Beijing Administrative Units and Urban Allocation

Source: Estimates compiled by authors with the following data sources: China 2000 County Population Census and GRUMP (CIESIN et al. 2004).

Spatial data can also shed light on the over-time dimension of city growth. Figure 6.3 presents a short spatially disaggregated time series for the São Paulo *municipio*, showing how rates of population growth have varied over administrative units from 1970 to 1996. This is a case in which growth rates plummeted in the core of the region while changing very little in its peripheries; had the boundaries of São Paulo been defined to encompass the core alone, a very different picture of the region's population growth would have emerged. Figure 6.4 situates São Paulo in relation to Rio de Janeiro, Belo Horizonte, and Campinas as well as myriad smaller urban places. One can imagine—and conceivably measure—the multiple networks that connect all these places and which may induce correlations (whether positive or negative) in their population growth rates.

Geographers have compiled a number of such special-case datasets like those for Beijing and southern Brazil, but clearly a more systematic and thorough effort is needed to create geo-coded data at this level of detail for all developing countries. Although most developing countries conduct national censuses, and an increasing number of them are beginning to map the results, the spatial display of census data is not yet widespread. Relatively few countries process their census data at the small-area level and fewer still make any sustained effort to place the disaggregated population data in the hands of local planners and policy-makers, many of whom must operate with rudimentary data that lack spatial content. While geographic information systems are being constructed at the national level, there will be an important interim role to be played by international geographic datasets that are organized on spatial lines.

One model for such a database is provided by CIESIN's (Center for International Earth Science Information Network) Global Rural-Urban-Mapping Project (GRUMP), described in detail in Balk et al. (2005). The GRUMP approach draws upon nighttime lights satellite data to approximate the spatial outlines of urban areas (Elvidge et al. 1997; Balk et al. 2005; Balk 2006) and then links the spatial imagery to rural and urban population data for administrative areas. As we have seen for the mainly rural counties of Beijing Province, administrative unit boundaries are sometimes too large to pinpoint the location of the urban settlements within the unit. When no finer boundary data are available, remote-sensing methods are helpful in locating and separating out these smaller cities and towns.

Another payoff to the spatial approach is evident in the global analysis conducted by McGranahan et al. (2007), who calculate the number of urban coastal inhabitants who live within ten meters of sea level, where they are likely to face rising risks from the storm surges and related

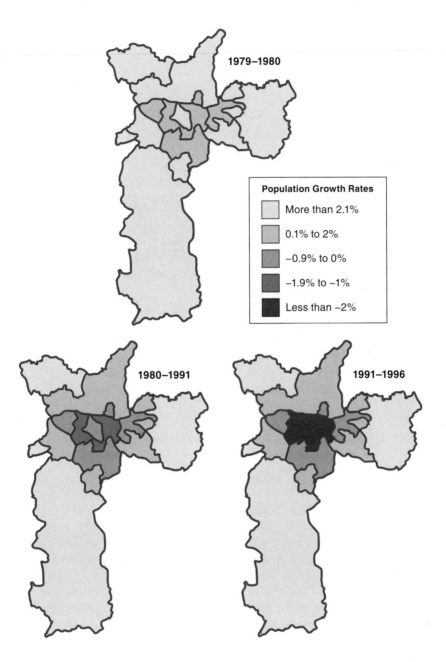

Figure 6.3. Population Growth Rates Change Within Urban Regions: São Paulo, 1970–1996

Source: Taschner and Bogus 2001.

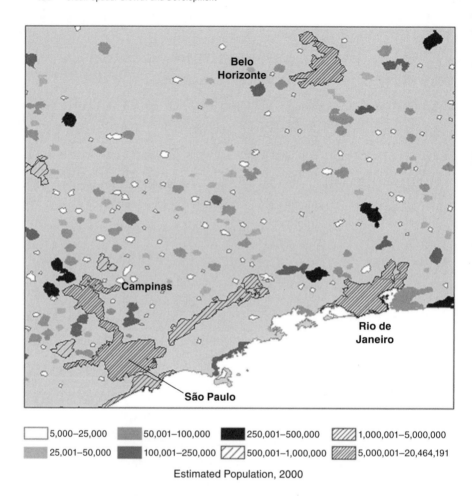

	5,000–25,000		50,001–100,000		250,001–500,000		1,000,001–5,000,000
	25,001–50,000		100,001–250,000		500,001–1,000,000		5,000,001–20,464,191

Estimated Population, 2000

Figure 6.4. Brazilian Cities Detected via the Night Lights Sensor

phenomena that are expected to accompany global warming. Much of southern Vietnam lies in the zone of risk, whose northeastern boundary cuts through Ho Chi Minh City, leaving the lower-lying quarters of the city in the risk zone and the more elevated quarters sitting above it. This application requires four types of data to be merged: population counts, administrative boundaries, night-lights satellite data, and data on elevation, also derived from remotely sensed sources.

This last example underscores a point that is sometimes overlooked by remote-sensing enthusiasts: relatively little of demographic interest can be gleaned from imagery alone. Administrative boundary data need to be overlaid upon satellite imagery if the images are to be linked to place-names and thereby to population. Furthermore, the difficulties entailed in making these linkages should not be underestimated. In the case of Nigeria, the country's national statistical office defines any place of 40,000 persons or more to be urban (United Nations 2005). However, its smaller cities and towns are not always detected by the night-lights satellite sensor—possibly because they are incompletely electrified. There are quite a number of settlements listed in the records of the country's statistical office for which no light emissions can be detected (the inset shows the details for the heart of Yorubaland). Conversely, of all the light sources that are detected by the satellite, approximately half emanate from locations in which the statistical office has no record of a settlement.

As the McGranahan et al. (2007) study demonstrates, measurement of urban spatial extents and population often requires multiple views of urban areas derived from a range of sources and sensors, including the night-lights satellite, radar, and Landsat (Angel et al. 2005). At the moment, the field of human settlement detection and classification is in a period of creative ferment, with several recent conferences specifically devoted to remote-sensing methods for urban classification. The sensors being considered differ significantly in their abilities to detect urban change and in their potential to be applied globally. Some of them do not provide temporally consistent, global data series at the intervals (such as mid-decade) that best complement the collection of population data. Others produce data that cannot be processed according to pro-grammable rules, requiring interventions and the exercise of judgment at key junctures in the analysis, which can make replication difficult (Small 2006). Some sensors are better at detecting the fine-grained intracity details and others (such as the night-lights satellite) at delineat-ing the broad outlines of urban settlements. As a rule, the sensors that excel at capturing fine detail tend not to be applicable globally. To sum up, there is at present no general agreement on how best to assemble a comprehensive spatial database for urban areas around the globe. The competition among methods now under way presents demographers and other social scientists with an opportunity to join physical scientists in a stimulating interdisciplinary conversation.

Conclusions

The urban demographic transition is unfolding amid three fundamental and related trends in economic development. The process of globaliza-tion is evolving in a way that binds cities to each other through international networks of production and communication, exposing more cities to the benefits and risks of the international markets. New decision-making roles are being thrust upon cities as national governments begin to decentralize and off-load responsibilities in service delivery (and revenue raising) to state and municipal governments (Panel on Urban Population Dynamics 2003). The decade of the 1990s saw an increasing quantification of development objectives taking place under the rubric of the Millennium Development Goals. This refocusing of development thinking is bringing international prominence to issues that are already core concerns in the cities of poor countries, both explicitly (in Target 11 on slum dwellers) and implicitly (in Targets focused on water supply, sanitation, and health). Together with the pressures being exerted by demographic change, these trends will likely force upon decision-makers and researchers a new recognition of the central roles of urban populations and governments in economic development.

As we have argued, a substantial workload awaits the demographic research community in assembling the data and methods needed for the upcoming urban era. Considerable effort will be required to clean the city population time series of its errors and inconsistencies. The performance of the UN forecasts of city and urban growth has been heavily criticized in recent years, and there is now general agreement on the need for a thorough critical review of forecast errors and the development of new methods (Panel on Urban Population Dynamics 2003; Bocquier 2005).

Further effort will be needed to bring spatial specificity to the city population estimates in the form of geo-coded databases. We would join Champion and Hugo (2004) in calling for a reorientation of international population databases to highlight space and geography, exploiting the most detailed available spatial units as containers for population data. These spatial "building blocks" must be defined in terms of a time series of boundary data and accompanied by demographic data at roughly the same level of detail. Remote-sensing methods will serve as increasingly valuable supplementary tools, providing easily updated information on urban spatial extents if not on population as such.

If the current level of effort continues, it may be possible in the not-too-distant future to define urban areas around the globe according to user-specified criteria for population density, contiguity, and distance. The GRUMP project shows that this is an attainable ideal. To achieve it, the city data for developing countries will need to be scrutinized by a wider set of local, country-level, and international experts than has been the case to date. For the past forty years, far too much of the urban demographic research burden has rested with the United Nations Population Division. In view of the challenges lying ahead, it is time for the burden to be more widely shared.

Chapter 7

Measuring and Modeling Global Urban Expansion

Stephen Sheppard

From the perspective of global urbanization, the first decade of the twenty-first century will be seen not as the time when the problems associated with urbanization first became apparent (these have been widely understood since the nineteenth century and perhaps earlier), nor as the time when the basic outlines of policy solutions first attained widespread recognition, if not agreement. The importance of infrastructure provision, the need for legal institutions that recognize and seek to internalize the externalities (positive and negative) intrinsic to high-density settlements, and the connection of housing provision to human health and social order have all been understood and discussed to some degree since the cities of the classical civilizations. What sets the present time apart are two facts: one is that for the first time in history these policies directly affect the welfare of a majority of humans living on earth. The other is that, for the first time, we have at our disposal—in the form of remotely sensed data and some basic theories of urban form—the opportunity to measure and model urban expansion on a global scale. The first of these facts is a central rationale both for increasing concern among policymakers and for publication of the present volume. The second is the central focus of this chapter.[1]

Like many other economic and public policies, urban development policies have often fallen prey to the tendency to assume that there must be a "local" explanation for what would be better understood as part of a global phenomenon. For example, internal migration from the countryside to an urban area increases the demand for housing and results in higher prices for dwellings in the city and conversion of land from nonurban to urban uses in and around the city. This in turn leads to demands for extension of infrastructure provision and complaints about loss of access to open space. This story has been repeated (and documented) in hundreds of places ranging from seventeenth-century London to twenty-first-century Beijing. Frequently, the explanation is that the unique attractions of the particular city under consideration relative to the rural origins of the migrants is the source of the problem, and a variety of rural development strategies coupled with building restrictions in the cities is offered as a solution. These are almost never successful in halting the urban expansion, although they may impose considerable costs on the citizens and generate a variety of rents to be dissipated throughout the economy.

In other regions where internal migration is less important or nonexistent, different local explanations become the focus of concern. There are many cities in North America and Europe whose populations have been stable or declining for several decades, but where new structures continue to be built on what was nonurban land. Perhaps the most obvious explanation for this is simply that land is a normal good and in these cities real household income has continued to increase. As their incomes rise, households purchase more of many different goods, but in particular they seek to purchase more housing and more land. This leads to lower-density, expanding cities even when population is constant or slightly declining. Because the policy implications of this explanation are not particularly palatable—since few would support putting the brakes on income growth—alternative local explanations are sought: road building and automobile ownership are identified as likely culprits, along with particular types of commercial development or general "white flight." Numerous campaigns and local organizations have come together to oppose road building, discount retailers, and a variety of other proposed causes of urban expansion.

From a policy perspective, the difficulty with such localized explanations is not so much that they are false (although they sometimes are) as that they are only partly true. Road building and other factors that reduce transportation costs probably do encourage urban expansion, as does population growth from internal migration. Understanding urban expansion requires that we be able to explain very different outcomes that emerge from apparently similar situations, as well as similar outcomes that emerge from very different situations. For example, Ibadan, Nigeria, and Seoul, Korea, have been experiencing urban expansion during the period of 1990 to 2000 of about 2.5 percent per year. Per capita GDP in Nigeria during this period was stagnant or declining slightly, but urban population grew at nearly 3 percent per year. In Seoul, urban population growth was a tiny 0.5 percent, but income growth was a robust 5 percent per annum during the period (World Bank Development Indicators 2010 website). To plan our cities and design effective urban policies we need to understand how a variety of factors combine and interact to produce urban expansion. Because of limits in the local variation in values for these contributing factors, we cannot hope to achieve such an understanding by examining what appear to be the localized causes of expansion.

The data to measure total urban land use in a format for comparison with other economic variables have been available for decades in selected cities or developed countries. What has not been available is consistently measured data on urban development from a global cross-section of cities over time. This has now changed. Using remotely sensed data we can assemble data on a global scale, and measure total urban land cover using the same type of data and same analytic approach in each urban area. These data are now available to cover a span of at least twenty years, so that for the first time we have the opportunity to measure and track the process of urban expansion in a very diverse cross-section of economic, social, and environmental conditions. This in turn permits us to test our models of urban expansion to a degree not previously possible. This has the potential to identify both strengths and weaknesses in our theories of these processes and promote the development and refinements of these models.

This chapter reports on one attempt at this kind of analysis. In the following sections we describe the data we have collected for this purpose and provide a summary of the techniques we have used to measure the urban footprint in a global sample of cities. We describe an approach for measuring the microstructure of each urban area using the data we have assembled and summarize our findings by global region. We then identify the primary driving forces for urban expansion that would be suggested by economic theories of urban land markets and explicitly identify a set of testable hypotheses implied by these theories. Using our data, we estimate the relation that holds between measured urban footprint and these variables as a way of testing the theory. Following this, we identify some policy implications of the research, and propose a simple rule of thumb for testing the extent of preparation for urban growth pressures as a way of helping to ensure that urban planning provides a realistic foundation for urban policy rather than wishful thinking about future scenarios.

Finally, we note that combining economically and politically important problems with the data and theoretical resources to do something effective about the problems provides an agenda for future research and study. We suggest a set of problems that are, at present, poorly understood, are significant for urban economic policy, and might benefit from study in the coming decade.

Data

In order to measure and model global urban expansion, we need to combine two types of data. The first is the information required to measure the expansion of urban land use, and the second is information on the economic and policy conditions that influence the pace of expansion so that we can test our models of urban expansion and determine the quantitative and qualitative nature of the relationships. For the first, we rely upon remotely sensed satellite data, and for the second, we rely upon a variety of sources, including data collected by field researchers deployed to each city in our sample. We discuss each in turn below.

Our data are collected for a global sample of 120 cities. These were randomly selected from a larger random sample constructed by UN-HABITAT for data collection in connection with their Urban Observatory program. The larger sample has been constructed to be representative of the global urban population in cities with populations over 100,000 persons.

Remotely Sensed Data

For each of the cities in our sample, we obtained Landsat thematic mapper satellite images for dates that are relatively near the national census dates and for which cloud-free images are available. Images were obtained for two time periods: approximately 1990 and approximately 2000. The actual image dates vary and the sample mean time period between images is just over eleven years. The images themselves provide data on reflected light intensity in seven spectral bands (three visual and four infrared). These data are used to classify each point as urban (covered with impervious built structures or surfaces), water, or nonurban (everything else) in each time period. The light intensity data that constitute the images provide values for grids of pixels each of which represents a square region 28.5 meters on a side.

There are several commercial and noncommercial data sources that provide information on global land cover. Some of these can be very useful, but we chose to develop our own classification for several reasons. First, many of the global land-cover classifications that have been undertaken have been done at relatively coarse scales (typically 1 km grids) that obscure the microstructure of the urban areas, including the open spaces interior to the built-up city. Even for those that are done at finer scale, the usual practice is to "fill in" small interior open spaces and classify them as urban. Our approach has been to regard such spaces as nonurban so that we can distinguish between new capital

Figure 7.1. Chicago, U.S.: Actual Landsat Image

investment and building at the urban periphery and infill development inside the built-up area. This will be discussed further below.

The actual classification of land cover was done using Erdas Imagine utilizing an integrated supervised cluster analysis approach. Three passes were used for each of the two images for each city. The goal was to provide a very simple classification suited to the purposes of our research: to classify each pixel as "urban" or "nonurban" and then in post-processing to remove water pixels (which are easily identified using unsupervised classification).

Figures 7.1 and 7.2 present stylized views of "before" and "after" classification using actual data for the Chicago metropolitan area. Figure 7.1 shows the actual Landsat image covering most of the city. After completing the analysis the result was the data shown in figure 7.2, where pixels are colored red if they were ultimately categorized as predominantly under urban cover and tan if not. The small insets showing a region in the southwestern suburban fringe show the image for the region available online from Google Earth (on the left of each figure)

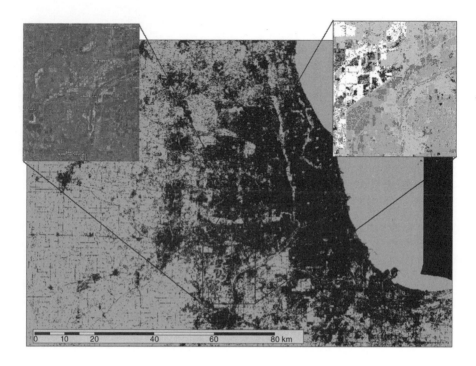

Figure 7.2. Chicago, U.S.: Image After Analysis

and the ultimate classification showing the urban dynamic discussed below.

All of the land-cover classifications produced for our study are available for download from http://www.williams.edu/Economics/Urban-Growth/DataDownload.htm in a format that will display in Google Earth. These images include links to photographs taken at "ground truth" points (used for evaluating the accuracy of our classifications). The areas representing urban land cover have been filtered to eliminate all areas that do not represent at least ten hectares of contiguous urban land cover. This greatly reduces the amount of data to be downloaded. The image for Chicago is shown in figure 7.3.

An important advantage of the approach we have followed is that *identical* procedures and *identical types of source data* were applied for all 120 cities in both time periods. This is essential if we want to reliably combine and compare data from different time periods for the same city, and also if we want to use the data to assemble a panel dataset that compares a cross section of cities around the globe over time. Such data

Figure 7.3. Chicago, U.S.: Image After Filtering

are central to our approach of measuring and modeling urban expansion. Further details concerning the remote-sensing data and classification procedure are provided in Angel, Sheppard, and Civco (2005).

Economic and Policy Conditions

The urban land-cover data described above are then matched with population data for jurisdictional boundaries in each area, obtained from the Center for International Earth Science Information Network's Global Rural-Urban Mapping Project. Using growth rates observed for each jurisdiction during 1980 through 2000, we interpolate to obtain population estimates for the dates of each image. There are many cases where the Landsat images did not provide complete coverage of the jurisdictional boundaries for which population data were available. In these cases we sometimes purchased additional Landsat images, but in other cases, we made use of an interpolation procedure using our land-cover classification and distance from the urban center to apportion the jurisdiction population between portions covered by our remote-sensing images and the portions not covered. In general the data not only include the jurisdictions covering the central city and largest contiguous regions of classified urban land cover, but extend to peripheral jurisdictions until the mean size of contiguous urban cluster falls below twenty-five hectares. This provides coverage that approximates a "metro area" definition for all cities, even though for most of the cities we lack the data on labor markets and commuting patterns generally required for the formal definition of such areas.

We also interpolate national per capita GDP to the date of the satellite image to provide an estimate of income levels in each city matched to the remote-sensing data. Data on biome type, availability of shallow groundwater aquifer, air transport links, and the value of agricultural land (approximated by agricultural output per hectare) were obtained from World Development Indicators or from sources described more fully in Angel, Sheppard, and Civco (2005).

Table 7.1 presents descriptive statistics for the central variables used in our modeling for two time periods and 120 cities. Use of a globally representative sample provides extensive variation in the data, with cities ranging from under 9 square kilometers to over 4,200, and population in the "metro area" ranging from 93,000 to over 27 million persons.

In addition to the variables used in the models of urban expansion presented below, table 7.1 provides information on additional variables that are likely to be of interest. While the sample includes many primate cities (of rank 1 in the national urban system), it includes cities down to rank 196 as well. The rate of automobile ownership varies across the sample even more than per capita income, although in general, it is income rather than automobile ownership that turns out to be the most important factor influencing total urban land cover. In part, this may be because increased automobile ownership does not necessarily imply reduced transportation costs, since congestion can slow travel considerably below the maximum speed of the vehicle. The average non-rush-hour travel speeds are seen to vary widely. These have been collected by our field researchers.

Measuring Urban Expansion

Before proceeding to discuss models of observed urban expansion, it is necessary to make a few observations concerning our measures of urban land, the calculations of urban dynamics, and the microstructure of urban land markets.

Urban Use and Urban Cover

Since our approach to measurement of global urban expansion relies upon the use of satellite images in order to have comparable data for all

Table 7.1: Descriptive Statistics for Sample

Variable	Mean	Std. Dev.	Min	Max	Obs
Total urban land (km²)	402.81	635.11	8.92	4,268.00	240
Total population	3,363,025.00	4,459,765.00	93,040.91	27,200,000.00	240
Per capita income (ppp$)	$9,914.08	$9,916.70	$609.88	$35,354.00	240
Agricultural rent (ppp$ / ha)	$3,347.65	$12,569.78	$68.84	$150,542.90	240
Fuel cost (ppp$ / US gallon)	$0.62	$0.36	$0.02	$1.56	240
Air linkages	108.21	133.39	0	659	240
Shallow groundwater	0.24	0.43	0	1	240
East Asia	0.13	0.34	0	1	240
Europe	0.13	0.34	0	1	240
Latin America	0.13	0.34	0	1	240
North Africa	0.07	0.25	0	1	240
South Central Asia	0.13	0.34	0	1	240
Southeast Asia	0.10	0.30	0	1	240
Sub-Saharan Africa	0.10	0.30	0	1	240
West Asia	0.07	0.25	0	1	240
Other developed countries	0.13	0.34	0	1	240
Years between images	11.24	2.21	5.19	16.97	240
Change in total urban land	115.21	126.09	3.19	549.66	240
Growth rate in urban land	0.05	0.05	0	0.36	240
Urban rank	19.09	38.05	1	196	240
Cars per 1,000 in country	139.47	180.55	0.39	573.28	238
Non-rush-hour travel speed (KPH)	27.11	13.64	2.61	75	198*
Maximum urban slope (%)	25.96	14.96	4.16	78	240

Source: Author's calculations based on modeling of urban expansion.

cities, we actually measure urban cover (buildings and roofing material, asphalt, concrete, and other impervious surfaces) rather than urban land use. What this means in principle is that we do not necessarily measure total land consumption by urban residents or producers. From the perspective of a satellite image, an urban worker who purchases a one-hectare plot adjacent to her home and plants a large and elaborate flower garden is essentially indistinguishable from a rural peasant who grows vegetables on the one-hectare field next to his farm house. From the perspective of urban land-use theory, however, these two are very different. Irwin, Bockstael, and Cho (2006), for example, are skeptical of reliance on urban cover as the measure of urban land use and criticize the work of Burchfield et al. (2006) and others for such reliance. They advocate instead the use of cadastral data with associated recorded types of activities and uses actually taking place on the land.

While the use of cadastral data is no doubt interesting, there are two responses to be made to its advocates. First is that many of the most interesting urban areas in the world have very limited cadastral systems, and the data recording actual land uses may either be nonexistent or so prone to error that they represent little improvement over remote-sensing data. Second, in practice at the scale of land use in modest to large urban areas, it seems to make very little difference. Irwin, Bockstael, and Cho (2006) compare remotely sensed with cadastral data in particular areas of the U.S., and while they find the total amounts of land in each category different, the qualitative nature of changes and even the rates of change of different types of land use are similar using either measure.

Finally, we note that if one is interested in the ecological, economic, or social value of open space, then use of urban land-cover data may be preferable. From the perspective of maintaining a habitat for a variety of species or providing positive externalities for which residents are willing to pay, our hypothetical urban gardener may be as productive as, or even more than, the peri-urban farmer. In any event, it should be acknowledged that the measure of urban expansion and urban land consumption used below is based on urban cover. We maintain the hypothesis that this measurement is very highly correlated with actual urban land use in consumption and production. In a sense, the empirical estimates derived below and compared with theoretical predictions of the comparative static properties of models of urban land use provide a test of this hypothesis.

Open Space and Infill Development

We referred above to the desire to provide measurements of the micro-structure of urban land markets and to characterize the dynamic of urban expansion. What do we mean by these terms? The simplest theories of urban land markets identify urban land use as clustered around a central business district of the city, with density of urban land use gradually diminishing as distance from the city increases. Eventually, the value of land in urban use falls to the level where land is more valuable in agricultural use than in urban use. That distance identifies the maximum extent of urban land use. Up to this distance, land should all be in urban use and after that distance all land should be in agricultural use.

Real cities, of course, are never like this. There are areas of open, unbuilt land within—sometimes deep within—the urban area. We might regard these as mild departures from the ideal type of human settlement represented by our theory. Alternatively, we might note that these spaces arise for several reasons: land may be preserved for use as a public good (like a park); land may be owned by a person with idiosyncratic preferences who prefers the land this way (like our urban gardener discussed above); the land itself may be heterogeneous so that some areas are more difficult to build on due to slope or drainage; and, finally, the dynamic structure of the urban economy may generate greater volatility of structure prices in some areas than in others. Areas with higher volatility present land owners with increased incentive to hold land vacant, since vacant land, as observed by Titman (1985) and others, is equivalent to an option to buy a building in the future with an exercise price equal to construction costs.

Sheppard (2006) considers this issue explicitly in modeling the microstructure of urban land use, in which different parts of the city have different levels of coverage by urban surfaces versus open space. The issue is certainly relevant for understanding why some cities achieve much higher gross population densities than others and exhibit more compact spatial structure. Measurement of this microstructure at different points in time allows us to describe more completely the emerging dynamics of urban expansion. In a simple von Thunen–style city, urban growth takes a very simple form: an increase in population or income simply adds another growth ring onto the periphery of the urban area. Again, actual cities exhibit more complex growth behavior because of the presence of interior unbuilt spaces. Using our classification of land use at two different points in time (T_1 and T_2), we can reveal considerable complexity. By combining the two classifications within a GIS system and calculating the differences between them, we divide the land in the urban area into nine categories and measure them. Figure 7.4 shows the final classification of Chicago into six land types.

Interestingly, there is considerable variation across the globe in the

Figure 7.4. Chicago, U.S.: Final Classification into Land Types

dynamics of urban expansion. In all countries, most urban expansion consists of outspill—new development on what was exterior open space. In some regions (such as North America and other non-European developed countries) urban expansion consists of a relatively high share of infill. In others (such as East Asia or South Asia) urban expansion involves very little infill. While Sheppard (2006) provides some discussion of how we might derive a theory to help explain these differences, and Cunningham (2006) provides suggestive empirical evidence on development probabilities for individual parcels in a single U.S. city (Seattle), at this point, it must be observed that standard economic theories have little to offer by way of an explanation for these differences.

Our main concern here, however, is with measuring and modeling overall urban expansion. Traditional monocentric urban models do make clear predictions about the variables that are likely to impact urban land use and the qualitative impacts of changes in these variables. The next section summarizes these.

Modeling Urban Expansion

There is no need here to derive a complete model of urban land use. Comparative static predictions are available from any of several thorough and clear presentations. Brueckner (1987), for example, derives urban land values and the extent of urban development $\bar{x}$ in the context of a closed urban model with housing producers. This model can be easily extended to include both a class of land consumers who are households purchasing housing from the housing producers and a class of firms who purchase land as an input used in production of an export good. Within this context, total urban land use will depend upon the urban population L, household income y, the value of agricultural rent r_i, transportation costs t, the productivity of land in making the export good f_i, and the productivity of land in production of housing h_i.

As noted in the above discussion, we have assembled measures of population and per capita income. In addition, we have relatively direct measures of agricultural rents (value added in agriculture per hectare of land in cultivation) and transport costs (price per gallon of motor fuel). As a proxy for the productivity of land in production of the export good, we use extent of air linkages between the city airport and other international airports. This is suggested by Wu and Yusuf (2004), who find a strong correlation between total freight shipments from cities and the extent of such air travel linkages. Finally, as a proxy for the marginal productivity of land in housing production we use the presence of shallow aquifers in the region where the city is located. Such aquifers make it relatively easy to dig wells to provide water for housing. The presence of such aquifers has been found (by Burchfield et al. (2006) to be strongly associated with urban expansion.

Table 7.2 presents the parameter estimates using our data for three models. We discuss each in turn. All the models share some basic similarities. The dependent variable is always the natural log of total urban land cover measured in square kilometers. The first five variables enter as the natural log of the variable named. All other variables are dichotomous.

The first model is the simplest: straightforward OLS estimates of the impact of the central variables of the model on total urban land use. We see that all variables are statistically significant at either the 10 percent level (single asterisk) or the 5 percent level or better (double asterisk). While results are not definitive, it is worth noting that, for such a simple model, the share of total variance explained by the central variables—82 percent—is surprisingly high.

The second model continues with simple OLS estimation but extends the specification to account for unmeasured factors that may be con-

Table 7.2: Model Estimates

Models of Total Urban Land Cover Variable	OLS Estimate	OLS Estimate	Instrumental Variables Estimate
Population	0.7405**	0.763**	0.3722*
σ	0.059	0.063	0.183
Income	0.5479**	0.5235**	0.5352**
σ	0.045	0.063	0.134
Agricultural rent	−0.2385**	−0.2315**	−0.1609*
σ	0.033	0.039	0.095
Fuel cost	−0.1212**	−0.1468*	−0.2072**
σ	0.061	0.065	0.059
Air linkages	0.0637*	0.0449	0.1451*
σ	0.038	0.044	0.071
Shallow groundwater	0.2452*	0.1336	0.0312
σ	0.128	0.127	0.175
East Asia		−0.0541	0.3209
σ		0.224	0.397
Europe		−0.2914*	−0.3082
σ		0.142	0.229
Latin America		−0.3643*	−0.3191
σ		0.159	0.272
North Africa		−0.3947	−0.4341
σ		0.288	0.395
South − Central Asia		−0.5336*	−0.2817
σ		0.222	0.364
Southeast Asia		−0.4025*	−0.2313
σ		0.226	0.364
Sub-Saharan Africa		0.0588	0.0048
σ		0.192	0.378
West Asia		0.1273	0.1179
σ		0.215	0.335
Constant	−8.8289**	−8.6998**	−3.8249
σ	0.885	1.010	2.670
Number of observations	240	240	240
Clusters	120	120	120
F	116.11**	75.25**	12.12**
R^2	0.82	0.84	0.77
Root MSE	0.55	0.52	0.62
H_0:Regressors are exogenous			
Wu-Hausman F test:			4.0171**
Durbin-Wu-Hausman χ^2 test:			12.3577**

Source: Author's calculations based on modeling of urban expansion.

stant over time and across all cities within a given region. This addresses the idea often put forward in discussion of global urban expansion, that "all cities in region X are special." This model changes very little in the values of the estimated parameters. We see that Europe, Latin America, and South and Southeast Asia all have cities that tend to be more compact (less urban land cover *ceteris paribus*) than the cities in other developed countries (the excluded case) but that inclusion of these variables adds little to the overall explanatory power of the model.

A natural concern in these types of models deals with the bias that arises from endogenous covariates. Population and income surely do appear to affect the overall level of urban land use. On the other hand, cities with large amounts of urban land cover might provide attractive locations so that population tends to move toward such cities. The result is a correlation between random variation in measurements of right-hand-side variables (such as population, income, etc.) and the error term of the model being estimated. The result is inconsistent estimation of the parameters.

To address this problem, we present as the final model an instrumental variables approach to estimation. For instruments we use the biome in which the city is located (a classification that reflects the local climate and types of natural plant life) as well as the location and measures of the topography. The Wu-Hausman and Durbin-Wu-Hausman tests given in the last two lines of the table easily reject the hypothesis of regressor exogeneity, suggesting that the IV approach is truly required in this case. Fortunately, the impact on parameter estimates is not large. The elasticity of urban land use with respect to income is almost unchanged. The elasticity with respect to population falls from around 0.75 to under 0.4. Overall, however, it must be observed that the hypotheses identified above are largely supported. This helps to build our confidence in using a standard theoretical approach in the analysis of global urban expansion and suggests at least tentative acceptance of these parameter estimates for some policy recommendations. We turn to these in the next section.

Policy Conclusions and Applications

In the introduction, we referred to policies to control urban expansion by limiting rural-to-urban migration or fighting road building, and noted that such efforts seemed to meet with very little success in actually limiting the extent of urban expansion. The model estimates presented above help us to understand, at least in part, why this might be true. The variation in urban expansion across global cities can be largely explained as a consequence of population and income growth, along with fuel prices, agricultural land values, and some other measures that define the economic context for the city.

It is instructive to identify the cities whose actual urban expansion from T_1 to T_2 was much less than would be expected from the model.

We calculate this difference as a percentage of the overall size of the urban area and rank the results in order of the difference between actual and expected urban growth. Table 7.3 below presents the twelve cities whose expansion was the smallest relative to model-based expectations and the twelve cities whose expansion was the largest.

The first thing to note is that these under- and overperforming cities are not uniformly the richest or poorest. Nor are they the largest or smallest in their countries. The less expansive cities do tend to be lower ranked in their respective urban hierarchies, and perhaps less affluent on average. Both groups, however, include a variety of cities. What we do note is that the cities that expanded less are often constrained by topography and coastal locations: Hong Kong, Victoria, Thessaloniki, Guaruja, and Palermo are all constrained in this way and therefore might be expected to expand less for a given level of income, population, etc. There are some coastal or port cities in the more expansive group as well, but many (like Chicago) are coastal but relatively unconstrained in terms of their ability to expand inland.

Several of the more expansive cities also clearly play major roles as world cities with influence far beyond their own national economies. London, Cairo, Beijing, São Paolo, and Chicago arguably fall into this category. There may be more to be learned about the factors that influence urban expansion through this type of evaluation and consideration.

One thing, however, is clear from the parameter estimates presented above. Economic development alone is likely to lead to urban expansion simply through the increase in per capita income. Whether it is possible for urban growth policies to limit expansion in the context of a developing economy city is not at all clear. There are many planning policies, particularly in developing economies, that seem to be predicated on the assumption that this is in fact possible, but even the most vigorous initiatives to limit urban expansion will have to contend with the processes of income and population growth, both of which tend to be relatively high in developing-country cities.

Whether one wants to call these initiatives planning policies is unclear. They are policies that identify what many urban designers regard as a desirable outcome, but the model estimates we present above call into doubt the extent to which they entail any planning (in the sense that planning involves, at least in part, a *preparation* for what is likely to take place in the future). The consequences of these "planning but not preparation" policies are often that cities, which do not want (or are unable) to incur the costs of providing infrastructure to newly developing areas, do not plan or set aside any areas for future development. This does little to stop the development from taking place, but

Table 7.3: Cities with More and Less Urban Expansion Than Expected

Expected Expansion Rank	City	Urban Rank	Urban Land T₁	Urban Growth Rate	Population T₁	Pop Growth Rate	Per Capita GDP T₁	Income Growth Rate	Growth Prep Rate	New Urban to Prepare	Prepare Actual
1	Hong Kong	4	75	2.19%	4,322,297	0.82%	$1,514	8.73%	4.77%	43	1.90
2	Songkhla	2	142	.92%	219,751	0.98%	$4,459	3.51%	2.24%	3	0.65
3	Victoria	16	81	2.85%	238,436	0.67%	$23,268	1.76%	1.21%	9	0.37
4	Guaruja	70	31	1.89%	798,401	1.15%	$6,727	1.29%	1.22%	3	0.59
5	Thessaloniki	2	52	2.33%	770,764	0.77%	$13,857	1.77%	1.27%	9	0.46
6	Saidpur	25	9	5.31%	502,692	1.39%	$1,184	2.43%	1.91%	2	0.26
7	Bacolod	7	13	11.56%	461,590	1.29%	$3,908	0.26%	0.78%	1	0.04
8	Palermo	7	74	0.74%	824,435	0.03%	$21,015	1.34%	0.68%	7	0.88
9	Chinju	24	32	5.43%	330,240	0.42%	$10,398	5.02%	2.72%	8	0.39
10	Kigali	1	11	9.28%	335,538	1.17%	$1,245	−0.85%	0.16%	0.3	0.01
11	Rajshahi	4	11	5.66%	490,564	1.82%	$1,155	2.43%	2.12%	3	0.27
12	Aswan	15	13	1.63%	225,969	2.29%	$2,727	1.90%	2.10%	4	1.14
109	Marrakesh	4	194	2.28%	613,373	1.94%	$3,326	0.31%	1.12%	28	0.42
110	London	1	1,573	1.49%	9,932,047	0.09%	$21,535	1.93%	1.01%	175	0.62
111	Cairo	1	366	2.73%	10,132,863	1.57%	$2,617	1.90%	1.73%	103	0.51
112	Coimbatore	23	99	4.56%	551,696	1.06%	$1,666	3.50%	2.28%	23	0.40
113	Zhengzhou	23	404	4.47%	3,457,936	2.47%	$1,326	8.73%	5.60%	294	0.92
114	Beijing	2	1,056	2.17%	8,639,446	2.13%	$1,399	8.72%	5.43%	603	2.23
115	Ipoh	2	145	3.61%	521,338	2.00%	$5,459	4.85%	3.43%	57	0.77
116	Chicago, IL	3	3,748	1.06%	7,550,456	1.04%	$27,884	1.80%	1.42%	650	1.25
117	São Paolo	1	1,264	1.76%	10,678,860	1.70%	$6,325	1.29%	1.50%	222	0.76
118	Tokyo	1	2,318	0.70%	25,106,290	0.56%	$22,641	1.12%	0.84%	279	1.13
119	Ibadan	3	209	2.38%	1,565,805	2.88%	$895	−0.12%	1.38%	44	0.48
120	Yulin	46	846	4.77%	4,065,112	−2.78%	$1,793	8.72%	2.97%	227	0.50

Source: Author's calculations based on modeling of urban expansion.

does ensure that it will be done in an uncoordinated fashion, so that when efforts are finally made to extend infrastructure to the newly built areas, it will be more difficult and costly than would be true if some minimal preparations for urban expansion were undertaken.

Using the estimated models presented above, it is possible to make forecasts of urban expansion that take into account all of the variables considered. It might be more helpful (and realistic), however, to propose an easily remembered and simple rule of thumb or reality check for planning policy. This might be conveniently designated as the 50–50 planning rule. It derives from the simple observation that, based on the models above, the elasticity of total urban land use with respect to population and the elasticity of total urban land use with respect to per capita income are both on the order of 0.5. The rule of thumb can be stated as follows: *Using recent history or reasonable expectations about the future, compute the sum of one-half the expected percentage rate of growth of population plus one-half the expected percentage rate of income growth. The result is an approximation of the percentage increase in total urban land to be expected* each year.

Because the result is expressed as a percentage increase, it can be applied to whatever type of measure of total urban land area is available to the planning authority. In the final three columns of table 7.3 this type of analysis is presented, using the actual rates of population and income growth observed from T_1 to T_2. Applying the 50–50 planning rule to these rates yields the annual percentage change in total urban land that might be expected—in the column labeled "Growth Prep Rate." Multiplying this rate by the size of the urban area and the elapsed time between T_1 and T_2 yields a suggested amount of new urban expansion for which preparations should be considered. Sometimes this amount is relatively modest—three to four square kilometers of new urban development for less expansive cities over a ten-year span. For more expansive cities, however, the areas can be very significant. Thus the 50–50 planning rule would suggest that São Paolo should be considering preparations for well over 200 square kilometers of new urban development during the next decade.

These amounts seem large, but in fact they are almost never sufficient! The final column in table 7.3 presents the ratio between the amount of urban expansion preparation suggested by the 50–50 planning rule and the actual amount of measured urban expansion observed between times T_1 and T_2. There are a few cities (Beijing and Hong Kong) for which such preparations would have been more than was required. For most cities, however, such preparations would still have been insufficient. Averaged over our entire sample of cities, the application of the 50–50 planning rule would have provided for about half of the actual urban expansion that took place.

Agenda for Research on Global Urban Expansion

The discussion above has presented an approach for measurement and modeling of global urban expansion. Using the measured urban expansion we have provided empirical tests of the models and found that our expectations are generally confirmed. There remain, however, several important avenues for future research and collaboration. We conclude with seven suggestions for consideration.

1. The collection and analysis of global data is expensive and difficult. There is a great need to coordinate data-collection efforts. This coordination could be promoted by UN-HABITAT, the World Bank, or a major foundation with interests in the area.

2. Determining the potential for urban growth policies to affect the levels of urban expansion is critical. If the variables used in the models in this chapter explain 80 percent of total variation in urban land use, does this imply that policies can explain at most 20 percent?

3. Several forces of social change continue to affect cities in ways that are not fully understood. Changing social and economic roles for women, for example, may have significant implications for evolving urban form. At present these are poorly understood, and need to be researched further.

4. Econometric techniques for evaluating the accuracy of land-use classifications are surprisingly limited. Most evaluations focus on the probability of correctly classifying individual pixels, but this is rarely the measure of accuracy of greatest interest for urban policy. What is important for policy analysis is to obtain accurate measurement of total urban land use at the geographic scale of interest to the policymaker. Sometimes this will be as small as a neighborhood, sometimes as large as the entire metropolitan area, but never as small as a pixel.

5. Examine the impacts various urban outcomes have on health and human welfare. For example, reductions in interior open space result in more compact cities with potentially less commuting, but also reduce the accessibility of open space to inner-city residents.

6. Analyze the potential for employment decentralization to reduce total commuting and hence total energy use in cities that are not compact and have relatively low densities.

7. Urban policies, particularly in settings where governments change frequently, can be a source of uncertainty and volatility in structure prices and expectations. It will be important to determine to what extent policy variability alters the microstructure of urban expansion.

Chapter 8

Urban Growth Models: State of the Art and Prospects

John D. Landis

Once known as urban activity models, urban growth models (UGMs) emerged in the mid-1960s out of advances in regional science, huge improvements in computing speed and storage capacity (or so they seemed at the time), a newfound surplus of detailed activity data, and federal mandates coupled with funding for metropolitan planning organizations (MPOs) to back up transportation funding requests with careful projections and hard-headed analysis. Overhyped and underdeveloped, early urban models soon proved unreliable. Their epitaph, "Requiem for Large-Scale Models," published in the *Journal of the American Institute of Planners* (Lee 1973), is still one of the most widely read and cited journal articles in planning.

By the early 1990s, UGMs had staged a small-scale comeback, buoyed by new modeling techniques—especially discrete choice models—further improvements in computing speed and storage capacity, the migration of GIS from mainframe to desktop, advances in data distribution channels (first CDs, later the Internet), and by the desire of local governments and MPOs to go beyond linear trend lines to investigate alternative planning scenarios. By 2000, a survey by the U.S. Environmental Protection Agency had uncovered more than twenty urban forecasting and simulation models, most of which had not existed just ten years earlier (U.S. EPA 2000). Recent and dramatic increases in the availability of high-resolution satellite imagery have given even greater impetus to urban modeling. Recent developments in urban modeling have been chronicled by Batty (1994, 2005) and Wegener (1994, 1998b). For the most part, UGMs have been developed and applied in the Global North, where their data needs can be more easily met. Recent improvements in remote sensing offer potential for their use in the Global South.

The allure of UGMs remains as siren-like today as in the 1960s. Foremost, they offer the promise of reducing huge volumes of local data into a few robust and understandable generalizations about processes of urban change. Second, they promise to facilitate thinking about the future of cities in ways that are new, nontraditional, *and spatial.* Third, with the addition of discrete choice modeling, they offer the ability to link the decisions and behaviors of individual agents to metropolitan outcomes; and this, more than any other capability, is the key to planning for sustainability. Fourth and most important, they provide a key analytical bridge between envisioning alternative urban development patterns and evaluating their impacts.

Promise and performance, however, don't always go hand in hand. Fifteen years after their resurrection, questions about UGMs still remain. Are they facilitating better metropolitan investment and policy decisions? Are they leading to a richer, more nuanced, and more comprehensive understanding of the effects of those investment and policy decisions? Are they helping open up local and metropolitan discussions about development to new ideas, approaches, and participants? Are they making the practice of local and metropolitan planning noticeably better? The answer to these questions for the most part is "no": UGMs are still too complicated, still too untested, and still too slow to adapt to local circumstances to be used regularly and reliably. Nonetheless, progress continues, and the state of the art of urban modeling advances daily.

This chapter takes a hopeful but critical look at UGMs through the lens of four archetypes: (1) the IRPUD (Institute for Regional Planning and Urban Development) model developed at the University of Dortmund, the best heir to the spatial interaction models of the 1960s; (2) the SLEUTH (Slope, Land Use, Exclusion, Urban extent, Transportation, Hillshade) model, an example of the use of cellular automata (CA) procedures to model urban change; (3) the California Urban Futures (CUF) family of urban growth models, the first to employ GIS; and (4) UrbanSim, the leading example of agent-based urban modeling.[1] All four share two essential characteristics: they are *calibrated,* which means their coefficients are estimated from historical experience and are therefore not ad hoc; and they are *spatially explicit,* capable of looking at urban change at the level of an individual parcel (or comparably sized grid cell).

This chapter is organized in four sections. The first, "Why Urban Growth Models?" explains UGM functions. The second, "Four Archetypal Urban Growth Models," introduces the four selected UGMs. The third, "Model Comparisons," looks at their respective structures, calibration procedures, ease of data assembly, and usefulness for simulation. The fourth, "A UGM Research and Development Agenda," offers ideas for future modeling developments and application efforts and reflects on the future uses of UGMs worldwide.

Why Urban Growth Models?

UGMs can serve four purposes—although not every UGM serves each equally well and different UGMs take different approaches, especially when simulating alternative policy interventions and urban futures:

1. *Providing key inputs into downstream impact assessment models.* UGMs provide key information on the intrametropolitan distribution of land uses and activities as inputs into impact assessment models, especially travel-demand forecasting models; and in the U.S., this remains their principal use. In recent years, the suite of impact assessment models for which UGMs provide inputs has expanded to include runoff and water quality models, land cover, habitat and soil-loss models, air and water pollution models, energy and water consumption models, environmental impact assessment models, and fiscal impact models.[2]

2. *Creating parameters of urban changes processes.* UGMs measure key drivers of urban change processes in order to identify their interaction with each other and with policy and planning variables. UGMs make use of mathematical models to generate estimates of the magnitude, location, and nature of urban change. Range estimates require a *calibration* process for estimating accurate and reliable parameters in order to correctly determine the magnitude and/or spatial contribution of a particular driver of urban change.[3]

3. *Developing baseline forecasts.* UGMs generate a "business as usual" or "continuation of current trends" forecast to make the case for or against proposed planning or policy interventions. Using a spatially explicit UGM to develop baseline forecasts permits policymakers and decision-makers to explore the spatial variations and incidence associated with particular trends.

4. *Simulating alternative planning and policy scenarios.* UGMs allow their users to rigorously consider processes of urban change. Users can identify whether and how changes to driver variables in the present will be consistent with a preferred end-state vision for the future; or they can see if a set of generated future outcomes is better or worse than the trend case. The second approach is commonly known as simulation. UGMs can simulate alternative futures in four ways: by imposing additional constraints upon the occurrence of particular outcomes (this is typically done by declaring certain sites, areas, or districts off-limits to certain forms of development, usually in the name of environmental protection); by specifying particular and spatially discrete interventions

at specific points in time (e.g., the construction of a new light-rail system down a freeway median, or the doubling of landing capacity at an airport, or the creation of a new regional park); by allowing one or more driver variables to increase or decrease in value or type (this can be done uniformly across the study area or metropolitan area—e.g., "increase suburban employment levels 20 percent over central-city employment levels"—or it can be done at particular locations—e.g., "increase densities 40 percent at locations adjacent to rail transit stops"); and by allowing the parameter estimates themselves to vary (e.g., increasing the parameter estimate associated with current densities—as a predictor of future densities—by 20 percent.) This is analogous to saying that future urban change processes will systematically and comprehensively vary from past processes, or, to put it another way, that the future *should not* resemble the past.

Four Archetypal Urban Growth Models

The IRPUD Model

The successive models developed by Michael Wegener and Klaus Spiekermann (Wegener 1998a) at the Institute for Regional Planning and Urban Development at the University of Dortmund are *spatial interaction models*. As such, they are direct descendants of the first generation of urban models developed in the 1960s. Spatial interaction models like IRPUD draw their name from the dominant role of travel times and costs in determining household and firm location decisions. The IRPUD model works as follows: for each forecasting period, the initial spatial distribution of households, persons, firms, and workers is passed to a series of travel-demand submodels which estimate commuter and freight transport activity by origin and destination zone, and then allocate that activity to the transportation network (figure 8.1). The resulting traffic flows, link loads, and travel times and costs are then fed back into a set of land-use allocation submodels, where they affect construction activity by developers and location decisions by households and firms during the next period. Households adjust their locations to maximize their housing consumption and accessibility to work, shopping opportunities, and public facilities. Firms adjust their locations and their space demands to minimize their shipment costs and real estate expenditures. Changes in traffic volumes, congestion levels, and the vehicle fleet mix (which is also modeled) affect vehicle-based energy use, noise levels, and air pollution emissions. Vehicle emissions are combined with household and industrial pollution emissions, causing ambient pollu-

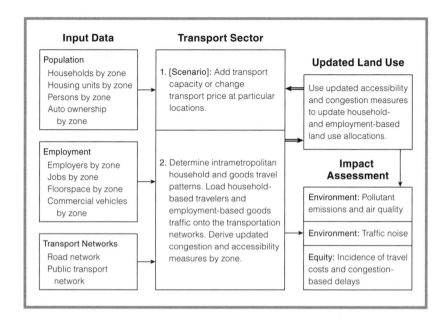

Figure 8.1. Logic of the IRPUD Model: ILUMASS Version

Source: Abstracted from Straunch et al. 2003. "Linking Transport and Land Use Planning: The Microscopic Dynamic Simulation Model ILUMASS," unpublished paper.

tion levels to change. New transportation facilities are constructed or existing facilities are upgraded at the points and for the locations where the aggregate travel time and cost savings exceed construction costs.

These different adjustment processes occur on different schedules. Travel times and costs are updated every period (i.e., every model year), as are air pollution emissions and ambient air quality levels. Firms and households are allowed to adjust their locations every period—although most do not—and to form, dissolve, expand, contract, or age into a different category every few periods according to their age (households) or economic competitiveness (firms). Developers update the building stock every three periods, and the transportation system can be expanded or changed every five years. Each IRPUD submodel is calibrated independently. The submodel results are then connected to each and checked against historical outcomes, a process known as historical validation.

IRPUD is used exclusively in Dortmund to test the spatial development and environmental impacts of a wide variety of transportation policy options (e.g., investments in highways versus public transit, changes in road tolls and transit fares, regulations restricting vehicle emissions). Unusual among urban modelers, Wegener and Spiekermann have long been concerned about the distributional dimensions of urban change and, through the use of location and income-specific impact factors, they try to sort out the effects of policy changes on different income groups.

SLEUTH

Developed by Keith Clarke of the University of California, Santa Barbara, and researchers at the U.S. Geological Survey, SLEUTH takes a cellular automata approach to modeling urban and landscape change (Couclelis 1997). CA models require that space be represented as a grid of cells that can change state as the model iterates. Rules specify a set of neighborhood conditions to be met before a change in state can occur (e.g., "If an undeveloped grid cell is adjacent to two or more developed grid cells and is crossed by a freeway, it will be developed in the next period.").

SLEUTH simulates four types of urban land-use change: spontaneous growth, new spreading center growth, edge growth, and road-influenced growth (figure 8.2). *Spontaneous growth* simulates the random urbanization of single pixels, captures low-density development patterns, and is independent of proximity to nearby urban areas or transportation infrastructure. *New spreading center growth* models the emergence of new urbanizing centers by generating up to two neighboring urban cells around areas that have been urbanized through spontaneous growth. A newly urbanized cluster can then experience edge growth, which simulates outward growth from the edge of new and existing urban centers. *Edge growth* is controlled by the spread coefficient, which influences the probability that a nonurban cell with at least three urban neighbors will also become urbanized. The final growth step, *road-influenced growth*, simulates the influence of the transportation network on growth patterns by generating spreading centers adjacent to roads. These four growth types are applied sequentially during each growth cycle—usually a year—and are influenced through the interactions of five growth coefficients: dispersion, breed, spread, road gravity, and slope. Each coefficient has a value that ranges from 0 to 100.[4]

SLEUTH's allocation rules and coefficients are allowed to change as a SLEUTH simulation progresses. When the rate of growth exceeds a specified critical threshold, the growth coefficients are multiplied by a factor greater than 1, simulating a development boom cycle. Likewise, when the rate of development falls below a specified critical threshold,

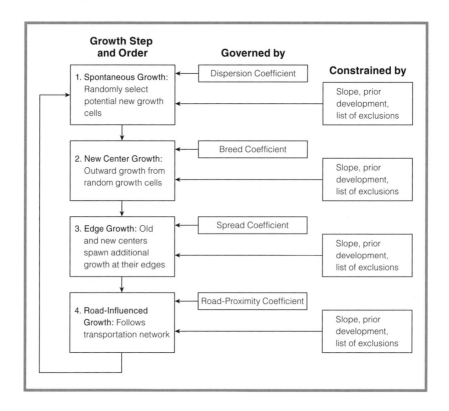

Figure 8.2. Logic of the SLEUTH Model

Source: Abstracted from Jantz, Goetz, and Shelley 2004.

the growth coefficients are multiplied by a factor less than 1, simulating a development bust cycle. Termed "self-modification" or "emergent behavior," these provisions allow for the possibility that SLEUTH simulations will not merely be linear extrapolations of past trends.

SLEUTH has been used to model and simulate land-use changes in the Baltimore-Washington corridor, in the San Francisco Bay Area, in the Chesapeake Bay region, and in California's Central Valley (Clarke and Gaydos 1998; Clarke, Hoppen, and Gaydos 1997; Jantz, Goetz, and Shelley 2003; Dietzel et al. 2004). SLEUTH (like CA models more generally) is most appropriately used for baseline forecasting,[5] and has limited application in simulating future land-use changes. Because of its black-box structure, SLEUTH has difficulty simulating real-world policy changes or providing inputs into impact assessment models.

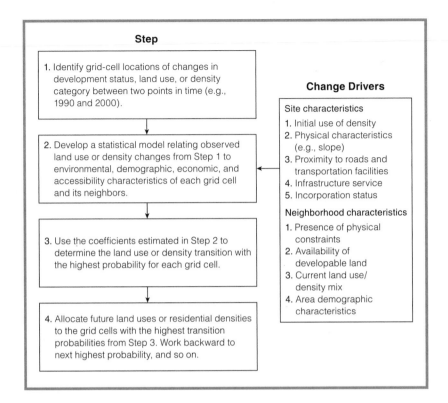

Step

1. Identify grid-cell locations of changes in development status, land use, or density category between two points in time (e.g., 1990 and 2000).

2. Develop a statistical model relating observed land use or density changes from Step 1 to environmental, demographic, economic, and accessibility characteristics of each grid cell and its neighbors.

3. Use the coefficients estimated in Step 2 to determine the land use or density transition with the highest probability for each grid cell.

4. Allocate future land uses or residential densities to the grid cells with the highest transition probabilities from Step 3. Work backward to next highest probability, and so on.

Change Drivers

Site characteristics
1. Initial use of density
2. Physical characteristics (e.g., slope)
3. Proximity to roads and transportation facilities
4. Infrastructure service
5. Incorporation status

Neighborhood characteristics
1. Presence of physical constraints
2. Availability of developable land
3. Current land use/ density mix
4. Area demographic characteristics

Figure 8.3. Logic of the CUF/CURBA/CURLA Model

Source: Abstracted from Landis and Reilly 2006.

The California Urban Futures Family of Urban Growth Models

Designed by John Landis and several associates at the University of California, Berkeley, the CUF family of UGMs (figure 8.3) is a series of spatially explicit models of urban growth and change. Except for CUF I (Landis 1994, 1995), all subsequent CUF models and variants have been *reduced-form* models using hundred-meter grid cells as their spatial unit of analysis (Landis 2001). They model site-level changes in land use, development status, or density as a statistical function of their physical characteristics, their proximity to regional infrastructure facilities and activities, the characteristics of neighboring cells, various demographic and economic characteristics, and local regulatory policies.

Using 1985 and 1995 land-use data for the fifteen-county Greater San

Francisco Bay Area, CUF II (Landis and Zhang 1998a, 1998b) modeled five categories of land-use changes ranging from undeveloped to developed and four categories of redevelopment. It did a good job explaining both the type and location of past land-use changes, a reasonable job predicting future amounts of land-use change, but a poor job predicting future land-use change locations.

An improved version known as CURBA (California Urban and Biodiversity Analysis) modeled changes in site-level urbanization between 1988 and 1998 using biannual land-cover data from the California Department of Conservation. Notably, it kept track of the land-cover and habitat characteristics of previously undeveloped sites, making it possible to evaluate how changes in the level and location of urban development affected farmland, wetland, and habitat fragmentation. Several state agencies used CURBA to generate urbanization footprint projections for California through the year 2100 (Landis and Reilly 2006). Because of input data limitations, the CURBA model could not account for exurban land-cover changes (development below a density of 1.5 houses per acre) or for redevelopment activity, both of which are fairly common in California. The latest CUF model, CURLA (California Urban and Rural Landscape Analysis), estimates the probability that a grid cell of a particular housing or population density in 1990 transitioned to a higher density category by 2000.[6] Landis and his team are now using CURLA to model density change for the entire Unites States to create a series of national population and employment footprint scenarios for 2050.

UrbanSim

Developed by Paul Waddell at the University of Washington, UrbanSim is an agent-based model that estimates the site-level behavior and location decisions of representative sets of households, employers, and developers. It incorporates the spatial interaction mechanisms of IRPUD and the grid-cell–based representation of space of SLEUTH and CUF. Like IRPUD, UrbanSim sees urban change as the outcome of a series of economic decisions. But whereas IRPUD models these decisions using tract or zonal aggregates, UrbanSim models them as the interactions of individual agents operating on the demand side (e.g., households and employers) and supply side (e.g., land developers).

Every model period, UrbanSim generates new sets of "mover" households and businesses (Waddell 2002). Movers are existing households and employers looking to change location, or households and businesses new to the metropolitan area as a result of population and economic growth (figure 8.4). Households choose a residential location

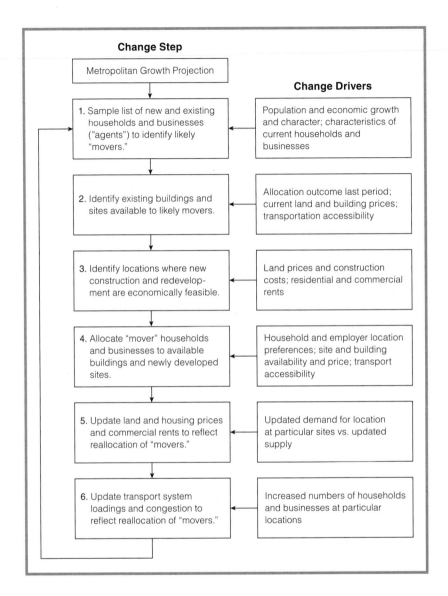

Change Step

Metropolitan Growth Projection

1. Sample list of new and existing households and businesses ("agents") to identify likely "movers."

2. Identify existing buildings and sites available to likely movers.

3. Identify locations where new construction and redevelopment are economically feasible.

4. Allocate "mover" households and businesses to available buildings and newly developed sites.

5. Update land and housing prices and commercial rents to reflect reallocation of "movers."

6. Update transport system loadings and congestion to reflect reallocation of "movers."

Change Drivers

Population and economic growth and character; characteristics of current households and businesses

Allocation outcome last period; current land and building prices; transportation accessibility

Land prices and construction costs; residential and commercial rents

Household and employer location preferences; site and building availability and price; transport accessibility

Updated demand for location at particular sites vs. updated supply

Increased numbers of households and businesses at particular locations

Figure 8.4. Logic of the UrbanSim Model

Source: Abstracted from Waddell 2002.

from a representative set of vacant dwelling units (including recently constructed homes) based on their demographic and economic characteristics; the price, size, and density of available homes; neighborhood characteristics such as land-use mix, density, and accessibility to retail locations; and regional accessibility to jobs. Employers choose where to locate or relocate based on the characteristics of their industries and markets; the availability and price of commercial space (including newly developed commercial buildings); selected neighborhood characteristics; and regional accessibility to the labor force. Developers choose where and how much new construction and redevelopment to undertake based on the market value of available land supplies and buildings; policy constraints such as zoning; and the physical and accessibility characteristics of available sites. The household, employer, and developer models are connected through a land price model which estimates current land and improvement values as a function of neighborhood quality and accessibility, policy factors, and the short-term difference between demand (from the household and employer models) and supply (from the developer model). Locations can be modeled as grid cells (easy) or parcels (harder). Households, employers, and development types are disaggregated into multiple subcategories depending on local data availability.

First applied to the Eugene-Springfield (Oregon) metropolitan area, UrbanSim has been subsequently applied in the Puget Sound (Seattle and Tacoma) region, in Amherst (Massachusetts), in Paris, and most recently in Tel Aviv (Waddell et al. 2001; www.urbansim.org). Unique among UGMs, UrbanSim's routines and linking utilities are available to any and all potential uses as open-source, and therefore modifiable, software through UrbanSim's Open Platform for Urban Simulation (OPUS) web page (www.urbansim.org/news/opus.html). UrbanSim's highly disaggregate structure and agent-based approach make it the most robust and potentially powerful of all current UGMs but also the most complicated and data hungry. Pulling together and organizing the many data layers needed to calibrate and run UrbanSim can take months of full-time work. In its initial application to the Eugene-Springfield MSA in Oregon, UrbanSim incorporated 300-plus combinations of household characteristics; fourteen employer types; and twenty-five land-development categories, including vacant and undeveloped land.

UrbanSim's disaggregate and behavioral structure—and in particular, its inclusion of a formal land price model—gives it the potential to simulate a wider variety of planning and policy interventions than any other UGM. These include the imposition of an urban growth boundary; area-specific changes in planning and zoning classifications and densities; investments in new transportation infrastructure or changes in gas prices, tolls, and transit fares; increases in the supply of affordable or subsidized housing; local economic development policies which subsidize particular businesses or earmark prime sites for specific industries; and public and private conservation programs which preclude environmentally sensitive lands from prospective urban development.

Model Comparisons

Figure 8.5 compares IRPUD, SLEUTH, CUF, and UrbanSim in terms of their model structure, calibration procedures, ease of data assembly, and usefulness for simulation. The purpose of these comparisons is to help readers better understand differences in approach, model design, and use, and not to identify which model is superior in one respect or another. Given that every UGM is unique, these comparisons are valid for these models only and would not necessarily apply to similarly structured UGMs.

Model Design and Processes

All four UGMs are spatially explicit—that is, they model urban activities at the site level—and all four rely on activity and spatial relationships that are calibrated against historical experience. However, each employs a different approach to modeling urban change. Since IRPUD is a spatial interaction model, the allocation of households and businesses is based on minimizing travel times and costs across origin and destination zones, and it is by varying those times and costs that it simulates alternative policies. SLEUTH is a cellular automata model, which means that it relies on a set of spatial rules for allocating new development to individual sites. Two features make SLEUTH unique among CA models. The first is that its governing rules are not heuristics—as is the case for most CA models—but instead are estimated from historical urbanization trends based on hundreds of thousands of Monte Carlo simulations. SLEUTH's second unique characteristic is that its rules can change and adapt as future circumstances change. This latter feature is also known as *emergent behavior*. SLEUTH is difficult to calibrate because of the huge number of required simulation runs but, once calibrated, is fairly easy to use. The CUF family of UGMs takes a reduced-form approach in which historical changes in site-level land use, development status, or residential density are statistically modeled from a set of explanatory variables describing site-level development opportunities and constraints, neighborhood-scale factors influencing development, driver (or demand-side) variables, and policy variables.[7] UrbanSim locates individual

	IRPUD	SLEUTH	CUF/CURBA/ CURLA	UrbanSim
Model type	Spatial interaction	Cellular automata	Reduced-form	Agent-based
Typical study area	Metropolitan area	Metropolitan area	Metropolitan area	Metropolitan area
Behavioral units	Zonal totals of different types of households and firms	Landscape cells of different development status	Landscape cells of different development, density, or land-use status	Representative and discrete household and business types ("agents")
Spatial units	Traffic analysis zone	100m grid cell	100m grid cell	Grid cells
Growth and change drivers	Exogenous population and employment growth, with income and cost feedback effects	Exogenous population growth totals	Exogenous population (and employment) growth totals	Exogenous population and employment growth, with income and cost feedback effects through increased moving activity
Activity/change allocation mechanism	Utility maximization: minimize travel time and cost; maximize location utility	Rule-based: (i) spontaneous growth; (ii) spread of existing centers; (iii) road-based growth; and (iv) edge growth	Reduced-form models of discrete changes in urbanization, density, or land use	Utility maximization: interaction of household and business demand for locations with additional developer-provided buildings, as mediated through land prices
Diversity of household and business types	Moderate	None	Varies	High
Incorporation of land prices or markets	Indirectly	No	No	Yes
Feedback mechanisms	Sequential	Rule-modification if change thresholds exceeded	Iterative	Sequential and simultaneous
Role of landscape and environmental factors	Small, as constraints	Mostly as constraints; may also be as allocation driver	As constraints and change driver	Mostly as constraints; sometimes as amenity into HH utility calculations
Calibration approach	Statistical: cross-sectional	Monte Carlo simulation	Statistical: cross-sectional for two time points	Statistical: cross-sectional for two time points

Figure 8.5. Four Urban Growth Models: Selected Comparisons

	IRPUD	SLEUTH	CUF/CURBA/ CURLA	UrbanSim
Model type	Spatial interaction	Cellular automata	Reduced-form	Agent-based
Availability of calibration data	High	Moderate: requires few data layers but for multiple time points	Varies by model	Moderate
Availability of spatial data	High	Low	Varies by model	High
Availability of tabular data	High	n/a	Varies by model	Moderate
Ease of data assembly	Moderate	Moderate	Moderate	Difficult
Ease of calibration	Moderate	Difficult	Moderate	Difficult
Generalizability of calibration results	Low	Moderate	Low	Low
Scenario simulation mechanisms	Adjustments from current accessibility and travel cost levels	Alter development constraints, add new roads	Infrastructure investments, constraint changes, alternative regulatory regimes, some sociodemographic change	Infrastructure investments, constraint changes, alternative regulatory regimes, some sociodemographic change
Ease of scenario construction and testing	Easy	Moderate	Moderate	Moderate
Impediments to use	Availability of transport network data	Availability of historical data for calibration	Availability of diverse spatial data	Availability of detailed spatial and tabular data

Figure 8.5. (Continued)

agents, chiefly households and businesses, in space and determines their behavior by a series of equations that balance land prices, regional job accessibility, preferences for different housing types and densities, and the quality of neighborhood services. These preferences for different housing sizes, types, tenure choices, and locations are mediated in UrbanSim—as they are in the world—through land prices. Like IRPUD, but unlike most other urban models, UrbanSim includes an explicit sub-model describing developer behavior. Like SLEUTH and CUF, Urban-Sim represents space and location as a series of grid cells. IRPUD uses travel analysis zones as its smallest spatial unit.

In none of the four models are population and employment growth completely endogenous. Instead, all four allocate externally specified metropolitan household and employment growth totals to individual sites. IRPUD represents sites as point locations; SLEUTH, CUF, and UrbanSim represent them as grid cells, typically on the order of 50 or 100 meters per side. IRPUD allows households and businesses to grow, shrink, form, disappear, and age as a simulation progresses. UrbanSim allows households to age and businesses to grow or contract. Like IRPUD, it also allows them to move in search of a newly preferred location. Both IRPUD and UrbanSim accommodate multiple household and business types (this is how UrbanSim differentiates between agents), while SLEUTH and CUF accommodate development with little regard to the specific mix of activities or agents. All four models simulate urban change iteratively: the IRPUD and SLEUTH models do so on a yearly basis; CUF and UrbanSim allow users to specify particular simulation intervals. Their iterative character allows the four models to affect some degree of path dependency, rather than simply replicating historical trend lines. All four models allow users to exclude environmentally important or sensitive sites from development, but only the reduced-form CUF model allows users to explicitly incorporate environmental factors as an amenity-attracting development.

Model Calibration and Data Requirements

All four models require calibration but use different techniques. SLEUTH uses Monte Carlo simulation procedures to compare the historical progression of development to what would occur based on various combinations of input parameters as sampled from statistical distributions. CUF uses logistic regression (i.e., "logit") procedures to estimate parameters based on their ability to fit observed changes in development status, land use, or density between two points in time. IRPUD and UrbanSim use both maximum-likelihood (logit or probit) and ordinary least-squares (regression) estimators.

Because the basic version of IRPUD is similar to models already used by many metropolitan planning organizations, assembling the input data layers required to calibrate and run IRPUD isn't difficult. More recent and complicated versions of IRPUD, however, require much richer and more detailed data. While SLEUTH does not require many spatial or attribute data layers, it does need multiple points in time, and at a fairly high degree of spatial resolution and accuracy. CUF runs with relatively few data layers—as long as the data are available for two points in time in order to observe changes—but multicategory versions require many more data layers. UrbanSim also requires many data layers for purposes of calibration and use, including hard-to-get information on housing and land transactions. SLEUTH and CUF use desktop GIS and database routines to assemble required calibration data. IRPUD and UrbanSim use their own utilities for that purpose. All of UrbanSim's code, including its many utilities, is open source.

None of the four models is easy to calibrate, and all require a moderate knowledge of statistical modeling. Except for SLEUTH, estimated model parameters are unique to particular times and places and cannot be applied in other circumstances. SLEUTH's coefficient estimates—there are only four or five of them—can be compared across different study areas but not used interchangeably for simulation.

Model Uses

IRPUD simulates and tests alternative transportation policy and investment scenarios and includes submodels explicitly designed for that purpose. SLEUTH prepares long-term projections of spatial development patterns and simulates changes in development patterns in response to new roadway investments and land exclusions. CUF and UrbanSim aim to identify and explain the parameters and relationships shaping urban development patterns; to provide key inputs into downstream impact assessment models; to prepare long-term baseline projections of likely development patterns; and to simulate alternative planning and policy interventions. Because it is agent based, UrbanSim offers the most potential avenues for users to run simulations—e.g., excluding sites from development, adding new roads and capital infrastructure, imposing new development regulations such as urban growth boundaries, subsidizing particular development forms or travel modes, or requiring that development patterns be consistent with transportation improvements. UrbanSim includes open-source utilities for specifying, running, and summarizing scenario simulations; CUF does not.

In terms of modeling downstream impacts, IRPUD and UrbanSim include their own integrated travel-demand forecasting and traffic assignment submodels. Later versions of IRPUD also include procedures for modeling energy and noise impacts. The results of SLEUTH and CUF are not sufficiently detailed in terms of household types and sizes or employment levels to be used with available travel-demand forecasting models. The CURBA and CURLA variants of the CUF model report on changes in land-cover fragmentation with a special focus on prime farmland and endangered species habitat lands.

None of the four models is easily transportable across study areas. Each new application requires fresh data collection, assembly, and calibration efforts. IRPUD requires detailed information on transportation network performance. SLEUTH, as noted above, requires fifty-plus years of high-resolution data on historical urbanization patterns. The CUF family and UrbanSim require multiple data layers for two (or more) points in time. Like IRPUD, UrbanSim also requires detailed transportation network and performance data.

Convergence or Divergence?

Short of applying IRPUD, SLEUTH, CUF, and UrbanSim—or any other UGM for that matter—to the same metro areas for the same period, it is impossible to compare them head-to-head. Since each model purposely takes a different approach, it is also difficult to identify whether the four models converge around similar driving factors, constraints, or processes that shape urban change. Indeed, except for the reduced-form CUF models, each of the models imposes its own structure on the process of urban change, with the result that estimated coefficients and parameters are comparable only to other runs of the same model. Nonetheless, with a little creative interpretation, it is possible to tease out a few commonalities (figure 8.6).

Looking first at the factors that most affect location outcomes— defined as a change in site use or density, or the allocation of activities to sites—two factors stand out above all others: proximity to roads, and initial site use or density. The closer a site is to a highway, the more likely it is to be developed (CUF and SLEUTH) or attract new households and jobs (IRPUD and UrbanSim). New activities and development are also attracted to sites abutting or adjacent to existing urban land uses. This preference for proximity to roads and existing development discourages leapfrog development in all four models. UrbanSim and CUF also model public transit accessibility and find it to have very localized effects on development and residential choice decisions. IRPUD finds that subsidizing transit service (or, conversely, increasing the cost of highway travel) has a significant effect on relative mode shares but a smaller effect on development patterns.

Turning to other factors, regional job accessibility is central to the operation of IRPUD and UrbanSim but only somewhat important in CUF;[8] SLEUTH does not model job accessibility. Accessibility to local shopping opportunities and public services are explicitly modeled in IRPUD and UrbanSim—where they moderately affect household location decisions—but not in SLEUTH or CUF. Land prices are likewise central to IRPUD and UrbanSim, where they serve to measure the balance between the demand for sites and the supply of sites. Land prices are not modeled in SLEUTH or CUF, but land supplies are: directly in CUF, and indirectly in SLEUTH through the dispersion and breed coefficients.

SLEUTH and CUF attach great importance to physical site characteristics, especially slope. In UrbanSim, physical site characteristics enter the developer submodel (as a cost factor) but do not affect household or business location decisions. Site and neighborhood amenities are important in the CURLA version of CUF (but not earlier versions) and in UrbanSim. Government regulations affect locational outcomes in UrbanSim and CUF but not in IRPUD. In SLEUTH, government regulation is one of several factors determining which sites may be excluded from development. Individual household and employer characteristics are of central importance in UrbanSim and the IRPUD model—although they are modeled differently. CUF includes neighborhood-level demographic and socioeconomic measures, but not individual household measures. SLEUTH sees households and businesses as units of growth, regardless of their characteristics.

All four models can generate sprawl (i.e., housing and job decentralization) and do so in much the same way: by building highways connecting residents and job centers to undeveloped lands at the metropolitan periphery. Unconstrained, none of the four generates recentralized activity patterns or compact growth. Substantially increasing the relative cost of auto travel gets drivers out of their cars in IRPUD, leading to a gradual increase in residential densities everywhere in the region, not just at the center. In CUF, rising household demand and limited land supplies cause densities to rise, while plentiful land supplies cause them to fall. Densities in UrbanSim can also go either way: up, if individual households and employers are willing to pay the location premiums associated with high-accessibility or -amenity locations, and down if they are not. SLEUTH allocates development to sites at fixed densities.

A UGM Research and Development Agenda

This brief review suggests a number of useful avenues for UGM development efforts:

1. *A UGM bake-off.* A competition to assess the usefulness and reliability of different UGMs—as well as to identify areas for development—by comparing their performance in explaining and recreating historical urban development patterns across a representative sample of metropolitan areas.

2. *Connections to macro-level policies and outcomes.* U.S. urban modelers have typically assumed that metropolitan household and employment growth totals were exogenous and have seen their function as distributing those households and jobs within a metropolitan area. This practice releases modelers from having to evaluate how alternative national or state scenarios might affect their areas. Determining the links between

	IRPUD	SLEUTH	CUF/CURBA/ CURLA	UrbanSim
Allocation outcome	Allocation of households or firms to zonal or point locations	Change in grid cell development status	Change in grid cell development status (CURBA), land use (CUF II), or density (CURLA)	Allocation of representative households or firms to grid cells
Factors affecting location outcomes (allocation of activity or land use to sites)				
Initial land use or density	Somewhat important	Unimportant	Very important	Important
Proximity to roads	Important	Very important	Very important	Important
Regional accessibility to employment (travel time and cost)	Very important	n/a	Varies	Very important
Local accessibility to shopping and public services	Somewhat important	n/a	n/a	Somewhat important
Land prices	Important	n/a	n/a	Very important
Physical site characteristics (e.g., slope)	n/a	Important, but principally as an exclusion layer	Very important	Varies with activity
Site and neighborhood amenities	n/a	n/a	Important	Varies with activity
Governmental jurisdiction and regulations	n/a	Unimportant, except as an exclusion layer	Varies by location	Varies with activity
Household or neighborhood demographic and socioeconomic characteristics	Important (households only)	n/a	Important (neighborhood only)	Both important
Business activity or sector	Important	n/a	Varies with model	Important

Figure 8.6. Four Urban Activity and Development Models: Common Factors and Drivers

local growth and sub- or international changes by comparing metropolitan growth and change across world cities is necessary to redress this issue.

3. *Better, cheaper, and more frequent image data.* With satellite-based remote sensing becoming ever more available and affordable, with data updates taking place more frequently, and with the tools for interpreting remotely-sensed images becoming more sophisticated and capable of

	IRPUD	SLEUTH	CUF/CURBA/ CURLA	UrbanSim
Allocation outcome	Allocation of households or firms to zonal or point locations	Change in grid cell development status	Change in grid cell development status (CURBA), land use (CUF II), or density (CURLA)	Allocation of representative households or firms to grid cells
Centralization and density drivers				
Centralization drivers	Relative accessibility and transport service quality and cost	Centralization drivers are inherent in dispersion, breed, and spread coefficients	Relative job accessibility, selected demographic characteristics, initial densities	Relative accessibility and transport service quality, household demographic characteristics, business agglomeration economies
Decentralization drivers	Relative accessibility and transport service quality and cost	Decentralization drivers are inherent in dispersion, breed, and spread coefficients	Supplies of easily developable land, selected demographic characteristics, initial densities	Relative accessibility and transport service quality, selected household demographic characteristics, lower land costs
High and "up-density" drivers	Relative accessibility and transport service quality and cost	n/a	Easy site developability, road proximity, socioeconomic diversity, initial density	Land prices
Low and "down-density" drivers	Relative accessibility and transport service quality and cost	n/a	Difficult site developability, poor road proximity, lack of socioeconomic diversity, initial density, lack of municipal jurisdiction	Land prices

Figure 8.6. (Continued)

higher-resolution images, the capability to capture short-term changes in urban development patterns—indeed, to measure the progress of construction projects—is just around the corner. These changes will open new doors to today's UGM as well as increase the need for bridging software to transform unprojected landscape-level image data (like that available from Google Earth) into projected and modelable spatial units for modeling neighborhood as well as metropolitan change.

4. *Incorporating feedback effects.* Urban growth generates large and predominantly adverse impacts on the natural environment. Urban growth typically causes or is accompanied by losses in farmland, open space, and habitat; by increases in air and water pollution and waste levels; by increased resource consumption[9]; and by increases in ambient temperatures—resulting in the so-called heat island effect. These changes not only reduce the metropolitan landscape's ability to support additional development, they also reduce the quality of life or add to the cost of living of existing residents. Over time, these unresolved externalities should negatively feed back into business expansions and household location decisions, slowing or even reversing urban growth rates. Modeling these feedback loops will require (a) developing better measurements of environmental quality at both the site and ecosystem levels; (b) developing a better understanding of whether and how rising development costs and different dimensions of environmental quality affect the behavior and location decisions of firms and households; and (c) robustly incorporating these improved measurements and behavioral dynamics into the structure of UGMs.

5. *Matching activities, buildings, and land uses.* For UGMs to become truly useful tools for analyzing alternative futures, they must do a better job matching contemporary households and business to contemporary buildings and land-use patterns. This improved activity-building-place matching must be analytically robust and easily visualized.

6. *Incorporating equity concerns.* The bottom line for a UGM should not be just whether it can explain and predict where and how much growth occurs; a UGM should also be able to investigate how and whether urban change makes residents and businesses better or worse off. That is, it should incorporate measures of equity. Equity can be measured on the income side and/or on the impact side. On the income side, equitable growth would benefit lower-income residents *proportionately more* than higher-income residents. On the impact side, equitable growth would adversely impact lower-income residents *proportionately less* than higher-income residents. Equity issues are especially important in rapidly urbanizing countries like China and India, where rapid economic development seems to be causing widening income inequality. No UGM we know of is currently capable of analyzing the equity or distributional effects of urban change. To do so, it would have to be able to reference panel data that properly tracked changes in the economic (and noneconomic) welfare of real households (and businesses) as a result of different types and forms of urban growth. Undertaking these panel studies should be a high priority.

7. *Improved impact assessment models.* Develop—in every area of impact

assessment modeling—robust and comparative validation studies across multiple trends, places, and circumstances.

Three questions about the usefulness and future of urban growth modeling remain. First, given their current capabilities and limitations, what roles should UGMs and related technologies play in metropolitan planning, and how might these roles differ between developed and developing countries? Second, how might these roles be realized? Third, how might international aid organizations help, and what forms should that help take?

Different Roles in Different Contexts

UGMs and related technologies take on different functions in different contexts. In the U.S., where metropolitan planning efforts are driven—and more importantly, funded—by federally imposed regional transportation planning requirements, the principal role of UGMs will continue to be to provide land-use and activity projections for regional transportation and air quality models. Along the way, some metropolitan planning organizations will also use UGMs to generate and evaluate alternative regional growth scenarios.

In Europe, UGM use will likely be driven by the desire to identify and evaluate effective policies or programs for reducing greenhouse gas emissions in compliance with international agreements. This particular application will favor models with a behavioral bent such as UrbanSim or IRPUD.

The principle difference between developed and developing counties with respect to metropolitan spatial planning is that the latter lack detailed, multiyear, and spatially tagged census data, and must rely instead on satellite imagery. This will make it difficult for metropolitan planners in developing countries to build behavioral models and to use them for forecasting, impact assessment, or detailed scenario building. The more appropriate use of UGMs in these circumstances will be to identify and parameterize the key drivers of urban expansion, and to help metropolitan policymakers better understand which types of planning interventions (e.g., transport and infrastructure investments, land-use regulation, or development subsidies) are likely to be most effective in shaping future growth increments and patterns. Reduced-form models like CURLA are most appropriate for this purpose.

Matching Models to Needs

Developing a workable UGM takes time, money, data, and people. It is not uncommon for metropolitan planning organizations in the U.S. to invest several years and several million dollars in the development of a locally useable UGM. The size of this commitment requires managers to think carefully about how UGM activities fit into their current and future work plans. As above, the choice of approach will be shaped by a combination of geography and development stage.

Most U.S. MPOs already have many of the data and many of the analytical procedures required to build and use a UGM; they may even have an existing UGM standing by. What many lack is land-use, land-price, and environmental data at the parcel level, making it difficult to identify which sites are ripe for market-based development (or redevelopment) or to simulate how particular planning interventions might affect individual sites and neighborhoods. Likewise, the environmental and impact assessment models used by MPOs are not sufficiently fine-grained or robust enough to reliably analyze community-level impacts. Rather than a new UGM, what most U.S. MPOs and community planning agencies need are up-to-date and high-resolution (e.g., three-meter or better) parcel and land-use data, as well as robust procedures for linking activity projections to likely land-use change and to potential environmental impacts.

The situation is similar in Europe and parts of Asia, where private developers and property owners have less say over development decisions than government planners. Planners in this context don't need to consider where development *might* go—it will go where they allow and enable it—but they do need to be able to simulate the environmental and community impacts of their decisions, as well as to very infrequently consider the desirability of alternative metropolitan development schemes.

The situation is very different in the developing world, where planners have a limited ability to intervene in formal land markets and virtually no ability to affect the growth or form of informal settlements. Here, UGMs are likely to be most useful for simulating how the development market is likely to respond to particular interventions such as the construction of a roadway, the extension of sewer and water service, or the designation of a greenbelt. The development of these capabilities is best coupled to existing or proposed efforts to create computer-based parcel registration and cadastre systems.

Getting the Ball Rolling

North America, Europe, and Southeast Asia have pressing needs for improved impact assessment models capable of identifying hotspot impacts as well as cumulative impacts. Achieving this capability will require building high-resolution databases that can be updated on a yearly or even monthly basis. Once improved data are available, the models themselves should be updated to better incorporate risk, exposure durations and effects, spatial processes, and spatial statistics. Researchers could help in this effort by convening international working groups to construct an agenda for data and model improvement. Once such efforts were underway, their results would quickly filter down to less developed countries.

In the developing world, improved data are also necessary, but of a different type. Here, the need is for high-quality and frequent land-use and parcel data so as to better track development trends and identify crucial urban service needs. The other major need in the developing world is for skilled GIS technicians able to organize available GIS databases into formats that support day-to-day urban management functions (such as providing and billing for basic infrastructure, managing transportation system loads, title recording, and land subdivision) as well as longer-term planning functions.

Better Data and Utilities, Not New Models

Institutions should think twice about funding a new generation of UGMs. As this review shows, the design and implementation of UGMs is still highly idiosyncratic and place dependent. Whether improving an existing UGM or developing a new one, current procurement practices—at least those in the U.S.—work quite well: a metropolitan planning organization or similar local agency facing a specific metropolitan planning or policy analysis task identifies the appropriate model. The resulting UGM application and results add real value to the planning process while also contributing to the agency's own knowledge and skill base. Instead of new models, what is needed is a better and timelier channel for disseminating results and developing common insights. Outside the United States and Europe it is unlikely that any UGM would pass a simple benefit-cost test.

In the developing world, the need for new and improved UGMs is less than the need for better and timelier spatial data and off-the-shelf tools and techniques for analyzing these data. Regardless of where they practice, urban planners and policymakers need to be able to visualize and measure the extent and characteristics of urban change. This means linking remotely sensed and interpreted land-cover and land-use data to sample survey data covering changes in population, economic, and social characteristics. In the United States, for example, this would be akin to linking the Quickbird satellite images with the U.S. Department of Agriculture's five-year National Resources Inventory with the Census Bureau's annual American Community Survey with the Commerce Department's annual County Business Patterns (zip code–level) jobs survey. The impediments to this type of coordination are not technological or even financial; they are principally institutional: data providers prefer that their data be used in the format in which it is provided, not the format that is most helpful to the user.

Beyond better data, planners and urban policymakers worldwide need better spatial analysis and impact assessment tools more than they need better models. These tools include *change detection utilities* to compare and parameterize changes in the spatial distribution of land uses and activities over time; *multilayer comparison utilities*, to compare changes in spatial patterns and intensity levels between different types of data (e.g., urban extent versus household income); and *international and intermetropolitan data retrieval utilities* so that changes and developments can quickly be compared across different spatial data frames and even countries. The development of these types of utilities would best be undertaken under the auspices of an international network of university, policy, and urban management researchers.

Chapter 9

Monitoring Urban Growth and Its Environmental Impacts Using Remote Sensing: Examples from China and India

Karen C. Seto

The size of the world's growing urban population gives urgency to the need for accurate estimates of the location, size, and growth of existing urban areas as well as forecasts of likely regions, magnitudes, and configurations of future urban growth. However, to date, there exists no global database that accurately describes and maps which portions of Earth's habitable land are urbanized, or how those portions have changed over the recent decades. Satellite remote sensing and spatial modeling offer tremendous opportunities to map historical patterns of urban growth, monitor urban areas, and forecast urban expansion. Satellite-based efforts at mapping global urban extents fail to agree on the size and pattern of urban land use, with estimates ranging from 0.2 percent to 2.4 percent of terrestrial land surface circa 2000 (Potere and Schneider 2007).

Recent advances in remote sensing—both in satellite hardware technology and image processing algorithm development—provide opportunities for collection and dissemination of timely information on urban form and size that can be useful for policy and planning. In spite of these developments, there are also limitations to remote sensing and its application in practice. In this chapter, I will describe some of the opportunities for, and limitations on, monitoring urban growth using remote sensing data, and I will provide examples of the environmental impacts of urban growth, as monitored with remote sensing.

Satellite Remote Sensing: Opportunities and Limitations for Urban Mapping

Satellite remote sensing affords a number of unique opportunities for monitoring urban growth. The internally consistent measurements and long observational record of satellite sensor data make it an attractive source of reliable information on urban extent and form. Beginning with the launch of the first Landsat satellite in 1972 and continuing through Landsat 7, satellites have provided more than thirty years of 30–80 m multispectral imagery for much of Earth's surface. Each Landsat scene covers approximately 170 km north-south and 185 km east-west, an area that easily encompasses a metropolitan area if the city is imaged near the center of the scene.

Satellite images are digital data of reflected energy collected across portions of the electromagnetic spectrum. Because most satellite data are multispectral, they contain information from the nonvisible portions of the electromagnetic spectrum (vegetation and soils are most reflective in the nonvisible range). Among the many types of information that can be derived from remote sensing, those relevant to the discussion of urbanization include local surface temperature, wildlife habitats and biodiversity corridors, and extent of impervious surfaces. Moreover, because satellite images are simply digital arrays of information, they can be reprocessed in the future as new digital image processing methods become available.

The ability of satellite data to identify urban areas rests on the unique spectral characteristics of urban areas relative to other land covers such as vegetation, water, or soil. Because urban areas are composites of other land covers (e.g., lawns, swimming pools, rooftops, concrete sidewalks, buildings, etc.), a single "urban pixel" in an image is likely to be a mix of composite land covers. Very few urban pixels will be "pure" (i.e., entirely pavement, entirely building, entirely roads). The purity of any given pixel will be determined by the scale of the urban elements (e.g., building, road) relative to the spatial resolution in the image (Woodcock and Strahler 1987). For example, the spatial resolution of Landsat makes it useful for mapping large urban areas and indicators of urban form and land use, but it does not lend itself to street-level urban mapping or differentiating between residential and commercial urban development, or between high-density and low-density urban development, unless additional ancillary data are available. Data from the first Landsat period, from 1972 to 1983, were imaged at 68 by 83 meters and commonly resampled to 57-meter spatial resolution. Since 1984 and Landsat 5, multispectral data have been collected at 30-meter resolution. For the purposes of urban mapping, these data are relatively coarse and cannot detect small-scale urban change. For example, intercity highways, isolated patches of small urban development, or urban infilling may not be distinguishable in a Landsat image. Where urban growth is occurring in agricultural regions, Landsat data may be too coarse to differentiate among irrigation ditches, dirt paths, and other types of land use that coexist in urban agricultural areas.

High-resolution urban mapping is best achieved with aerial photographs or commercial-grade satellite data such as IKONOS or Quickbird, but these data are significantly more expensive than Landsat data and have small area coverage: a single IKONOS image covers an area of 16.5 km by 16.5 km. With 4-meter multispectral and 1-meter panchromatic spatial resolution, these data can be used for city-level urban mapping. However, IKONOS was launched only in 1999 and has an anticipated lifespan of nine years, thereby limiting its utility for historical mapping. Moreover, IKONOS images are priced between $350 and $1,800 per scene, compared to Landsat data, which are now available at no cost; this difference suggests another limit on use of IKONOS data. DigitalGlobe's Quickbird also has high resolution data (at 2.4 meters in the multispectral mode and 60 centimeters in the panchromatic mode) and is priced similarly to IKONOS. The satellite has been operational since 2001 and is fueled for seven years.

Despite their low spatial resolution, Landsat data can provide useful information for a wide range of urban applications, including analysis of historical urban growth; modeling and forecasting future urban growth; predicting and planning for infrastructure needs; assessments of impervious surfaces and runoff in watersheds; identification of agricultural land, forests, and other places vulnerable to urban envelopment; conservation planning; and land management. Some of the most valuable information that can be extracted from remote sensing includes the size and spatial configuration of urban areas. No other information source can provide a similarly consistent dataset that can be used for inter- and intraregional comparative studies. Data on urban extent, or "built-up area," provided by national statistics often suffer from being aspatial; information is provided in terms of total area without any reference to location, making it harder to measure urban growth patterns over time or space.

One of the biggest challenges in urban remote-sensing research is how to map urban growth dynamics. Some cities are growing rapidly and require frequent acquisition of satellite data over short time intervals. For example, mapping the growth dynamics of one of the fastest growing cities in the United States, Las Vegas, Nevada, would require the use of interannual images. Using only a few images to describe the city's growth patterns may not adequately reflect the temporal and spatial patterns of change. Yet, most remote-sensing urban change studies utilize only two or three satellite images because a majority of image-processing algorithms are designed to analyze landscape change between two periods. Computationally, the same image-processing algorithm can be applied to more than three images, but the repeated application can introduce errors. It is widely recognized that the accuracy of a change analysis made from two separate classifications will be at best the product of the two individual classifications (Singh 1989). For example, if each individually classified map has an accuracy of 90 percent, a change map made with these two maps will have at best 81 percent accuracy if the errors are spatially correlated. Therefore, it is important to use algorithms that process all the images simultaneously rather than sequentially or in a pair-wise fashion (Kaufmann and Seto 2001; Seto and Kaufmann 2003; Boucher et al. 2006). Such algorithms do exist and more are currently being developed, but their use is limited to a small community of specialized researchers, and their widespread adoption by the larger remote-sensing community is unlikely to occur soon due to technical and human resource constraints.

With increasingly long time series images, change-detection accuracy may not just be evaluated for two time periods, but may include multiple time points. That is, one must ensure accuracy through time. Temporal accuracy becomes as important as spatial accuracy, especially when linking landscape changes with policy or socioeconomic data.

In terms of mapping and monitoring of "urban hot spots"—areas of rapid urban change—perhaps the most significant limiting factor is the need to do a geographic sampling of existing urban areas. It is estimated that the fastest-growing urban areas are medium-sized cities. Global-scale monitoring efforts with coarse-resolution imagery may not detect small-scale changes that occur in these cities. However, due to technical and fiscal constraints, it is impossible to do a comprehensive study using moderate- or high-resolution images. Therefore a sampling scheme is required. How should this sampling be achieved, by population size or area? Areas with large urban populations are not necessarily areas that are large in urban extent. Similarly, large urban areas do not indicate large urban populations. Currently, global estimates of urbanization are based on population size, and there are no reliable or consistent global—or even regional—estimates of urban extents.

Finally, other obstacles to the use of satellite imagery to map urban growth include the limited availability of this imagery, especially for tropical regions where presence of cloud cover in the images is prevalent; the level of technical expertise required to utilize the data beyond visual interpretation; and the costs associated with developing and maintaining extensive geospatial databases. Although the Landsat record extends back to 1972 with a repeat cycle of sixteen days, in reality, for most locations outside the United States, there exist only a handful of images for the Landsat 1 through 3 missions. The dearth of data during this period is due to a combination of poor and inconsistent archiving methods and the lack of cloud-free data for many regions of the world. In terms of technical expertise, there is a growing community of remote-sensing users, but algorithm developers and remote-sensing specialists remain in limited supply, especially outside of the industrialized countries. While remote-sensing researchers develop increasingly more specialized and technical methods, the vast majority of the remote-sensing community continues to use time-tested algorithms that are easy to implement but may not be the most advanced. Lastly, the development of geospatial databases is a costly effort, in terms of both human and financial resources. Maintaining and archiving these databases is often comparable to, if not more expensive than, their development.

Urban Growth and Environmental Impacts in the Pearl River Delta, China

The Pearl River Delta in South China is one of the most economically vibrant regions in China (figure 9.1). For over a decade, my research group has used remote sensing to monitor urban growth in the region and assess associated environmental impacts. In a country where an average of twenty new cities are being built each year (*People's Daily* 2000), timely monitoring of urban growth is critical for sustainable urban development. In this chapter, I describe work in the Pearl River Delta that focuses on four of the fastest growing cities in the region: Guangzhou, Shenzhen, Dongguan, and Zhongshan.

Guangzhou (Canton), capital of Guangdong Province, is the oldest among the four cities in the study. Located at the mouth of the Pearl River, it has a long-established park system and a rich assemblage of vegetation, especially in the older districts where dense tree cover is common. Traditionally, Guangzhou has been considered the cultural, economic, and industrial focal point of southern China. It is also a transportation hub; it has an international airport, one of the most active regional seaports, and railroad connections to all regions of the country. Just a small fishing village until it was declared a Special Economic Zone in 1979, Shenzhen is located on the Hong Kong–China border and has experienced the most dramatic economic growth and landscape changes of the cities in the study. Regionally, it receives the bulk of foreign direct investment (FDI) and has a large population (estimated to be between 5 and 10 million) of temporary workers.

Located between Guangzhou and Shenzhen in the northeastern part of the Delta, Dongguan is a leader in export-oriented industries such as textiles, toys, and food processing. It has developed rapidly in part because of its proximity to Hong Kong. The soils in Dongguan are well suited for agriculture, and lychees from the region are famous through-

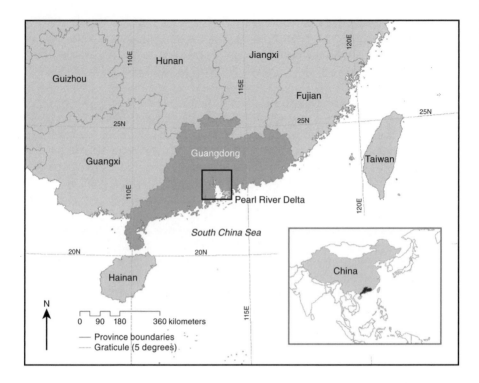

Figure 9.1. Pearl River Delta Study Area

Source: Seto and Fragkias 2005.

out the country. Zhongshan is located in the low-lying western mouth of the Pearl River Delta, approximately 80 kilometers south of Guangzhou. It differs from the other three cities in that it has received relatively little foreign direct investment, and a shift from the primary to the secondary and tertiary sectors of the economy has been led by a mix of both domestic and foreign enterprises. These differences have resulted in a city that has developed more slowly and with a more domestic Chinese character than the other three cities.

We used ten Landsat Thematic Mapper (TM) images, covering the period from 1988 to 1999, to develop maps of urban extent (Seto et al. 2002). Following the remote-sensing analysis, we calculated landscape metrics for each of the maps. The characterization of landscape mosaics and patterns has a long tradition in ecological studies, where understanding habitat fragmentation, landscape heterogeneity, and the distribution of landscape disturbance is important for understanding ecological processes (Ives et al. 1998). Landscape metrics can be used to characterize how the landscape has developed. For example, they can empirically describe the shape, complexity, compactness, patchiness, linearity and squareness, and size of urban areas (Riitters et al. 1995; Schneider et al. 2005). We calculated six landscape metrics to describe the spatial and temporal patterns of urban land development and to identify common patterns in the shape, size, and growth patterns across cities at different stages of economic development. We chose metrics that describe three aspects of the urban landscape: absolute size, relative size, and complexity of urban form. Absolute size is described by two metrics: total urban area and number of urban patches. As urban growth occurs, total urban area continually increases due to the highly nonreversible nature of urbanization. The number of urban patches is a measure of discrete urban areas in the landscape and is expected to increase during periods of rapid urban nuclei development, but may decrease if urban areas expand and merge into continuous urban fabric.

Relative size is described by the mean urban patch size and urban patch size coefficient of variation. The mean urban patch size is a function of the number of urban patches and the size of each urban area and can either increase or decrease through time. Decreasing values of mean urban patch size imply that new urban centers are growing faster than existing urban areas. That is, urban growth occurs more as a process of new and multiple urban nuclei formation than of envelopment or annexation. The urban patch size coefficient of variation is a normalized metric of the urban area and can either decrease or increase through time.

Urban edge density measures the total edge of urban areas relative to the total landscape and should increase with new urban nuclei, but may decline as urban areas fuse together and boundaries dissolve. The metric for the area-weighted mean patch fractal dimension describes the degree to which the shape of an urban area is simple versus irregular or complex. The more irregular the shape of the urban area, the higher the value of the fractal dimension. Of the many shape and complexity measures available, we used the area-weighted mean patch fractal dimension because it is normalized. Values range between 1 and 2, with values closer to 1 indicating areas with relatively simple shapes such as squares or circles. Values that approach 2 represent complex and irregular shapes. The area-weighted mean patch fractal dimension is hypothesized to increase during the early periods of urban land-use change when new urban nuclei and expansion of existing urban space create irregularly shaped landscape patterns. This metric is expected to decline as urban form becomes more regular.

We calculate the six landscape metrics for each of the ten years of satellite data for three buffer zones drawn at 0–3 km, 3–10 km, and 10–20 km from the city centers. Our rationale for a concentric ring partitioning of urban space and the selection of buffer size was based on three criteria: (1) the need for a standard buffer size to which the cities in the study could be compared through time; (2) the need for each buffer to capture variation within and among cities (drawn too close to the city center, the buffers would capture variations only within the central business district; drawn too distant from city centers, the buffers would capture variation over too large of an area); and (3) our interest in the boundaries of the urban-rural fringe and the forces that drive landscape changes at the edges of cities.

Urbanization Impacts on Agricultural Land and Local Precipitation

Results from the analysis indicate that the average annual rate of urban growth for the four cities between 1988 and 1999 was 17 percent, with the largest growth of 32 percent between 1992 and 1993 (figure 9.2). Total urban land for the four cities nearly quadrupled during the study period, from 290 km^2 in 1988 to 1,122 km^2 in 1999 (figure 9.3). Most of the new urban development has been at the expense of agricultural land. Four major types of agricultural land loss have occurred. First, the construction of industrial centers, residential complexes, and factories has led to the conversion of large tracts of agricultural land. Second, on a smaller scale, improvement of houses owned by farmers and agricultural workers has also reduced the amount of land available for agriculture. Third, highway development has divided agricultural plots and removed them from cultivation. Fourth, the flooding of fields for water reservoirs and dams has also taken farmland out of production. Reservoirs and dikes have been constructed to support the booming residential and industrial sectors. Despite a 1985 moratorium in the region that limited the amount of agricultural land that could be converted for nonagricultural purposes, remote-sensing analysis reveals that the loss of agricultural land is more than 11 percent greater than the amount reported in statistical yearbooks (Seto et al. 2000).

The higher estimates of loss of farmland may be due to the coarse resolution of the Landsat data, which cannot differentiate among irrigation ditches, dirt paths, small houses, and other land uses that coexist with agriculture. Yet even with this potential bias, there are reasons to believe that the total amount of agricultural land was systematically underreported by farmers due to institutional factors such as the tax system and historical grain quotas. Since 1958 with the Great Leap Forward, farmers have had strong incentives to underestimate their agricul-

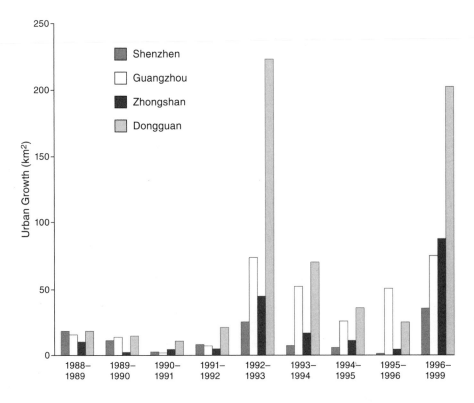

Figure 9.2. Annual Urban Growth (km²)

Source: Author's calculations based on Seto and Fragkias 2005 and Seto et al. 2002.

tural land. During this period, grain quotas were based on total farmland acreage. Therefore, underestimates of agricultural area reduced a farmer's grain quota. Although this production quota has been eliminated, the regional moratorium has also had the effect of causing farmers to underestimate the loss of farmland.

Urban growth rates are strongly related to foreign investments, politics, and policies (Seto and Kaufmann 2003). Immediately following the Tiananmen Square incident in 1989, foreign investments dropped significantly and some large-scale development projects were suspended in the delta. In January 1992, Premier Deng Xiao Peng visited the delta to reassure investors that China would continue to pursue reform. This led to the resumption of foreign investments and development projects.

The region's long history of agriculture and human settlement resulted in extensive deforestation that occurred well before the current

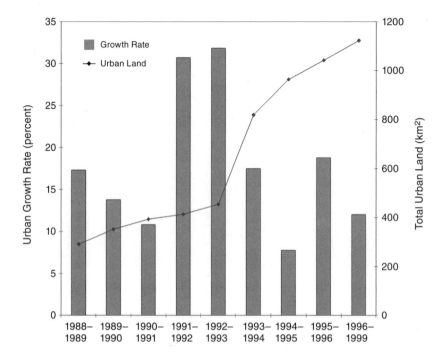

Figure 9.3. Total Urban Land and Urban Growth Rate for Four Case-Study Cities

Source: Author's calculations based on Seto and Fragkias 2005 and Seto et al. 2002.

period of economic development. Little urban growth has recently occurred in forested areas. Most of the large intact tracts of forests are located in the mountainous regions north of the delta's basin, away from the major cities and industrial zones. The conversion of natural vegetation to urban areas that occurred in the delta consisted mainly in small patches of forests and hills. Urban development has led to the quarrying of hills and has caused widespread soil erosion. A preliminary analysis of the topography in the region shows that the region has become more leveled over the last two decades as a result of quarrying and new construction. Soil erosion has become prevalent, and the Chinese Academy of Forestry has engaged in collaborative reforestation projects with international organizations. The Chinese government's Ninth Five-Year Plan increased forest coverage by planting 1.2 million hectares of forest in the delta. Plantation efforts have focused on fast-growing species of *Eucalyptus, Acacia,* and native Chinese pine. Especially prevalent is *Acacia mangium,* which is tolerant of poor soils and has grown successfully under similar conditions in other tropical environments. The introduction of nonnative tree species and reforestation efforts are two unintended effects of urbanization in this region. Whether these efforts will abate soil erosion is unclear, especially given that large-scale land-use change and urban development continue in the region.

The results of the study on the spatial and temporal patterns of urbanization highlight a few points about the patterns of urban development in the region (Seto and Fragkias 2005). First, urban growth in the four cities occurred through two primary processes: envelopment—the annexation of the surrounding landscape through the growth of extant urban areas—and multiple nuclei development. In South China, most of the area surrounding urban centers is used for agriculture. Therefore, urban growth through envelopment occurs mostly at the expense of cultivated land. Multiple-nuclei urban growth occurs when new urban centers are developed in areas disconnected from existing urban areas. This development occurs mainly as result of high-tech zones that are financed primarily by foreign direct investment. These clusters of industrial zones were initially constructed in rural communities distant from the urban core, usually on agricultural or unproductive land. The trend of multiple-nuclei urban development has been documented in a number of other cities throughout China (Schneider et al. 2005).

The spatial pattern of development reflects land-use decision-making that occurred at all levels of the Chinese administration and at different stages in the evolution of development policies. The original 1987 land administration law allowed development zones to be sanctioned by the central government's State Council. The land law also allowed various lower-level administrative units, such as municipal and local governments, to develop industrial zones. This gave rise to internal competition across multiple administrative levels to develop specialty zones, which led to a polynucleated urban space. Town and municipal governments competed directly against each other in their attempts to establish high-tech and industrial zones to attract foreign investments.

Incorporating a temporal component to landscape metrics reveals that the urban form of cities can change relatively quickly over short time periods. It is widely noted that the patterns of cities change slowly, primarily because the establishment of infrastructure such as roads limits the direction in which urban growth can occur (Henderson 1988). Once the basic form of a city is in place, it is difficult to alter the trajectory of city structure. Although there is a certain level of urban growth path dependency, however, the results from Seto and Fragkias (2005) show that urban form can vary greatly during the early stages of economic development.

The expansion of these cities follows a particular spatial and temporal form. Despite differences in levels of economic development and local policies, there are common patterns in shape, size, and growth of urban land across the four cities. There is also evidence that disconnected urban areas converge toward a pattern of contiguous urban fabric.

Modification of land cover through urban growth changes the biophysical attributes of the land surface and ecosystem functions. These changes then contribute to regional and global climate change by modifying surface energy and water budgets and biogeochemical cycles. Building cities on land that was previously vegetated modifies the exchange of heat, water, trace gases, aerosols, and momentum between the land surface and overlying atmosphere (Crutzen 2004). In addition, the composition of the atmosphere over urban areas differs from vegetated and nonurban areas (Pataki et al. 2003). These changes imply that converting vegetated land to urban areas can affect local, regional, and possibly global climate at diurnal, seasonal, and long-term scales (Zhou et al. 2004; Zhang et al. 2005).

Research over the last two decades has generated significant understanding of the relationship between urban areas and climate. There is now a well-established urban heat island (UHI) effect that appears stronger during the night than the day (Lo et al. 1997). The urban heat island effect is thought to be created by the interaction of many factors, including building geometry, land cover, and urban materials (Oke 1976). In terms of the relationship between urban areas and precipitation, there is general consensus that urbanization affects precipitation, but the mechanisms by which urbanization affects precipitation are not well understood (Lowry 1998). Possible mechanisms include (1) enhanced convergence due to increased surface roughness in the urban environment (Thielen et al. 2000); (2) destabilization due to UHI-thermal perturbation of the boundary layer and the resulting downstream translation of the UHI circulation or UHI-generated convective clouds (Sheppard et al. 2002); (3) enhanced aerosols in the urban environment for cloud condensation nuclei sources (Molders and Olson 2004); and (4) bifurcating or diverting precipitating systems by the urban canopy or related processes (Bornstein and Lin 2000). It is also hypothesized that urban areas serve as moisture sources needed for convective development (Dixon and Mote 2003). Even less is understood about the relationship between urban growth—or urban land conversion—and local climate. While numerous studies focus on urban climate, few examine urban growth explicitly (Tereshchenko and Filonov 2001).

Given the rate and magnitude of urban growth in the Pearl River Delta and its likely impact on local climate, we evaluated the relationship between urban growth patterns and precipitation and temperature. We coupled the satellite-generated urban growth analysis from 1988 to 1996 with monthly climate data from sixteen local meteorological stations. A statistical analysis of the relationship between climate and urban growth in concentric buffers around the meteorological stations indicates that there is a causal relationship from temporal and spatial patterns of urbanization to temporal and spatial patterns of precipitation during the dry season (Kaufmann et al. 2007). The results suggest an "urban precipitation deficit" in which urbanization reduces local precipitation during the dry months of October through April. This reduction may be caused by changes in surface hydrology that extend beyond the urban heat island effect and energy-related aerosol emissions. No causal relationship is found between urbanization and precipitation during the rainy season. The rainy season occurs from May through September, when the effects of the Asian monsoon dominate and may overwhelm local urban impacts. During the dry season, cold fronts from northern China bring rainfall to the region, but with a much smaller magnitude than during the summer months. Therefore, local urban effects may be more pronounced during the dry season. This may explain why the urban heat island is most visible in winter (Zhou et al. 2004).

Urban Growth and Environmental Impacts in Bengaluru, India

The urban landscape of Bengaluru (formerly Bangalore), India, has been transformed since the central government initiated policy reforms in 1991. Reforms of industrial, trade, and agricultural policies at both the central and state levels have created an investor-friendly environment that has encouraged foreign direct investment and fostered economic and urban growth. Located in the South India state of Karnataka, Bengaluru had an estimated population of 6.5 million in 2006, making it the fourth-largest city in India (Mumbai, New Delhi, and Kolkata are larger). After liberalization of the Indian economy, foreign direct investment has increased significantly, from $200 million U.S. in 1987–1990 to $4.1 billion U.S. in 2001–2004 (UNCTAD online database). Since the mid-1990s, FDI has shifted from the agriculture and manufacturing sectors to services. Citing Bengaluru's numerous technology institutes, learning centers, and large skilled labor pool as comparative advantages, multinational information technology (IT) and high-tech corporations such as IBM, Microsoft, and Motorola now have major operations in the city.

The development of Bengaluru's IT and associated industries has reshaped the urban environment. Industrial parks that house multiple high-tech companies to create a research campus environment are akin to those found in Silicon Valley (O'Mara 2004). These research parks represent only one dimension of the new urban fabric. Other pieces of the urban mosaic include new residential communities that house high-tech workers and upper and middle management, along with premium transportation corridors that connect different districts of the metropolitan area. The new residential communities range in style and size, with the most opulent targeting senior management nonresident Indians and expatriates. These "master-planned" developments are similar in style to those in the United States, complete with exclusive, limited-access facilities such as tennis courts, golf courses, swimming pools, and even schools. They do differ from American-style suburban developments in that their scale is vastly smaller, with pedestrian-friendly streets and homes that are designed to house multigenerational families.

Our analysis of urban growth in Greater Bengaluru uses Landsat TM imagery from 1973, 1992, 2000, 2005, and 2006. Preliminary results indicate that the period 1992 to 2000 was the most significant in terms of urban expansion, with most change occurring on the edges—most notably on the southern edges—of the city rather than through infilling in the city core. Urban growth during this period is characterized by intensive road building, especially around the city in an effort to connect Bengaluru to other major cities around the country. For the period 2000 to 2006, growth is evident in the east and south, following the development of industrial parks and residential communities (figure 9.4). New growth is also evident in the northeast near the proposed new international airport. Like that in the Pearl River Delta, most of the urban expansion in Bengaluru has been at the expense of agricultural land.

Challenges to Mapping and Monitoring Urban Growth

Urban areas in China and India pose mapping challenges unique to their environments. In both case studies, the biggest challenge lies in identifying urban growth at small scales. Peri-urban growth takes place contiguous to as well as in agricultural areas. Agriculture occurs at small scales, which can be likened to household gardening with respect to the size of plots and the variety of crops produced. Multicrop fields, terracing, and small field sizes produce texture and tones that can be difficult to differentiate. Agricultural plots are generally small, less than an acre, but the plots of a village are usually adjacent to each other. The smaller plots, and the variety of crop types (vegetable fields, fish ponds, and fruit orchards often abut each other) within the plots, create heterogeneous surfaces which are more difficult to characterize than large-area plots of a single crop.

Detection of urban growth in agricultural regions in China and India

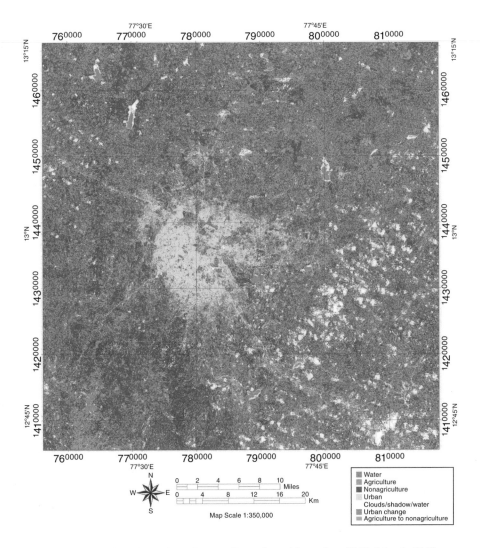

Figure 9.4. Urban Growth in Greater Bangalore, November 2000–March 2006

Source: Author's calculations, unpublished.

is inherently difficult because significant landscape changes result from both traditional and novel practices. In both case studies, an increase in farmers' disposable incomes has permitted the refurbishing of old homes and the construction of new homes. The use of new materials often creates a change in spectral signal distinct from the surrounding agriculture. On the other hand, the cycle of planting, growth, plowing, and harvesting introduces an element of change to multidate images independent of urban growth dynamics. For instance, after rice has been harvested, rice fields are essentially bare plots of soil, which spectrally look similar to land which has been cleared for construction of new buildings. Only when rice fields maintain a high level of moisture are they spectrally distinct from bright, dry soils. Therefore, the phenological and planting cycles of rice can be confused with new urban development. Located in tropical and semitropical regions, South China's and South India's agricultural fields often support multiple crops per year, and the timing of crops varies among individual fields. Under these conditions, individual satellite images will include fields at all stages of the agricultural cycle, and it is easy to confuse recently plowed, planted, or fallow agricultural fields with new urban land.

Although the spatial resolution of Landsat data allows for discrimination of urban features, such as large road networks, the spatial variance of urban environments in China and India is also high. The heterogeneous nature of urban areas in these countries makes it particularly difficult to generate accurate urban maps. Moreover, magnitudinal changes, such as increases in urban density, are much more difficult to identify with remote sensing than wholesale changes.

In terms of integrating remote sensing and socioeconomic data to understand the drivers of urban growth, work in both countries has been limited by a lack of spatially explicit socioeconomic data and reliable administrative boundaries. In China and India, new cities emerge from existing villages and towns, and city growth often occurs as small towns are enveloped by larger municipal units. As a result, administrative boundaries are frequently adjusted and redrawn. Accurate administrative boundaries are critical to urban growth forecasting because urban land-use data derived from remote sensing are linked to socioeconomic data through governmental units. Without digital representations of administrative boundaries, it is difficult to integrate satellite data with socioeconomic data. The challenge ahead is to develop analytical tools and approaches that can be applied across regions.

Our experience in China and India shows that remote sensing can contribute significantly to the understanding of the patterns of urban development and their environmental impacts. The effects of urbanization on precipitation in South China suggest that urban growth in semitropical areas could have major effects on local precipitation worldwide. Given that urban growth is rapid in many developing countries, it is critical to develop a global database of urban growth patterns. Only when we monitor the scale, pattern, and rate of urban change can we begin to understand their potential impacts on the earth's functioning as a system.

Chapter 10

Tracking Regional Growth and Development: The Nairobi Case

Wilber K. Ottichilo

Fast-growing Nairobi, Kenya, the most populous city in East Africa, offers an important example of how a municipality that lacks modern maps and databases turns to spatial technologies, especially remote-sensing and geographic information system (GIS) technologies, to track urban growth and development and inform public and private infrastructure investments and other decision-making. The recent adoption of these tools has assisted in the management of a city that in less than one hundred years has burgeoned from a British colonial capital of 10,500 population to a modernizing metropolis with over 3 million inhabitants. This case can serve as a guide to other cities, especially in Africa, with rapid but inadequately documented growth.

Background on Nairobi

Founded in 1899, Nairobi has experienced a population trajectory through the twentieth century that has accelerated in the past four decades. Between 1906 and 1936 the number of its inhabitants grew threefold; between 1936 and 1962, fourfold. But after independence in 1963, the increase was tenfold as the city moved from a quarter of a million to its current 3.1 million people (Molumbe 2000). Land consumption accompanied the population growth. In 1906, Nairobi covered an area of 18 square kilometers. However, there have been several boundary expansions since then. In 1927, the town area was extended to 78 square kilometers. In 1963, it grew to approximately 690 square kilometers (UNDP 1997).

In addition to population and geographic changes, other unrecorded

Table 10.1 Population Growth in Nairobi, 1948–2010

Year	Population	Change per period (percent)	Change since independence (percent using 1965 base)
1948	119,000		
1955	186,000	56%	
1957	221,700	19%	
1960	251,000	13%	
1962	266,800	7%	
1965	380,000	42%	
1969	509,300	34%	34%
1979	827,775	63%	118%
1989	1,324,570	60%	249%
1995	1,810,000	37%	376%
1999	2,143,254	18%	464%
2005	2,750,561	28%	624%
2010	3,240,155	18%	753%

Source: Kenya National Bureau of Statistics 2010.

demographic conditions complicate management of this city and occasion administrative difficulties in planning and implementing local public services. For example, the daytime population or transients commuting from the surrounding regions is higher than the resident population. In another example, rural-urban migration continues alongside natural increase to contribute to population growth, but neither the number of newcomers who settle in new or existing squatter settlements nor the newborns are recorded very frequently (Obudho 1999).

Nairobi is divided into several districts: residential, the CBD, and industrial areas. The residential areas hold low-, middle-, and high-income households. It is estimated that 80 percent of the population living in high-density settlements occupies less than 20 percent of the residential land area; but about 55 percent of the urban population is housed in unplanned, informal settlements/slums (Badiane 2008, 7). The main feature of these informal settlements is the lack of such infrastructure and services as water, sewage, and solid waste disposal.

The original frame of the city was determined by the dictates colonial practice. Racial segregation was paramount and lasted to the early 1960s. Enforced by zoning and property laws, these policies created land-use patterns that prevail to the present (Emig and Ismail 1980). Nairobi was systematically racially zoned in the major plans of 1905, 1927, and 1948. In 1902, as the colonial government claimed ownership of all land under its jurisdiction, it enacted the Crown Lands Ordinance that granted long-term leases to Europeans and short-term "licenses" to natives. Further, this law stated that each "native license," or permit to use the land, allowed only a five-acre plot maximum. It was not until 1954 that Africans were allowed to own leasehold property in Nairobi (Amis 1990). The predictable result of these residential planning processes is an extremely unequal land distribution. Evidence of this inequality is evident in Nairobi today, where, even after independence, the availability of land remains severely restricted by previous contractual agreements and high prices.

As for Nairobi's socioeconomic role in Kenya, the city's functions have expanded to such an extent that it has become the country's primate city. It holds 38 percent of Kenya's urban population and is three times more populous than the next largest city, Mombasa (Badiane 2008, 14). It produces 45 percent of the nation's gross domestic product and employs 25 percent of all Kenyan workers (and 43 percent of all urban laborers.) In addition to being the capital city of Kenya, it serves as the regional and international headquarters for several commercial and public institutions, including many multinational companies and United Nations agencies (Badiane 2008, 127).

These growth patterns and the functional evolution of the city have not been accompanied by systematic planning and development of physical infrastructure and social amenities, and inadequate attention has been paid to the conservation of natural resources and the environment. As a consequence, the city is currently faced with numerous problems including poor urban infrastructure (water, sewer, waste disposal, transport); substandard social amenities (schools, health facilities); inadequate and inappropriate housing; especially the mushrooming of slum dwellings or urban sprawl; poor transport system; environmental deterioration; and personal insecurity.

Furthermore, Nairobi suffers, along with most of urban Africa, from a lack of accurate and up-to-date maps and information, a phenomenon that has rendered its planning and management problematic. For most urban areas, it is difficult to find maps that are less than ten years old. In the case of Nairobi City, most of the maps available are outdated (over ten years old), lack detail and accuracy, and are mostly in hard-copy form, rendering them static and cumbersome to interpret and analyze.

Methods Used to Track Urban Growth and Development

With no systematically developed and managed urban database, Nairobi recently turned to three synergistic geographic information technologies—satellite remote sensing, geographic information systems (GIS), and the Global Positioning System (GPS)—to meets its urgent needs to develop cost-effective, rapid-mapping methodologies that yield timely data for planning and decision-making. Satellite remote sensing guarantees timely repetitive data acquisition for continual map updating, while GIS enables spatial database creation and management. GPS facilitates the acquisition of higher geometric accuracy for both satellite imagery and GIS databases. Given that these datasets are in digital format, and that current technological developments ensure data access through the Internet, data sharing among stakeholders, however distant, has become a real possibility. Details of this work follow below.

High-resolution satellite data were used in the development of a multi-user digital spatial database to map land cover, update the city cadastre and develop other applications with information gained with the launch of the QuickBird satellite in October 2001 by DigitalGlobe (DigitalGlobe 2003). This satellite currently has the highest spatial resolution (60 cm) of the commercially available satellites and competes directly with medium-scale aerial photography. The applications of QuickBird imagery are further enhanced by the satellite's five-band multispectral characteristics—one panchromatic and four multispectral (blue, green, red, and infrared). Due to its high resolution and its synoptic view (16.5 km x 16.5 km), the data are particularly useful for basic city-based work described above but can also be used for large-scale natural resources mapping, disaster management, utility mapping, hydrological studies, agriculture, real estate, and insurance.

The land-use/land-cover map of Nairobi was developed by interpreting the QuickBird image digitally. First, road centerlines were digitized from the images and the roads were buffered according to their classes. From these road buffers, general land-use blocks were delineated and consequently interpreted using a predefined land-use classification system. A database of land-use classes and other associated data were finally produced in a GIS environment. Other features mapped in the Quick-Bird image are rivers, railways, schools, hospitals, and police stations. A field exercise was conducted where feature names (roads, rivers, estates) were recorded and positions confirmed using GPS. Stakeholder organizations also participated in the collection of data. For instance, the Kenya Police provided crime data, Ministry of Education staff provided schools data, and Kenya Telkom provided data on telephone infrastructure.

To update the city's old cadastral maps, baseline data were acquired by digitizing existing cadastral maps of scale 1:10,000 acquired from the Survey of Kenya (Kenya 1981). These data were then overlaid on the QuickBird image and the changes mapped. Despite having a substantial nonlinear shift between the two datasets, near-perfect matching was achieved through individual block shifting. Further, the cadastral data contained the following information: plot sizes, plot numbers, plot owners, postal addresses of owners, and plot status. Using this database a simple interface was then developed to enable data access and query to be undertaken by individuals not skilled in using GIS.

Results and Discussion

Over nearly a decade of work, the following digital databases were developed:

1. Digital QuickBird image of Nairobi.
2. Updated digital cadastral maps of Nairobi (digitized from the 1:10,000 scale cadastral maps provided by the Survey of Kenya and updated by QuickBird satellite imagery).
3. Digital thematic maps of Nairobi that were digitized from the QuickBird image. These include roads, railways, rivers, academic institutions, health centers, police stations, buildings, and land use/land cover.
4. A water management database and application for the Nairobi City Council.

In addition, the following were developed:

1. Customized GIS software. Simplified GIS software called Prompt-info has been developed for users among the GIS community who may not necessarily be GIS experts. This software enables them to access and query the data (Maps Geosystems 2004).
2. Land parcel locator to enable quick access and identification of land parcel information (Maps Geosystems 2004).
3. Community GIS toolbox developed by Maps Geosystems (2004) and basically comprises hardware, software, and data that can easily be installed in an organization's local area network. The toolbox can be used by anybody within an organization with the right access authorization and therefore guarantees optimal data use and data security. It can be configured to prevent unauthorized data access.

The toolbox software can be easily customized for a wide range of applications. An essential element of the customization is an investigation into the needs of the end user that is made through consultation by a system engineer. This idea is to customize the software to perform what the user wants, rather than training the user to operate the software.

Conclusion

Remote-sensing and GIS technologies offer the practical possibility of resolving the shortcomings in the efficient, effective, and rapid generation of maps for resource and environmental information in Africa. The past two decades have witnessed dramatic advances in resource data collection by space satellites as a result of major developments in cameras, sensors, and other remote sensing devices. Space platforms provide bird's-eye views of the earth's surface never available before, and the new sensors provide better resolutions and synoptic perspectives covering thousands of kilometers in single views. The satellite data are now readily available and the cost of acquiring data has drastically fallen in the last five years. Therefore satellite data and GIS can efficiently and cost-effectively be used to update the old maps and to generate new resource maps for sustainable development (Alexandrov et al. 2004).

Especially useful is QuickBird satellite data that offers high planimetric detail nearly as good as aerial photographs. However, the QuickBird image cannot be seen as a substitute for aerial photography. Whereas QuickBird imagery is good for thematic mapping, aerial photography is good in both thematic and topographic mapping.

This study has demonstrated that high-resolution satellite data—particularly the QuickBird data—can be rapidly and repeatedly used to generate data and maps essential for urban planning and management. For example, the data and maps generated in this study are being used along with other available information (e.g., on population, crime) by the city authorities to update the cadastre; identify for demolition of illegal structures; plan for provision of more social amenities, including city beautification and environmental conservation; enhance crime prevention; and manage water and sewer—particularly repair and maintenance work (EIS-Africa 2002).

Despite the advantages of using geographic information technologies for sustainable development, a number of factors militate against their broad application, particularly in Africa. First, there is a serious lack of updated large-scale topographic and thematic maps as well as integrated digital geospatial databases suitable for resource planning purposes. Second, there is inadequate awareness among decision-makers about the importance of geo-information technologies in sustainable resource assessment, mapping, and management. Third, there is a lack of national policies on geo-information/spatial data infrastructure and consequently an inadequate level of capacity-building (human resources and infrastructure, including hardware and software) in geo-information technologies at all levels. Fourth, high-resolution satellite data is expensive, and such technical problems as poor coverage and limited Internet connectivity due to bandwidth problems are significant.

Nonetheless, on balance, the use of geographic information technologies in sustainable development is recommended, particularly in urban planning and management. These technologies should be aggressively promoted in developing countries, specifically in African countries where the rate of urbanization is currently very high. These promotional efforts should focus on the importance of geo-information to decision-making and capacity-building.

PART III

Urban Governance and Finance

Chapter 11

Strategic Directions for Local Public Finance in Developing Countries

Paul Smoke

Fiscal decentralization and local government finance in developing countries have received considerable scholarly attention in recent years, particularly with respect to urban areas. A well-developed literature focuses on policy and institutional-design concerns driven by public finance/fiscal federalism and new public management principles (Bahl and Linn 1992; Shah 1994; Ter-Minassian 1997; Bird and Vaillancourt 1998; Litvack, Ahmad, and Bird 1998; Smoke 2001; Ahmad and Tanzi 2002; Ebel and Yilmaz 2002; Ebel and Taliercio 2005; World Bank 2005; Bardhan and Mookherjee 2006). Actual performance, however, has been weak in terms of both policy formulation and outcomes (weak local tax yields, wastage of intergovernmental transfers, and failure to obtain or repay loans). In addition, the dynamics underlying this disappointing performance have been poorly researched. Indeed, the current literature largely explains unsatisfactory outcomes as a result of problematic central design and management of intergovernmental fiscal structures, and the inability or lack of "political will" among local government officials to improve fiscal performance.

This chapter argues that researchers have not sufficiently considered four aspects of fiscal reform: the politics of revenue generation, the use of incentives, capacity-building, and reform implementation. This oversight has constrained efforts to improve performance. This chapter analyzes the importance of these four aspects, provides some limited empirical evidence about them, and suggests a research agenda to advance a deeper understanding of local public finance issues in developing countries.

Mainstream Fiscal Decentralization and Its Challenges

Researchers have commonly identified several elements critical in establishing an enabling environment for local government fiscal performance (Shah 1994; Litvack, Ahmad, and Bird 1998; Ebel 2003; Rodden et al. 2003; Shah 2004; Ebel and Taliercio 2005; Smoke 2006). They have particularly focused on the need for defined constitutional and/or legal provisions for fiscal structures, property rights, freedom of information and association, and electoral structures that support effective local government performance. However, even if legal elements of a fiscal framework are in place, their implementation can be a challenge. Central agencies may resist losing power and resources; local governments may not have capacity or incentive to assume new functions. Service assignment is complex. Indonesia, for example, is engaged in a lengthy, contentious process of defining local functions on a sector-by-sector basis (Smoke 2004); South Africa remains in the process of refining detailed responsibilities for constitutionally assigned municipal functions (Bahl and Smoke 2003).

Basic principles for local revenue assignment are generally followed, with some exceptions, but problems persist (Shah 1994, 2004; Bird 1999, 2001; Lewis 2005, 2006; Ebel and Taliercio 2005). Assigned revenues rarely match budget requirements, creating incentives for unofficial revenues and heavy need for intergovernmental transfers. Finally, implementation takes time—too much rapid reform can overwhelm local taxpayer tolerance and local government capacity.

These challenges have led mainstream thinkers to recommend various revenue reforms for local and central governments (Shah 1994, 2004; Bird 1999, 2001; Bahl 2000). Common recommendations include that local governments should focus on generating revenue and not pursue other objectives through tax policy; concentrate efforts on a few potentially productive sources; improve records and information; and simplify tax structures (bases and rates) and administration. The central government is called on to better harmonize central and local taxes on the same bases; provide more revenue generation autonomy/flexibility to local governments, without forgoing all central regulation; support local governments in their efforts to pursue tax reform; and address weaknesses in intergovernmental transfer and subnational borrowing frameworks and mechanisms.

Gaps in the Mainstream Approach

Although the value of the mainstream approach to fiscal decentralization and local government finance is not in dispute, it ignores four realities that are particularly important for achieving better performance in developing countries.

First, since revenue generation is inherently political, political concerns commonly dominate reform considerations for everyone but the technicians designing reforms. Although this is widely understood in a general sense, the politics of local government revenue generation is poorly researched and even more poorly recognized in formulating fiscal reform efforts.[1]

Second, performance incentives in the fiscal system have often been weak. Despite decades of reform, local governments continue to receive substantial resources through intergovernmental transfers and loans from central lending mechanisms that they know they will not have to repay, thus limiting any incentives to tax constituents for repayment or to meet often onerous fiscal reform mandates. In addition, grants to fund potentially self-financing development projects in creditworthy local governments undermine local incentives to borrow.

Third, weak capacity is an important concern. Many deficiencies in local revenue generation are related to the dearth of relevant skills required to design and manage subnational tax policy. Poor management of transfers and loans may also be at least partially attributable to inadequate skills at the local level. Although such constraints are often recognized, approaches to dealing with capacity-building have been problematic.

Finally, even the best-designed intergovernmental revenue system can rarely be fully implemented quickly. Very rapid implementation of complex reform programs will quickly run into problems in all but the most advanced situations. Thus the strategy, pace, and sequencing of reforms can be critical matters, yet they have received limited research attention.

The Politics of Revenue Generation

Higher-level governments may limit local government revenue autonomy for political reasons, and transfers and loans to local governments can easily become politicized.[2] Recommended adherence to more rule-based and transparent systems can help, but there is often political resistance. Typically such resistance can be overcome only through a realignment of political dynamics and governance reforms, which requires both time and strategic attention to fostering change.[3]

The most important political obstacles to local revenue generation and use are rooted in local conditions: the visible nature of property tax and the concentration of base ownership among powerful elites; political resistance to charges for services that people have received free of charge; the politically motivated substitution of transfers for local tax revenues; etc. Although fiscal federalism implicitly assumes some means for local governments to discern and respond to citizen preferences in how revenues are raised and used, political issues receive limited explicit attention. Indeed, the mainstream approach to local revenue analysis barely addresses governance and accountability beyond promoting elections and recognizing the need for transparent, rule-based procedures.

Some emerging research provides useful insights into the political nature of local revenue generation in a number of countries and raises a key question about why residents either pay or try to evade local taxes. In Tanzania, for example, local tax compliance is positively related to factors such as ability to pay and the (perceived) probability of prosecution, and negatively related to oppressive tax enforcement, taxpayer harassment, and weak satisfaction with public services (Fjeldstad and Semboja 2001). In Uganda, where tax compliance is poor, only 11 percent of respondents felt that local tax payments were substantially dedicated to service improvement, and 75 percent of respondents said that they would pay more if local governments did more for the community (Kjær 2004, 2005). Compliance in South Africa depends on the degree to which citizens perceive local governments to be acting in their interest—in terms of providing services, equitably collecting revenues and providing services, and convincing them that other citizens pay a fair share (Fjeldstad 2004, 2005).

Some evidence shows that when increasing the revenue role of local governments the details of local tax collection are important. In Tanzania, for example, enforcement works best where revenue collection is insulated from influence by elected councilors, who presumably shield constituents from compliance (Fjeldstad 2001). In Senegal, tax compliance decreased substantially after collection was devolved to local councilors (Juul 2006). Further, respondents to a survey indicated broad dissatisfaction with service delivery and a weak confidence in the new local governments. In contrast, the city of Porto Alegre (Brazil), well-known for pioneering participatory budgeting, used local participation to mobilize tax compliance substantially (Schneider and Baquero 2006).

Recent work documents that the structure of local government revenues influences how local politicians spend them. Local governments in Tanzania and Zambia, for example, devote a larger budget share to public service delivery as local taxes increase. As the share of resources from transfers and foreign assistance rises, so does the share of the budget devoted to employee compensation and administration (Hoffman and Gibson 2006). This suggests that local governments that raise more resources from constituents may feel obligated to provide visible public services.

A small body of empirical work considers how donor-driven revenue reforms affect performance, and suggests that there are significant consequences if state-of-the-art approaches to reform do not include political and institutional considerations. Privatization of local tax collection in Uganda, for example, modestly enhances revenue growth and stability (Iversen et al. 2006). Revenue leakage, however, remains significant although altered—instead of occurring in the revenue collector–taxpayer transaction, it is shifted to the point at which the contracted private collector turns over revenue to the local government. Recent research on the Uganda Revenue Authority (URA), which was established to reduce corruption and improve yields, finds that social relations are more important than loyalty to URA in determining staff behavior (Fjeldstad 2006). Initially, improved working conditions and incentives adopted under the URA model increased revenue generation, but eventually staff learned how to work within the system to favor certain taxpayers over others.[4]

Although this empirical literature is limited in volume and scope, it suggests a number of lessons relevant for local government revenue improvement. First, citizens seem to avoid paying local tax if they do not feel they are being well-served or fairly treated, and there is some evidence that they would pay more for higher benefits. For this reason, it is imperative to think beyond standard prescriptions for credible elections, which are a blunt accountability instrument. Other mechanisms—such as town meetings, oversight boards with private-sector and NGO representatives, participatory planning/budgeting, and social auditing of local resource use—can be useful in promoting public understanding of how revenue sources are defined and levied and how proceeds are being used for local expenditures.[5]

Second, the existence of local accountability mechanisms does not guarantee their beneficial use. Rules and processes for citizen engagement in budgeting or planning can be token, noninclusive, and/or captured by local elites. Such factors limit or alter the intended role and impact of participatory mechanisms.

Third, the use of accountability mechanisms requires a minimum of citizen awareness, capacity, and interest. People may not know what citizen engagement mechanisms exist or how to get involved, or they may face intimidation or other barriers to using them.

Finally, high-profile technocratic reforms pushed by international donors and only halfheartedly or opportunistically supported by local bureaucrats do not adequately recognize that progress in revenue-generation depends on stimulating changes in the behavioral culture of the public service. This does not happen easily or quickly even with major changes in formal structures and procedures.

Performance Incentives

The pursuit of better local revenue performance has recently begun to include more vigorous use of explicit incentives, such as political competition, rule enforcement, better pay, rewards for local government staff, and intergovernmental transfers. Although each of these can be important, the focus here is on the last approach.

Concern with how intergovernmental transfers affect local government incentives for revenue-generation is a long-standing issue. Many transfer formulae do not include a revenue-performance variable, and little evidence exists about the impact of transfers on local revenue yields. Without such evidence, it is difficult to make recommendations about how to better structure transfers.

Among the latest innovations in intergovernmental transfers are performance-based grants (PBGs) (Steffensen and Larsen 2005). PBGs aim to promote a positive change in some aspect of local government performance by making access to at least a portion of grant resources conditional on achieving certain goals defined by a central government authority. In short, PBGs penalize undesirable behavior (as defined by the center), and reward desirable behavior.

It is important to emphasize that such grants are generally not intended to infringe on local government autonomy with respect to how transfer resources are spent, but only on whether local governments have met legal requirements and adopted critical institutional or managerial reforms in decentralizing environments. For example, Kenya's Local Authority Transfer Fund (LATF) uses a formula to allocate government expenditures on local priorities, withholding a portion for noncompliance (e.g., failing to submit final accounts for audit or meet fiscal accountability reporting requirements) or new reforms (e.g., demonstrated adoption of new local government budgeting regulations or civic engagement mechanisms).

Critics worry that PBGs undermine local autonomy and are subject to abuse in the absence of clear guidelines. While these are legitimate concerns, in newly decentralizing environments, there is also danger in cutting lines of local accountability to the center before downward accountability to citizens has been adequately established. The granting of complete local autonomy as has been done in some cases of decentralization has led to misuse of resources, which has in turn resulted in partial return to centralization (Smoke, Gomez, and Peterson 2006). This suggests that central attempts to foster responsible local-government fiscal behavior are worth considering, at least where there are legitimate concerns about the willingness and ability of local governments to adopt key reforms and behave responsibly.

Although experience with PBGs is limited, recent work suggests early positive outcomes in a number of countries, including Bangladesh, Kenya, Tanzania, and Uganda (Steffensen and Larsen 2005; Steffensen 2006). In many cases, the results have mostly involved modest changes in behavior, such as adoption of new procedures, submission of required reports, and use of transfer funds according to agreed plans and budgets. In others, the modifications are more substantial. In Uganda, for example, local governments must meet minimum conditions before transfers are provided. The central government also provides capacity-building grants to help localities meet entry requirements. Where providing new resources, PBGs have also been successful in expanding service delivery and sometimes meeting other goals, such as pro-poor orientation.

Other types of incentives also improve local fiscal performance. For example, where local governments collect revenues shared with higher levels, central governments can structure the arrangements to create incentives. An important case is China's fiscal contracting system, which uses a high marginal revenue retention rate and other incentives to stimulate municipal revenue generation and improve fiscal behavior (Chang and Wang, 1998; Jin, Qian, and Winegast 1999; Bahl and Martinez-Vazquez 2003; Hsu 2004; Ping and Bai 2005). In addition, local governments can strictly enforce repaying municipal loans in order to meet debt service requirements (Peterson 2000; Peterson 2002; Friere and Petersen 2004).

Appropriate Capacity-Building

Fiscal experts commonly emphasize the need for capacity-building so that local employees can manage revenue-generation effectively. Central governments supported by international assistance commonly provide training and technical assistance but often formulate them in a mechanical, classroom-based, blueprinted way (Green 2005). Consensus is growing that the on-the-job capacity-building—related to current functions that local governments are implementing or reforming—is likely to be a better way of developing and retaining required skills than the traditional approaches. Thus, having a general course at a training institute on valuing property or setting user charges may be less useful than, or should at least be supplemented by, hands-on training and technical assistance provided as local government employees are in the process of undertaking these functions. While little is written about this alternative approach, some efforts in this direction have been reported in Kenya (Smoke 2003), Cambodia, Thailand, and Vietnam (Green 2005).

Implementation

Designing fiscal reform in developing countries has commanded far too much attention, while implementation at both the central and local level is almost universally underemphasized. Increasing recognition, however, that fiscal decentralization is often complex, contentious, and dependant on a level of capacity that does not broadly exist has prompted scholars to look more closely at implementation. The recognition that decentralization often requires behavioral changes that are unlikely to occur easily or rapidly has increased the sense that a deliberate strategy to implement fiscal decentralization is as important as the decentralization plan's design (Smoke and Lewis 1996; Litvack, Ahmad, and Bird 1998; Burki, Perry, and Dillinger 1999; Falleti 2005; Bahl and Martinez-Vazquez 2006; Ebel and Weist 2006; Shah and Thompson 2004; Smoke, Gomez, and Peterson 2006; Smoke 2007).

Where decentralization is beginning, the center must decide how to devolve new functions and resources.[6] At one extreme, the center may believe that implementation is entirely the responsibility of individually acting central ministries and local governments, which must develop the capacity needed to assume their mandated roles in the decentralized fiscal system. In other words, local governments must "sink or swim." At the other extreme, a "paternalistic" central government could pursue a highly managed process for gradually decentralizing to meet the provisions of the new system at a pace determined by the center.

The sink-or-swim approach places great expectations on all involved parties. Central ministries must comply with decentralization mandates even though they are giving up power and resources. Local governments need adequate capacity to assume new functions. Civil society needs to have sufficient power and experience to demand local government accountability. In contrast, the paternalistic approach gives too much power to the center, which may withhold power from local governments that are capable of responsibly managing new functions and resources independently.

A better path in many cases would be to pursue a compromise "developmental" approach of asymmetric treatment of local governments as they individually evolve their capacity to assume new functions. Capable local governments could be left to sink or swim, while others might more gradually assume new functions in conjunction with appropriate capacity-building and technical assistance. The central government could provide incentives for progressive adoption of key fiscal reforms and improved performance. Without an objective basis for classifying local governments and certifying when they are ready to progress, however, this approach could be politicized and local governments could stagnate at early stages that leave them with limited authority and autonomy.

Local governments also face implementation decisions when undertaking local public finance reforms. Even the most developed and capable local governments may need to be strategic in implementing broad reforms that require either major changes in the nature and level of what residents pay for local services or new staff skills. Local governments may, for example, face resistance in moving toward fuller collection of major revenues. Thus, they need to prioritize and make decisions about how to build the capacity of local staff to undertake them. (Priority steps need not always be the most important ones for fiscal performance. Sometimes it is better to tackle simpler and more politically acceptable reforms before taking on more complex or controversial ones that may be more productive.) Local governments could also test new systems and procedures in a few neighborhoods, allowing space for improvements before widespread application.

Forward-Looking Innovations

The weaknesses in the mainstream efforts toward intergovernmental fiscal reform outlined here, along with some recent developments in a number of countries, suggest various modified or alternative reforms that might be more productive. Some are specific to one aspect of local revenues—own-source revenues, intergovernmental transfers, or loans—while others bridge reforms across areas and lead to a more synthetic approach to overall reform. In addition, some involve central actions in decentralizing systems, while others involve actions that local governments can take independently.

Local Own-Source Revenues

A number of approaches may help local governments improve own-source revenue-generation. First, political and capacity constraints can be somewhat overcome by gradualism and flexibility. For example, when Indonesia moved to market-based capital value as its property tax base, it started with a low assessment ratio and increased it incrementally. Similarly, new-user charges could move gradually toward cost recovery in order to limit harsh equity effects, undesirable changes in service use, and administrative and political resistance. Flexibility in payment schemes could also improve compliance, especially where large lump-sum payments are expected as betterment levy assessments or connection charges for new water or sewerage infrastructure.

Second, it is useful to link new efforts to generate local revenue as directly as possible to service delivery expansion and quality improvements. Sometimes this can simply involve public education campaigns; in other cases, local governments may negotiate revenue increases with affected groups. For example, some municipalities in Kenya have negotiated central-business- or manufacturing-district tax or fee increases with chambers of commerce and citizen groups and have negotiated market-fee increases with market-user associations (Smoke 2003). More generally, local governments can use participatory planning and/or budgeting mechanisms to determine priority expenditures and to secure acceptance of and compliance with new or expanded local revenue sources. Local user committees for specific services have been used to connect citizens to local government service delivery and associated revenue-generation, although they can also bypass and undermine local governments (Manor 2004). Working with community groups on service delivery and revenue-generation for services such as trash collection can be productive and benefit local governments and community groups.

Third, given citizen expectations of fair treatment, local governments need to worry about developing and enforcing acceptable rules of the game. Thus some efforts to publicize reformed procedures, to create and support mechanisms for citizen appeals and complaints, and to enforce the rules consistently could be productive, assuming political support for them is present.

Intergovernmental Transfers

Since intergovernmental transfers are a central-government instrument, most new approaches to improve their allocation and use must come from the center. Beyond traditional recommendations for objective, transparent formulae for resource allocation that do not undermine local tax efforts, the adoption of performance-based transfers described earlier can be productive. Rewarding notably good and penalizing notably poor local government performance can push local governments to be more fiscally responsible and to improve accountability to their constituents. Where decentralization is beginning, initiating reform with very modest transfers subject to central control and monitoring may be possible. The size of transfers and level of autonomy can increase as local governments develop capacity and learn to behave in a fiscally responsible way. Although a substantial degree of flexibility in resource allocation is an important element in promoting local autonomy, it is perfectly acceptable for central governments to use unconditional transfers to help local governments to meet broader national policy goals.

It is important to emphasize that performance-based grants require additional central mechanisms and capacity to define and monitor performance. Monitoring the use and effects of transfers is notoriously weak in many developing countries. Better oversight would provide information that is useful not only to the central and local governments, but also to citizens seeking information on the fiscal behavior of their elected officials.

Although transfer reforms are primarily a central function, local governments can have a role. Including an element of negotiation in setting specific performance objectives a local government is expected to meet in any given year may be productive. When local governments play a role in defining what is to be achieved, it is possible to move away from a paternalistic "the-center-knows-best" approach to what can be done and to place responsibility on local governments for meeting agreed-upon targets. Using citizen consultation mechanisms to help define and monitor goals as well as to decide how portions of intergovernmental transfers will be used could also help to improve the local government's political credibility with its citizens.

Local Borrowing

A growing number of countries have improved local government access to development finance by adopting frameworks for sound local government borrowing and fiscal responsibility, by opening market borrowing opportunities to eligible local governments, and by pushing public mechanisms for lending to local governments to operate on more market-based principles. While these efforts move in a productive direction, they do little for the majority of local governments in many developing countries that are not creditworthy. A good intergovernmental fiscal system in such circumstances requires an appropriate spectrum of public investment finance options, from grants and subsidized loans for poorer local governments and non-self-financing projects, to various types of loans for more fiscally sound local governments and self-financing projects. Where local governments are relatively strong, efforts to develop access to capital markets make sense if the central government regulates borrowing and enforces hard budget constraints. In more typical developing countries, where local governments have fewer functions and are fiscally weaker, even in many urban areas, some type of special credit institution or government arrangements with private credit providers are required. Initial public management or regulation of these institutions or arrangements gives the center some needed control over local borrowing, although care must be taken to develop structures and procedures that minimize politicization of lending and loan repayment operations. Public sector–dominated institutions can be increasingly privatized as local governments develop creditworthiness.

Perhaps the most critical challenge in developing an intergovernmental finance system is how to "graduate" weaker local governments from grants and subsidized loans to greater use of credit markets. This requires coordinated development of grant and loan options.[7] It is critical to ensure that wealthy governments do not use grants for self-financing projects or divert scarce resources from poorer governments unable to borrow. At the same time, grants and subsidized lending mechanisms must create incentives for weak local governments to improve fiscal discipline and begin to borrow on more market-based terms. If, for example, even weak local governments are required to borrow a small percentage of development project finance and with support to build capacity are required to manage that loan, including raising revenues for loan repayment, they can begin a trajectory of building creditworthiness.

Risk mitigation strategies can be used to facilitate access to municipal credit. These include comprehensive and partial credit guarantees from the central government, cofinancing initiatives, secondary market support, and the use of bond banks and credit pooling (Estache 2004; Kehew, Matsukawa, and Petersen 2005; Petersen 2006; Matsukawa and Habeck 2007). A number of countries have made advances with some of these innovations through various institutional mechanisms, including FINDETER (Colombia), the Tamil Nadu Urban Development Fund (India), the Infrastructure Finance Corporation of South Africa, and the Local Government Unit Guarantee Corporation (Philippines).

Future Research

Although some empirical evidence on positive experiences exists, many proposals for local government finance reform are based primarily on an analysis of weak performance rather than on documented successes. Further research is needed on how to improve local government finance in developing countries in order to derive more generalizable, concrete recommendations. A number of areas of focus seem productive.

First, extensive and multimethodology-based research on the political dimensions of fiscal decentralization, both in terms of central-local relations and political dynamics at the local level, would offer a better understanding of how central governments can be encouraged to pursue fiscal decentralization. At the local level, learning more about the determinants of local revenue compliance and the effects of the local government revenue mix on service delivery composition, coverage, and quality would be useful. Understanding the role and impact of citizen-engagement mechanisms in making fiscal decisions and how these have influenced results is of particular importance.

Second, much more formal work is required to understand the practices and impacts of performance-based grants. Although PBGs are growing in importance and influence, their use in less developed environments has primarily been to promote the adoption of basic procedural reforms. The potential for and pitfalls of using such transfers and other mechanisms as incentives for more effective local government fiscal performance are not well understood.

Third, the focus on improving local borrowing has been on establishing strong fiscal accountability frameworks and "marketizing" traditional public or quasi-public lending institutions. These are important, but they will not meet the pressing infrastructure finance needs of the many noncreditworthy local governments in developing countries. More work is needed to understand how to improve fiscal performance and to help local governments evolve to a point where they can borrow on more market-compatible terms. The grant-loan linkage and risk-pooling mechanisms outlined earlier are worth exploring further, but there may also be other ways to approach this massive challenge.

Fourth, there has been inadequate effort to understand capacity-building efforts, particularly with respect to evaluating the role of classroom versus on-the-job efforts and general training versus task-specific capacity building. More formalized research into the effectiveness of various options and how best to approach them for fiscal reform would add to knowledge about how to foster effective capacity-building for local government fiscal performance.

Finally, with growing agreement that implementation is as important as design, more documentation of experience is needed. Understanding the strategic elements of central government approaches to fiscal decentralization and local government responses would be helpful in answering key questions, for example: Does asymmetric treatment (based on capacity and/or performance) of local governments improve the prospects for reform? If so, how might it best be structured? Do gradualism and strategic sequencing at the local level help to promote sustainable reform, and how are the specific steps taken related to often-neglected political considerations? How should incentives and capacity-building activities be used as part of more strategic approaches to reform? There is some promising evidence on all of these questions, but it is largely anecdotal and the degree to which these approaches can be used more generally is unclear.

The traditional approach to developing effective local public finance has been around for a long time, and it still has considerable relevance.

But the reality of often-disappointing performance in developing countries calls for going beyond the mainstream approach in understanding how to improve local fiscal behavior and performance. Current research provides some clues to productive avenues for reform, but additional investigation is needed to better understand practice and to form the basis for more definitive policy recommendations.

Chapter 12

Public-Private Partnerships and Urban Governance: Coordinates and Policy Issues

Lynne B. Sagalyn

Policymakers, practitioners, and academics around the world make compelling arguments for bridging public and private sectors through alliance, collaboration, and partnership. Based on the logic of pragmatism, they cast these arrangements as innovative and resourceful ways of dealing with the intensifying demands of urbanization. Infrastructure policy specialists in particular, citing a combination of economic and institutional forces, emphasize the central role public-private partnerships (PPPs) can play in meeting the pressing need for new large-scale investments and the equally urgent need to refurbish existing systems. Construction engineering experts support the paradigm shift as a new way to solve particular problems in contracting for large-scale construction projects.[1] For governments and international donor organizations eager to enhance productivity and stimulate economic growth, PPPs represent an efficient means to expand the scope of their development investments while securing advanced technological expertise.

The driver of change, typically, is financial. Worldwide, governments face fiscal constraints from limited (or cash-starved) budgets and heightened voter sensitivity to taxes. For the past several decades, fiscal pressures have prompted government officials to experiment with innovative approaches to the intense technical challenges of planning, designing, financing, and executing large-scale infrastructure projects for the development and delivery of urban services. The ensuing big-three PPP formats—asset-sale privatization, contracting out, and cooperative or joint venture agreements—comprise an alphabet-soup list of acronyms affording public officials diverse alternatives to the traditional public-sector procurement model, which many experts benchmark as bureaucratically inefficient and costly.

The worldwide momentum for PPPs has emerged from the support of a broad and diverse coalition that sees the strategy as a reform of urban governance as much as a pragmatic fiscal imperative. Complex urban problems and a better quality of urban services, policy reformers argue, are no longer solvable solely by traditional state intervention. Multifaceted approaches are required, including new institutional arrangements that devolve power from the national center to local government and reinvent government by engaging the private market to deliver urban services in cooperation or competition with public agencies (Osborne and Gaebler 1993; Moore and Pierre 1998; Engberg 2002). International funding organizations like the World Bank, the Asian Development Bank, the Japan Bank for International Cooperation, and the Inter-American Development Bank have entered the PPP advocacy tent, seeking to promote and expand the development of needed infrastructure around the world (USFHWA 2007a). And relatively recently, the European Union (EU) accepted the PPP as a "complementary implementation tool," linking PPP use to its initiatives for economic development and competitiveness (EC 2004; EC 2003; Newman and Verpraet 1999; Elander 2002; Grimsey and Lewis 2004).[2] In the U.S., the Department of Transportation, through its surface transportation administrations, aims to expedite urban transportation projects by encouraging state and local transportation agencies to consider the "selective use" of PPP approaches (USFHWA 2007b, 4–2). On the political front, some leading politicians have adopted PPPs as a central tool of governance within their ruling party's wider "modernization" agenda, as did Labour's Tony Blair when he became prime minister of the UK in 1997 (Flinders 2005). In short, the collaborative approach of the PPP paradigm theoretically affords government several strategic advantages, albeit with a trade-off: growing unease over traditional public-sector values that seem to get jettisoned on the path to collaboration.

Policymakers have fed upon the optimism about PPPs to accelerate applications to broad and diverse urban problems across the globe. Between 1985 and 2004, worldwide PPP infrastructure projects worth more than $2 billion had been planned and funded, with 53 percent of them completed by the end of 2004 (USFHWA 2007a). In some countries, PPP has been an experimental innovation (Netherlands, Spain, Finland); in others, an ideological force (United Kingdom, Canada, Australia); and in still others, a variant on a history of mixed enterprise (United States, France, Singapore). PPP slogans often reveal these political drivers: "A New Framework for Infrastructure" (Asian Development Bank et al. 2005); "PFI: Meeting the Investment Challenge" (HM Treasury 2003); "Partnerships for Progress" (National Council for Public Private Partnerships 1998); "Working Together" (Farlam 2005).

Whether for urban redevelopment/regeneration, transportation and environmental infrastructure, housing and homelessness, hospitals, schools, or economic development, the PPP model and its many variants has become the policy of choice for municipal government in the U.S., and an increasing number of countries in Europe and Asia. As practiced today, public-private collaboration marks a broad convergence of current economic forces and changing political paradigms. For the public sector, PPPs symbolize the search for greater efficiency of urban service delivery and resourceful mobilization of private capital to ease financial constraints and strengthen weak fiscal positions. For the private sector, PPPs represent an economic cornucopia of potential opportunity in urban markets across the globe.

Evidence of the strategy's effectiveness is not extensive (though it is growing) relative to the number of PPP initiatives, and what exists is mixed (Daniels and Trebilcock 1996; Boase 2000; Public Citizen 2003; HM Treasury 2003; Flinders 2005; Siemiatycki 2006; Koppenjan 2005; Murray 2006; Cambridge Systematics 2006; USFHWA 2007a, 2007b). I can offer several (less than satisfying) explanations for this state of affairs. First, a PPP project takes a long time to execute before data can be marshaled for evaluation, and the full implications of performance may not even be understood for many years after a project's completion. Second, in the absence of a statutory or administrative mandate or a political decision to repurchase a concession or provide a subsidy, government stakeholders do not have strong motivation to undertake ex post evaluations that might reveal disappointing results or embarrassing and costly construction overruns. Third, the information needed to assess performance of a PPP project is, more often than not, confidential. Fourth, because each project has a nearly unique set of complexities, general lessons are hard to come by (Sagalyn 1990, 2007), especially from experiences in emerging market economies.

Nevertheless, experience with PPPs in the U.S., Europe, and Asia has consistently brought to the fore common issues of governance, which are the focal point of this chapter. These public policy concerns are not particular to the PPP model, but the political rhetoric and elevated expectations for performance from cooperative (as opposed to adversarial) sector relationships add tension to the issues of accountability. In so doing, they amplify the political risks of adopting the PPP model as a governance reform.

In this chapter, I describe the coordinates of the global application of PPP and identify central commonalities of sector collaboration for both infrastructure development and urban redevelopment/regeneration projects. The comparison across these two types of "hard" asset-based initiatives will, I hope, highlight the central issues of implementation and underscore the need for policymakers to address the nature of risk sharing, which I believe is central to the PPP strategy at the project level. It should also provide an understanding of how weak management of accountability concerns is likely to intensify the political risks of the PPP strategy.

Partnership Coordinates

Government officials have rapidly expanded application of the PPP model to an ever-broadening set of urban service needs. In the realm of service infrastructure, asset-based partnership projects take in waste water and sewage treatment works, power plants, pipelines, telecommunications infrastructure, public-use motorways, toll roads, toll bridges, tunnels, road upgrading and maintenance, railways, subways, light-rail systems, airport facilities, harbors, affordable housing, student housing, school buildings, government offices, fire and police stations, hospitals and other health services, social housing, prisons and secure training centers, parking stations, and museum buildings along with other projects for recreation and tourism. (See table 12.1 for a list of illustrative PPP projects.) In the realm of urban redevelopment, what began with initiatives for downtown development would now include waterfront transformation, historic preservation, brownfield development, neighborhood commercial-center revitalization, community development lending, and military base conversions. The open character, flexible format, and customization of project-specific business terms and conditions for public-private sharing of risks and responsibilities make the PPP model highly adaptable (Sagalyn 2006). Some PPP projects, like prison services, remain controversial (Grimsey and Lewis 2004; Verkuil 2007), while certain others, like information technology and small capital projects, are not particularly amenable to the PPP strategy (Kumaraswamy and Morris 2002; Koppenjan 2005; Flinders 2005).

In theory, the market-based logic of PPP promises to deliver design and management innovations as well as economic efficiencies. In practice, the institutional architectures needed to execute these multiple objectives are complex. The processes and procedures necessary to select private concessionaires, services providers, or real estate developers willing and able to operate in the public interest pose a challenge to existing public expertise, and the contract arrangements and joint-venture agreements necessary to implement these projects are exceedingly difficult to design and negotiate. Public players must be skilled politically as well as technically versed in the details of what it takes to deliver the infrastructure service or redevelopment/regeneration project. The

Table 12.1: Illustrative Scope of PPP Projects

Projects	PPP Format	Date Project Begun
42nd Street Development Project (New York, USA)	Redevelopment PPP	1980
A1, A2, A4 Motorway Toll Roads (Poland)	Concession	1997
A59 Road (Netherlands)	DBFM	2001
Abbotsford Hospital (British Columbia, Canada)	DBFOM	1987
Alliance Airport (Texas, USA)	Development PPP	1989
Atlanta Water Service (Georgia, USA)	O&M Contract	1998
Asia World Expo (Hong Kong, China)	BOT	2003
Bangkok Elevated Transport System (Thailand)	BOT	1991
Battery Park City (New York, USA)	Redevelopment PPP	1969
California Plaza (Los Angeles, USA)	Redevelopment PPP	1981
California State Route 91 HOV lane (USA)	BTO	1995
Castlemaine Sewage Treatment Plant (Australia)	BOOT	1998
Channel Tunnel Rail Link (England / France)	BOT/PFI	1988
Charleswood Bridge (Winnipeg, Canada)	DBFO	1993
Chengdu No. 6 Water Plant B Project (China)	BOT	1997
Chicago Skyway Lease (Illinois, USA)	Concession	2004
Country Park Motorway (Hong Kong, China)	BOT	1993
Dartford Crossing Bridge (London, UK)	DBFO	1986
Debrecen Municipal Waste Water System (Hungary)	Joint venture	1991
Delfland Waste Water Purification Plant (Netherlands)	DBFO	1999
Dulles Greenway (Virginia, USA)	DBFO	1988
E-470 Tollway (Colorado, USA)	DBO	1985
Franklin Waste Water Treatment Plant (Ohio, USA)	DBFOT	1995

Projects	PPP Format	Date Project Begun
Helsinki-Lahti Motorway (Finland)	BOT	1995
Highway 407 (Ontario, Canada)	DBO	1993/4
Hudson-Bergen Light Rail (New Jersey, USA)	BOT/DBOM	1994
Indiana Toll Road Lease (USA)	Concession	2005
Labin B Power Plant (Guangxi, China)	BOT	1997
JFK Airport Terminal 4 (New York, USA)	Development agreement	1995
Labuan Water Supply (Malaysia)	BOT	1993
Las Vegas Monorail (Nevada, USA)	BOT/DBOM	1993
M1-A1 Link (Leeds, UK)	DBFO	1993
M5 Transport (Hungary)	Concession	1992
M4 Toll Motorway (Sydney, Australia)	BOT	2003
Maasvlakte II (Netherlands)	Combination model	2001
Melbourne CityLink Toll Road (Australia)	BOOT	1994
Melbourne Convention Center/ Development (Australia)	Development agreement	2004
Millau Viaduct (France)	Concession	1998
New Dockland Stadium (Melbourne, Australia)	BOT	1996
Phoenix Water Treatment Facility (Arizona, USA)	DBO	2000
Pipeline Rehabilitation Services (Bucharest, Romania)	Concession	2000
Pocahontas Parkway Route 895 (Virginia, USA)	DBFO	2004
Prince Edward Island Fixed Link (Canada)	DBFOT	1985
Olympic Stadium (Sydney, Australia)	BOOT	1995
Pearson International Airport Terminal 3 (Toronto)	DBFO	1986
Richmond-Airport-Vancouver Line (BC, Canada)	DBFO	2001

Table 12.1: (Continued)

Projects	PPP Format	Date Project Begun
Rosario-Victoria Bridge (Rosario/Victoria, Argentina)	DBOM	1997[a]
Route 28 (Virginia, USA)	DBT	2002
Schwerte Municipal Waste Water System (Germany)	Joint venture	1993
Second Vivekanda Bridge (Kolkata, India)	BOT	2004[a]
Shajiao B Power Plant (China)	BOT	1984
Sijtwende Road (Voorburg, Netherlands)		1999
Sofia Water and Wastewater Project (Bulgaria)	Concession	2000
South Bay Expressway SR 125 (California, USA)	DTO franchise	1991
Sydney Harbor Tunnel (Australia)	BOOT	1987[a]
Sydney SuperDome (Australia)	BOOT	1997
SH 130 (Texas USA)	DBFO concession	2006
Union Station (Washington, D.C., USA)	Redevelopment PPP	1981
Yeuba Buena Center (San Francisco, USA)	Redevelopment PPP	1980
Yitzhak Rabin Trans-Israel Highway (Tel Aviv, Israel)	BBFO	1999[a]

Sources: Various.
Note: Date project begun generally means date the public sector started planning the project; in select instances where that date is not available from online information, the date begun represents the date the private vendor was selected. [a] Indicates start of construction; start date of project planning and/or public-sector initiative unavailable.

details of specific project conditions and public objectives matter a lot. Political cultures vary and shape the institutional context of contracting. Rate-setting constraints on cost recovery or profits, extraordinary programmatic public benefits, or other policy mandates can create potential losses in economic efficiency and reduce private investment value (Daniels and Trebilcock 1996). When PPP projects carried out by numerous independent public agencies proliferate, fragmentation of policy coordination is another potential problem (Flinders 2005). Alternatively, when driven by a central government, as in the case of airport privatization in Australia, the process might "quarantine" adjacent commercial development from the scrutiny of state and local planning processes (Freestone et al. 2006). And as nearly all reviewers of case-based experience point out, sector partnerships cloud accountability.

To what extent might any of these unintended consequences induce a political backlash or counterproductive trend undermining the broad convergence behind and potential gains of the PPP strategy (Engberg 2002)? The question holds practical consequence because the ways in which policymakers address the governance issues inherent in policy trade-off of PPPs are likely to influence the political legitimacy of the reform approach.

Political Economy

Rooted political traditions and institutional cultures of both business and government distinguish different forms of privatization and partnership in countries around the world. Statutorily and politically, a spectrum of weak to strong PPP environments exists (Van Boxmeer and Van Beckhoven 2005). In the U.S. a long tradition of public-private interplay exists, in contrast to Europe, where centrist models of national-local government relations and active government intervention in social welfare and economic markets have been dominant. Comparatively placed by a number of researchers, the UK, for example, is somewhere between the strong-state European model and the market-oriented U.S. experience (Newman and Verpraet 1999).

Culturally constrained powers can readily limit what a PPP can achieve. For example, Adams and Hastings (2001) analyzed the performance of Hong Kong's Land Development Corporation (LDC) prior to 1997 to evaluate how the U.S. pattern of public-private development translated into local experience. Their detailed case analysis revealed that specific development powers and resources mattered, not just the institutional model of action. Culture mattered too because it influenced the powers and resources government was willing to give to public-private entities. Lacking eminent domain powers and resources for rehousing those displaced limited the LDC's accomplishments; the corporation did not have legal powers to acquire sites and so could assemble land only by negotiation and pay market (and, in practice, above-market) prices, which limited its financial performance. The Hong Kong government insisted on very close ongoing scrutiny of the LDC's operations and mandated specific bureaucratic procedures because of its commitment to public accountability and the fear of corruption. The LDC produced much-needed housing, but this outcome "merely replicated the kind of small-scale redevelopment produced by the private sector elsewhere" (Adams and Hastings 2001, 483). As a result, the authors found little benefit beyond what the market would have produced without the LDC.

Political economies at the national level of government aside, researchers studying redevelopment/regeneration continue to find a "convergence in practice" at the municipal or community level. They trace this to the idea of market-led project feasibility and its corollary practice of interfacing with private interests early in the planning and implementation process (Moore and Pierre 1988, 169; Frieden and Sagalyn 1989; Van Boxmeer and Van Beckhoven 2005).

Allocating risk between public and private sectors is the core of the PPP strategy. The precise mechanisms of ownership, financing, usage rights, and obligations for production, delivery, and service can be rearranged into different allocations of public and private responsibility, which is what government officials in the United Kingdom, North America, Europe, and Asia have been experimenting with for the past three decades. This experimentation has produced diverse public-private business models, especially in the area of service procurement, as shown in table 12.2. Pure privatization—when government disengages totally through transfer of ownership to a private firm which takes over assets and assumes responsibility for service delivery—differs from the many formats of contracting out, which in turn differ legally and financially from the joint venture.

Substantial variations in procurement laws and procedures exist worldwide (and within federalist government systems such as the U.S.), making generalizations about contracting out tenuous. Yet more than the involvement of private enterprise per se, what distinguishes PPP infrastructure contracting arrangements is bundling. Bundling ties together traditionally discrete procurement processes of design, financing, construction, operations, and maintenance. By vertically integrating some or all of these functions, bundling creates the potential for greater economic efficiency because private companies have a financial motivation to think in ways that might generate greater productivity and cost efficiencies *over time*, that is, for the duration of their service contract (Daniels and Trebilcock 1996). It also can open up to competition a set of economic activities previously excluded from that process (Grimsey and Lewis 2004).

Project-level PPPs for infrastructure delivery represent an array of contract arrangements differentiated by three elements: the services bundled (the degree of private control over service delivery and level of policy control retained by the public entity), the level of private-sector financial commitment (risk-taking), and the ability and willingness of the public sector to share these risks. In each variant of contracting out,

Table 12.2: Range of Public-Private Business Models

Type of PP Model	Acronym	Public Interface
Public provision of collective goods		Complete public provision
Outsourcing/contracting		Generalized procurement
Service provision contracts		Service procurement
Design and construct	D&C	Service procurement
Sale and leaseback	S&L	Ownership transfer and contracting
Operate and maintain	O&M	Service procurement
Operate, maintain, and manage	OM&M	Service procurement
Build transfer operate	BTO	Service procurement and capital asset
Build operate transfer	BOT	Service procurement and capital asset
Build lease transfer	BLT	Service procurement and capital asset
Build lease transfer maintain	BLTM	Service procurement and capital asset
Build own operate	BOO	Service procurement
Build own operate maintain	BOOM	Service procurement
Build own operate remove	BOOR	Service procurement
Build own operate transfer	BOOT	Service procurement and capital asset
Build own operate train transfer	BOOTT	Service procurement and capital asset
Design build operate	DBO	Service procurement
Design operate transfer	DOT	Service procurement and capital asset
Design build finance operate	DBFO	Service procurement
Design construct manage finance	DCMF	Service procurement
Design build finance operate manage	DBFOM	Service procurement
Lease renovate operate transfer	LROT	Service procurement and capital asset
Rehabilitate own operate	ROO	Service procurement
Rehabilitate operate transfer	ROT	Service procurement and capital asset
Private finance initiative	PFI	Service procurement (U.K. model)
Franchise		Licensed service agreement
Concession		License service agreement
Business Improvement District	BID	Special taxation and codecision making
Joint venture	JV	Co-investment "mixed enterprise"

Table 12.2: (Continued)

Type of PP Model	Acronym	Public Interface
Community development bank	CDB	Cocapitalized lending venture
Redevelopment partnership		Co-investment "mixed enterprise"
Outright privatization		Complete private ownership and provision

Source: Grimsey and Lewis 2004, 54; Kumaraswamy and Morris 2002, 95; Briffault 1999, 368; Flinders 2005, author.

Notes: **Outsourcing or contracting out:** arrangement in which the public sector maintains ownership or policy control (for example, rate setting) of a function but contracts with a private operator to discharge that function through some type of procurement process over a contractually defined period of time.

Procurement process: arrangement in which the public sector decides on a mix of rights and responsibilities—risk allocation, operation, financing, maintenance, performance—of a service over a contractually defined period of time.

Private Finance Initiative: formal UK model in which the private sector provides capital for a project as well as builds and often manages a facility in turn for a long-term (twenty-five years or more) contract in which the government commits the state to pay an annual fee for the use of the facility. This is akin to a long-term service lease arrangement.

Franchise: arrangement in which a private firm is granted a license to operate/provide services in a particular territory for a contractually defined period of time.

Concession: legal arrangement in which a private firm is granted land or property for a particular purpose for a contractually defined period of time in return for services; in France, which has a long history of concession contracting, entrepreneurs are given a franchise to provide services such as water and electricity for a specific period of time, after which the infrastructure is returned to the public entities.

Business Improvement District: business-initiated territorial arrangement within a city in which all property owners or businesses are subject to additional tax assessments that are used to fund services and improvements within the district and to pay for the administrative costs of the BID operations.

Joint venture: arrangement in which private and public entities jointly undertake the development (and perhaps operation and maintenance) of a facility that will provide services.

Community development bank: lending venture jointly capitalized by government and private sector funds designed to leverage private capital for loans, guarantees, venture capital, grants and technical assistance to small businesses in disadvantaged neighborhoods. The Los Angeles Community Development Bank, created by the U.S. government in 1995, was capitalized with $435 million from the U.S. Department of Housing and Urban Development and $210 million from regional commercial banks.

Redevelopment partnership: a project-based arrangement that typically involves co-investment by the public sector. The public investment may involve all manner of direct or indirect financial assistance as well as regulatory relief, bureaucratic expediting, and related forms of project assistance. The public entity (or entities) may or may not be a co-owner of the project in the legal sense, notwithstanding profit-sharing arrangements.

Outright privatization: sale of an asset to private ownership, which delivers services from that asset under terms that may involve subsidization and/or regulation by the public sector.

though, the public-private relationship redirects service delivery from unidirectional agency to public-private coproduction—an institutional move challenging the structure and values of public-sector agencies (Engberg 2002). Politically, the emphasis shifts as well: "What matters is what works," said Britain's former prime minister Tony Blair in an often-quoted phrase (*Financial Times* 1998, cited in Newman and Verpraet 1999, 489).[3] In short, adoption of the PPP strategy signifies regime reform.

The joint venture or development agreement partnership differs from contracting-out formats, which circumscribe the nature of the public-private relationship to what is specified in the contract. Regeneration and economic development PPPs, for example, typically involve more of a commitment than what transmits in the development agreement. In practice, they include what cannot be anticipated—an implicit mutual commitment to deal with unexpected project-threatening crises if and when they occur, which may mean renegotiating the agreement if necessary to ensure successful execution of the project (Frieden and Sagalyn 1989; Bovaird 2004; Sagalyn 2001). All types of public-private ventures share a significant commonality: the negotiated allocation of risk and control between public and private partners. This is the core of the PPP business relationship, in theory and practice, so much so that it even shapes the potential for partnership.

For example, in a comparative analysis of nine transport projects in the Netherlands, Koppenjan (2005) asked what made for the successful *formation* of a PPP project. Because not all projects or public entities are amenable to PPP, understanding the determinants of successful formation is actually a more important research question than might be apparent at first blush. Koppenjan wanted to understand the nature of the problems encountered in creating these partnerships and how they should be dealt with. He identified three formation patterns: quick take-off; early private involvement supported by interactive decision-making techniques, but difficult movement forward; and hesitant and risk-avoiding behavior, resulting in disappointing outcomes, followed by unilateral public planning, then stagnating contract negotiations. Success was most apparent when the decision-making process embedded active engagement of the partners, which he termed "interaction." Financial reasons are typically the strongest motivation behind infrastructure transport PPPs, for both public and private entities. Whether or not they could be achieved in every instance turns on market-based potential trade-offs supporting a project's financial feasibility. Expensive projects, he argued citing numerous sources,[4] are capable of being made affordable and/or generating cost savings for government through several channels: gains in efficiency, the creation of cash flow between construction and market delivery, financial trade-offs between profitable and nonprofitable project parts, value capture from increases in property values near infrastructure used to contribute to the financing of a project's construction, and benefit sharing whereby public authorities share in the profits of the private partners. Many of these trade-offs involve the potential for commercial real estate development, which does not calibrate the same way across all types of infrastructure. For example, because it is spatially spread out, line infrastructure like roadways and railway links appear to offer less trade-off potential than point infrastructure, such as traffic intersections, railway stations, and airport terminals.

Complexity

Considering how players handle implementation, partnerships for redevelopment/regeneration and infrastructure projects share a number of common traits that make them complex undertakings. The product is typically complicated in its technical specification. It is demanding in terms of public policy ambition as well as financial feasibility. Each side of the partnership is typically populated with multiple players, public and private entities themselves representing infrasector collaborations. With infrastructure bundling, for instance, bidding private partners often form consortia ("virtual corporations") because "the functions involved are highly specialized and entail deployment of quite different bodies of complementary expertise and resources" beyond the capabilities of individual firms unless a firm is vertically integrated (Daniels and Trebilcock 1996, 390). For redevelopment/regeneration projects, state and local government entities regularly collaborate to facilitate funding, marshal powerful financial incentives, or expedite entitlement approvals (Sagalyn 2001). The whole gets fashioned into a project-specific organizational network governed by the business terms and conditions of the contracting arrangement, concession or franchise agreement, long-term ground lease, or disposition and development agreement. These organizational networks make confronting public officials responsible for managing a PPP project negotiation a rather complex operation, since they must secure agreement to not one, but a series of consistent and interlocking agreements detailing each participant's rights and obligations in implementing the project. "The complexity of intergovernmental relationships should make one wary of over-generalizing typologies," two researchers cautioned in their assessment of the impacts of European regeneration PPPs on urban governance—an observation that could just as easily apply to the U.S. experience (Newman and Verpraet 1999, 487).[5]

Government detachment is the linguistic myth of "privatization," in any contracting-out format. In practice, contracting out may involve government-backed financing, regulatory restrictions, and ongoing subsidy, or it may implicate other public policy concerns that involve ongoing monitoring of governance. Government actions create assets with pri-

vate-sector value and embed economic rights—long-term fee-based revenue streams, special development incentives, and opportunities to
capture value from adjacent real estate development—that can readily
beget political risks.

A compelling set of experiences comes from a detailed review of three
high-profile Canadian infrastructure projects.[6] In this study, Daniels and
Trebilcock (1996) found that despite the depiction of economic benefits to the government from private-sector efficiency and risk-bearing,
each project included some significant role for government in project
financing or long-term subvention. Their analysis of primary project
documents also revealed that "each of the projects implicated a range
of public policy concerns that could not be sidestepped by the decision
to develop the project through a public/private partnership" (387).
These policy concerns included right-of-way and eminent domain issues,
the effectiveness and transparency of levers for government action after
construction had been completed, network externalities, monopoly
pricing concerns, and operator compliance with specific governmental
laws. The need to respond to these policy concerns, they saw, "was often
in direct tension with the need to provide credible assurances to the
developer/operator (as an inducement to investment) that the franchise value of the undertaking would not be debased ex post by direct
government action" (388).

What these legal scholars emphasize and elaborate on in their thorough analysis is how, beyond the technical character of the capital asset
or flow of services to be provided, the status of government as a partner
imposes particular and complex demands on contracting arrangements
used to implement public-private partnerships.[7] Government, as other
researchers similarly concluded from case analyses of PPP projects, can
be "a capricious partner" (Van Ham and Koppenjan 2002, 600; see also
Levy 1996, cited in Kumaraswamy and Morris 2002; Bassett et al. 2002).
That unanticipated government action creates problems for private
market investments is not unique to PPP circumstances. Rather, as Daniels and Trebilcock (1996, 388) emphasize, these problems are "particularly acute" in PPP situations because private investors are asked to sink
large up-front costs in physical bricks-and-mortar facilities, which, once
in place, cannot be moved if underlying economic conditions shift. The
same is true for both physical infrastructure and redevelopment/regen-
eration projects.

Complexity is the structurally bedeviling feature of public-private partnership arrangements. It impacts the chances of successfully forming a
partnership. It influences how partnership decisions get made. It has a
cost in attenuating potential efficiency gains (often presciently evident
in the size of a project's legal fees). Deals *become* complex, I wrote in

1990, based on research for *Downtown Inc.: How America Rebuilds Cities*: "Most cities do not set out to make public/private deals complex, to obscure costs, or to confound critics. Rather, the deals become complex as cities try to match their many policy goals against the constraints of public financing and the demands of private real estate investment" (Sagalyn 1990, 437). In this early work on public-private redevelopment, I also explained the political purposefulness of complexity and how it confounds rational approaches to greater accountability. "The lack of comprehension of complex deals acts as a shield against close scrutiny: what is difficult to understand is more likely to be left alone. With such compelling forces at play," I wrote, "where are the incentives for change" (437)? Seventeen years later, I am still grappling with this question and the range of accountability issues complexity begets, as I will discuss in the next section.

Governance Agitations

The theory and rhetoric behind the PPP movement set up high performance hurdles for these projects. They were promoted as a means of providing more cost-efficient delivery of urban services, stimulating innovations in technology and the design of complex physical infrastructure projects, shifting the very substantial risks of public capital investment to private ownership, reducing the bureaucratic snags in the approvals system, and expediting the implementation of large-scale public initiatives in city building, regeneration, or economic development. In short, carrying promise as a multifaceted reform remedy for urban governance at a time when direct government action needed both a new cloak of political optimism and a deep source of capital funding, PPPs were bound to disappoint many in government, policy circles, and the academy, especially skeptics waiting in the wings. The limited evidence on performance from detailed case studies of ambitious and complex PPP projects, mostly for physical infrastructure, consistently reveals that results have been considerably less than the theoretical and rhetorical claims. But in what ways, and by what dimensions, has the reality fallen short of expectations? Where are the weak or naïve links between theory and practice in plan, design, and execution? What lessons can we take away from these case experiences to improve our understanding of what is realistically possible and probable in complex PPP projects?

Risk and Economics

On risk transfer and cost efficiencies, the results present a weak story line, so far. For the majority of case studies discussed in published research, academics found that government ended up sharing significant financial risks, either in the form of a long-term public subvention (in Canada: Prince Edward Island Fixed Link/Confederation Bridge and the Richmond-Airport-Vancouver Line; in the United Kingdom: National Air Traffic Services, Devonport Dockyard; in the United States: Tacoma Narrows Bridge project); or takeover (UK: Channel Tunnel Rail Link; Hungary: M1-M5 Motorway; Texas: Camino Columbia project); or government-backed financing for the entire project (Canada: Highway 407);[8] or government payment of compensation for contract cancellation (Canada: Redevelopment of Pearson Airport Terminals 1 and 2).

PPP is not a one-size-fits-all strategy. The type of project and service delivery shapes the reality of risk transfer. Case evidence suggests that substantial risk can be transferred to the private sector in transport projects *provided* that demand forecasts and revenue streams are well identified. Case evidence also demonstrates the potential for failure if demand forecasts are exaggerated and other fundamental issues (cost control and rigorous planning and financial preparation) are not carefully addressed or if sustained and committed political support is absent. And case evidence further demonstrates the risk of not transferring enough risk and responsibility or, conversely, transferring too much (EC 2004). Certain public services, like the London Underground, for example, are highly capital intensive and present a formidable challenge to risk transfer because the level of user charges necessary to cover capital and operating costs would either dramatically reduce demand, thereby exacerbating the financial problem, or create a politically untenable situation. Other services like air traffic control, policing, water supply and solid waste management, and highway safety are essential to a functioning civil society. When PPP projects in the essential service realm are in danger of failing, government has little choice owing to legal or political consequences but to bail out PPP contractors who get into trouble, as the U.K. Public Accounts Committee noted in its 2002–2003 report on the nation's high-profile Private Finance Initiative (PFI) (Flinders 2005).[9] As guarantor of essential services, government is always the supplier of last resort.

The scope and complexity of PPP projects generate other types of economic problems, most of which cannot be edited away through careful and detailed contracting design and documentation. These include delays and additional costs associated with time-consuming bidding and negotiation processes (which can be more costly than traditional public procurement) and persistent stakeholder resistance and opposition. Economic efficiency is often compromised by an attenuation of private asset value from regulatory restrictions imposed by government upon PPP operators[10] and low levels of competition from the small number of bidders who actually progress to the final stage of the PPP tournament. Finally, contractual guarantees to deliver complex projects "on time and on budget" are likely to carry built-in risk premiums since private entities are likely to anticipate potential contract-penalty costs in advance.

The economic advantage in PPP infrastructure projects does not come from privatizing the financing component per se, not even in these hugely capital-intensive projects and not even from a theoretical perspective. Regardless of whether its bonds are backed by tax-revenue general obligations or project-specific revenue streams, government typically borrows at more advantageous rates than private entities. Rather, the case for privatizing urban service delivery "necessarily turns on the efficiency and incentive effects" that flow from bundling elements of the procurement process into privatization contracting, including the financing piece (Daniels and Trebilcock 1996, 409).[11]

Divergences between PPP theory and practice in the case of the Richmond-Airport-Vancouver (RAV) Link in British Columbia tell a cautionary story. Based on a careful and seemingly comprehensive economic and institutional analysis, including an examination of the political donations of RAV proponents, Siemiatycki (2006) concluded that the RAV PPP failed to drive technological innovation or limit cost escalations during the planning process. On the first point, the performance specifications of the RAV line, whose technology and route had been studied for more than a decade, left little room for private-sector innovation. On the second, price escalations from late-scope changes and other financial attributes of the project forced the public sector to take on additional financial risk (as has been the case with other PPP experiences). Again, the evidence is mixed. Other case experience suggests that PPPs do facilitate a transfer of technological expertise, especially in transitional and developing economies (EC 2004).

To date, the case-study evidence clearly demonstrates that the actual benefits of contracting are not automatic: they do not flow robotically from the bundling format of privatized infrastructure projects. Much the same could be said for PPP redevelopment-regeneration projects, which, in comparison, are technically less specified and programmatically more fluid during the early stages of developer selection and design and development. In both instances, public-sector players are put in the position of having to acquire or rapidly develop sophisticated institutional skills and the political acumen necessary to execute agenda-setting, contract negotiation, and policy oversight of PPP projects. These are public-sector responsibilities that no government official can formally delegate to the private sector (and expect to keep governing) with any type of PPP format for any type of public service. This mandate for policy performance includes coping with the demands for transparency, the dilemma of confidentiality, and the politics of consultation with a wide range of stakeholders.[12]

Transparency, Confidentiality, and Accountability

Risk-sharing in public-private partnerships places a heavy emphasis on confidentiality, particularly when the business terms and conditions of an agreement are being negotiated. Hammering out the details of complex agreements requires meeting behind closed doors. The issues raised by closed-door negotiations for redevelopment deals remain unchanged since I first wrote about the accountability dilemma (Sagalyn 1990, 435):

> Eventually, when local government has to give formal approval, the city council will learn about the bargains that were struck; the public-at-large may have access to the agreement through summaries deposited at libraries or reported in the press. But alternatives dropped along the way seldom come to light, and the complexity of the business deal increases the likelihood that few people will understand it well enough to raise informed objections. The city, after all, is usually trading current costs against future returns that are necessarily uncertain. Besides, the deal that reaches the members of the city council is a fully negotiated agreement that they cannot take apart and amend piece by piece; so they have the choice of accepting it as it is or becoming the spoiler of a project that has been years in the making.

For infrastructure projects the accountability dilemma embedded in confidential partnership agreements poses a distinct and intellectually challenging problem involving proprietary rights. When government entities contract for urban service delivery through long-term concessionary agreements with private entities, they are extending ownership rights and facilitating asset creation for these private-vendor entities. Drawing a comparison through a metaphor with patents,[13] Ghere asks us to consider what such ownership could mean in the case of a large-scale municipal water operation or state corrections facility (Ghere 2001, 444):

> First, partnerships may involve the sale of existing capital facilities (such as a water treatment plant) or provide for the private partner to finance and own a new facility. Second, a fee-for-service partnership might convey a fee-based revenue stream to the private firm. In such an arrangement, the private partner could be viewed as "owning" a customer base and, indeed, may exercise rate-setting authority. Third, control over operations—including assumption of a public-employee workforce—could also constitute a form of asset creation. And fourth, it is conceivable that, in certain cases (for example, with park systems, toll roads, or corrections), partnerships could arrange for real estate transactions accruing to the private firm.

Operating for profit under market conditions, a private vendor understandably wants to protect its competitive position. Acting rationally, it will condition its engagement in bidding and negotiation on some type of confidentiality agreement restricting the sharing of proprietary technical, business, financial, or legal information, if not over the term of the long-term agreement, then as long as it can and certainly for specified durations related to project-sensitive phases, including planning and contract negotiation.

This was the case with Vancouver's RAV project, where, Siemiatycki (2006) explains, the "confidentiality screen" may have kept the city manager from sharing information about the vendor consortium's controversial cut-and-cover construction method with the Vancouver city council, "even if there were parts of the plan that could be to the detriment of constituents," because that information was part of the proprietary bid. "The level of secrecy required to maintain the integrity of the private-public-partnership delivery model," he wrote, "calls into question whether the RAV-project governance structure threatened the fiduciary responsibility for the civil service or provided the necessary accountability to the elected officials who were responsible for deciding whether to approve the project" (148).[14] Strict confidentiality agreements can also shield the full costs of these projects and obviously make difficult, if not impossible, the task of evaluating the actual efficiency gains from privatization contracts.

But as with other aspects of PPP implementation, procedural variations in practice shape the governance implications (see Briffault 2000). Confidentiality need not be total or coterminous with the contractual term. By limiting the scope and timing of confidentiality, greater transparency can be built into the PPP process. For example, under the procedures established by the state of Texas in 2003 authorizing PPPs through comprehensive development agreements, information submitted by bidders remains confidential until a final contract is signed with the winning bidder. More to the point, the State Department of Transportation can provide modest compensation (up to $1 million) to losing bidders for use of intellectual property included in the proposal (Durbin Associates 2005, cited in Buxbaum and Ortiz 2007).

On the other side of the balance sheet, government brings political skill in mobilizing community support and managing opposition to the partnership table. Its unquestioned role is to manage the process of consultation among a wide range of stakeholders, however willingly, ably, and skillfully individual public managers carry it out. As a participant observer at several annual meetings of the National Council of Public-Private Partnerships, a U.S. trade group of private-vendor advocates, Ghere explains that despite rhetoric generally characterizing "grass-

Table 12.3: Governance Concerns

Public Governance Norms	PPP Issues
Accountability	Procedural fairness
Ban on conflicts of interest	Transparency
Administrative and judicial appeal	Confidentiality / proprietary rights
Disclosure	Confidentiality agreements
Rights protection	Information imbalances
Stakeholder participation	Normative regime change:
	Devolution / policy fragmentation
	Centralization / "quarantine effect"
Social equity	Social equity

roots politics as an unfortunate and troublesome deviation from enlightened rationality," private partners "cultivate a regard for government's political brokerage skills as an indispensable resource" (Ghere 2001, 446). Bassett et al. (2002) find the same sentiments in their study of the Bristol Harbourside waterfront regeneration project. Scholars of infrastructure PPPs also see the political risks of these projects as being the hardest to manage, even in comparison with the technical risks and the harder, but often manageable, financial risks (Tam and Leung 1999, cited in Kumaraswamy and Morris 2002; EC 2004).

Like many investments taken on by government, PPP projects confront a well-established list of political hazards: failure to complete, project-threatening stakeholder resistance and opposition, overgenerous economic incentives, political interference, and favoritism or corruption. Because PPPs represent a paradigm shift, political risks specific to the PPP strategy—most notably, financial failure reverting to public takeover or buyout—are potential liabilities capable of inducing backlash and pushback. This is where the processes and procedures aligned to traditional norms of governance and designed to address specific PPP issues, identified in table 12.3, can help shield the PPP strategy from a premature abandonment.

Toward an Agenda for Policy Performance

In the U.S., Europe, and Asia, experience with PPPs has brought to the fore common issues of governance, independent of performance results. PPPs represent a political challenge to the structure and values of public-sector agency. They involve difficult issues of contracting compared to the traditional model of public procurement. Public-private risk-sharing places a heavy emphasis on confidentiality and heightens the role of disclosure and oversight. Because the policy strategy leverages private capital, PPPs are biased toward market-based investments and only secondarily, if at all, address social equity concerns.

On the other hand, the strong case for PPP has gathered widespread support from a number of conceptually compelling arguments, accelerating applications across the globe, and case-based results that selectively demonstrate efficiencies and innovation. As a powerful means for government to expand its capacity to ensure provision of urban services and stimulate economic productivity through investment, PPPs have become an essential instrument in the tool kit of policymakers. They are evolving. The biggest promise is still in the future as public and private players alike work through the kinks of complex risk-sharing agreements, and policy analysts mine the experiences for insights to improve efficiencies in practice.

How stakeholders respond to the governance issues of PPPs will inevitably depend on both the cultural traditions and policy context of country-specific public-private initiatives. But the mandates central to the agenda for policy performance are universal: PPP governance protocols, PPP capacity-building for public officials, and comparative research on PPP results.

Chapter 13

City Building in China:
Implications for Urban Form Efficiency

Douglas Webster

Current Chinese city-building processes can be viewed from a land efficiency perspective and through the prism of the key actors, particularly (1) local governments (municipal, urban district, county), (2) the national government, which has become increasingly interventionist in response to energy efficiency, agricultural land protection, and housing-affordability issues, (3) developers (ranging from small-scale, local to large-scale, international developers), and (4) China's emerging civil society.

Two cases, Xi'an and Tianjin, are illustrative. Xi'an was a staid interior city from 1949 until the late 1980s. Over the last two decades, however, the city has been impacted by global industry, particularly by tourism (after the discovery of the Terracotta Warriors) and by software development drawn by a strong educational base and the Xi'an High Technology Development Zone (XHTDZ). The second case, Tianjin, is an established coastal city and a former treaty port, whose economic growth was modest over the last twenty years (in Chinese terms), but it has recently been designated by the current (Hu Jintao) Chinese government as a priority target for urban development as part of a larger-scale focus on the Beijing-Tianjin-Hebei megapolitan region.

The two case studies are presented from different perspectives. The Xi'an case study focuses on the role of actors, while the Tianjin case study focuses on land-use issues resulting from the behavior of key actors.

The research underlying this chapter is driven by the Chinese national government's concern to achieve more efficient land use in metropolitan areas measured in terms of energy consumption, human travel time, unit infrastructure investment costs, logistics (distribution) costs, and loss of fertile agricultural land. In regard to the last, China's national target is to protect 121 million hectares of agricultural land nationwide in perpetuity.[1] As such, the chapter emphasizes understanding the potential of vacant land within the built-up city, rural-urban land conversion, and the degree and spatial distribution of nodality. Of particular concern is the role of drivers affecting the foregoing, particularly land markets, transportation systems (routes, mode, alignment with land use and employment), and large-scale public investments, e.g., construction of urban subcenters.

This chapter is a follow-up to research the author undertook earlier on city-building in Bangkok (Webster 2000). Comparing China with Bangkok and other East Asian extended urban regions raises the question: is the Chinese city-building process substantively different from earlier city-building processes in East Asia, or is it simply at an earlier point on the trajectory?

A Typology of Chinese Cities

Although political decision-making affects urban outcomes (both systems of cities and intra-urban patterns) worldwide, political and administrative decisions have had a stronger impact in China than in comparable continental-sized nations such as the United States, Canada, and Australia. In post-1949 China, the spatial nexus of economic power shifted substantially, especially in terms of manufacturing. (As the country is known as the "factory of the world,"[2] manufacturing is important in Chinese urban areas, constituting as much as 70 percent of gross economic product in peri-urban areas.)

For example, immediately after 1949, the northeast (centered on the Harbin-Qiqihar Corridor) was the industrial center of the country, given its closeness to the Soviet Union. But by the 1960s, the "Third Line" policy had resulted in massive relocation of heavy and strategic industry to the west, e.g., rural Sichuan. (China feared attacks by the Soviet Union over land and by the U.S. along its coasts.) The opening up during the early 1980s brought the coast into a lead role, starting with the four Special Economic Zones in Guangdong Province (Pearl River Delta) and Fujian Province. By the 1990s, the action had moved up the coast to the lower Yangtze Delta (Shanghai), with the designation of Shanghai as the "gateway to China" in 1992. From 2006 onward, the action shifted to the Beijing–Tianjin–Hebei megapolitan area, again the result of public policy.

At the intra-urban-region scale, policy decisions can play a similarly dramatic role. For example, approximately 80 percent of urban manufacturing (former work units) has not only been dispersed out of core cities since 1980, usually to surrounding peri-urban areas, but has also been concentrated in Economic and Technological Development Zones (ETDZs) or High-Technology Development Zones (HTDZs). Decisions about where to locate these massive zones can play a dramatic role in reshaping an extended urban region. Over the same period, large institutions—major universities, municipal and provincial government complexes, health clusters—have also been dispersed, dramatically influencing metropolitan spatial arrangements.

Accordingly, it is difficult to forecast land use in, and the physical form of, Chinese urban regions. Deep local knowledge is needed. Conventional modeling techniques, including agent-based models, have significant limitations under such conditions. However, certain infrastructure drivers, such as expressways, do exert rather predictable effects. As the market plays a larger role in city-building, moreover, the future form of Chinese cities may become easier to forecast.

The View from Above

China's urbanization can be viewed from the bottom up, that is, as a set of *cities proper, county-level cities,* etc. This was the way Chinese officials and academics viewed the Chinese urban system until approximately ten years ago. In other words, a *county-level* city of 500,000 was viewed as a self-contained midsized city, even if it was an integrated component of an urban system containing millions, or even tens of millions, of people. Now, the Chinese urban system is increasingly viewed from the top down by both the national government and leading Chinese urban analysts; it is defined by functional linkages as a set of *metropolitan* areas (usually defined by municipal boundaries which considerably exceed the built-up area, as in other communist states such as Vietnam). Of late, the perspective has widened further, with *megapolitan* regions, composed of at least two metropolitan areas (which invariably cross *municipal* and often *provincial* boundaries),[3] as an increasingly important geographic unit of analysis. This paper focuses on the metropolitan scale, although both metropolitan areas assessed, Xi'an and Tianjin, are in embedded in megapolitan regions as described by figure 13.1.

Drivers of Form in the Chinese City-Building Process

The macro drivers of China's metropolitan and megapolitan development include rural-urban migration focused on a limited number of destinations (Chan and Hu 2003); concentrated foreign and domestic

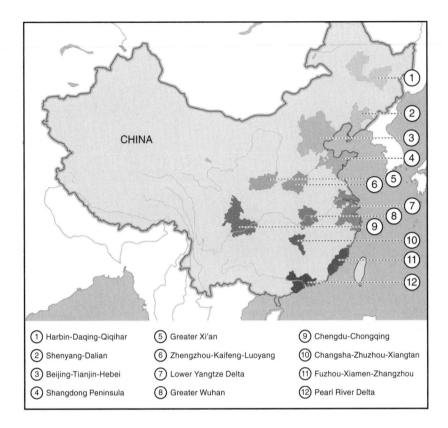

Figure 13.1. Megapolitan China

Source: Cai Jianming, Chinese Academy of Science.

investment in manufacturing in peri-urban areas spurred by the dynamics of the international division of labor (Duranton and Puga 2004); the rise of new tertiary activities (Yusuf and Nabeshima 2006); massive construction of expressway systems (Liu and Smith 2006); and the rush of talent (and investment) to cities offering more or better amenities, be they climate, scenery, or environmental quality (Webster and Muller 2004). These drivers are mediated by top-down national directives and municipal policies as noted above.

Establishing reasonable estimates of future urban-region land-use demand by function is possible. Figure 13.2 describes the current land-use allocation system in China. It reflects the fact that market forces play a larger role on the demand side than the supply side under current city-building processes in China. Most land released by local govern-

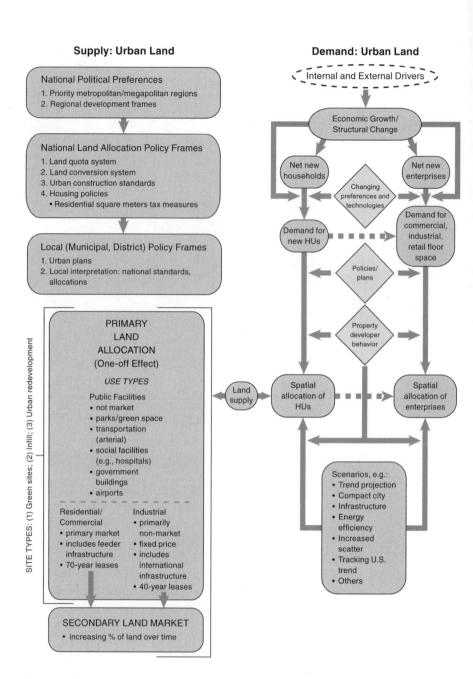

Supply: Urban Land

National Political Preferences
1. Priority metropolitan/megapolitan regions
2. Regional development frames

National Land Allocation Policy Frames
1. Land quota system
2. Land conversion system
3. Urban construction standards
4. Housing policies
   • Residential square meters tax measures

Local (Municipal, District) Policy Frames
1. Urban plans
2. Local interpretation: national standards, allocations

PRIMARY
LAND
ALLOCATION
(One-off Effect)

USE TYPES

Public Facilities
• not market
• parks/green space
• transportation (arterial)
• social facilities (e.g., hospitals)
• government buildings
• airports

Residential/ Commercial
• primary market
• includes feeder infrastructure
• 70-year leases

Industrial
• primarily non-market
• fixed price
• includes international infrastructure
• 40-year leases

SECONDARY LAND MARKET
• increasing % of land over time

SITE TYPES: (1) Green sites; (2) Infill; (3) Urban redevelopment

Demand: Urban Land

Internal and External Drivers

Economic Growth/ Structural Change

Net new households

Net new enterprises

Changing preferences and technologies

Demand for new HUs

Demand for commercial, industrial, retail floor space

Policies/ plans

Property developer behavior

Land supply

Spatial allocation of HUs

Spatial allocation of enterprises

Scenarios, e.g.:
• Trend projection
• Compact city
• Infrastructure
• Energy efficiency
• Increased scatter
• Tracking U.S. trend
• Others

Figure 13.2. Urban Land Allocation System, China

Source: D. Webster and S. Guhathakurta.

ments (the *primary land market*) is still not the subject of open lowest-bidder auction processes, despite national regulations encouraging such processes (Bertaud et al.).[4] Primary market land can be allocated through auction or bidding (invited bidders are judged on the merits of their proposed development—often against existing conceptual plans—as well as on bid price). Industrial land, however, has tended to be provided, through negotiation, free or at very low cost to ETDZs and HTDZs controlled by local governments (usually municipalities), or even to freestanding factories. However, in 2005, national regulations were put forward to curb this practice.

As seen in figure 13.2, on the supply side, local governments release land (the primary land market) within the context of three nested sets of policy frameworks. At the national level, certain geographic areas are given preference, such as access to credit and land quotas, as explained above. Also at the national level, administrative measures, including land quotas and rural-urban land conversion criteria, are promulgated by the Ministry of Land and Resources, and are enforced, to varying degrees, down the vertical hierarchy of governments. Below that, local governments, with municipal governments exerting the most power, especially in western China, formulate master plans (which are differentially enforced nationwide) and decide (in consultation with the provincial and national governments for large projects) on the spatial allocation of public investment. Primary land allocation, through forty- to seventy-year leases (the municipality is the key actor) covers (1) peripheral "green field" and rural collective land; (2) infill (vacant and precleared sites); and (3) designated urban redevelopment sites (to be cleared). In turn, property on land allocated through the primary market may later be resold, creating a secondary property market similar to that in the U.S., characterized by higher churn for residential properties.

Given that China's urban economy is experiencing accelerating structural change, demand and location preferences for floor space for manufacturing, service, and residential uses will continue to change rapidly. Demand for more floor space by households is expected to continue, although at a decelerating rate; over the past twenty-five years, the per-person consumption of residential floor space has increased from 3.6 to 18 m². The service sector is expected to be the area of greatest change over the next decade. New business and producer services that did not exist in China—advertising and management consulting—are being created at a rapid pace, and new types of commercial and mixed-use space—lifestyle-oriented, themed shopping malls and tourism complexes—are being built. At the same time, office workers and retailers demand more space. The third important variable affecting demand is access—that is, the availability of different modes of transportation and the preference for using cars to commute (as in North America) versus reserving them primarily for leisure travel (as in Japan and Europe). A fourth major factor is the behavior of land developers. Developers, especially more cosmopolitan ones like those from Hong Kong, introduce new products such as "live-work" loft residential units, which change consumers' perspectives and demand.

Determining how future floor space demand (by use category) will be manifest in spatial patterns is especially difficult since official spatial plans have limited future explanatory power (Schneider et al. 2003; Schneider, Seto, and Webster 2005a). Furthermore, lifestyles are changing rapidly, as are urban economic structures, expressed in changing location preferences in the former case and impacting spatial outcomes in the latter. A scenario approach is the best route forward. Different future scenarios could be developed based on consumer preferences, public policies, and market prices; examples include (1) a status quo/trend scenario, (2) a compact-city scenario, (3) a scenario tracking the U.S. trajectory, and (4) an infrastructure/energy efficiency scenario. Depending on which scenarios best explain the future, efficiency impacts will vary widely. For example, a dense city will use different building materials and have different energy characteristics than a sprawling city (Goldstein and Watson 2002). Similarly, different urban form scenarios will result in different levels, rates, and patterns of rural-urban land conversion.

Xi'an: China's Compact City

Although Xi'an's urban economy is still largely state driven, new drivers, such as software, higher education, and related high-tech activity, are to a large extent reinforcing core-oriented development rather than fueling centrifugal forces. The result is that Xi'an is one of the only major urban regions—along with Wuhan, another interior urban region with similar economic and spatial dynamics—where the built-up density is essentially not decreasing.[5] Most of the new economy (high tech, education, tourism, energy) is core centered, being dependent on access to talent and knowledge services. The strong centripetal orientation can be explained by walled-city ambience and access to hotels in the case of tourism, proximity to the knowledge institutions (particularly leading universities) in the case of high tech, access to business and producer services in the case of the oil/gas cluster (located in the Weiyang area just north of the city wall), historical railroad access in the case of textiles and machinery, and the slow dispersal of traditional industry relative to most other Chinese cities. The only strong drivers of peripheral development is aerospace, located in the Yanliang satellite city and to a lesser extent in the airport corridor. However, even in the case of the aerospace, of the 200,000 new jobs forecast to be created by 2020, 80,000 will be in the core city.

Drivers of Urban Form

The unattractiveness of Xi'an to foreign direct investment (FDI) in the post-1980 period has been a key factor shaping the city's structure—both economically and spatially. Xi'an—perceived as a land-locked, polluted, state-enterprise-dominated city—has had little FDI. This lack of FDI had a major impact on Xi'an's current spatial structure, given that industrialization has been the main driver of peri-urbanization in China.[6] The peri-urban area is industrialized, with 57 percent of peri-urban economic product from manufacturing—thus the lack of importance of Xi'an's peri-urban economy (relative to most other Chinese metropolitan areas) is not related to its economic structure per se, but rather to lack of scale. The lack of scattered peri-urbanization, combined with the centripetal bias of its emerging economy, explains Xi'an's compactness.

The close correlation between economic function and urban form in Xi'an has been reinforced by the fact that the city's development over the last twenty-five years has been driven by seven major special development zones. Essentially, these zones have replaced large-scale work units, the primary building blocks of the city during the planned economy period. Three of these special zones (the XHTDZ, the ETDZ, and the Aircraft Industry Zone) together account for 27.2 percent of the economic product of the municipality.

Special Economic Zones—quasi-autonomous institutions created by the municipality—have special strong powers to make master plans, allocate land, and grant investment approvals, literally within days. This contrasts with the relatively weak spatial planning at the metropolitan level, which tends to focus on site development, rather than the macro strategic level.

Because the special zones tend to compete with each other, the city is developing as a set of relatively uncoordinated modules, leaving "orphan" areas not included in the special zones to stagnate, although this is starting to change with the emergence of *self-organizing* spatial clusters in parts of the city. For example, each special zone attempts to create its own urban center, often resulting in duplication of function and dilution of each subcenter's importance.

Spatial Dynamics: Xi'an's Future Development

Looking into the future, Xi'an's spatial development is likely to be driven by the following key drivers.

1. The emergence of a strong software cluster in the Xi'an High Technology Development Zone, established as a national zone in 1991, to the immediate southwest of the walled city. This zone ranks second in China in terms of HTDZ employment. It accounts for one-fifth of municipal economic output and 280,000 jobs (about 40 percent of which are high-quality, high-end jobs), and has 70,000 residents. The XHTDZ has become so dominant that it is constructing a new central business district (CBD) in the zone, with Greenland Property developers of Shanghai playing the lead private-sector role. Within the XHTDZ, software development is especially important, and is expected to grow rapidly, with the value of production increasing from 4.9 to 30 billion RMB between 2003 and 2020, and employment increasing from 40,000 to 200,000.

2. Growth to the north will be driven by the manufacturing-oriented Xi'an Economic and Technological Development Zone, which consists of two components: a suburban center close to the northern wall, where the municipal government will move from within the walled city, and the Jingwei Heavy Industry industrial zone further north, emerging as a center for the manufacture of heavy vehicles and oil field equipment.

3. Tourism has emerged as a major component of the economy (Xi'an attracts over 23 million tourists per year, of whom approximately 750,000 are foreign), centered on the walled city as well as the Terracotta Warriors and the Tang Dynasty Huqing Lake summer palace sites near Lintong to the east. Tourism is contributing to pressures to redevelop the city's historic core. In addition, it has driven the creation of the Lintong Tourism Corridor, defined by an expressway that connects the city to the Terracotta Warriors site. Most tourists base themselves in or near the walled city and travel out to the Terracotta Warriors; thus the net impact of tourism is centripetal.

4. The continued strength of the oil industry (Xi'an is the third most important petroleum cluster in China) is driving the Weiyang Business Corridor, located immediately north of the wall's North Gate. High-rise corporate buildings of Petro China, Sinopec, etc., plus associated hotels and business services, are contributing to the dynamism of this corridor, which is located between the northern wall and the suburban center anchored by the municipal government. Interestingly, the Weiyang Business Corridor has emerged through self-organizing dynamics, outside the special zones.

5. The organic, or self-organizing, rise of a business subcenter,

anchored by the Chang'An financial complex and two five-star hotels, immediately outside the South Gate of the wall.

6. More typically, the high-end residential district, which Xi'an has lacked to date, is being developed under the Special Economic Zone model. It is situated in Qujiang New District, along the southern arc of the beltway (third ring road) and proximate to the university and research district, the XHTDZ, and civic and leisure facilities.

7. The growth of a large aerospace economy in Yanliang (in the northeast peri-urban area), which employs 60,000 workers and houses 100,000 residents, anchors peri-urban development to the northwest of the built-up city. However, this cluster zone, anchored by this state enterprise, is facing strong competition from emerging aerospace centers such as Harbin (Embraer) and Tianjin (Airbus), as it attempts to place more emphasis on civil aircraft through international joint ventures.

Income Distribution and Urban Characteristics

Of particular note is the relatively uniform nature of the urban environment in terms of design quality, local densities, mix of uses, etc. There are few distinctive neighborhoods and relatively low levels of socioeconomic residential segregation. In part, this reflects a relatively low level of income inequality compared with other Chinese cities, thanks to significant state control of the urban economy.[7] (As late as 2003, only 28 percent of the urban economy was in the private sector; Xi'an was one of the last cities in China to become an open city, in 1992.) Although positive from an equity perspective, this situation has a related downside in that distinctive "up market" urban neighborhoods and a vital (day and night) CBD have failed to develop. The situation is exacerbated by high levels of air pollution and a harsh climate, constraining the desired shift to a high-tech economy, which demands increased amenities. Unless the city as a whole, and some of Xi'an's neighborhoods in particular, are made more livable, further rapid restructuring to a higher-quality economy is likely to be stymied. While in some senses a positive factor, low property values, even for high-end residential properties (<6,000 RMB per square meter), constrain the development of high-end communities (though this is starting to change with the development of the up-market Qujiang New District).

Between 2001 and 2007 urban and rural incomes within the municipality have grown at almost an identical pace, so that relative spatial disparity has remained the same. Rural incomes were 37 percent of urban (core city) incomes in 2005.[8] Higher incomes are associated with central city location, with very little change in the relationship over time; by 2003 urban incomes were 1.43 times suburban incomes, a slight decline from 1.51 in 1990. However, if we use the ratio of mean-to-median income as a crude indicator of income inequality,[9] the ratio has increased in the core area from 1.08 in 1990 to 1.5 in 2003. In other words, the core urban area appears to be experiencing increased household inequality and is more unequal than the suburban area (a ratio of 1.22 in 2003). This is not unexpected; Chinese households, in general, still prefer to live in the central city (unlike in much of the United States), so those with money generated during Xi'an's recent economic transformation are likely to live in high-quality *pocket* developments in the core city near better middle schools, parks, and restaurant districts, and to intermix there with long-term residents, the latter often with lower incomes.

Housing is considerably less expensive in suburban and peri-urban areas than in the urban area. In 2003 (the last year for which complete data are available), suburban housing costs (per square meter) were 59 percent of urban housing costs, while peri-urban housing costs were only 43 percent of urban housing costs. In other words, consumers can save on housing costs by moving to the periphery but, in doing so, they generally lose status, have to cope with poor public transportation or high vehicle operating costs (including increasing fuel costs), and face higher crime rates. There are similarities to the U.S. situation where potential buyers often drive outward until they qualify for a mortgage.

Chinese cities are remarkable in the developing world in that they do not, with minor exceptions, contain squatter housing or self-constructed slums. However, they do contain sizeable areas of aging substandard housing, typically seven- to eight-story buildings. In addition, substandard "farmers'" housing is found in peri-urban areas. Substandard urban housing in Xi'an (and nationwide) is generally poorly constructed, often dating from the 1950s, 1960s, and 1970s, particularly just before and after the Cultural Revolution.[10] Since economic take-off came late to Xi'an, and there is relatively limited capital for urban redevelopment (from both the public and private sectors), Xi'an has more substandard housing than most Chinese metropolitan areas, with a few exceptions such as Zhengzhou.

In Xi'an, redevelopment of substandard areas has been under way over the last decade, although high relocation and compensation costs now threaten to slow several urban renewal processes indicated below. In central Xi'an, large-scale urban redevelopment (to replace substandard housing) has already occurred, affecting 3.3 percent of the urban population (95,565 people) and 12.2 percent of the land area. This drops off to 1.5 percent of the population (35,242 people) and 0.9 percent of the land area in the suburban area and to 0.8 percent of the population (17,008 people) and 0.4 percent of the land area in the peri-urban area.

Market Incentives and the Growth of Civil Society

It is not financially feasible for private developers, under market conditions, to redevelop the historical walled city in a manner respecting the area's heritage. Growth of population in deteriorated worker housing from the 1960s and 1970s, often informally modified, within the walled city, combined with increased informal neighborhood organization (growth of civil society), has dramatically increased the cost of relocating existing residents and altered the municipal government's plans to move 200,000 people out of the walled city to undertake heritage restoration. The implication is that new mechanisms for urban redevelopment (land readjustment, for example) that better align the interests of developers and current residents need to be implemented in Xi'an and China as a whole, creating win-win situations. Other Chinese cities such as affluent Qingdao—trying, so far without success, to restore its historical Zhongshan (former treaty port) area utilizing market-based approaches—face a similar situation.

Lack of Sustainable Municipal Finance

In Xi'an, off-budget revenues, the dominant source being from land lease transactions, constitute more than 25 percent of official revenues. Because land taxes have been growing at a slightly faster rate than overall revenues (11.8 percent versus 9 percent overall during this decade), their share of on-budget revenues has increased from 11 percent to 12.5 percent. However, if we include land lease revenues (off budget), assumed to be in the range of $250 million U.S. in fiscal 2005, land development accounts for approximately 29 percent of Xi'an's revenue. The city-building process is highly important to Xi'an's revenue generation. However, because city-building, especially on the periphery, entails high costs to the municipal government (developers do not pay impact fees so the municipality is responsible for providing access roads, sanitation infrastructure, etc., financed from land lease revenues), it is not clear that land lease revenues cover the real costs of city-building, especially when the costs of maintaining infrastructure systems are included.

Implications: Actors

As indicated by the Xi'an case, Chinese cities contain both areas that are highly planned, like the Special Economic Zones, and areas that are developing more organically, such as the business clusters emerging just outside Xi'an's north and south gates. Economic function significantly determines the overall form of the city, much more so than, for example, in Latin American cities such as Quito, where residential preferences and effective demand of the rich, the middle class, and the poor play a much more dominant role in shaping urban form. In Xi'an the rise of the software and tourism clusters are contributing to the strength of centripetal forces, while the lack of FDI is manifest in a relatively subdued level of peri-urban development. In general, the role of the state is declining in city-building, whereas the role of private property developers and civil society is increasing. The latter is indicated by the important role of organized local residents in determining the fate of urban redevelopment within the walled city. As the market economy becomes more important, the impacts of more inequitable income distribution are being manifest in physical form, even in a city such as Xi'an, which came late to the market economy.

Tianjin: Embedded in China's New Priority Megapolitan Region

Tianjin Municipality contains approximately 10.75 million people; a former treaty port, it is a leading global container port, ranked ninth in the world in throughput. Its economy has been stagnant until recently but is currently taking off, in part because of its designation as the "new coastal agglomeration," as expressed in the National Eleventh Five-Year Development Plan and, in part, because of closer integration with the Beijing metropolitan area. Reflecting this policy decision, a new coastal manufacturing and port city, the Binhai New Area, is being built in Tianjin Municipality.

Land Efficiency Dynamics

Tianjin is increasingly becoming an integrated component of the Beijing-Tianjin-Hebei megapolitan area, with its spatial form and transportation system being shaped by *megapolitan*-scale flows. A second expressway (private concession/toll) connects Tianjin and Beijing, and the high-speed rail (HSR) system that began operations in 2007 has reduced the trip from Tianjin to Beijing to approximately thirty minutes. The impacts will likely result in both metropolitan areas becoming more specialized; Tianjin's CBD is expected to lose some high-end services and become more specialized residentially (attracting those seeking more sedate lifestyles) while gaining in its share of manufacturing (particularly in the Binhai New Area).

Given the increased importance of manufacturing in Tianjin, the Binhai New Area (2,270 km²) will attract over half the public investment in Tianjin Municipality over the next five years (1,170 billion RMB). (The eight functional zones identified for immediate development total 400 km²) A very strong corridor is emerging between the central Binhai New Area (Tanggu) and Tianjin's current CBD; the corridor is served by an operating light rapid transit (LRT), three expressways, and numerous highways. Figure 13.3, based on Google Earth imagery, describes the form of the Tianjin metropolitan region and current land use.

Densities

Tianjin Municipality is expected to experience slow demographic growth of about 1.1 percent annually. At present, approximately 4.3 million live in the core city (within the third ring road), an area of 340 km² (not including the greenbelt), generating an overall density of 12,647 people per km². It is forecast that 4.7 million people will live within the third ring road in 2020, implying a density increase to 13,824 people per km². This density increase will be supported by a planned 230 kilometers of metro (subway plus LRT) lines within the third ring road by 2020.

While density in the core will increase, as will densities in the planned eleven new towns (essentially, the existing county-level towns) and the thirty smaller towns that will become officially urban (tripling floor area ratios (FARs) in their built-up areas), overall density of urban development beyond the third ring road will be much lower than in the core.[11] In part, this reflects fragmented land development processes on the periphery.

If the municipality gains approximately 3 million people by 2020, with essentially all of this increase urban,[12] and if it adds 389 km² of new built-up urban land (based on municipal forecasts), and we subtract out the 0.4 million who will be added to the core, *the 2020 densities in the new areas urbanized will be 6,684 people per km²* in 2020, or 48 percent of 2020 core area densities. By global standards new development will remain relatively dense, although the density of the new urban fabric will be halved, an outcome largely explained by the development of the Binhai New Area. Over half of the municipality's incremental urban population will be added to the central Binhai New Area—it is forecast to be home to 1.6 million people by 2020. In the central Binhai New Area, densities will be approximately 4,000 persons per km² in 2020, although this is a somewhat misleading measure given the high space requirements of contemporary just-in-time industries. However, it also reflects the underpricing of industrial land in China. Furthermore, a high percentage of

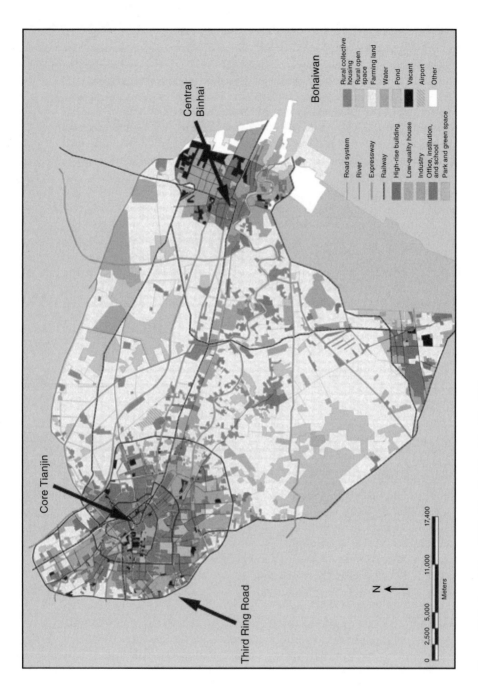

Figure 13.3. Land Use, 1997, Tianjin Municipality, China

Source: Y. Zhenshan for World Bank.

land (approximately one-third) will be in green space or covered by water, e.g., ponds in parks—an ostensibly "green" environment, but one that may exert environmental costs through lower densities.

As in most new towns throughout China (but not including the Zhengdong New District in Zhengzhou), densities in Binhai will be much lower than in the traditional built-up city. In part, this is a reflection of the industrial land-use effect. However, even controlling for this and other factors, densities will be dramatically lower than in the core city. The impact is partially ameliorated by the fact that most of the land to be urbanized is highly saline, reclaimed from the sea, and of little value agriculturally.

Rural-Urban Land Conversion

Based on Land Resources Bureau statistics, Tianjin currently contains 4,456 km² of officially protected *basic agricultural land*.[13] Essentially, none of this land is available for urbanization under present policies and administrative guidelines. Accordingly, it is forecast by the Land Resources Bureau that the amount of cultivated land will remain essentially the same in 2020: 4,371 km². New urban land will be converted from land classified as *other*, totaling 1,882 km², plus some infilling of the ocean. If land continues to be converted to urban uses at the rate forecast for the 2005–2020 period, all *other* land will be converted to urban uses in seventy-three years. The nature of land conversion or urban construction would then have to change dramatically, either by consuming *basic agricultural land* or accommodating all future urban growth through densification. However, the situation is likely to be less dire than implied, as population growth and urbanization will dramatically level off (and decline in some urban areas) by midcentury in China. Furthermore, it is expected that land will continue to become available for urban redevelopment (recycling) as the city's urban fabric ages.

Land Fragmentation

Figure 13.4, a satellite image, illustrates land fragmentation in the northern periphery of the city resulting from a variety of causes, significantly including mechanistic adherence to *basic agricultural land* regulations. High-rise residential buildings are progressively replacing villages outside the third ring road, while large pockets of agricultural land are left undeveloped within the third ring road itself. This is a very costly practice, as utility networks and transport lines have to be extended, bypassing large pockets of empty land. It is clear from the image that the

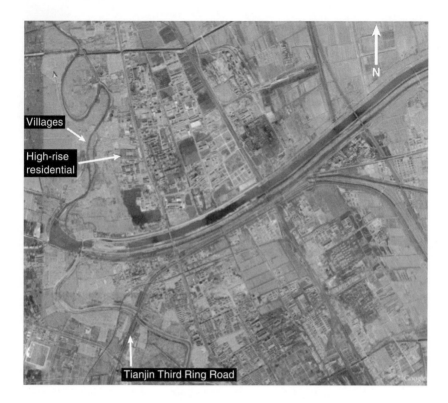

Figure 13.4. Fragmented Land Use, Vicinity of Third Ring Road, Tianjin, China

Source: Google Earth imagery.

productivity of the agricultural enclaves within the third ring road must be greatly reduced by the lack of access for agricultural machinery, distortions to the irrigation system, etc. Although the underlying principles of the Basic Agricultural Land Protection Regulations are valid, present practices lower both agricultural and urban productivity.

Transportation Characteristics

Tianjin is a unique city in transportation terms.[14] It has been slow to embrace the private automobile, despite its relative prosperity. It may have the potential to leapfrog from bicycles/walking to buses/rapid transit, acting as a model city. It is the number one city for the use of bicycles in China. Its monocentric structure—now becoming bipolar with the development of Binhai New Area—supports alternatives to motorization.

In 2005, there were only 480,000 private cars in Tianjin (4.6 households per car),[15] while, at the same time, nine metro lines were operating or planned (in the National Eleventh Five-Year Development Plan) within the third ring road.[16] A central stacked intermodal transport facility, opened in July 2008, is likely to reinforce Tianjin's monocentric structure.[17] Significantly, public transportation is being put in ahead of development in the Binhai area. By 2010, Tianjin hopes to have a 30 percent bus mode share (currently 12 percent).

Infill Potential

There is moderate amount of infill land available within the city proper (figure 13.3). If developed at reasonably high densities, it could play a significant role in reducing pressures on the periphery. We have identified 28.4 km² in the city proper with potential for infill. This represents 9.7 percent of the land area within the third ring road.[18] If the 28.4 kilometers of land were developed at the densities expected to obtain within the ring road in 2020 (13,824 per km²), the land could accommodate 392,600 people.[19] However, if these infill sites were strategically developed as high-density nodes at the highest prevailing densities (47,000 per km², found in Tianjin's Heping District), they could accommodate 1,335,000 people.

Assuming a middle range infill absorption number of 700,000 people, this would be equivalent to 23 percent of all municipal population growth to 2020. If developed at this density (which is high but still does not compare to Hong Kong), existing potential infill land could accommodate 45 percent of all population growth to 2020, while at the same time significantly improving the cost-effectiveness of rapid transit systems, lowering infrastructure costs, etc.

As is generally the case in China, FARs are not assigned in the urban (master) plan; rather they are determined project by project at the detailed planning level. In Tianjin, within the third ring road, there are 176 detailed planning areas,[20] where FARs are worked out on an ad hoc basis (developers negotiating with the local government, for example).

This situation does not maximize returns to transport systems because it discourages nodality. The objective should be transit-oriented development: greater variance in FARs in Tianjin and other Chinese metropolitan regions, with high FARs near transit stations to encourage high levels of office employment, residential densities, and retail/services.

Implications: Land Efficiency

In Tianjin and even more in Xi'an, given its higher densities, basic agricultural land does not, even under status quo (trend) scenarios, need to be encroached on. Enough *other* land is available until at least the late twenty-first century. Urban built-up land of the 268 prefecture-level cities in China in 2005 constituted only 0.26 percent of China's land area. Officially defined cities proper, which considerably over-bound actual built-up areas, constituted 6.2 percent of China's land area.[21] And, after midcentury, urban population growth will level off dramatically. This is not an argument for lower densities, or continued low variance in FARs. However, there may be stronger reasons for promoting efficient urban form than loss of agricultural land, namely rapidly rising costs of energy, transportation-related pollution and greenhouse gas emissions, and loss of human time. Importantly, in China, the cost of human time is likely to rise at a rate similar to, or even faster than, energy costs.

Since Chinese urbanization will level off near midcentury, gains made in developing infill land at relatively high densities can be significant in terms of saving significant amounts of peripheral land into the late twenty-first century, and perhaps in perpetuity, for agricultural, recreational, and environmental services as well as for other uses.

If *basic agricultural land* is protected in a mechanistic manner and land quotas remain in place, it will lead to a new urban form in China. Until the early 1990s, China's cities grew contiguously in virtually all directions; but since then, peripheral development has become patchier, leapfrogging far out from the edge of the built-up area. Although many factors are involved, including construction of intercity expressways and motorization, mechanistic protection of *basic agricultural land* and *land quotas* appear to be significant factors contributing to this *two-ring* pattern of urbanization in China.

The challenge is to steer urbanization away from extensive zones of high agricultural fertility while concentrating urban growth in vectors with lower agricultural fertility and/or environmental services value, even if it means sacrificing some high-capability agricultural land in the designated vectors. Land should be serviced in an orderly, phased manner, moving outward along corridors (infrastructure-led development) with higher densities around mass-transit stops and expressway exits and entrances. This development pattern is known as the *necklace* form and is highly efficient.

Introduction of growth boundaries, such as those employed in Portland, British Columbia, in the Netherlands, and in other locations, should be considered in the Chinese context. The distinction between what is urban and rural is more important than the details of urban land use per se.

Chinese metropolitan areas have high densities by global standards and, as indicated by Tianjin, relatively little vacant land exists in the built-up city. Vacant land in Chinese metropolitan areas is close to the global norm of approximately 8 percent (Shepperd 2008). Thus, it is inevitable that considerable land will need to be developed on the periphery of Chinese cities over the next fifty years. At the same time, peripheral development is becoming less efficient. Spatial outcomes on the periphery are a product of a policy environment that leads to targeting (legal or illegal) of "farm villages" (rural collective villages) for redevelopment because their conversion is not counted against land quotas and they are not considered to occupy *basic agricultural land*. Considerable land in the *other* category almost always exists in large quantities around Chinese cities, and it should be developed first. Automatic targeting of existing "rural" villages, given their preexisting scattered spatial patterns, becomes reflected in the city's outward expansion.

The development of civil society, evident, for example, in the formation of informal neighborhood groups, is making it more difficult for the public sector to redevelop areas in need of urban renewal and to rationally develop on the periphery of cities. The growth of civil society is a desirable trend. However, as indicated by the case of Xi'an's walled city, the rise of civil society means that new mechanisms need to be initiated, such as land readjustment, to enable situations to benefit all parties—existing residents, the government, and developers—and free land for public purposes and/or to upgrade the quality of life.

Although densities are high in the built-up city, densities and FARs do not vary to the degree one would expect with properly functioning land markets. *Nodality* is not occurring to the degree expected under market conditions. (For example, in cities such as Bangkok, other factors being held constant, property within 500 meters of rapid transit stations sells for between 30 and 100 percent more than otherwise comparable land and property.) The current situation in China has serious implications in terms of ridership and the financial viability of rapid transit systems. Lack of policy support to *nodality* also constrains investment by qualified investors who could create highly livable, high-profile, high-density communities in CBDs and other prominent nodes. Higher FARs aligned with high-access conditions would also result in lower unit infrastructure costs—we estimate at least 30 percent lower (Bertaud, Webster, and Cai 2007); the facilitation of vital innovation and leisure/entertainment environments; savings in human time; energy and emission savings; and affordable housing.

A hierarchy of FARs should be planned—from highest to lowest: (1) intersections of rapid transit rail systems and HSR megapolitan rail systems (usually in the CBD); (2) intersections of rapid transit rail lines; and (3) "normal" rail stations.

There should be much greater variance in FARs. For example, in large

U.S. cities these may vary from 0.5 to 18 (as in New York City). In China, the range is much narrower, between 1 and 3, typically about 1.8. Higher FARs or no FARs in areas with high accessibility will enable transportation infrastructure to be self-financing. Urban plans should indicate FARs, rather than their being designated on a project-by-project basis in detailed plans.

State subsidies are often targeted to land, especially in industrial areas and new districts; if such subsidies were *selectively targeted to transportation systems instead*, with land being leased at market value, a more efficient pattern of urban development would emerge, driven to a greater extent by market drivers. New development areas, e.g., Binhai, are often the least efficient in use of land. Ironically, this is often because large amounts of land are designated as green space, often in inefficient, e.g., rectangular, shapes.

There is considerable variation in the role of markets by type of land use and history of urban development in an area. Key stakeholders, including local governments, state enterprises, property developers, bankers, and consumers appear to not be fully aware of the present discounted value of accessibility and other amenities. This results in the underpricing of land with significant location or amenity advantages. Industrial land is allocated outside the market, resulting in wasteful use. Close to 22 percent of built-up urban land in Tianjin is devoted to manufacturing (slightly lower than the 25.7 percent of Chinese urban built-up land is devoted to manufacturing); compared with 6.9 percent in Seoul (a comparable case), and even lower percentages in Western Europe and North America.[22] On the other hand, the new apartment market is buoyant and relatively efficient. However, old housing blocks, although privately owned, may not reflect market forces. Often work-unit housing was sold to employees at below-market price with constraints (prohibiting, for example, sale within five years) reducing market liquidity. Furthermore, typical of East Asia as a whole, the reluctance of consumers to purchase used housing constrains the efficiency of urban property markets.

Public-private partnerships and land readjustment should be considered by Chinese authorities to take advantage of access to create high-quality nodal developments. There are many East Asian examples, particularly from Japan, of effective use of land readjustment and public-private partnerships.

Given the high economic and financial value of land in China, green-space planning should emphasize linear parks, which maximize perimeters, and thus household access to parks. Greenbelts should be avoided as they increase commuting costs enormously—as the built-up area expands, traffic must jump over them. Rather, green wedges, as in Chengdu's and Wuhan's new plans, which follow ecological systems, e.g., river valleys, are superior both in land-use efficiency and ecological terms.

Awareness of the high quality of life achievable at high densities should be spread to city-building officials throughout China. A well-designed community, designed by leading architects, with a high FAR, e.g., 8, containing high-rises, gardens, schools, recreational facilities, and convenience services, will deliver a higher quality of life than a typical 1960s–1970s six-story walk-up neighborhood with an FAR one-quarter as high.

Last, but not least, the dependency on land lease revenue, almost invariably paid up front by developers, encourages governments to release more land than may be optimal. An alternative strategy would be to hold out for higher prices by releasing less, as Hong Kong does. Excess release of land may discourage densification and nodality.

Given the lack of property tax, local governments favor manufacturing activity (which generates shared corporate and excise tax) over residential and other uses. Since local officials are still (though decreasingly so) evaluated to a significant extent on the GDP growth in their jurisdictions, local officials chase manufacturing. As a result, industrial land (economic zones) proliferates in Chinese urban regions and is found in virtually every jurisdiction (city districts, counties, townships, etc.) within the municipality, often to the detriment of real economic efficiency (impeding economic cluster development and causing inefficient commuting along with higher logistics costs) and amenities (juxtaposing industrial and residential land uses) (Webster, Cai, and Maneepong 2006).

Conclusions

A variety of actors shape Chinese cities with their relative powers shifting rapidly. In general, in areas where market forces operate, e.g., in the residential market, relatively dense development is the result. However, policy frameworks often do not create incentive structures that maximize land efficiency. Of particular concern in this regard is increasingly scattered peripheral development, the lack of variance in FARs and densities, and inefficient industrial land allocation.

Chapter 14

Financing Housing and Urban Services

Kyung-Hwan Kim

Bertrand Renaud (1987) said that cities are built the way they are financed. The financing of housing and of urban infrastructure and services is crucial to the functioning of cities. Housing finance and urban finance share several characteristics. First, both are instruments that can be used to increase the overall standard of living. The ultimate goal of housing finance lies in improving the overall housing standards of the society and possibly contributing to financial sector development, and that of urban finance lies in providing high-quality urban infrastructure and recurrent services to the residents and businesses. The demand for housing finance derives from the demand for housing, especially owner-occupied housing, and the demand for urban finance comes from that for urban services. These demands are influenced by changing demographics, income, and prices of housing and urban services, respectively.

The second shared characteristic concerns their macroeconomic dimension. Price stability is a precondition for well-functioning long-term mortgage markets, and the stability of housing finance systems affects the stability of housing markets and thus the wider economy. Mismanagement of subnational finance may impair the soundness of public finance and hence macroeconomic stability.

Third, in recent years technology has improved the efficiency of both housing finance and urban finance. The widespread use of credit-scoring techniques and automated underwriting systems facilitates the mortgage loan origination process, while GIS (geographic information system)-aided tax cadastre and mass appraisal help administration of property taxation.

Finally, financial discipline is important in both housing finance and urban finance. The recent U.S. subprime mortgage crisis has demonstrated that the consequences of over-indebtedness of the household sector can posit a systemic risk for the entire financial system and the macroeconomy. Large fiscal deficits and the debts of state and local governments can become a drain on the whole economy. Beyond these similarities, it is also clear that the operations of housing finance and urban finance are closely interrelated. The combination of decent housing finance and inadequate urban finance may lead to housing development without adequate urban services. Improved housing finance makes homeownership feasible for more people, and the increase in owner-occupied houses leads to a larger property tax revenue base that can, in turn, be tapped to maintain and upgrade urban services. This chapter looks at the current state of housing finance and urban finance, keeping their close linkages in mind.[1]

We begin with a common framework for housing finance and urban finance and apply the framework to address the following questions: What is the context in which housing/urban finance operates? What do we know about a well-functioning housing/urban finance system? How do actual practices compare with an optimal or ideal state, and how do they vary across countries and cities? What should be done, and what barriers need to be overcome, to improve the current situation?

Housing Finance

At least two important factors can be identified as defining the context of housing finance. The first concerns the socioeconomic dimension of housing demand. It varies from country to country: the growth of population and household formation remain strong in developing countries, while the aging of the population is proceeding rapidly in many developed countries. The overall growth of income in developing countries will increase the demand for housing of better quality, while changes in income distribution toward a greater concentration of high-income households in particular cities will affect the composition of housing demand. The second factor concerns the fundamental changes that housing finance systems have been going through. Financial deregulation has led to an increase in the number of institutions providing housing finance, and to a wider range of loan products being made available to borrowers. Specialized housing finance circuits have become less important in the housing finance market, as it becomes more closely integrated into the overall financial system. The growing integration of global financial markets and the expansion of cross-border finance have enabled some housing finance institutions to tap international capital markets, though in a limited way.

Some Basic Points

Access to credit is more important than the terms of credit. The reason is simple: if one is denied credit, the terms of credit such as interest rate or loan maturity are irrelevant. This point is most relevant for a housing finance system dominated by a special-circuit housing finance institution which rations below-market-rate mortgages to a fraction of potential borrowers using nonprice criteria, while leaving the vast majority of potential clients unserved altogether. Subsidized special-circuit institutions fail to reach the requisite scale, since they cannot mobilize sufficient amounts of "low-cost" funds without subsidies. Market-based competitive lending offers a more effective alternative to extending credit. Recently, risk-based pricing practice has helped expand access to mortgage credit by providing loans at different prices according to the creditworthiness of borrowers. The effects of this development will be elaborated on later.

Improved housing finance is expected to make homeownership more affordable, but the increased supply of mortgages does not necessarily translate into a higher rate of homeownership. Although the rapid expansion of subprime mortgage finance enabled more than 1 million American households, including low-income and minority groups, to buy their first homes during the latest housing boom (Jaffee 2009), the feat did not last long. A recent study of European countries finds no firm correlation between owner-occupation rates and mortgage penetration rates (Scanlon et al. 2008). In a housing market with inelastic supply, the supply of loans at more favorable terms may not make home purchases more affordable, as the increases in house price can offset the benefits of more affordable finance (Renaud and Kim 2007).

Mortgage Finance

There are some prerequisites for a well-functioning market-based mortgage system. The first one is macroeconomic stability. High and variable inflation rates make long-term mortgage development very difficult. Workable legal systems are required to secure property rights and enforce foreclosures on defaults. Lenders should be allowed to compete on level playing fields, while subsidies should be separated from finance to avoid distortion.

There exist several models of mortgage lending: there are those relying on retail deposit taking (e.g., building societies/savings and loans, commercial banks or savings banks), there are those in which specialized mortgage banks mobilize funds through issuing their own securities, and there are those that fit the originate-to-distribute model with secondary markets through which the ownership of mortgages and the risks associated with them can be transferred to capital market investors (Lea 2009). It is most important to note, however, that there is no single model that suits the needs of every country.

The various models of mortgage lending differ according to the way the four functions of mortgage delivery are organized. The four functions are origination, servicing, risk management, and funding. There is a trend toward unbundling according to the comparative advantages of the relevant institutions. For example, mortgage companies specialize in originating loans, while the secondary mortgage market is utilized for mobilizing long-term capital.

Beginning in the 1980s and continuing throughout the late 1990s and early 2000s, mortgage markets have expanded substantially in both developed and developing countries. Financial deregulation and low inflation have been the key drivers of this expansion. Financial deregulation broadened the base of the housing finance industry, and low inflation led to low interest rates and, hence, to increased demand for mortgages. However, the depth of the mortgage market varies enormously across countries. Figure 14.1 illustrates outstanding mortgage debt as a percentage of gross domestic product (GDP) in various developed and developing countries as of 2006. The sample is concentrated in European countries, but it also includes the U.S., Australia, Japan, China, Indonesia, and Korea. The average for the twenty-seven EU countries is 50 percent. Iceland tops the list with 121 percent, followed by the Netherlands at 100 percent, Denmark at 93 percent, the United Kingdom at 86 percent, Australia at 78 percent, and the U.S. at 77 percent. On the other extreme, the figure is less than 5 percent in Russia, Indonesia, and Serbia. An analysis of a larger global sample of countries reveals that mortgage debt outstanding is less than 1 percent of GDP in some developing countries (Warnock and Warnock 2008).

In addition to the growth in the sizes of the mortgage markets, the range of mortgage options has expanded in recent years as new products have been introduced and mortgage terms modified. For example, interest-only, or "bullet," loans were introduced in Denmark, France, Finland, Australia, the U.S., and Korea. In the United Kingdom, where endowment mortgages, or interest-only loans with a separate vehicle for repaying the principal, have been available for a long time, pure interest-only loans increased substantially over the past decade or so. In the U.S., the new products include payment-option adjustable rate mortgages and piggyback mortgages. Mortgage terms were lengthened in Australia, Denmark, Finland, Greece, Portugal, and the United Kingdom (Bank for International Settlements 2006). A wider range of choices is accompanied by greater risk. For example, borrowers of inter-

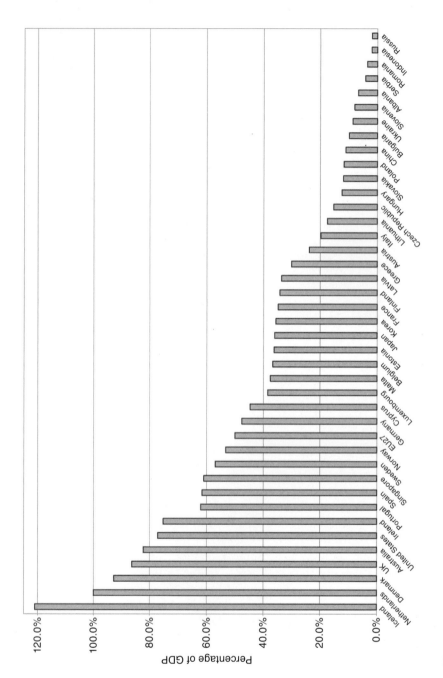

Figure 14.1. Mortgage Debt Outstanding (as a Percentage of GDP)

Source: Warnock and Warnock 2008.

est-only mortgages at variable interest rates are more vulnerable to interest-rate or house-price shocks than borrowers of traditional mortgages. A rise in market interest rate increases the level of payment, and a drop in house price may move the borrower into negative equity since such loans involve no equity build-up (Scanlon et al. 2008). This has been clearly demonstrated by the latest U.S. subprime mortgage crisis.

A new trend in housing finance is risk-based lending. Under this system, most applicants are offered loans at differential rates commensurate with their credit score, although a small fraction of applicants are rejected. One important factor that made this possible in the U.S. was the abolition of the usury laws on first-lien mortgages (Gramlich 2007). The risk-based lending is more efficient and has a potential to reach the larger clientele, but there are dangers from mispricing, principal-agent distortions and asymmetric information problems (Collins et al. 2004).

The subprime mortgage market has grown very rapidly in the U.S. in recent years, especially between 2004 and 2006. But the poor loan quality due to lax origination standards and the design of the hybrid adjustable rate mortgages (ARM) with the initial teaser interest rate that necessitates refinancing or default after two or three years from origination led to a precipitous rise in foreclosures as house prices took a downturn in mid-2006. The subprime mortgage market virtually disappeared after that. Although the consequences of the U.S. subprime mortgage crisis are still unfolding,[2] some important questions emerge from the experience of this apparent failure. They include those about proper regulations and supervision of the lenders and about promoting financial literacy and ensuring consumer protection. But one fundamental question to be asked is how far the market-based housing finance system can go toward increasing homeownership in a sustainable way.

Housing Microfinance

In many developing countries, formal housing finance often fails to serve the low-income clientele, especially those without adequate collateral and verifiable income. An important issue is how to address the housing needs of these potential borrowers. Housing microfinance (HMF), which provides small, short-term loans to support incremental home building and home improvement, has surfaced as a response to this demand. HMF evolved as a spin-off of microfinance for economic livelihood, such that microfinance institutions lend to those who have already borrowed from them and established their credit record by repaying the loans. Table 14.1 compares the main characteristics of HMF with conventional mortgage loans. It shows that the average HMF loan amount is in the range of $1,000 to $2,500 and the loan term aver-

Table 14.1: The Growth of Microcredit Lending

Characteristics	Housing microfinance	Mortgage loans
Target income group	Low-and moderate	Middle to high
Term	Short (less than 5 years) Average 2–3 years	Long (more than 10 years)
Interest rate	inflation plus 15~45% Average 36% p.a.	Inflation plus 8~15%, varies depending on macroeconomic and housing finance market conditions
Loan amount	$250~7,000 Average $1,000~2,500 (ACCIÓN $2,280)	$10,000 and above
Underwriting criteria	Borrower's income and creditworthiness	Borrower's income and creditworthiness Property title and value
Use of loan amounts	Home improvement Progressive building	New construction House purchase
Guarantee	Co-guarantors, some proof of secure tenure	Formal mortgage

Source: Daley-Harris 2009.

ages two to three years. Loans are made based on the evaluation of borrower's income and creditworthiness, and alternative forms of collateral and some proof of tenure security are required.

Housing microfinance has expanded substantially over the past decade as can be inferred from figure 14.2, which is based on the data provided in the Microcredit Summit Campaign Report 2009 (Daley-Harris 2009). The figure shows that the number of verified microcredit institutions increased from 618 to 3,552 between 1997 and 2007. During the same period, the total number of clients increased from 13.5 million to 154.8 million, a more than tenfold increase, while the number of poorest clients reached by these loans increased somewhat faster still, from 7.6 million to 106.6 million.

Despite the impressive performance in terms of the number of programs and the number of clients served, the total size of housing microfinance loans remains very small compared with potential demand. According to a survey of partners of ACCIÓN, a nongovernmental organization operating in Latin America, existing housing activity accounted for only 5.7 percent of the total microfinance portfolio and 2.3 percent of their active clients in 2005, although HMF's share of the total microfinance portfolio went up substantially, from 6.4 percent

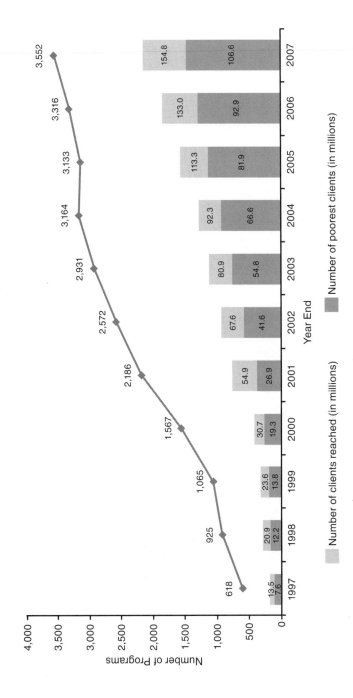

Figure 14.2. Growth of Microcredit, 1997–2007

Source: Daley-Harris 2009.

in 2002 to 11.5 percent in 2005 (Mesarina and Stickney 2007). Considering an estimate that 50 to 80 percent of the population in most emerging countries build their homes progressively, which translates into financing needs exceeding $330 billion worldwide, the total HMF loan volume will be trivial relative to demand even if the remarkable pace of growth continues (Ferguson 2008).

There are several barriers to scale. On the demand side, housing is a low-priority item for some low-income households. On the supply side, lenders tend to favor existing microenterprise clients with good credit history and such clients are relatively few. Given these conditions, the increased scale of HMF might have to come from the overall growth of the microfinance industry as a whole.

Another way by which housing microfinance can go to scale would be through its integration into the mainstream financial sector. Although it is argued that neither funding mismatch nor term mismatch poses serious problems (Mesarina and Stickney 2007), the size of HMF operation will expand substantially as the HMF lenders form partnerships with the formal financial institutions in mobilizing deposits and reaching out to a wider pool of borrowers. Littlefield and Rosenberg (2004) document some efforts for collaboration between microfinance institutions (MFIs) and commercial banks. At a low level of engagement, commercial banks can make wholesale loans to MFIs so that they can on-lend to HMF customers. At a higher level of engagement, commercial banks can make equity investments in MFIs or create microloan service companies. Martin (2008) reports some examples from Peru, where large microfinance institutions have "upscaled" or transformed themselves into commercial banks or where commercial banks have entered the housing microfinance sector. Despite these promising examples, globally speaking, commercial banks remain hesitant to develop the HMF offerings.

Nevertheless, there exist more critical views about housing microfinance. The first one is that HMF fails to reach the poorest of the poor. But even if this is the case, it is currently unclear what better mechanism is available. The second point is that a vacuum exists between the clientele served by HMF institutions and that served by the formal housing finance institutions. This vacuum arises because formal-sector housing finance does not go down market fast enough, and HMF does not go up market to close the gap. In this regard, Hassler (2006) suggests that some grassroots financial institutions with a capacity to mobilize savings, such as credit unions, can serve low-wage earners and informal sector workers with housing loans that are not microcredit (exceeding $2,000) using some guarantees. Such institutions can also tap secondary markets or guarantee funds to mobilize HMF loans.

One final observation about the future of HMF concerns the level of expectation about it. By its very nature, HMF serves the financing needs of low-income households for progressive homebuilding or upgrading. In this context, HMF should not be expected to fill the gap left by the formal housing finance system, which aims at financing home purchases or home construction (Martin 2008).

Rental Housing

In most countries, both general public opinion and government policy favor homeownership over renting. However, it is the case not only that homeownership rates vary greatly across countries in both the developed and developing worlds but that international comparative studies have failed to establish a clear relationship between homeownership rates and per capita income (Gwin and Ong 2004; Fisher and Jaffe 2003). In any case, there is a realistic limit on expanding homeownership in any country, and homeownership may be risky for certain types of households, a lesson clearly taught by the U.S. subprime crisis.

A well-functioning rental housing sector absorbs the pressure of owner occupation by providing a viable alternative to homeownership for those who do not wish to or cannot become homeowners. Rental housing is even more important in developing countries, where housing finance systems are not well developed and the vast majority of would-be home buyers do not qualify for mortgages made by the formal-sector financial institutions.

Although rental housing is financed by various equity and debt instruments in developed countries, it is financed mostly with equity in developing countries. This is, in part, because a large share of rental housing is in the informal sector and investments in the informal rental housing stock are typically financed by landlords (Le Blanc 2009).

Government intervention abounds in rental housing markets even in developed countries. In the case of the U.S., the earliest approach to policy was the direct provision of low-rent public rental housing, but it proved to be a failure. It was then followed by capital grants to support the construction of rental housing. The Low-Income Housing Tax Credit (LIHTC) introduced with the 1986 tax reform is considered quite successful, but it is much more costly than a demand subsidy (Quigley 2008).[3] In fact, a demand-side subsidy in the form of general income support has been advocated by economists. It is well known that the public budget required to attain a given level of consumer satisfaction is smaller for an income subsidy than for an in-kind subsidy. A demand subsidy also provides the beneficiary with more flexibility in choosing the house to rent. Quigley (2008) recommends switching the U.S. program of supply and demand subsidies for rental households to an entitlement program for shelter subsidies, similar to the food stamp program or the Earned Income Tax Credit. He argues that this is a much more efficient way of addressing the problem of the high rental burden of low-income households. But whether such a proposal is politically feasible is unclear, and its applicability to developing countries may be constrained by the fact that the majority of low-income households work in the informal sector and often have incomes that are not easily verifiable (Arnott 2009).

Although a demand subsidy is more efficient than a supply-side approach, it cannot succeed if the supply of rental housing is inelastic. An increase in the demand subsidy in such a market will lead to rising rents. Therefore, in order for rental subsidy reform to be successful, simultaneous efforts should be made to make the supply of housing more elastic. This could be done by removing the various barriers, including the unrealistic building standards and other regulations, which raise the cost of housing.

Urban Finance

The context of urban finance has been changing for several reasons. First, increases in urban population, especially in the developing world, and the aging of the population in developed countries have a significant impact on the nature of the demand for urban services. Second, decentralization of government functions and finances tends to entail greater responsibilities for municipal revenue generation, although decentralization should ideally accompany additional revenue allocation from the central government. Third, globalization puts greater pressure on cities. Major cities around the world are trying to enhance their competitiveness by improving the quality of life for their residents and creating a business environment conducive to existing firms and more attractive to new firms. These efforts involve operation and maintenance, upgrading, and expansion of urban infrastructure and services. Fourth, financial deregulation has opened up new opportunities to tap the capital markets, but this requires that municipalities be bankable.

Some Basic Points

The ultimate goal of improving urban finance is to make cities more livable and competitive, as well as more equitable and inclusive, by providing adequate services. Urbanization generates enormous income and wealth, but many cities have difficulty tapping these resources to finance their services and infrastructure investments. The problem is particularly acute in the developing world for various reasons. Revenue assignment may be obsolete or inadequate to meet expenditure requirements. Collection of taxes and user charges may be poor because taxpayers are not convinced that they get their tax money's worth from local governments. Another important constraint is the existence of the large informal sector in cities in the developing world. Since tax can be levied only on the formal sector, a government's ability to raise taxes is limited by the size of the informal sector (Arnott 2009).

Coordinated efforts are needed to address the financial challenges facing the cities. Cities themselves need to strengthen their capacity to raise revenue from existing sources as well as to explore new revenue sources. Central governments should get the revenue and tax assignments right, grant greater financial autonomy to local governments, and rationalize intergovernmental transfer systems.

Own-Source Revenues

The own-source revenues of a typical local government consist of local taxes and nontax revenues such as user charges. Ideally, user charges should be used to finance services whose beneficiaries are clearly identified, whereas local taxes should be reserved for general services benefiting the general population.[4]

The tax base in a country is shared among all levels of government according to a system of tax assignments that reflects a history of decentralization. Table 14.2 illustrates the indicators of fiscal decentralization on the expenditure and revenue sides, defined as the share of subnational government expenditure and revenue as a percentage of total government expenditure and revenue, respectively. The countries represented in the figure cover both OECD countries and developing countries.[5] The figure exhibits a wide range of both decentralization indicators across countries in the two country groups. It also shows that in most countries represented, expenditure is more decentralized than revenue, implying that the gap between expenditure and own-source revenue should be filled by fiscal transfers from the national government. Moreover, actual control over local taxation might not follow the nominal assignment of taxes because the institutional details of local taxation, such as the authority to set the tax rate and to establish the tax-base assessment, might be restrained by the national government.

Among local taxes, the land tax is the most efficient and equitable. This is the well-known single tax proposition advanced by the nineteenth-century political activist Henry George. A tax levied on land in all uses at the same rate does not cause any distortion and is also equitable since land ownership rises with income. In practice, however, prop-

Table 14.2: Indicators of Fiscal Decentralization

	Expenditure Share	Revenue Share
OECD Countries		
Luxembourg	16.5	6.4
Norway	38.3	20.6
Switzerland	58.2	38.5
Denmark	57.4	30.3
Sweden	41.8	31.0
Ireland	30.1	3.1
UK	29.5	8.6
Finland	43.2	25.8
Austria	33.6	21.3
Netherlands	36.4	2.3
Germany	46.3	29.8
Belgium	12.9	4.9
France	17.5	8.8
Italy	25.0	5.2
Spain	23.7	10.5
Greece	4.2	1.0
Portugal	8.4	3.4
Japan	40.5	39.6
U.S.	51.9	32.1
Canada	68.0	49.0
Australia	50.6	20.7
New Zealand	11.6	6.6
Korea, Rep	41.8	10.5
Argentina	38.2	31.9
Brazil	39.0	27.7
South Africa	33.3	6.4
Developing Countries		
Indonesia	11.3	3.1
Malaysia	7.0	6.5
Thailand	8.0	7.7
Bulgaria	12.5	8.7
Czech Republic	17.3	12.1
Hungary	21.1	14.6
Lithuania	19.1	15.2
Poland	27.5	15.8
Romania	17.9	17.7
Russia	21.6	19.7
Slovakia	35.1	23.4
Bolivia	23.1	23.6
Chile	34.5	24.3
Mexico	41.4	32.6
India	52.0	33.6

Source: Thiessen (2008) for OECD countries, World Bank (2004) for developing countries

erty tax is levied on both land and structures, and at different rates across land-use categories, and hence is not distortion free. The share of property tax out of local government revenue varies substantially across countries. In the U.S., where property tax is also regarded as a benefit tax to finance local public services, property tax is the predominant local revenue source. On the other hand, in the European Union the share varies across countries but is, in general, declining (Dirie 2006). In many developing countries, the property tax remains underutilized. In order to exploit this revenue source more fully, assessments should be updated with tax mapping, and collection efforts should be strengthened.

User charges assessed at full cost of services are an ideal way of financing those services for which beneficiaries are clearly identified and the quantity of usage can be measured accurately. Efficiently administered user charges also serve as a mechanism to manage demand and avoid waste. But there are at least two practical constraints that limit the active utilization of user charges. First, there is a concern that full cost recovery might make basic services such as water unaffordable for the urban poor. On the one hand, some case studies indicate that the urban poor end up paying much more to water vendors than it would cost to pay for the full cost of piped water. Other studies show that subsidies are equivalent to about 3 to 4 percent of income or expenditure of the urban poor, implying that transition to full cost recovery may be painful to some members of this population. A recent World Bank study shows that the feasibility of cost recovery on water varies with income levels (Foster and Yepes 2006).

Second, there is the issue of low willingness to pay by the service users. People may refuse to pay for services for political reasons or out of dissatisfaction with the quality of services provided. This can lead to a vicious cycle: as residents do not pay for municipal services, municipalities fail to recoup sufficient revenue, which in turn leads to deterioration of the quantity and quality of services, lowering the consumers' trust in municipality's ability to provide adequate services and making the consumers even less willing to pay their dues. Municipal governments should effectively communicate to the residents the close linkages between what they pay and what they get. Also, special service districts could be established and the residents permitted to sort themselves out so that they live with people with similar capacity and willingness to pay for services. This might be an efficient approach but would raise equity issues.

Fiscal Transfers and Other Sources

Grants-in-aid or transfers from higher-level government are a major revenue source of local government. The general grants are given by the central government to alleviate vertical imbalances between revenue and expenditure responsibilities or horizontal imbalances across local government bodies. A formula-based general grant with no strings attached to it can arguably be considered almost equivalent to local own-source revenue. Specific grants are provided to stimulate local spending on particular services, but matching requirements could impose a financial burden on the recipient local government.

There are some additional sources of revenue for urban finance. For example, Chinese cities generate substantial revenue for infrastructure finance from the leasing and sale of land. Introduced on an experimental basis in 1987 in Shenzhen and other coastal cities, land leasing or the up-front sale of long-term (forty to seventy years) occupancy and development rights have become a major source of urban infrastructure financing. Since the supply of municipality-owned land is limited, land leasing is a transitional financing strategy for infrastructure investments. In fact, those Chinese cities that pioneered land leasing have become more dependent on the income streams provided by infrastructure assets to recover capital costs (Peterson 2007). It should also be noted that revenue generated through land leasing can be volatile, reflecting the changing conditions of land markets. For example, an economic downturn may reduce the demand for land, which will make land leasing unattractive. Land can also be used as collateral for urban infrastructure financing. Municipalities in California, constrained by Proposition 13 from raising revenue from property tax, allowed developers to issue land-based bonds to finance roads, sewer, and water systems.

Tapping the Capital Markets

Capital markets offer an important funding source for long-term investments whose beneficiaries include both current and future generations.[6] However, local governments are often constrained by higher-level government restrictions on borrowing. In other countries, urban local governments are allowed to borrow, but their revenue base is too poor and their dependence on the central government is too heavy to make themselves bankable.

There are two possible ways to tap capital markets: borrowing from banks and issuing bonds. Municipal banking builds on the private relationship between the municipality and the bank, whereas the municipal bond market is competitive by nature. The creditworthiness of the municipality is monitored by municipal banks in the banking model, while in the bond model it is based on the disclosure of financial information about the municipality. Municipal banks provide the municipality with support services bundled under one price, but the municipal bond market provides support services unbundled and separately priced. However, these two methods are not mutually exclusive, and some combinations could be appropriate for individual countries.

There have been many experiments with municipal development funds (MDFs). An MDF is a parastatal institution, essentially a financial intermediary that lends to local governments for infrastructure investments. There are cases of successful MDFs, such as the Territorial Financing Institution (FINDETER) of Colombia and the Tamil Nadu Urban Development Fund (TNUDF) of India. FINDETER is a market-based rediscount window for commercial banks lending for municipalities, i.e., a second-tier specialized development bank. FINDETER raises funds from public sources in debt and equity as well as from private sources in debt. It uses the funds to make discounted loans to the first-tier financial institutions that deal with subnational governments. TNUDF is a government-sponsored MDF that has been converted into a public-private funding/management and loan-pooling scheme. Tamil Nadu Pooled Financing Authority raises funds from investors at market rates and uses the funds to finance various local government projects. Sovereign government transfer payments are used as a safety mechanism.

Although MDF is intended to be an intermediate step allowing local government to become a responsible borrower from the capital markets, successful cases of such transformation are not plentiful. There are several reasons why the success of MDFs is not translated into a municipal credit institution (MCI). A main factor is the lack of safety features available for the private-sector players. The central government may intercept the amount due to it from the grants-in-aid being allocated to the local government, thereby ensuring that the municipal government repays debt to the MDF. Private sector MCIs cannot do so. Another problem is the inadequate capacity of the municipal governments to identify and prepare fungible projects. Also the lack of reliable and up-to-date information about municipal finance makes accurate credit rating of municipalities very difficult.

Finally, developing countries have become more reliant on private participation in infrastructure (PPI) during the 1990s. This trend represented a response by many cities unable to mobilize sufficient funds in the face of increasing financing requirements for urban infrastructure investments. However, PPI has been a disappointment in mobilizing private finance for urban infrastructure. Among the five countries studied by the World Bank, investments in urban infrastructure have played a minor role in the overall PPI flows except in one case. The main reason for such a disappointing outcome is that there are many features that raise the risk profile of urban infrastructure for private investors. One such factor is the difficulty of achieving full cost recovery. Even in high-income countries, only half the water utilities can cover both their operation/maintenance costs and their capital costs. In low-income countries, only 3 percent of the water utilities are able to cover these costs (Annez 2007).

Conclusion

This chapter describes the context and the current state of housing finance and urban finance and tries to draw implications for policy. A few concluding remarks are in order. The first point is that financing needs are diverse in both housing and urban finance and vary across income groups and across cities. This implies that a mix of various approaches is needed. In the case of housing finance, standard long-term mortgages, hybrid mortgages, and housing microfinance all have a place. Housing microfinance represents a promising new avenue for supporting incremental housing investments by low-income households, but the challenge of bringing such models to scale remains. Rental housing is a viable option for many households, especially low-income ones in developing countries (UNCHS 2003). Policies should facilitate the development and the functioning of a rental market. Some of the government resources devoted to promoting home ownership could be channeled to rental programs. In urban finance, some combination of taxes, user charges, and prudential borrowing from capital markets should be pursued. Efforts should be made to improve revenue administration by utilizing available technology and by trying to recover cost from urban services to the extent possible, as well as by cultivating a culture in which taxpayers grow accustomed to paying for services. Intergovernmental transfers are also an important revenue source, but they need to be made more transparent and predictable.

Second, subsidies should be separated from finance, made transparent, and targeted well. Interest rate subsidies make housing loans affordable to the lucky few, but they cannot reach the vast majority of low-income borrowers. Subsidized loans are usually raided by the middle-income households. A one-off capital grant to qualifying first-time homebuyers is much more efficient than subsidized loans offered at below-market rates. Efforts should be made to replace supply-side subsidies with demand-side subsidies as well as to make the supply of housing more responsive to market signals.

Many of these recommendations are not new, and they appear in policy documents prepared by various international agencies and are discussed at meetings of government officials. Then why has there been so much talk but so little action? There are several reasons for this. First, the reform plan might be unrealistic, and unlikely to be implemented due to various constraints. Second, changes in economic conditions or the political landscape may weaken the momentum for reform. For example, government and municipalities come to an agreement for a reform in a crisis situation and later change their minds once the crisis is overcome. Third, government may lack the political will to implement the proposed reform. Pricing services at full cost is politically difficult to carry out. Fourth, inadequate capacity, especially at the local level, can be a problem. Finally, consultants and outside experts advising on the reform can fail to follow through the implementation process until actual changes take place on the ground.

What needs to be done going forward? A strategic plan for implementation of a reform package should be drawn with a clearly defined timeline for each phase, taking into consideration the legal and regulatory barriers as well as country- and city-specific constraints. Next, capacity-building programs should be made an integral component of the implementation plan. Third, it is important to find a way to build momentum in the early stages of reform, accumulating a record of early success by making those reforms most readily available. This will help draw attention to the reform effort. Finally, the implementation process should be open for monitoring and evaluation by the relevant bodies of government, outside experts, and the media

Although housing finance and urban finance will remain crucial in making the cities more livable and productive in both developed and developing countries, their role will be more critical in many developing countries, where urbanization will continue in the years to come. Providing adequate housing and basic services to the growing urban populations in the developing world, a large fraction of which is not capable of paying for them, is an overwhelming task (UN-HABITAT 2005). Such challenges require, at a minimum, a concerted effort engaging both the private and public sector with a proper division of labor. The knowledge base on the theory and practice of housing finance and urban finance, as well as the lessons learned from policy experiences in various countries in both developed and developing worlds, could serve as a valuable resource to support such an endeavor.

PART IV

Cases in Urban Development

Chapter 15

Managing Urban Infrastructure and Services in India

Vinod Tewari

India, with an urban population of about 341 million (2007 estimate), is challenged with how to provide adequate levels of infrastructure and services in its many rapidly growing cities. Although only 29.2 percent of the total population is urban, in absolute terms that population is huge, almost equal to the combined urban population of the United States, France, and Italy.[1] Moreover, its urban population is growing at a high rate, projected at about 2.46 percent/year for the next twenty-five years. Currently, India represents 12 percent of total global urban population growth; three of its cities (Mumbai, Delhi, and Kolkata) are among the world's eight largest (United Nations 2008). Thus, the task of providing adequate levels of urban infrastructure and services in the country is immense, comparable only to provision in China.

India has 4,378 urban agglomerations/cities/towns (5,161 if all constituent cities/towns in urban agglomerations are counted separately), of which 35 have more than a million people and 393 have more than 100,000 (Census of India 2001). The provision of water, sewerage, drainage, solid-waste management, city roads, and transport has failed to keep pace with this growth. Among the reasons for this are past underinvestment in urban areas, inadequate attention to infrastructure in urban policies, failure to recognize commercial viability of service delivery, and poor managerial capabilities of urban local institutions.

The economic reform process that started about a decade and a half ago has given rise to an increasing demand for improved services both from the general public and the business community. Having one of the fastest growing economies in the developing world (in excess of 8 percent/year for the last four years (2004–5 to 2007–8)[2] and a current GDP of almost a trillion dollars (*Financial Express*, 26 April 2007)), India is now recognizing that its cities, focal points of this economic revolution and responsible for 60 percent of national GDP, will have to be more wisely managed and governed.

For the newly affluent, changing lifestyles, increasing trade, globalization, and international competitiveness have all contributed to their willingness to pay for an urban service, provided they get the required quantity and quality of the service. This is a significant change in mindset from the days when people assumed public services should be supplied by the local government at no or only nominal cost or when an increase of just a cent in city bus fares generated loud public outcry. Nonetheless, city governments remain reluctant to increase service charges, partly because officials are not able to improve the management of the services and partly because elected representatives fear losing political support.

This unprecedented demand for infrastructure like roads and housing and services like water supply and urban transport and increasing affordability and willingness of urban inhabitants to pay for these are not only creating large challenges but also opening up ample opportunities to transform the nation's urban infrastructure and services. Economic prosperity is providing new funding sources, including foreign investment in improved infrastructure and services, provided there is an institutional, legal, and political environment conducive to commercial interests.

Infrastructure and Services Situation in Indian Cities

Although housing, roads, water supply, and sanitation in urban areas have all improved significantly in recent years, the overall situation remains far from satisfactory. India's Planning Commission has recently argued that the state of urban infrastructure is weakening the country's ability to benefit fully from the economies of scale provided by its large urban agglomerations. Congested roads, poor public transport, inadequate water supply, improper sewage treatment, uncollected solid waste and, above all, grossly inadequate housing (in some metropolitan areas as much as 50 percent of the population lives in slums) severely decrease the urban quality of life. The commission's report holds that if Indian cities fall behind those in other developing countries the investment climate could become more hazardous (Government of India 2006b).

Though overall statistics on the status of public services present a satisfactory picture, they do not indicate the serious shortcomings in both quality and access. For example, the National Institute for Urban Affairs reports that the water supply situation is reasonably adequate but hampered by poor management (NIUA 2005). While 95 percent of the urban population has access to potable water, gaps in spatial coverage and system function lead to unequal water distribution and unreliable water quality. Lacking accurate figures on water unaccounted for because of leakages or unauthorized use, NIUA estimates that about 40 percent of the water in large cities is unaccounted for or nonrevenue generating. It also reports that water meters are rarely provided and, where provided, often do not work. Typically, urban residents supplement the supply by constructing bore wells and underground and overhead storage tanks, installing water pumps and water purifiers, and buying water from private vendors.

Wastewater disposal and treatment is also a very serious problem. Noncollection of wastewater and the discharge of untreated wastewater into rivers, other water bodies, and low-lying areas cause severe water and land pollution problems, reducing the potable water supply. NIUA (2005) estimates that while all India's cities of 1 million or more have sewerage systems, only one-third of the cities with populations exceeding 100,000 and less than one-fifth of the smaller urban centers have them. Where sewerage systems are present, coverage remains partial, with wastewater collection not usually exceeding two-thirds and treatment coverage of only 25 to 40 percent.

The main method of solid-waste disposal is open dumping. According to NIUA, while many cities have distant sanitary landfill sites, due to high transportation costs many dump waste in more proximate low-lying areas or just outside the city periphery (NIUA 2005).

The overall transportation situation in most cities is chaotic. Streets, particularly in the inner city areas, cannot meet the traffic requirements, and rampant encroachment severely reduces whatever capacity is available. Public transport is highly inadequate and motor vehicle activity is making traffic unmanageable. Multiple modes of transport and lack of modal separation reduce motor vehicle speeds to as low as 10 km/hour in city centers, and rates of fatal accidents are among the highest in the world. Around 15 percent of the nation's 100,000 annual estimated road traffic fatalities occur in its twenty-three metros. Nonmotorized transport users—pedestrians, cyclists, and users of other slow vehicles—are the most vulnerable group, accounting for 60 to 80 percent of all traffic fatalities (Mohan 2004).

The inadequacy of institutional, technological, financial, and administrative resources severely constrains efforts to augment the urban transport infrastructure to meet the challenge of growing mass mobility. Investments focus on street improvements for motorized vehicles and not on pathways for pedestrians, nonmotorized transport, or parking. Bus-based public transport systems are limited to major metropolitan cities, while other cities and towns rely on unsafe and unregulated paratransit modes. Encouraged by the recent success of a partially implemented rail-based mass transport system in Delhi, several cities are now considering implementing such public transport systems. However, views diverge on the ability of mass transit to reduce personal motor vehicle activity and to be financially viable (Badami et al. 2007).

Institutions Responsible for Managing Urban Infrastructure and Services

Under the Constitution of India, state governments are responsible for urban development and management. They delegate functions, authority, and financial powers to municipalities and other local bodies. As a result, urban infrastructure and services are managed by a mix of government departments, specialized state-level agencies, and local bodies and authorities. These various actors often undertake similar (even redundant) functions (see table 15.1) in frequently overlapping jurisdictions.

The multiplicity of institutions responsible for urban infrastructure development and service delivery has been a result of ad hoc management and regulatory approaches. The country has not yet evolved a comprehensive and integrated urban development policy that could provide a rational institutional structure. States often authorize institutions whenever a need arises to focus on a particular area, but the old institutions continue to operate, often with reduced functions, mainly due to political considerations. Further, local management institutions have weakened over the years due to a host of factors, including parastatal or urban development authority encroachment on traditional and legitimate functions of municipal bodies, a weak executive system, fragile fiscal health, and inadequate staffing and expertise in municipal management. Although recognized as the third governmental tier by the Constitution of India, local elected governments have grown so weak that enormous efforts are needed to bring them back to a position befitting their due roles.

Issues in Managing Urban Infrastructure and Services

Interinstitutional and interjurisdictional conflicts have become common in the management of urban infrastructure development and service delivery. The cities in the country lack effective mechanisms for departmental and agency coordination. This gap often results in infrastructure development projects being inordinately delayed or unnecessarily costly. Furthermore, the proliferation of managers makes urban service delivery and infrastructure management highly complex and difficult.

Table 15.1: Managing Urban Infrastructure and Services in Indian Cities/Towns

Institution	Main Functions
1. Municipality (municipal corporation/municipal council/town *Panchayat*)	Identify obligatory municipal services such as water supply, solid-waste management, street lighting, maintenance of drains, roads, etc.
2. City development authority (in large cities)	Urban development planning (master plan preparation), new area development—including provision of basic infrastructure
3. Improvement trusts (in small cities/towns)	Urban development planning, new area development—including provision of basic infrastructure
4. City-level water and sewerage board	Operations and maintenance of water supply and sewerage system, collection of water tariffs
5. State-level institution (parastatal) for water and sewerage	Water source development and networks design for water and sewerage system
6. Public health engineering department (in smaller cities/towns)	Water source development and sewerage system development including networks
7. State-level housing development board	Planning, designing, construction and development of housing projects
8. State public works department	Construction of main roads and transport infrastructure including construction and maintenance of government housing
9. State-level development authority for basic services to poor	Development of slums, construction of community toilets, assistance for housing and services, community development
10. State- and city-level road transport corporations	Intracity and statewide public transport; maintenance of buses, bus stands
11. State town and country planning department/ directorate of town planning	Preparation of development plan taking into consideration the needs of industrial, residential and commercial sectors
12. State pollution control board	Prevention and control of pollution in regard to groundwater, ambient air, compost quality, transport and processing of solid waste
13. Central archaeological agency	Maintenance of heritage areas and historical monuments and supporting infrastructure
14. Industrial areas development board	Provision of infrastructure in industrial areas

Table 15.1: (Continued)

Institution	Main Functions
15. Office of divisional/district commissioner	Coordination of the infrastructure development activities of various agencies/departments
16. State department of urban development	Policy aspects relating to urban infrastructure and services and overall control on most of the above mentioned institutions

Source: Compiled by the author using data provided in the CDPs of sixty-three cities prepared under JNNURM (Government of India 2006a).

The absence of the institutional capability to structure commercially viable infrastructure projects discourages the private sector's participation in infrastructure planning and management. Weak financial health, lack of authority to set rates and user charges, and inefficient methods of tax and fee collection hamper local urban bodies' performance in this area. Only the revision of the legal frameworks relating to urban infrastructure development and the facilitation of public-private partnership to increase market efficiency will solve this problem (Government of India 2006a, Tewari 2004).

Urban local bodies are often without complete information on their assets, lack skilled manpower and resources for operations and maintenance, and often fail to control unauthorized use and waste in the delivery of services. Such limitations have resulted in lack of transparency and accountability in their functioning and consequently encouraged corrupt practices. Addressing this issue will require an enormous effort to build the capacities of the local bodies and improve their governance systems.

Another important issue related to managing urban infrastructure development and service delivery is that it requires a huge investment of funds both for managing the current assets as well as for augmenting the deficient infrastructure systems. In 1996, the Expert Group on the Commercialisation of Infrastructure Projects (1996) estimated an investment of $69 billion U.S. (at 1995 prices) for the ten-year period 1996–2006 in key urban infrastructure relating to water supply, sewerage, solid-waste management, and roads in the country. The group observed that funds available for the same period were about $12 billion U.S.

Recently the Jawaharlal Nehru National Urban Renewal Mission (JNNURM; see detailed discussion below) updated these figures based on city development plans (CDPs) for sixty-three cities, a group that includes the thirty-five largest urban agglomerations, all the state capitals, and some other cities of tourist and religious importance. These CDPs detail costs for developing key infrastructure and improving service delivery for the period 2006–2012, worked out through consultations with key stakeholders and, in many instances, from detailed project reports (DPRs) for specific infrastructure projects. In making these estimates, JNNURM considered water supply, sewerage and sanitation, solid-waste management, drainage, urban roads and transport, inner-city renewal, urban environment improvement including restoration of water bodies, heritage conservation, and basic services to the urban poor. Besides the project costs, the JNNURM estimates also included the cost of improving the management and governance capabilities of the urban local bodies and developing the requisite information systems (though they do not include mass rapid transport systems, like metro rail systems). The total for the sixty-three cities is about $89 billion U.S. at 2006 prices. The per capita requirement is $655 U.S. Assuming that the estimated per capita requirement is similar in other urban areas, the total investment for all urban areas would be $211 billion U.S. for the six-year period (see table 15.2).[3]

In the past fifteen years, the national government has envisaged that the traditional system of funding infrastructure based on planning and budgetary allocations will have to be minimized and gradually withdrawn, and that it will give way to new fiscal instruments which require reduction in subsidies and plan allocation and improved pricing and cost-recovery mechanisms. Therefore, innovative strategies and financial instruments need to be developed to generate resources to finance sustainable urban infrastructure development. This would include attracting investment from the private sector and developing capital markets for urban infrastructure financing. However, attracting private sector investment in infrastructure is not easy, as the institutions responsible for providing and managing the infrastructure in most cities/towns are not creditworthy. They need to be strengthened both financially and functionally.

Further, there are issues related to developing an inclusive approach to the delivery of urban services to ensure that the urban poor, estimated at 81 million (27.7 percent of the urban population), have access to adequate infrastructure and basic services (Government of India 2006). Almost all the urban poor and a sizeable number of lower-middle-class urban residents tend to live in unauthorized/illegal settlements without municipal services. In many metropolitan areas, 40 to 50 percent of residents live in slums often unfit for human habitation. Current subsidies and programs to improve these conditions rarely benefit the targeted groups. The slum dwellers often illegally tap urban services, increasing the unaccounted-for component in the service delivery. Getting services

Table 15.2: Total Investment Requirements for Urban Infrastructure Development and Service Delivery, 2006–2012

Investment Requirement as Estimated in the 63 CDPs	
Total investment requirement (Rs million)	3,615,082
Total investment requirement (US$ million)*	89,261
Population of the 63 cities as per 2001 Census of India (million)	119.6
Estimated population 2006 of the 63 cities— 2.46 percent growth rate (million)	136.2
Total investment requirement per capita (Rs)	26,546
Total investment requirement per capita (US$)	655
Estimated Investment Requirements for All Urban Areas Based on Per Capita Estimates	
Total urban population as per 2001 Census of India (million)	285
Estimated total urban pop 2006—2.4 percent growth rate (million)	321.8
Investment requirement for all urban areas (Rs million)	8,543,103
Total investment requirement (US$ million)	210,940
Requirement for water supply (in US$ million)	24,259
Requirement for sewerage (US$ million)	24,110
Requirement for solid-waste management (US$ million)	4,349
Requirement for drainage (US$ million)	12,548
Requirement for urban roads/transport excluding MRTS (US$ million)	90,486
Requirement for basic services for the poor (US$ million)	34,139
Requirement for others including capacity building of local bodies (US$ million)	21,049
* 1 US$ = Rs 40.5	

Source: Compiled and estimated by the author using the data from the CDPs of sixty-three cities selected under JNNURM (Government of India 2006a) and Census of India (2001).

to the poor is a complicated task, as the services must be accessible, affordable, and of a reasonable quality and quantity (Tewari et al. 2007, Laquian 2007, Asian Development Bank 2009).

National Strategies to Address the Issues

Recognizing that urbanization is inevitable, is associated with the country's economic development, and should be supported by adequate levels of infrastructure and services for sustainability, central, state, and local governments have initiated several innovative strategies. These include (1) decentralizing urban local governance and empowering urban local bodies; (2) improving urban governance and management systems; and (3) providing reform-linked financial support to state and local governments for infrastructure projects.

Decentralization of Local Governance

In 1992, India passed the Constitution Seventy-Fourth Amendment Act to elevate local urban governments, enabling them to function as effective democratic institutions of local self-government. Recognizing urban governments as the third tier of the government, the amendment introduced fundamental changes: it ensured periodic and fair conduct of elections to municipalities in each state, to be overseen by statutorily constituted state election commissions, and provided protection to elected bodies against supersession, suspension, or arbitrary dissolution by state government. It required elected bodies to have adequate representation of women and scheduled castes and tribes, and it provided for ward committees to ensure popular participation in civic affairs and for metropolitan planning committees and district planning committees to prepare and consolidate urban development plans.

The amendment also specifies a set of functions, listed in the Twelfth Schedule of the Constitution, that the state may devolve, to urban local bodies, including urban planning, planning for economic and social development, and urban poverty alleviation. Further, it expects states to endow the municipalities with the necessary powers and authority to function as institutions of self-government. Finally, each state must constitute a finance commission every five years to review the financial positions of the municipalities and recommend improvement measures including assigning taxes, duties, tolls, and fees, and sharing state revenues and grants-in-aid.

The amendment intends to empower municipalities financially and build their capacity to manage the functions they are to perform. To date the results are these: all states have taken the steps necessary to implement its various provisions, including the creation of finance commissions whose recommendations are relayed to state legislatures, though not all of them are accepted; and all municipalities now have elected bodies that adequately represent the issues and concerns of all sections of society.[4]

NIUA's evaluation of how well the provisions of the amendment have been implemented concludes that while compliance with certain provisions (the constitution of municipalities, regular municipal elections, reservation of seats in the elected body, constitution of finance commissions, and actions taken on their recommendations) has been satisfactory, the implementation of other provisions (like functional devolution and constitution of ward committees, district planning committees, and metropolitan planning committees) has been slow and half-hearted. Implementation has also varied from state to state; some have made good progress while others have lagged behind (NIUA 2003, 2005a).

Notwithstanding the amendment, most municipal bodies remain weak, with state governments reluctant to devolve the required functions, financial powers, and authority to them. None of the state governments has given serious attention to the requisite change in the institutional arrangements for urban infrastructure and the role of municipal government vis-à-vis that of the other agencies, operating either at the state level or at the city level in carrying out various functions. Many vested interests and political considerations are to blame in retaining the traditional institutional arrangements as they are. Further, the states argue that municipal bodies lack capacity to shoulder any additional responsibility and the amendment prescribes no time limit for the devolution and the associated institutional changes.

Improving Urban Governance and Management Systems

The Expert Group on the Commercialisation of Infrastructure Projects (1996) first highlighted the need for new approaches to financing infrastructure development, and the magnitude of the report's estimated funding requirements for urban infrastructure generated a wide debate. Urban policymakers, particularly in the Ministry of Urban Development of Government of India, in emphasizing the huge funding requirements and needed urban sector reforms, suggested developing public-private partnerships, and building the capacity and creditworthiness of local bodies. Subsequently, a technical assistance project, Financial Institutions Reforms and Expansion—Debt (FIRE-D), launched in 1995 with USAID support, has contributed significantly to the policy advocacy efforts (NIUA 2000). Several other international agencies like the World Bank, ADB, CIDA, and DFID also advocated various urban sector reforms during this period.

In 2002, the finance minister of Government of India used his annual budget speech to announce a number of reforms, including the most important measure, the Urban Reform Incentive Fund, to provide assistance to the states to accelerate urban institutional and legal changes identified by the national government (Government of India 2004). These included (1) repeal of the Urban Land Ceiling and Regulation Act of 1976 at the state level; (2) phased reduction of stamp duty (duty on conveyance of land) to no more than 5 percent by the end of 2007; (3) reform of rent control laws to stimulate private investment in rental housing; (4) introduction of a computerized process for land registration; (5) reform of property tax structure to make it a source of revenue for local urban bodies and improve collection efficiency to 85 percent by the end of 2007; (6) levy of reasonable user charges by urban local bodies to collect the full cost of operation and maintenance by the end of 2007; and (7) introduction of a double-entry accounting system for local urban bodies.

Other policy measures included establishing a city challenge fund to facilitate city-level reforms by funding the move towards sustainable systems of municipal management and service delivery, and a pooled finance-development scheme to facilitate access to capital markets by smaller local urban bodies. The central government also permitted the local bodies to issue tax-free municipal bonds according to national guidelines. The central government has also developed a model municipal act, advising state governments to modify theirs accordingly. The model act enables urban local bodies to leverage funds and to introduce improved accounting systems and private sector participation in urban infrastructure development and service delivery. These modifications are aimed at providing the legal environment necessary to carry out various reforms at the municipal level.

In 2001, the comptroller and auditor general of India (C&AG) constituted a task force to recommend improvements to the municipal accounting and financial reporting systems, especially the replacement of cash-based systems with accrual-based accounting systems. C&AG's report provided guidelines for accrual-based accounting, budget and accounting formats, accounting policies, and costing of urban utilities and services. Some state governments adopted the guidelines, and Tamil Nadu became the first state to switch to an accrual-based accounting system. However, overall progress was quite slow because state governments believed they needed a generic framework of national municipal accounting. With this objective the Ministry of Urban Development in cooperation with the C&AG produced the *National Municipal Accounts Manual* (Government of India 2004).

The manual comprehensively details the accounting policies, principles, and procedures designed to ensure correct, complete, and timely recording of municipal transactions and to produce accurate and relevant financial reports. It contains the required forms and formats, and a section on "chart of accounts." The manual is to be adopted and followed by the various state governments while drafting their state-specific municipal accounts manuals.

The Government of India has also developed a number of other manuals and guidelines to help the state governments and the cities to implement the urban reform agenda, including (1) a draft citizens' charter; (2) a manual on water supply and treatment; (3) a manual on solid-waste management; (4) a manual on sewerage and sewage treatment; (5) guidelines for sector reform and successful public-private partnership in urban water and sanitation services; and (6) guidelines for property tax reforms. Further, the government has announced a number of fiscal incentives to facilitate urban infrastructure development, including permission for foreign direct investment in the development of integrated townships, fiscal incentives for urban infrastructure in the form of a tax holiday for solid-waste management and water-treatment systems and exemption of custom duty on equipment imported for water, sanitation, and solid-waste management projects.

The government also initiated two major projects aimed at improving urban governance and information management systems. One was the National Urban Information System project, launched in 2003 with the objective of developing various levels of spatial and attribute data for urban planning efforts. In 2006, the government selected 137 towns/cities to develop GIS databases at 1:10,000 and 1:2,000 scales and 24 towns for utility mapping at 1:1,000 scale. The attribute data component of the scheme was designated as National Urban Data Bank and Indicators (NUDBI). These databases are expected to facilitate master plans and town planning schemes and also serve as decision-support systems for e-governance. The total outlay of the scheme is Rs 662.8 million (about $16 million U.S.), of which 75 percent will be borne by the central government and 25 percent by the state governments.

The other project, e-governance in municipalities, part of the national e-governance initiative, was launched in 2004. By that time some municipalities, including Visakhapatnam, Hyderabad, Bangalore, Coimbatore, Surat, Ahmedadad, Delhi, Nashik, Kalyan-Dombivali, Navi Mumbai, Vijayawada, Guntur, and Indore, had already developed computerized systems for select municipal services like registration and issuance of birth and death certificates, payment of utility bills and property tax, building plan permission, public health and sanitation, and grievance redress. The e-governance project was established, in part, through financial support from the central government and, in part, through resources generated through developing partnerships with the private sector.

Most of the above-mentioned initiatives aimed at improving the governance and management systems of urban local bodies were initiated from 2002 to 2004. However, as the central funds allocated to implement these reforms were quite limited, the state governments did not have much incentive to implement the reform agenda.

Reform-Linked Financial Support for Infrastructure Projects

By 2005, policymakers realized that, while upgrading the country's urban infrastructure was an urgent need, the states were in a position neither to mobilize the required investment nor to attract investment from elsewhere. At the same time, the government was committed to ensuring environmental sustainability including access to basic services to meet the Millennium Development Goals. Thus, to integrate various reform initiatives and scale up the effort to catalyze investment in urban infrastructure, the government launched the Jawaharlal Nehru National Urban Renewal Mission (JNNURM), an ambitious program to provide reform-linked financial assistance to state governments and local urban bodies for urban infrastructure development. The Ministry of Urban Development and the Ministry of Housing and Urban Poverty Alleviation are the responsible ministries, expected to formulate and implement the program during 2005–2012.

JNNURM identified an initial group of sixty-three cities for integrated infrastructure development and service delivery. Eligible cities include seven cities with populations of more than 4 million according to the 2001 Census of India, twenty-eight cities with 1 to 4 million, and twenty-eight cities that are either state capitals or cities with religious, historic, and tourist importance.[5] The program has substantial central assistance, estimated at Rs 1205 billion, or $30 billion U.S., linked to state- and city-level policy and structural reforms (Government of India 2005). (Most of the other urban development schemes previously in operation have now been subsumed under JNNURM.) The central government is providing grants covering from 35 to 90 percent of the costs of the projects in specified areas, depending on the city size and location. The balance of the investment is shared, as specified by the program guidelines, by the state where the city is located and the local urban body responsible for implementing the project.

The main goals of JNNURM are (1) improving and augmenting the economic and social infrastructure of the cities; (2) ensuring basic services to the urban poor, including security of tenure at affordable prices; (3) initiating wide-ranging urban sector reforms; and (4) strengthening municipal governments. The specific infrastructure development and reform activities have been grouped under two sub-missions—the Sub-Mission for Urban Infrastructure and Governance, and the Sub-Mission for Basic Services to the Urban Poor.

The program is designed to achieve its objective through a strategy comprising reform-driven, fast-track, and planned development of identified cities with a focus on efficiency in service delivery, community participation, and increased transparency and accountability. As described earlier, the JNNURM approach consists of preparing city development plans and detailed projects reports for the projects identified in the plans by the cities, and motivating the cities to incorporate private sector efficiencies through public-private partnership arrangements. JNNURM

has issued toolkits to assist in formulating CDPs and DPRs and in identifying fundable projects. After a review of the CDPs and the DPRs,
the central government releases its share of the project cost to a state-
designated agency that, to the extent feasible, leverages additional
resources from the financial institutions, private sector, or capital market and disburses soft loan or grant-cum-loan or grant, depending on
the case. The national government also requires that private sector participation in development, management, and financing of the project
be clearly delineated and that the state-designated agency also set up a
revolving fund to meet operation and maintenance costs of the assets
created under JNNURM-supported projects.

A number of committees, including the National Steering Group,
Central Sanctioning and Monitoring Committee, Technical Advisory
Group, and Program Management Unit will review quarterly state progress reports. In addition, specialized technical agencies will monitor the
overall performance as agreed to in memorandums of agreement that
are signed between the central government, state government, and the
concerned local urban body for the projects sanctioned under the program.

Major components of the reform agenda include (1) strengthening
urban local bodies by devolving functions and financial powers as envisaged in the Constitution Seventy-Fourth Amendment Act, changing the
legislative landscape to facilitate reforms; (2) improving their financial
management and accounting systems; (3) reforming property tax
administration and assessment to increase coverage and compliance; (4)
rationalizing user charges, duties, fees, etc.; (5) improving governance
and service delivery through ICT applications; and (6) improving access
to basic services by the urban poor and providing them affordable security of tenure.

JNNURM covers about one-third of India's urban population. The
remaining two-thirds, inhabiting 4,313 urban agglomerations and
towns, probably require greater attention, as infrastructure and service
level is worse in these places. For instance, none has an underground
sewerage system. The central government has initiated an Urban Infrastructure Development Scheme for Small and Medium Towns (UIDS-
SMT) to support urban infrastructure and services in these cities and
towns. Its objectives are (1) to improve infrastructural facilities and help
create durable public assets and quality-oriented services; (2) to
enhance public-private partnership in infrastructural development; and
(3) to promote planned integrated development in the towns and cities.

The main features of UIDSSMT are similar to those specified under
JNNURM, with the exception that preparation of city development
plans is not required and the shared funding pattern is 80 percent cen-

tral, 10 percent state, and 10 percent local. Also, under this scheme, yearly allocations for the grants are not earmarked clearly. In the three years after the scheme was launched, about 500 projects, covering just one-tenth of the total number of eligible towns, have been approved with a total cost of Rs 80 billion ($2 billion U.S.). This is a much smaller amount compared to what has been provided for the sixty-three JNNURM cites. One reason is that UIDSSMT cities and towns do not have the capacity or awareness to seek funds under the scheme. For example, even in a few towns near Delhi, where a fair amount of real estate development is taking place, local leadership was unaware of the scheme.

The nation's small and medium towns require greater attention because, with improved accessibility due to road development, their economies are primed to grow and real estate development is taking place rapidly. Without timely action, the very rudimentary transport and service infrastructure of these settlements could quickly collapse.

The most important outcome expected from these reform-linked infrastructure grant schemes is that the urban local bodies will become more efficient, transparent, accountable, creditworthy, and financially self-sustaining, which would lead to sustainable urban development in the country. Further, the efforts to establish a citywide planning and governance framework and to improve access of the urban poor to basic services would ensure better planned, more efficiently managed, and more equitable urban service delivery systems.

Progress So Far and Emerging Trends

In the past fifteen years, the initiatives taken by the central government, some of the state governments, and some of the cities to improve the urban infrastructure and services management in the country have been quite commendable. However, the progress so far—in implementing the initiatives, improving service management and delivery, and strengthening local institutions—has been slow and limited considering the scale of the urban infrastructure problem.

A key factor responsible for the slow pace of urban reforms, particularly the lagging implementation of the constitutional amendment, is the lack of political will at the state level to restructure institutions and the unwillingness of the state bureaucracy to transfer the power of urban governance to elected local bodies. The urban infrastructure management powers are still concentrated in the hands of state-level politicians and bureaucrats who use the city commissioner/chief executive to forward their—and not the city's—vested interests.

Another important factor is the pervasive corruption in the infrastructure development process. The rapid economic development in many cities and surrounding areas is providing unprecedented opportunities for the private sector in real estate development in the form of huge concentrations of commercial and residential spaces, but in the absence of any transparent regulatory mechanisms, there is no way to ensure that the developers provide the required support services such as water supply, solid-waste management, road space, and parking. The city managers responsible for regulating such developments often relax the service norms and approve irregular and even unauthorized development in return for monetary considerations, which are proportionately shared by the functionaries at various levels of the government. Similarly, the elected members of urban local bodies have found ways to exploit the situation to their advantage. The mayor of the elected body typically does not enjoy much planning or financial power but uses his or her clout to influence the process of awarding infrastructure project contracts to benefit relatives or friends, which often results in poor-quality urban infrastructure assets. Based on several public interest litigations in recent years, the judiciary in the country has taken great interest in urban policy matters; but given the strong nexus between the unscrupulous builders, politicians, and bureaucrats, it may take several years before the situation improves. The reforms addressing the transparency and accountability aspects are absolutely crucial in this regard.

The elected councilors are typically first-time local politicians who have little understanding of urban issues, a failing often cited by state leaders as a reason for not empowering them. By contrast, the mayors of large cities in China are typically powerful political leaders who can express a larger vision for city growth and provide for it in terms of resources and other wherewithal (Mohan 2005). Constitutional provisions in India now provide for creating such a political and executive environment for city-level local management. The process needs to be expedited by building human resource capacity, not delayed on the pretext that local urban bodies are without sufficient capacity. The municipal governments, as the lead agencies, must be made accountable for the planning and development of all the urban infrastructure and services in a city through a mechanism as close to self-financing as possible.

Notwithstanding these issues, numerous urban sector reforms and practices have improved the management and governance in many Indian cities (table 15.3). The list provided here is not exhaustive.

Progress in implementing the JNNURM program appears quite satisfactory, according to the claims made by the central government. Although all the sixty-three cities have prepared their city development plans (available on JNNURM's website, http://jnnurm.nic.in), the qual-

Table 15.3: Key Urban Sector Reforms and Their Implementation

Reform	Examples of States/Cities Implementing the Reform
Regular conduct of municipal elections	In urban local bodies of all states where 74th Amendment is applicable, a few newly carved out states are in the process of conducting elections (some areas are exempt).
Constitution of state finance commissions	All states where 74th Amendment is applicable.
Constitution of district planning committees (DPCs) and metropolitan planning committees (MPCs)	Most states have constituted DPCs but they are not functioning as envisaged in the amendment; MPCs are constituted only in West Bengal (as a result the planning process as envisaged in the 74th Amendment is not being followed).
Reforms in property tax assessment and administration	Several states have introduced area-based property tax assessment, and cities like Ahmedabad, Bangalore, Hyderabad, and Delhi have made significant progress.
Reforms in municipal accounting and financial reporting systems	All urban local bodies in the state of Tamil Nadu (a most successful example) and cities such as Hyderabad, some cities in the state of Maharashtra, Ludhiana, Jaipur, Indore, Bangalore, Tumkur.
Improved management of municipal assets	Ludhiana, Indore, Bangalore, Ahmedabad.
Revisions of municipal acts	Several states have started the process; states like Tamil Nadu, West Bengal, Delhi made significant changes.
Raising resources through municipal bonds (some tax-free, mostly private placement issues)	Ahmedabad (only area that had part public issue), Bangalore, Vijayawada, Ludhiana, Nagpur, Madurai, Nashik, Indore.
Market-based pool financing	In Tamil Nadu and Karnataka states—small municipalities around Chennai and Bangalore.
Rationalization of user-charges	Progressive increase in user charges in many cities particularly for water; good examples are Vishakhapatnam, Ahmedabad, Bangalore.
Urban infrastructure projects with private sector participation (PPP)	Unbundling of services for some components of water supply in cities like Tirupur, Alandur, Ahmedabad, Pimpri-Chinchwad, Vijayawada, Bangalore; PPP in several roads projects in slum development projects, and in solid waste management projects; PPP in street lighting in Vijayawada.

Table 15.3: (Continued)

Reform	Examples of States/Cities Implementing the Reform
Improved solid-waste management practices	Better compliance with Municipal Solid Waste Management Rules (Government of India 2000) in states such as Karnataka, Gujrat, Rajasthan, and Maharashtra, and in cities of Vijayawada, Chennai, Surat, Nagpur, Ahmedabad, Hyderabad.
Access of the poor to basic services	Kerala state, Ludhiana, Sangli, Pune.
Remote sensing and GIS applications	Several attempts in the last ten years (mostly unsuccessful; much talk, little meaningful output).
E-governance and IT applications	A number of cities in the state of Andhra Pradesh (best examples are Vishakhapatnam and Hyderabad), Delhi, Coimbatore, Indore, Ahmedabad, and some cities in the state of Maharashtra including Kalyan-Dhombivili.

Sources: 3inetwork 2006; NIUA 2005a; http://jnnurm.nic.in; and author's fieldwork.

ity of the CDPs varies from city to city, partly because of the short time frame in which many were prepared. In cases where cities could provide the required data (because they already had some information collected and/or projects prepared through earlier international or donor agency grants), the quality of the CDP is reasonable. But in others the data quality is not as good.

The DPRs submitted to the Government of India for funding are not public documents, so no assessment can be made about their quality. As of March 31, 2009, the central government had sanctioned 461 projects for urban infrastructure and governance for sixty-one of the sixty-five JNNURM cities. The total value of the projects sanctioned is about Rs 494 billion ($12 billion U.S.). Ninety percent of the sanctioned projects are in water supply, sewerage, drainage, roads/flyovers, and solid-waste management sectors. The progress under the Urban Basic Services to the Poor component that was relatively slow in the beginning of the program has improved in the past year. Most of the projects sanctioned under this sub-mission are for construction of housing units for the poor and resettlement of slum dwellers. The information on projects submitted and cleared under both the sub-missions is periodically updated on the JNNURM website (http://jnnurm.nic.in). The information on how many of these projects have any private sector involvement, which in any case is not significant, is not available publicly.

Also, not much information is yet available on the progress of the projects and the implementation of the reforms. Therefore, at this stage it is not possible to assess the success of the program. The progress so far in terms of preparation of the CDPs and sanctioning of the projects cannot be taken as an indicator of overall success, as it could be largely due to the keenness of the states and cities to access central assistance and the desire of the central government to show significant progress for one of its flagship development initiatives. Under several earlier schemes, the state governments, promising urban sector reforms, took first installments of central assistance but could not show much progress, and, therefore, never sought further grant installments. Such schemes are often restructured and renamed and the disbursed components of the grants written off.

Under JNNURM, the grant-receiving cities and their states have signed detailed memorandums of agreement (http://jnnurm.nic.in/MoA) with the central government, but the timelines for many intended reforms are spread over the program's entire seven-year period. Typically a committee will be set up in the second year to examine a particular matter in detail and prepare draft legislation, which will be adopted by the state government and then implemented in the fifth year of the program. Further, in the absence of accurate data on the present state of affairs in several areas, both the central and state governments are likely to manipulate or exaggerate the progress of reforms in their attempt to claim successful implementation of the program. It is, therefore, very difficult to monitor real progress and ensure that the final outcome is as envisaged in the reform agenda. However, it is hoped that, with all the institutional arrangements being made for monitoring this program, the compliance, though partial, will be better than under the earlier schemes.

The urban infrastructure and services scenario in the country may considerably improve if all the reforms envisaged under JNNURM and UIDSSMT are implemented in a true spirit of accountability and transparency by state and city governments. Sustainable urban infrastructure depends on judicious planning, efficient management, and transparent and accountable governance. Therefore, huge efforts are needed to build the capacities of urban local bodies and create the regulatory mechanisms needed to ensure better compliance from all players. Successful reform will also require process reengineering and improved information systems amenable to integration with information and communication technology applications. Considering the scale and complexity of urban infrastructure development, the ongoing reform process has to be vigorously scaled up and sincerely implemented by state governments and local bodies, not just in the cities selected under

JNNURM but in all urban areas. The central government can play only advisory and guiding roles.

The Urban Research Agenda

The urban reform initiatives discussed above have mostly been based on the experience gained from past initiatives and outcomes of some best practices or technical assistance provided by international agencies like the World Bank, Asian Development Bank, USAID, and DFID. However, to date, the use of an indigenous research base in policy and program development has been quite limited, leading to the withdrawal or redesign of many policy and legislative initiatives. Further, lacking data, some states are reluctant to adopt the reform policies. For example, in the absence of any evidence showing that a reduced stamp duty on land transactions leads to better compliance and increased state revenue, many states initially did not come forward to accept the idea. In fact, certain states, like West Bengal, openly opposed it. The time now is ripe to analyze the impact of the reform in the states that have reduced the duty rates and estimate the financial gains of the states in real terms.

Contemporary research in India has focused on the urbanization process, migration, industrialization, urban poverty measurements, rural-urban relationships, decentralization, the informal sector, housing and land markets, urban environment, performance indicators, municipal finance, infrastructure financing, and willingness to pay. The research output is based on easily available secondary data from such sources as Census of India or National Sample Surveys, and thus not on primary data. This points to the insufficient funding and facilities available to the very few researchers in the area, despite the scale and complexity of urban research requirement in the country.

India has no major specialty institutes of urban research, teaching, or training in urban development and infrastructure management. Existing urban research comes from geography, economics, sociology, academic urban planning, a few small research institutes/centers, and, sometimes, from a select number of bureaucrats who develop interest in the area. The prospects for future research in the area are grim. The government policies in this regard are faulty and lack vision. For example, under JNNURM, a significant amount of funding is available for technical assistance but the government is not making adequate efforts to build technical institutions that could provide assistance. Instead, it is funding a number of consultancy firms and NGOs that have no or little expertise in the area. These entities are producing products that are actually a set of strategies, rarely based on any scientifically collected data or analytical research, which provide quick-fix solutions to the urban problems. There are very few attempts to conduct any knowledge-building research that would provide guidance to urban policymakers and managers.

India badly needs the kind of urban research that can be useful in formulating urban infrastructure policies, assisting city managers in decision-making and process reengineering, structuring and implementing projects, and evaluating the impact of various policies and programs. Interpretative and analytic approaches based on high-quality information need to be developed. The research agenda should also include documentation of best practices based on a critical analysis and impact assessment rather than on the claims made by a practice's originators.

Specific areas requiring research include local institutional structures, manpower planning, impacts of various reforms, financing of urban infrastructures, project cost-benefit analyses, appropriately structured public-private partnerships, community participation structures, process reengineering, environmental and sustainability issues, financial implications of urban policies, information management and decision support systems, applications of GIS, asset management, tax assessments and administration, and the role of globalization in changing urbanization processes. The roles of citizens and nongovernment organizations—particularly in urban service planning and delivery, local political processes, and dynamics of interest groups—are other important areas that need research. Increasing poverty and lack of access to basic services are serious urban issues; developing sustainable solutions requires in-depth research. Finally, high-quality research can be conducted only with high-quality and comprehensive urban databases; the production of the needed data will require serious efforts at the national, state, and local levels.

Chapter 16

Sustainable Urban Development: Managing City Development in Uganda

Shuaib Lwasa

Although traditional urban centers existed in Uganda before colonization, developing around the seats of reigning kings and their governments, urbanization with a western touch only surfaced in the nineteenth century as administrative centers and agricultural markets were established. This history is important in understanding the evolution and management of urban development in Uganda because the development pathway was influenced by the colonial legacy. Urbanization has accelerated recently as migration into towns increases driven by civil crisis, environmental problems, and natural growth. This rapid urbanization has increased the imprint of urban settlements across the country and raised sustainability issues that require innovative management strategies.

Urban centers are legislatively categorized as city, municipality, town council, town board, and trading center. Uganda has only one city, Kampala; it continues to exert its primacy over lower-level urban centers, absorbing 39.6 percent of the nation's urban population. A key feature of urban management in Uganda is the decentralized political power and devolution of decision-making to democratically elected councils. Although these local council-based decisions are expected to improve urban management, decentralized urban administration faces challenges of adequate social service provision, promotion of economic development, housing delivery, urban governance, spatial development guidance, and environmental management. This chapter addresses urban management issues and how they relate to sustainability in Uganda. The chapter also compares Uganda's experience with cities in sub-Saharan Africa.

Evolution of Urban Development in Uganda

"Urban" is subject to a broad range of definitions (IBRD 1994). In many countries, the definition is based on a threshold number of inhabitants in a defined geographical expanse, ranging from a few hundred to more than ten thousand. Some countries define urban using a combination of criteria, such as population density, political function, and/or predominant economic activity of the area. In Uganda, the Local Government Act 2002 defined Kampala as the only city, with the remaining municipalities or town councils making a total of seventy-four urban areas. But it is important to note that there are many centers with urban tendencies that are not defined as urban in Uganda. The definition of urban has been changing over time. In 2002 urban areas were divided among cities, municipalities, and town councils; the 1991 census even included trading centers with more than 1,000 people as part of the urban population (UBOS 2002). "Urban" is, therefore, largely a statistical concept determined by the country's policy. A city, on the other hand, is more than just large numbers of people living in close proximity to one another; it is a complex political, economic, and social entity (World Resources Institute 1997). As noted, Kampala is the only city and is the administrative, commercial, and industrial hub of the country. Its size, nature of development, and national importance provide a basis for evaluating sustainable development.

In Uganda, the population living in urban areas has increased from 635,000 in 1969, to 938,000 in 1980, to 1.9 million in 1991, to 3.7 million in 2007 (UBOS 2002). Urbanization has been slow in Uganda but despite the slow rate, it poses the challenging task of ensuring environmental sustainability, especially in metropolitan areas. Due to changes in the criteria used to define urban centers, it is difficult to compare regional and countrywide urbanization, a difficulty that obscures the increasing densities of settlements defined as urban before 1991 by the national census. Changes in the administrative boundaries of certain urban areas also make such comparison challenging.

Although it is not properly documented, urbanization did occur in the precolonial period. In Buganda, where administration was based on the institution of kingship, the seat of the king was a settlement sufficiently orderly and populous to count as urban. Settlements were laid out systematically for different classes of the population. The 1900s saw deliberate efforts to establish towns that were planned from Western perspective, and throughout the period up to the 1970s, urban development revolved around the legacy of controlling development with stringent laws that also segregated social groups.

A clear and elaborate urbanization process took shape during Ugan-

Table 16.1: Growth Rates of Selected Urban Centers in Uganda (in percent)

Urban center	1948–1959	1957–1964	1969–1970	1980–1991	1991–2002
Kampala	10.5	6.8	3.1	4.9	3.7
Jinja	4.7	2.0	−0.6	2.8	2.4
Masaka	10.0	8.9	7.8	4.9	1.8
Mbale	5.5	3.6	1.7	6.1	2.3
Fort Portal	−0.5	5.7	11.7	1.8	1.8
Mbarara	14.3	8.8	3.5	5.1	4.5
Entebbe	7.5	3.7	0.1	6.3	2.5

Source: Uganda Bureau of Statistics 2002.

da's colonial period. Over the past three decades Kampala has expanded from a township of 0.69 sq km gazetted in 1902, 12.95 sq km by 1929 and 195 sq km by 1968 growing into a metropolitan area of about 839 sq km (Nyakaana, Sengendo et al. 2004). This expansion occurred as Kampala annexed adjacent townships. As the city boundaries were extended, Kampala's population also kept increasing at an average annual rate of 3.7 percent. Meanwhile, for the rest of Uganda, urbanization occurred mainly through the establishment of administrative centers that were centers for exchange of produce and industrial activity. These centers have grown sluggishly over the past thirty years but still have an influence on the urbanization of Uganda. The urban population has grown from 6.6 percent of the total population in 1969 to 12.3 percent in 2002 (UBOS 2002).

The reasons for this trend include population dynamics, industrialization, rural-urban migration, and economic growth and its attendant labor shifts. These factors remain present and forecast fast-paced urbanization. Although urbanization need not be taken as a problem, it does entail significant challenges. As shown in table 16.1, the growth rates for major towns in Uganda indicate a steady increase in the urban population. Still, the most striking feature of Uganda's population is the small size of its urban population. Although the urban proportion of the population doubled between 1980 and 1991 as shown in table 16.2, the proportion of the urban population was still relatively low. Table 16.2 further indicates that the urban population is concentrated in a few areas: 76.7 percent of the total urban population in the twenty largest towns. It is also important to note that the service centers—which are located between dispersed rural settlements and urban centers—are often too small to be defined as urban and yet too nucleated to be rural.

What is being experienced in Uganda is a strong rural-urban migration that has often kept urban growth rates between 4 and 6 percent. There is also growth of secondary urban centers often adjacent to the

Table 16.2: Urbanization in Uganda, 1969–2002

Index	1969	1980	1991	2002
Number of Towns	58	96	150	74
Urban Population	634,952	938,287	1,889,622	2,921,981
Proportion Urban (%)	6.6	7.4	11.31	2.2
Urban Growth Rate (%)	8.17	3.93	6.35	3.73
Percentage in Capital City (%)	53.9	47.9	310	40.7
Percentage in 20 Largest Towns (%)	87.4	80.4	74.4	76.6

Source: Uganda Bureau of Statistics 2002.

administrative boundary of the city. This expansion is associated with poor services, informal (emerging) economic growth, and segregated spatial distributions of housing and services. This presents challenges in the planning and management of urban areas—not only the major cities but the secondary urban centers as well.

Looking at Uganda's urban population by region, more than half (54 percent) of the urban population lives in the central region, while other regions have slightly differing proportions of the urban population (17 percent for the northern, 14 percent for western, and 13 percent for eastern). Uganda has experienced an urbanization process characterized by exploding urban centers in a steadily growing economy since 1989. Ideally urban centers are meant to be centers of production, employment, and innovation, but rapid urbanization has had negative consequences, including alarming and increasing incidence of poverty, urban sprawl, and deficient social services and infrastructure. The negative consequences have led to deterioration of settlement conditions, depletion of natural resources, and pollution.

Like other East African countries, Uganda has pursued a policy of urbanization as a means of achieving development through the "growth pole" centers. It was assumed that if urban centers were established, new markets would be created for the produce from the rural areas, industries would be established to offer employment to the immigrants into the urban centers, and the new urban centers would promote the diffusion of ideas and techniques to the rural areas (Obudho and Peter 2002). What has happened is the growth of an emerging, informal economic sector that not only contributes to the national economy but also provides employment and livelihood for many urban dwellers.

Urbanization in Uganda has two dimensions: an increasing growth path that continually presents urban management problems and sustainability challenges, and the issue of districting, which is creating more urban centers without ensuring the capacity to manage the areas administratively, financially, socially, and economically. Estimates indicate that the urban population will grow more than fourfold in the next twenty years (UBOS 2009). This is an opportunity, but it implies that sustainable urban development and management must be high priorities on Uganda's urban agenda. Since urban areas are crucial engines of economic growth, urban centers need to be managed properly in order to enhance and promote national development. Failure to initiate an adequate urbanization policy, including developing the systems and laws that will allow for continued, sustainable urban growth, will have far-reaching and strongly negative implications for national and regional development.

Drivers of Urbanization in Uganda

Urbanization in Uganda is driven by both underlying and proximate factors. The underlying drivers include the natural increase of the urban population and rural-urban migration. Through natural increase—due to a high fertility rate of 6.7, a decline in mortality, internal migration, and international migration (Nyakaana, Sengendo et al. 2004)—the urban population has, for the last three decades, grown steadily faster than the pace at which urban services and housing are provided. For example Jinja, which is the third-largest town according to the 2002 census, is experiencing growth that is largely driven by rural-urban migration. According to the 2002 census, 42 percent of Jinja's population was born in the municipality and 58 percent migrated into the municipality. Kampala is also experiencing a similar situation. According to the same census, 53 percent of the persons in the city were born outside of its administrative boundaries. Although disaggregated data are unavailable and the contribution of rural-urban migration cannot be precisely determined, the contribution of urban-urban migration should not be overlooked. These phenomena emphasize the importance of demographic dynamics to Uganda's urbanization.

One of the proximate factors influencing urbanization in Uganda is the economic policy of industrialization pursued for the last five decades. Although this industrialization policy apparently shifted the focus from the formerly industrial city of Uganda (Jinja) to Kampala, industrial development in smaller towns in Uganda is also contributing greatly to urban growth. Kampala City is the major industrial and commercial center in the country and has attracted an increased population. Industrialization due to globalization has led to an increase in consumption levels and the establishment of numerous industries and commercial centers. There has been proliferation of the emerging economic sector, which absorbs most of the economically active population in urban areas. It is important to note that the growth of the emerging sector is not necessarily a problem—it provides employment to many in urban areas and contributes to the national economy—but the challenges of integrating this kind of economy into spatial planning and policy development are more evident. The expansion of urban areas is therefore steadily advancing, engulfing adjacent rural areas and other urban centers. Kampala city and its metropolitan area have extended into an area of approximately 839 km^2, engulfing what were hitherto satellite towns and rural areas. The significant ramifications such changes have for both environmental and social well-being make them a great challenge to sustainable development.

The other proximate driver for urbanization is the balkanization of administrative regions as smaller districts have been carved out of larger districts. The number of districts in Uganda increased from thirty-five in 1986 to forty-five in 1998 and fifty-six in 2002, and currently stands at seventy-five. The headquarters of each district is automatically defined as a town council, which qualifies the population to be counted as urban. Several of these towns have rapidly expanded beyond their originally stipulated boundaries, and without administrative control over these adjacent areas, the towns instantly experience social, environmental, and economic problems. Unemployment, poor sanitation, inadequate social services, and environmental degradation have become common features of urbanization in Uganda. The adaptive coping mechanisms of the urban population have included reliance on urban natural resources such as wetlands to provide alternative livelihood strategies (Nyakaana et al. 2004). These alternative strategies are not sufficient, however, and the provision of adequate services—schools, health facilities, environmental infrastructure (drainage, water supply, sewerage networks, street lighting, and security)—remains a challenge.

The political landscape associated with civil strife is also speeding Uganda's urbanization as well as taking its toll on social well-being. The increased urbanization in the northern region is partly due to insecurity, which has resulted in the population moving to towns and the creation of camps for internally displaced persons (IDPs). For example, the Gulu and Lira municipalities and a number of towns in the Katakwi district have high populations mainly due to the influx of people seeking security in these urban centers, while the political situation in Southern Sudan is responsible for the high densities in northwestern Uganda, in the districts of Adjumani and Moyo. The movement of IDPs creates a need for urban services and has put pressure on local government

Table 16.3: Number of Businesses and Employment by Region, 2001–2002

| Region | Number of businesses | Employment | | | Average Number of Employees per Business |
		Total	Male	Female	
Central	96,991	281,456	163,412	118,044	2.9
Eastern	29,839	65,830	45,170	20,660	2.2
Northern	9,763	23,206	15,313	7,893	2.4
Western	24,290	73,626	47,353	26,273	3.0
Total	160,883	444,118	271,248	172,870	2.8

Source: Uganda Bureau of Statistics 2002.

resources. This has been a continually stressing problem for urban authorities.

The influence of the private sector on urbanization should also not be underestimated. Associated with strategies for national economic rehabilitation and development, the private sector contributes to urban expansion through establishment of industries, housing estates, higher education institutions, and commercial agricultural entities. This contribution is most marked in the major towns, which double as hubs for the provision of education services. Jinja, Mbale, Kampala, Mbarara, Soroti, and Mubende are all experiencing growth driven by the establishment of educational centers. The rush for educational centers is, in turn, driven by the liberalization of the educational sector which has allowed the existence of private education providers. These private education providers have typically been established at the fringes of Kampala City and other major towns such as Mbarara, Jinja, Masaka, and Mbale. Likewise, the real estate business is establishing ultramodern residential neighborhoods amidst impoverished peri-urban and rural settings. These planned neighborhoods exist around Kampala, most especially along the Kampala-Entebbe corridor. The growth of the private sector has influenced labor migrations into urban areas as rural populations search for employment, accelerating the housing sector development and the proliferation of the urban informal sector but also further limiting service availability.

The regional distribution of business establishments indicates that the central region surpasses all other regions in economic terms. Over 50 percent of the nation's registered businesses are in the central region (table 16.3); Kampala has the highest number of businesses, and they employ over 40 percent of the total labor force (UBOS 2003). A range of informal artisanal industries exists in Kampala alongside the formal

Table 16.4: Number of Businesses and Employment in Kampala by Industry Group, 2001–2002

Industrial Group	Number of Businesses	Employment		
		Male	Female	Total
Agriculture	449	9,736	5,047	14,783
Fishing	174	903	96	999
Mining and Quarrying	427	1,235	374	1,609
Manufacturing	11,968	70,588	16,543	87,131
Utilities	23	2,829	615	3,444
Construction	247	6,633	707	7,340
Wholesale and Retail Trade	107,486	102,222	76,053	178,275
Hotels, Restaurants, and Bars	20,483	16,269	37,862	54,131
Transport and Communications	834	10,161	3,737	13,898
Finance	417	4,107	2,916	7,023
Insurance	122	635	442	1,077
Real Estate and Business Services	2,414	15,871	4,308	20,179
Education	479	5,873	3,730	9,603
Health and Social Work	3,273	7,480	9,916	17,396
Community, Social, and Personal Services	12,086	16,706	10,524	27,230
Not Defined	1	0	0	0
Total	**160,883**	**271,248**	**172,870**	**444,118**

Source: Uganda Bureau of Statistics 2002.

industrial and business areas of Ntinda, Nakawa, Luzira-Port Bell, Kawempe, and Namanve. These industrial areas accommodate 93 percent of Uganda's formal industries and employ 66 percent of Uganda's industrial labor force (as quoted in UIA 2005). Since 1991, the Uganda Investment Authority has licensed a total of 1,561 industrial businesses falling into more than sixteen categories, including manufacturing, advertisement, leather tanning, food processing, beverage companies, and industries dealing in petrochemical products. Out of the total, 424 were established by securing land and building infrastructure and 448 not implemented, while 689 have the production lines operational. These industries range from wet (implying the use and/or generation of liquid) to dry (nonliquid inputs and outputs). Service industries are of differing sizes in terms of production output and demand for human resources.

Numerous medium- and small-scale industries are involved in food processing, metal fabrication, wood works, and the production of wine and soft drinks as indicated in table 16.4. These industries contribute to the migration into the city, which entails the absorption of externalized fertility. A total of 1,500 planned employment opportunities were expected to be generated by the licensed industries (UIA 2005). This level of employment generation implies better opportunities for labor in Kampala, which acts as an attraction for more migrants, but is not sufficient to the influx of population needing employment, even once the indirect opportunities (trading in products or linking economic activities) have been included. This raises questions about the sustainability of employment creation necessary to deal with higher rates of urbanization.

Urban public policy in Uganda is a domain of the central government and to some degree the local government authorities. Public policy to guide urban development is provided for in the constitution as well in supportive laws. Urban development has, however, suffered from a lack of vision at the national level to steer the formulation of appropriate and sustainable urban development policy. The political leadership reduced the ministry responsible to a single department, while between 1986 and 2000, the ministry has been switched and merged with other sectors several times. This seeming lack of direction and vision has put urban guidance in the balance, and this partly explains the lack of a national urban development policy to guide urbanization and manage city growth and development. Currently, responsibilities overlap between the Ministry of Lands, Housing, and Urban Development (with urban development reinstated in April 2006) and the Ministry of Local Government. Despite several public and professional calls for a national urbanization policy and guidance system, a couple of efforts to kick-start the policy formulation have either been derailed or abandoned. This situation has also contributed to the urbanization trends, especially sprawl, with no controls to address challenges. Currently, however, a land policy is being formulated, and the Ministry of Lands, Housing, and Urban Development was recently created with some promises that it would craft policies and frameworks for sustainable urban development.

Sustainable Urban Development Compared to Other Countries

Uganda's urbanization level is low—less than the 20 percent and 22 percent, respectively, for Kenya and Tanzania. Tanzania, Kenya, and Democratic Republic of Congo (DRC) have more urban population than Uganda and Zimbabwe. The urban growth rates are also high for Kenya and Tanzania compared to Uganda and DRC. But the challenges of sustainable urban development each country faces appear to have similarities. Except Zimbabwe, all the other countries have staggering proportions of the urban population without improved sanitation, despite higher proportions with access to safe water. The challenge of slums and associated social and environmental burdens is even more evident. Whereas this may reflect previously unsuccessful attempts to manage urban development sustainably, it actually underlines the present and future challenges of making cities in the region livable to all social groups while embracing sustainability principles. Although the comparative literature of regional urbanization experiences is scanty, micro-urban studies indicate similarities in the nature of urbanization, features of urban growth, country-specific urbanization trajectories, and integrated sustainable principles in urban development (Obudho and Peter 2002).

Since the Brundtland Report of 1987, the concept of sustainable development has attracted considerable debate, which is reflected in the vast amount of international literature on its interpretation and feasibility (Enyedi 2003). According to the report, sustainable development is meant "to ensure that development meets the needs of the present without compromising the ability of future generations to meet their own needs." From this point of view, several definitions have emerged, raising the difficulty of assessing the needs of future generations. Indeed, it would seem that the conflict arising between the protection of the biosphere and the continual demand for growth is not resolvable. Debate has increasingly drawn attention to the *societal* conflicts of environmental sustainability. With urbanization, the intertwining of societal and environmental conflicts is evident in cities (IHDP 2005; IDRC 2006). In the developing world, the environmental considerations are continually challenged because they have not been coupled with an efficient program of easing urban poverty. Improvement in the urban infrastructure, education and health care service, housing, transportation, and communication cannot be done without giving equal rights to the poor and other disadvantaged social groups, and without recognizing their organizations (Enyedi 2003). In other words, no environmental policy can be efficient without a social policy.

Recognizing that sustainable development is multidimensional, encompassing social, economic, and environment sustainability, sustainable urban development can be seen as encompassing six areas: (1) governance, (2) social and cultural considerations, (3) social infrastructure and public services, (4) urban land use and housing issues, (5) urban transport and urban natural resource management, and (6) employment and the enhancing of economic growth. These six areas form the framework for understanding the sustainability of urban development and also offer pointers on how to achieve sustainable urban development. Evaluating the sustainability of urban development requires robust but flexible methodologies and the formulation of indicators along which the six areas would be assessed. With the current urbanization trends, urban sustainability remains a challenge due to spontaneous developments, peri-urban developments, urban environmental change, land-use change, and industrialization (Enyedi 2003). This is because environmental burdens intertwine with poverty in a concomitant and reinforcing manner (IDRC 2006). In Uganda, research into these challenges has intensified and scaled up to the national level (Lwasa 1999; NEMA 2000/01; UBOS 2002). Due to the increasing complexity and interactions at all scales of urban development, the need for connections between research and policy in this area has become more pronounced. The subsequent sections of the paper focus on social services and infrastructure issues in urban management and how the provision of these services relates to environmental and social sustainability.

Urban Management in Uganda

Urban development in Uganda is experiencing changes in nature and direction. Currently, urban development is guided by the Town and Country Planning Act (1964), supported by the Public Health Act (1964) and the Local Government Act (1997). The Town and Country Planning Act defines the procedure for declaring an area as a planning area and the process for formulating spatial schemes as a framework for urban service provision. The Public Health Act details standards and requirements for buildings. Whereas these two legislations are focused on spatial development, the Local Government Act focuses on the provision of services (such as street lighting, solid-waste management, environmental management, infrastructure development, and governance) in an urban setting. These laws are also complemented by other laws for environmental management, water resources management, and wetland management. Gazetted towns have the liberty to make ordinances, which translate the rules and regulations concerning specific urban management issues. These are developed to implement the laws and or address the challenging issues that have emerged. For example, in 2005, Kampala City Council passed five ordinances on urban agriculture that had long been contested in lieu of the Urban Authorities Act (which was repealed but strictly made any form of farming, expect for planting flowers and keeping pet animals, illegal).

Translating laws and regulations for urban management has largely been pursued through two approaches, the project-based approach and the sector-wide approach. The project-based approach is the most common in Uganda, while the sector-wide approach has only recently been introduced at the national level. One of the disadvantages of the project-based approach is projectization with limited scaling out, which has left some communities unserviced compared to the pilot communities. But

Table 16.5: Summary of Expenditure on Urban Services by Major Urban Authorities, 2006–2007

City	Population	Expenditure in Ugandan shillings	Equivalent in dollars
Mbarara	69,208	773,481,473	465,953
Mbale	70,437	374,413,801	225,550
Kampala	1,189,142	35,867,679,200	21,607,036
Jinja	86,520	561,549,044	338,283

Source: Uganda Bureau of Statistics 2002.

the urban services and infrastructure developed in piloted communities become unsustainable in relatively short time periods.

At the national level, urban development has not proceeded in a balanced way. The central region has registered substantial infrastructure development in terms of transportation, communication, and sociophysical and environmental infrastructure, as well as social services. For Kampala, the World Bank has spent more than $10 million U.S. over the last ten years on solid waste management, drainage, spatial planning, and building capacity. While Kampala received these resources, other major towns remained underfunded by the central government, which explains the lesser levels of development compared to Kampala. But the services and infrastructure development has not corresponded to the 4.9 percent annual growth rate of the city, living urban service gaps and accentuating urban poverty (UBOS and ILRI 2004), in which 16 percent of Kampala's population is under the poverty line. As indicated in table 16.5, there is a huge variation between the major urban authorities in terms of budget expenditure on urban services in the period 2006–2007. This is partially because of the population, but it is also because of the priority of investment projects. Roads, construction of school classrooms, and drainage take the largest share in all cases. But despite these investments, deplorable conditions exist among urban population sections in these urban centers.

The sector-wide approach has been pursued at the national level, where the need for guiding urban development and ensuring sustainable national development has been recognized. Among several sectorwide programs is the Land Sector Strategic Program, which recognized the need for land-use planning at the national level, especially managing urbanization. The other sector-wide programs have embraced the principles of sustainability to ensure a participatory identification of solutions to social and environmental conflicts. Three national development policy initiatives are under way: the National Land Use Policy, the National Land Use Plan, and the National Land Policy. The National Land Use Policy has been approved by the cabinet, while the other two are in draft form and the stage of consultation. But all three recognize the importance of sustainable urban development.

Decentralization Policy and City Management

Although an effective urbanization policy is one of the key factors in national development, such a policy is not in place to guarantee an orderly and sustainable urban development in Uganda. The current Local Governments Act has succeeded in the devolution of powers to local governments for effective planning, implementation of plans, and delivery of services to the urban populations. Analysis of its effectiveness indicates that it has fallen short of the requirements for sustainable urban development. Since its implementation was in 1993, however, it is also possible that it is still in the gestation period. Rather than focus on how effective the law has been in the past, it is important to focus on the current and future challenges of urban development—effective and efficient provision of urban services, governance, and infrastructure development. These are key issues of urban development, because of their influence on the economic and social development and the environmental status of an urban area. Social and economic development needs a spatial framework, but decentralization has led to competitive allocation of resources with little consideration of the spatial development of the city. One of the key consequences of this is marginalization of large sections of the urban population, leading to polarization.

Urban Health Service Provision

Urban health in Uganda has been compromised by the nature of urban development, due to the increased exposure of city dwellers to health risks. The urban environment in Uganda, characterized by informal settlements with inadequate infrastructure and sanitation facilities, is conducive to disease outbreaks (Rugadya 2006). Despite huge investments in urban infrastructure, pockets of poverty "hot spots" are spread around the country in the urban areas. In these "hot spot" areas, urban services and infrastructure are inadequate, leading to the accumulation of wastes, flooding, and poor sanitation (UBOS and ILRI 2004). Drainage channels are also open sewers that run through the neighborhoods, scattering organic and inorganic wastes that contaminate water sources when they overflow during the rainy season. In Kampala, for example, cholera outbreaks have occurred every year since 1997; an outbreak between October 30, 2006, and mid-January 2007 registered 634 cases with nine deaths. In regard to service provision and access, planning has been decentralized to subcounty level but still requires improvement. For example, in a Kampala study on health service provision, the proliferation of private clinics has shifted service provision from the public health facilities to the private sector. Although the private sector has its merits, including more drugs and physicians, it also acts as a conduit for inappropriate treatment, poorly trained professionals, and expired drugs. Although statistics indicate that urban populations have access to health services within 5 km from their residence, the quality of services provided is low. The shift to the private sector implies less control over the quality of services provided by authorities, making urban populations vulnerable, yet providing much-needed services.

Urban Education Services

Under the decentralization policy, education service provision is also a responsibility of the municipalities/cities in regard to planning, resource allocation, human resources, and supervisory roles. The privatization of education services has ushered in private educational institutions. Education is categorized as preprimary, primary, secondary, vocational, and tertiary. Preprimary is a sole responsibility of the private sector and only guided by a national guidance system; primary is universal, but the number of public schools with universal primary is superseded by the privately owned primary schools. Universal secondary education just began at the beginning of 2007 on a pilot basis, and has been rolled out in the last three years nationally. Vocational education is largely provided by the central government through the Ministry of Education, while tertiary education is largely private, with a few public universities. According to the Ministry of Education, 56.7 percent of the education facilities are provided by government, including local governments such as municipalities and the city, while 34.7 percent are provided by the private sector (MOES 2007). This distribution is likely to increase with the introduction of universal secondary education because parents prefer private institutions to public ones.

Urban Transportation Services

Public transportation planning in Uganda is a responsibility of the Ministry of Works and Communication Technology, but the municipalities have responsibility for providing public transport services (Mukwaya 2001). As in other public services, the decentralization policy passed on supervisory responsibilities to the local governments, which engage the private sector to directly provide services on their behalf. The idea is to reduce the costs for the local government/municipality to directly provide the service. Public transport provision is dominated by minibuses with a seating capacity of fourteen. When coupled with the mean growth rate of cars by 10.9 percent, it is obvious why traffic congestion is a common feature of urban transportation, especially in Kampala. With an energy consumption rate of 0.00012 ton/vehicle km, the demand for energy for the public transport sector is ever increasing, as urban development accelerates. In 2002, the total energy demand for the Kampala region was estimated at 33.12 million gigajoules (mgj); this is expected to increase to 81.8 mgj in 2010 (UBOS 2002). This level of energy use places an enormous toll on the environment through greenhouse gas emissions. Due to the type of public transport and the huge energy demand, the sector is largely inefficient and unsustainable. (Mukwaya 2005) notes that the performance of the transportation sector to users in terms of costs, travel time, and level of choice is rated low, while a detailed zonal analysis of greenhouse gas emissions based on intensity of urban development reveals that CO_2 emissions range from 0.11 kg CO_2/liter to 3.54 kg CO_2/liter of diesel (Mukwaya 2001; Mukwaya 2005). This raises sustainability questions and the need to revisit the public urban transportation sector for managing urban growth and development.

Urban Water and Sanitation Services

Urban water service provision in Uganda is a responsibility of the National Water and Sewerage Corporation (NWSC). The NWSC is a public corporation wholly owned by the government of Uganda. The principal business of the corporation as defined in the National Water and Sewerage Corporation Act is to operate and provide water and sewerage services in areas entrusted to it under the Water Act. The National Water and Sewerage Corporation effectively operates in seventeen towns, namely Kampala (including Kajjansi and Nansana), Jinja/Njeru, Entebbe, Tororo, Mbale, Masaka, Mbarara, Gulu, Lira, Fort Portal, Kasese, Kabale, Arua, Bushenyi/Isahaka, Soroti, Mukono, and Malaba. Final preparations are under way to take over the towns of Iganga and Lugazi. Despite its existence for thirty-three years and its concentration on urban centers, only 67 percent of the population in Kampala is served with water. Though this percentage has increased over time, the remainder of the unserved are largely the urban poor and residents of the peri-urban fringe.

Urban Waste Management

Urbanization is also closely associated with high densities, which has implications for waste generation and management. Waste management in the city is still a daunting and challenging task for the city authority and population. Waste generation rates are high mainly due to the high population; with an average household size of 5.7, the generation rate per capita is 0.069 kg for households and 0.213 kg for commercial units per day (KCC and BTC 2008). Although generation of wastes would not be a problem, it becomes so if the means for storage, transportation, and disposal are insufficient and therefore overwhelmed. This presents serious environmental and health implications to the urban population.

Until 2002, solid-waste collection, transportation, and disposal has been the responsibility of the municipal authorities. Under the Local Government Act 1997, it is one of the services listed as the mandated role of urban authorities. The current practices have separated roles in the solid waste management model (SWM). For example, Kampala City Council passed a revised Solid Waste Management Ordinance in 2002, in which the principle of the "generator pays" was established as the basis of the current solid-waste management systems. Many other municipalities are revising, or considering revising, municipal ordinances to pursue the "generator pays" principle. The solid-waste ordinances led to privatization of garbage collection, and this was coupled with the private sector-led development policy, which supports procurement of services from private organizations by the local governments. Privatization has increased refuse collection coverage in one of the municipal divisions from 10 percent to 80 percent, while the unit cost of collection was reduced from Uganda shillings 11,300/m³ to 4,500/m³ ($8 U.S./m³ to $3 U.S./m³) (Rugadya 2006). An estimated 20 to 30 percent of the population is served with the solid waste management services in Kampala (UBOS 2002). There are several private garbage collectors that provide door-to-door solid waste collection services at fees ranging from 20,000 to 30,000 Ugandan shillings ($12–$20 U.S.) per month for biweekly service. The city council subsidizes these fees for the urban poor settlements. Private collectors are now experimenting with a clustered hold method that enables a group contribution to the monthly fee.

Urban Sustainability in Ugandan Context

Urban sustainability, as indicated earlier, embodies several thematic areas that should be the focus of urban development. These areas also fit very well with the Millennium Development Goals and, if pursued, could help Uganda achieve these goals. But given the current urban development experience in Uganda, sustainable urban development needs to be stepped up, for several reasons: increasing social polarization of urban communities; environmental degradation; increasing burdens (sanitation, flooding, waste accumulation, public health, and disasters) on large proportions of the urban populations in Uganda; regional imbalances in urban development (industrialization in Kampala); and the challenge of labor migrations to the central region. Urban sustainability challenges are summarized below:

- Increase in urban population, industrialization, and the associated demand for housing have ushered in a process of land-use and land-cover changes in the urban areas in Uganda.
- The nature of urban expansion and extension around major urban areas is putting pressure on peri-urban areas, with social and environmental consequences.
- Natural disasters in urban areas are also increasing with urban growth and expansion. Flooding in Kampala, for example, has become an expected phenomenon when even a slight downpour occurs, affecting economic productivity and the livelihood of people, and affecting their health, housing, and ability to access their neighborhoods.

A Future Trajectory of Urbanization in Uganda

Uganda's path to urbanization is characterized by a mixture of processes. The forces driving Uganda's urbanization are intertwined, propelling rapid growth in urban areas previously unaccustomed to it. Therefore the urbanization process in Uganda is characterized by five important dimensions of change: (1) population densities, (2) urbanized and chronic poverty, (3) social spatial polarization, (4) urban environmental degradation, and (5) services and infrastructure gaps. The challenge of sustainable urban development is likely to become more overwhelming as urban populations continue to expand. With this background, the future of Uganda's urbanization path seems to be comprised of significant but uncontrolled and undirected change. Additionally, the current policy of decentralization has implications with respect to urbanization. Gazetted urban centers are likely to increase, as local governments increasingly advocate for control of resources.

In conclusion, despite the potential for realizing sustainable urban development, this path remains elusive for Uganda and sub-Saharan Africa more generally. Social sustainability for urban areas would require an adequate and cross-sectional distribution of urban services to ensure accessibility and to improve the conditions of many urban dwellers. Although the rate of urbanization is low in Uganda, the challenges to sustainability posed by urban growth and expansion are daunting, given the current experiences of populations with inadequate access to urban services, including a water supply, sanitation, education, and health. Meanwhile inadequate infrastructure, such as drainage systems and roads, is exposing urban populations to environmental burdens. The consequence of these conditions is increasing urban poverty as well as the urbanization of poverty. The intertwining of urban poverty and environmental challenges calls for innovative research into alternative urban development approaches and policy. This will require a concerted effort that should bring together researchers, policy actors, communities, and governments to address the challenges.

Chapter 17

Thinking About Urban Services Needs in Fast-Growing Cities: Housing in São Paulo

Suzana Pasternak

The prevalent forms of housing among low-income groups in Brazil vary according to the city and period considered. In each place and time, a specific form of housing has been prevalent in the urban landscape. Three basic types of housing stand out: slums (*cortiços*), squatter settlements (*favelas*), and peripheral land developments, with home ownership and self-construction.

Interventions for the provision of low-cost housing have changed throughout history. Slave quarters gave way after 1888 to the solutions of industrialized cites: the spontaneously developed slums and the government-backed factory villages. Renting was by far the primary means of having a roof. From the 1930s onward, sharp industrial growth and expansion above 5 percent gave rise to increasing rural-urban migration and to the growth of large cities, especially in the southeast region. Interventions in the relationship between lessor and lessee discouraged the construction of rental housing units. The urban settlement pattern had three pillars: low-cost land development, home-ownership, and self-construction. The urbanized area expanded horizontally, thus increasing the city's periphery.

During the Vargas period (1930–1945), government concerns over housing issues prompted interventions in the rental housing market and the creation of construction programs sponsored by Retirement and Pension Institutes. During the "populist period"[1] (1945–1964), the "entrepreneur state" created the Fundação da Casa Popular (Popular Housing Foundation), for low-cost housing, which became the seed of the military government's housing policy. After the military coup in 1964, the federal government set up an ambitious system to finance and build mass housing. The choice of housing policy to be the central axis of the government's social policy was determined by the military government's need to legitimize itself with the low-income population. According to one of the creators of the system, Minister Roberto Campos, "the solution to the problem of home ownership has the specific allure of encouraging savings that would otherwise not exist, and contributes a lot more to creating social stability than rental property. Homeowners think twice before getting into trouble or vandalizing the property of others and become allies in order maintenance" (Banco Nacional da Habitação 1966, 20–21).

In the beginning of 1985, when the so-called New Republic came about, the National Housing Bank was going through a deep institutional crisis which eventually brought it to bankruptcy; in 1986 it closed. The following year, CEF (Caixa Econômica Federal), a federally owned savings bank and commercial bank, incorporated the activities of the National Housing Bank. The federal government's policy was primarily based on alternative programs, within an ideological framework of compensatory policies. During the Sarney administration, federal housing programs focused on the National Program for Collective Home Building (Programa Nacional de Mutirões Habitacionais).

The Collor administration, which followed the Sarney administration, innovated very little in its two-and-a-half-year term. The state and municipal governments, however, made interventions in the low-cost housing market, adopting their own criteria. This was possible because of the decentralization provided for in the Constitution of 1988. With the inauguration of President Itamar Franco (1992), decentralization increased further.

The Cardoso administration began in 1995 and sought to implement a new financial system, the SFI (Sistema Financeiro Imobiliário, or Real Estate Financial System). It also designed new capital funding systems, implemented mortgage securitization, and prioritized the granting of credit directly to the buyer (and not to a real estate developer or construction company, as was the case with SFH (Sistema Financeiro da Habitação, or Housing Financing System). Now, in the Lula administration (which began in 2002), the SFI has still to be fully implemented and decentralized policies continue to prevail.

The problem of home financing remains unsolved. There are efforts in place to create a specific system for the medium- and high-income population based on the SFI—that is, on mortgage refinancing—and another system for the low-income population, with heavy subsidies. But social housing is still in very short supply. In short, there are macrostructural limitations that make squatter settlements a possible housing solution for the low-income population.

The problem of squatter settlements has grown to unprecedented proportions in Brazil. The 2005 PNAD Survey (the national household sample survey) points to the existence of almost 2 million households in squatter settlements in Brazil, totaling over 6.5 million dwellers. In some cities, such as Rio de Janeiro and São Paulo, there are approximately 1 million people living in the *favelas*, and in others, such as Belém, households in the *favelas* account for 35 percent of the total housing units.

To quote Cardoso, "How and why have squatter settlements become a problem of [this] magnitude?" (Cardoso 2007, 4). Until the 1980s, the growth of squatter settlements was thought to be related to the high rates of rural-urban migration. Squatters were thought to be primarily those recently arrived in town, especially from backward rural areas. This interpretation was challenged in the late 1970s and early 1980s by research showing that a significant part of the squatter population was not made up of migrants seeking social ascent but, rather, included many in the process of social descent (Pasternak Taschner, 1978). To quote the administration further:

> The Brazilian model of development led to the formation of a social pattern that associates a reasonable degree of economic growth (especially from the 1940s to the 1970s) to a high degree of inequality and a significant portion of the population living below the poverty line. Poverty and inequality, structural characteristics that have marked Brazilian development, have been associated with increasingly deteriorated and informal employment relations in the last 25 years. This is why a significant portion of the population has insufficient or insecure income, which greatly limits their possibilities of contracting debt and thus of having access to the formal housing market. (Cardoso 2007, 4)

Additionally, Brazilian economic development was marked by the focus of public authorities on investment to support the industrialization process, to the detriment of investment in services designed to reproduce labor power. Public authorities were therefore unable to invest in infrastructure or to increase their ability to regulate the land and housing markets. As a result, cities grew in a poorly planned manner, and there was rampant land speculation. The land market was, up until the 1960s, one of the few alternatives for capital investment. Since the 1970s, the financial market has been organized and consolidated as an alternative for investment. Land speculation generated huge disparities between the price of land in the formal market and the creditworthiness of the majority of the population, thus prompting informal takeovers and putting a huge mass of urban workers at risk. Ineffective low-income housing policies are also associated with these facts. In short, there are a large number of squatter settlements which will be around for a long time.

The Squatter Population in Brazil

Squatter Settlement and Squatters per Metropolitan Region

Squatter settlements are present in all Brazilian regions, though they are unevenly distributed. In 1991, there were 3,187 squatter settlements, according to the Demographic Census. According to the Population Count of 1996, the number of such settlements had risen to 3,348, and it reached 3,906 in 2000.[2]

Just as the number of settlements has been increasing since 1980 at higher rates than the total population, so too has the number of squatters and households of squatters. From 1980 to 1991, the total number of households in Brazil grew by 3.08 percent yearly, whereas the number of households in squatter settlements grew by 8.18 percent yearly. In the following period—from 1991 to 2000—total households grew by 0.88 percent yearly, whereas households in settlements grew by 4.18 percent. Estimates for 2005 point to a 3.45 percent yearly growth rate for total households, with the number of households in settlements increasing at a similar rate, 3.46 percent yearly for the period. The squatter population in 1980 was 2.25 million people; in 1991, more than 5 million; in 2000, approximately 7.2 million; and, in 2005, it was estimated at more than 8.5 million, for a total of 1,956,331 households in subnormal settlements.

The only Brazil-wide information available on squatter settlements is included in the Demographic Census. Therefore, this data has been used to measure the size of the phenomenon in Brazil, despite the conceptual and methodological problems of such information. Some municipalities, such as São Paulo, Rio de Janeiro, Belo Horizonte, and others, have built a historical series based on field surveys conducted by the academy or funded and organized by the local government itself. However, these surveys were carried out using specific dates and methods, and the data they obtained are therefore difficult to compare. Thus, using the census is the only alternative for making estimates at a national level.

Tables 17.1 and 17.2 make it obvious that the highest percentages of squatter households are located in the north and southeast regions. In the north region, the squatter household growth rate is fairly high and increased between 1991–2000 and 2000–2005. The percentage of households in squatter settlements in this region is growing: 1.04 percent in

Table 17.1: Percentage of Households in Squatter Settlements per Major Region in Brazil, 1980, 1991, 2000, 2005

Region	1980	1991	2000	2005
North	1.04%	4.11%	6.35%	7.61%
Northeast	0.87%	2.62%	2.69%	2.90%
Southeast	2.60%	3.59%	5.14%	4.96%
South	0.62%	1.11%	1.53%	1.02%
Central-West	0.58%	0.42%	0.53%	0.62%
Brazil	1.62%	2.76%	3.69%	3.69%

Source: Fundação do Instituto Brasileiro de Geografia e Estatística Demographic Census of 1980, 1991, 2000, 2005.

Table 17.2: Geometric Growth Rate for Squatter Households per Major Region in Brazil, 1980–2005

Region	Squatter Household Growth Rate		
	1980–1991	1991–2000	2000–2005
North	20.37%	6.91%	9.63%
Northeast	13.66%	0.76%	4.79%
Southeast	5.96%	4.89%	2.55%
South	8.44%	4.65%	−5.01%
Central-West	0.64%	4.55%	7.33%
Brazil	8.18%	4.18%	3.46%

Source: Fundação do Instituto Brasileiro de Geografia e Estatística Democratic Census of 1980, 1991, 2000, 2005.

1980, 4.11 percent in 1991, 6.35 percent in 2000, up to 7.61 percent in 2005. It is the region with the highest percentage of squatter settlements in Brazil, and this percentage has been growing alarmingly.

In the northeast, historically Brazil's poorest region, the percentage of households in squatter settlements has also been growing (see Table 17.2), but at lower rates than in the north. Even so, the growth rate of squatter households—4.70 percent at the beginning of 2000—is higher than the growth rate for total households (3.21 percent yearly). The squatter population is growing faster than the total population. The northeast region is believed to have the greatest census data discrepancies; if so, the total number of subnormal settlements has been underestimated and the difference should be even higher than the figures indicate.

In the southeast region, the growth rate for total households, after a relative decline in the 1990s, went back to a 3 percent yearly increase. The pace of growth for households in squatter settlements in the early 2000s slowed down and was lower than the overall growth rate. As a result, in 2005, squatter households made up a smaller percentage of total households than in 2000.

In the south, the percentage of squatters decreased to approximately 1 percent of total households. And finally, in the central-west region, just as in the north, the rates have been increasing, although the percentage of households in squatter settlements is still small, approximately 1 percent.

Squatter settlements in Brazil are a predominantly metropolitan phenomenon: in 1980, 79.16 percent of the households in squatter settlements were located in the nine federal metropolitan regions, as seen in table 17.1. In 1991, 2,391 squatter settlements (74 percent of the total) and 817,000 squatter households (78 percent of the total) were located in these metropolitan regions.

In 2000, the percentage of squatter households located in metropolitan squatter settlements increased to 87.15 percent. In that same year, squatter settlements were described as a clearly metropolitan phenomenon, and their percentage continued to rise. In 2005, the percentage of squatter households located in metropolitan areas dropped to 75.15 percent, thus indicating a certain reversal in the trend. Although squatter settlements are mostly a phenomenon in large urban areas, they are spreading rapidly in other, smaller cities. Squatter settlements can be considered a problem in medium-sized cities; in 2000, 26 percent of the squatter population was found in cities with a population between 100,000 and 500,000.

Throughout the twentieth century, squatter settlements have clearly been the norm for a large portion of the urban poor population. In some state capitals, such as Belém, the percentage of people living in such settlements has reached 35 percent of the local population. In metropolitan centers such as Rio de Janeiro, the absolute number is in excess of 1 million people, almost 20 percent of the households. São Paulo, the capital itself, in addition to Guarulhos and São Bernardo, has a large number of squatters.

Squatter Population in the São Paulo Metropolitan Region

The São Paulo Metropolitan Region has the largest concentration of squatter settlements in Brazil, as seen in Table 17.3. The cities of São Paulo, Guarulhos, Osasco, and Diadema alone had, in 2000, 938 squatter settlements—approximately one quarter of the country's squatter settlements according to the Demographic Census. Among the fifteen municipalities with the largest number of squatter settlements in 2000, five are in the state of São Paulo; of these, four are located in the São Paulo Metropolitan Region (São Paulo, Guarulhos, Osasco, and Dia-

Table 17.3: Total Population and Population Living in Subnormal Settlements in 10
        Municipalities with the Largest Population Living in Squatter Settlements, 2000

Municipality	Population	Squatter Population	Percentage
Rio de Janeiro	5,580,544	1,092,476	18.7
São Paulo	10,348,736	909,628	8.8
Belém	1,275,622	448,723	35.2
Fortaleza	2,125,111	353,925	16.6
Belo Horizonte	2,229,697	268,847	12.1
Salvador	2,418,440	238,342	9.9
Manaus	1,401,567	167,774	11.2
Guarulhos	1,066,065	163,757	15.4
S. Bernardo	695,586	147,483	21.2
Curitiba	1,578,506	145,242	9.2

Source: Costa 2005, in Cardoso 2007.

Table 17.4: São Paulo Metropolitan Region Households: Total and Number in Squatter
        Settlements, 1991 and 2000

Geographical Unit	Total Households		Households in Squatter Settlements	
	1991	2000	1991	2000
São Paulo Municipality	2,630,138	3,039,104	146,891	225,133
Other Municipalities	1,580,306	2,040,084	93,972	188,220
Total for the São Paulo Metropolitan Region	4,210,444	5,079,188	240,863	413,353

Source: Fundação do Instituto Brasileiro de Geografia e Estatística Demographic Census
of 1991 and 2000.

dema) and one in the municipality of Campinas, with 117 squatter settlements. The following is a ranking of the municipalities with the
largest number of squatter settlements: São Paulo (612), Rio de Janeiro
(513), Fortaleza (157), Guarulhos (136), Curitiba (122), Campinas
(117), Belo Horizonte (101), Osasco (101), Salvador (99), Belém (93),
Diadema (89), Volta Redonda (87), Teresina (85), Porto Alegre (76),
and Recife (73). It should be noted that these data are indicative,
because the number of squatter settlements is not directly proportional
to the squatter population and there are no records of its growth. It is
also worth noting that among these fifteen municipalities, Teresina,
Volta Redonda, and Campinas are the only ones that are not located in
federal metropolitan regions.

As shown in table 17.4, the percentage of households in squatter settlements in São Paulo has been increasing since 1991. This percentage
relative to the total households was 5.72 percent in 1991, rose to 8.14

percent in 2000, and then rose again to 9.29 percent in 2005. The housing scenario in the metropolis has clearly deteriorated.

This growth was not consistent throughout the greater São Paulo area. The 2005 data cannot be broken down, but the census information of 1991 and 2000 shows that the growth rate of households in squatter settlements in peripheral municipalities was almost twice that of the capital city, a sign that squatter settlements are spreading throughout the metropolitan region (the so-called process of *favelization*). Not only is the population living on the periphery of the metropolis growing more rapidly than the population of the capital city, but squatter settlements in peripheral municipalities are also growing faster than those located in the capital. Even when absolute numbers are considered, the number of households in squatter settlements in peripheral municipalities has increased faster than in the capital city: the number of settlements increased by 94,248 on the periphery, more than doubling, whereas in the capital the number of households in squatter settlements increased by 78,242, an increase slightly above 53 percent.

This fact may reflect a trend toward the expansion of poverty into the periphery, which is represented here by the territorial expansion of poor housing. In addition to poor housing conditions, distances to work also increase, thus rendering the life of the poor living in metropolitan regions even more difficult.

Squatter Settlements in the São Paulo Municipality

Different Estimates

The number of squatter settlements, households, and individuals in the São Paulo municipality varies according to the source of data used. There is much discrepancy regarding the number of squatter settlements in São Paulo: according to the 2000 census (preliminary data), there were 612 squatter settlements in the municipality, with 932,628 dwellers. According to the 1991 census, this figure was 629; according to the 1996 Population Count, it was 574. It is worth noting that the census records only settlements with over fifty households and mixes the so-called subnormal sectors with the normal ones. According to the 2001 municipal profile, there were 387,863 households in squatter settlements. Actually, the municipal profile was based on the information of the Fundação Instituto de Pesquisas Econômicas e Secretaria da Habitação do Município de São Paulo (FIPE-SEHAB)/Secretariat of Housing survey, which was later refuted by the SEHAB itself and replaced by the estimates of CEM. This is why we have adopted the census information.

Thus, we can conclude the following:

- The squatter population in São Paulo Municipality has increased at a higher rate than the population of the municipality;
- The squatter settlement area grew substantially in the 1990s;
- In addition to the increase in the area used by squatter settlements, there is strong evidence of an increase in their average density. Squatter settlements are now denser, with their empty spaces being occupied, and squatter settlements are undergoing a process of verticalization;
- Difficulties in accessing land put up for sale, in addition to the impoverishment of the dwellers, have made squatter settlements a possible housing alternative for the poor. We should add the lack of housing units for the low-income population and the relative improvement in housing conditions in squatter settlements in the city of São Paulo to these factors, so that living in a squatter settlement is not as hard as it used to be decades ago;
- The policy of upgrading and maintaining squatter settlements within the urban fabric—although legitimate—has encouraged land takeovers.

Spatialization of Squatter Settlements in the City of São Paulo

The squatter population growth rate from 1980 to 1991 was 7.07 percent yearly, significantly higher than the growth rate of the population of the municipality for the same period (1.16 percent yearly). From 1991 to 1996, the squatter population continued to grow at a higher rate than the population as a whole: 1 percent yearly, whereas the total population grew at a meager 0.4 percent yearly. And from 1996 to 2000, rates for squatters were higher than municipal growth rates: 5.07 percent for the squatter population and 1.49 percent for the municipal population as a whole.

Over the last decade of the second millennium, the yearly growth rate for the squatter population was approximately three times higher than that for the population as a whole: 2.82 percent for the squatter population compared with the municipal rate of 0.93 percent from 1991 to 2000. Because the number of people per household has decreased in squatter settlements as well, the growth rate for households in squatter settlements was even higher than that of the squatter population, reaching 3.96 percent yearly, and 5.06 percent yearly for those settlements in the peripheral ring, between 1991 and 2000.

Just as in the municipality, squatter settlements grow at a faster pace in the urban periphery. Preliminary spatialization using the rings (Pasternak and Bogus 2006) shows that growth of the population as a whole,

Table 17.5: São Paulo Municipality: Percentage of Squatter Population per Ring, 1991, 1996, 2000

Ring	Percentage in 1991	Percentage in 1996	Percentage in 2000
Central	0.05	0.00	0.00
Inner	0.90	0.48	0.78
Intermediary	5.28	4.79	7.19
Outer	7.06	6.80	8.03
Peripheral	10.32	10.59	11.53
Total	7.39	7.60	8.73

Source: Fundação do Instituto Brasileiro de Geografia e Estatística Demographic Census of 1991 and 2000; 1996 Population Count.

and in squatter settlements as well, takes place primarily in the so-called peripheral ring.

The percentage of the squatter population relative to the total population has been increasing since 1991 and rose from 7.39 percent to 8.73 percent in 2000. The reversal in the trend for the inner and intermediary rings stands out: in these two rings, between 1991 and 1996, the percentage of squatters had decreased only to rise again at the end of the decade. In the outer and peripheral rings, the percentage showed an upward trend. There may be problems with the 1996 data, as it was collected via a population count, not a national census. In the population count some of the data were collected by phone, a methodology that may have caused problems with accuracy, as some results have been questioned by scholars familiar with the data.

As shown in Table 17.5, there are districts in the city of São Paulo where half the population lives in squatter settlements, such as Vila Andrade, in the south zone. In 1991, 42.73 percent of Vila Andrade's population lived in squatter settlements, a percentage that increased to 45.69 percent in 1996 and to 52.11 percent in 2000.

In 1991, 1996, and 2000 alike, Vila Andrade, in the south zone, Jaguaré, in the west zone, and Pedreira, also in the south zone, had the highest percentage of their populations living in squatter settlements (in 2000, this percentage was 33.48 percent for Pedreira and 29.18 percent for Jaguaré). Vila Andrade was the district with the highest percentage of squatter settlement dwellers throughout the decade. From 1996 to 2000, the district of Jaguaré dropped to third place among the districts with the highest percentage of squatter settlements, and Pedreira, in third until 1996, went to second place.

In many districts in the south zone of São Paulo, 20 percent of the population lived in squatter settlements: Cidade Dutra (20.04 percent in 1991, 21.22 percent in 1996, and 21.80 percent in 2000); Capão

Redondo (20.78 percent in 1991, 18.65 percent in 1996, and 20.99 percent in 2000); Jardim São Luís (19.62 percent in 1991, 21.01 percent in 1996, and 19.90 percent in 2000); Grajaú (18.95 percent in 1991, 19.50 percent in 1996, and 17.85 percent in 2000); Jardim Ângela (18.24 percent in 1991, 15.75 percent in 1996, and 19.40 percent in 2000). In Vila Sônia, in 2000, 19.62 percent of the population lived in squatter settlements, a significant increase from the past, since in 1991 this percentage was 12.71 percent and in 1996 it was 14.93 percent.

In the north zone, Brasilândia, with 13.07 percent in 2000, and Cachoeirinha, with 17.63 percent in 2000, were the districts with the highest percentage of squatters. In the west zone, Jaguaré continued to have a high percentage of squatters: 29.18 percent in 2000, whereas in 1996 the percentage was 26.73 percent and in 1991 it was 33.89 percent. In Rio Pequeno, the percentage of squatters, which had been below 20 percent (18.15 percent in 1991 and 19.67 percent in 1996), rose to 20.52 percent. In the east zone, Sapopemba ranked first, with 12.32 percent in 2000. It becomes apparent that the squatter settlements tend to be established and grow in environmental preservation areas, particularly in water-source areas in the mountains of northern São Paulo.

The conclusions are as follows:

- The municipal population and the squatter population alike grow in the periphery. The number of households in squatter settlements from 1991 to 2000 increased by 78,237 units, of which 58,868 households, i.e., 72.24 percent, were located in the peripheral ring;
- The squatter population grows even more in the periphery than the total population in the municipality: the growth rate of the squatter population in the peripheral ring was nearly 1.5 times higher than the total population growth rate (3.98 percent yearly compared with 2.71 percent between 1991 and 2000);
- There are almost ten districts, among the ninety-six that make up the municipality, where more than 20 percent of the population lives in squatter settlements. In 2000, these districts were Vila Andrade, Pedreira, Jaguaré, Sacomã, Cidade Dutra, Vila Jacuí, Capão Redondo, Rio Pequeno, and Jardim São Luís;
- The squatter population is concentrated in the municipality's southern districts.

Myths About Squatter Settlements and Squatters

Valladares (2000) and Pasternak (2001) have commented on some "myths" that have influenced scholars' thoughts about squatter settlements and squatters.

Myths About the Space in Squatter Settlements

The first myth has to do with the specificity of the space of squatter settlements. The myth holds that they occupy urban space in a unique manner. According to this myth, the streets have an irregular design and are narrower. The architectural design and the construction techniques used in squatter settlements are also supposed to be specific, from the design—which does not comply with building codes and land-use regulations—to the use of specific construction materials and techniques.

As regards morphology, houses in squatter settlements in 2000 are usually made of brickwork, often with two stories, are served by electricity (more than 99 percent), drinking water (approximately 98 percent), and garbage collection (more than 80 percent of the units). Of course, there are wooden shacks, but these shacks do not prevail as they did until 1987 (when approximately 50 percent of the housing units were built of wood). Shacks no longer prevail in the landscape, which now has a grayish and reddish tone due to the concrete blocks used on the floor and walls of the lower stories and the red perforated bricks used on the upper stories. In terms of infrastructure, the critical housing issue in squatter settlements concerns the disposal of domestic sewage: only 51 percent of the households were connected to the public wastewater system in 2000. For the city as a whole, this percentage was 84 percent in 1991 and 87 percent in 2000 (Pasternak, 2001).

As regards household occupancy, there has been continual improvement over time: whereas in 1973 houses with a single room prevailed, in 2000 only slightly over 1 percent of the households had a single room; 84 percent have more than two rooms. Household crowding indicators have been improving, with the number of people per room decreasing threefold from 1973 to 2000, and the percentage of crowded households, with more than two people per bedroom, decreasing from 35 percent in 1991 to 19 percent in 2000 (Census 2000).

Although use value has been the main factor in the appropriation of the land taken over, both plots and houses have become merchandise. There are "formal" systems to sell housing units, especially in larger squatter settlements. Baltrusis (2000) analyzed the squatter settlements of Nova Conquista (in Diadema) and Paraisópolis (one of the largest in the São Paulo municipality, with approximately 40,000 dwellers) and noted that in the latter 110 (1.2 percent) of the properties were put up for sale. "In the 1990s, D. Helena established the first real estate dealer in the squatter settlement. There are currently three such businesses that make most of the transactions involving property there" (Baltrusis 2000, 46). Prices are fairly consistent among different squatter settlements, with the modal price of the four-room house ranging from

R$12,000 to R$15,000, a selling price of approximately R$250 per square meter. Data from EMBRAESP (Brazilian Company of Real Property Studies) indicate that the average price per square meter of a household in low-income districts in the capital city of São Paulo was approximately R$967 (roughly eight times the minimum salary of 1998). Therefore, the price charged in squatter settlements was 25 percent of the price of newly developed properties in low-income districts.

Even plots of land are oftentimes sold: The plots are "reserved" during the takeover and are sold later. Because this merchandise is scarce and there is a growing demand for it, a price has emerged where before there was none: In 1987, 4 percent of the respondents to the survey of 1987 declared that they had paid money for a plot; in 1993, 14 percent had, an indication that the land market in squatter settlements is growing.

The land and home market in squatter settlements, though specific, has players that are very much like those of formal markets. Baltrusis (2003, 226) states that "the informal real estate market in squatter settlements works as an extension of the formal market. It is a submarket with specific characteristics. D. Helena's testimonial reflects this. She says that her business works just like an ordinary real estate dealership, with brokers, a promotional strategy, and real estate management services, in addition to the purchase, sale and rental of different types of property."

Squatter settlements, just like the poor periphery of the city, always look like a construction site. Narrow and irregular streets are reminiscent of medieval towns, with winding and confusing roads, not designed for automobiles.

Table 17.6, which compares household indicators for squatter settlements in the capital city, in the peripheral ring, and in the municipality as a whole, shows that, in 2000, the condition of the infrastructure differed very little between these different spatial segments. The percentage of households with piped water was higher in squatter settlements than in households in the peripheral ring. Electric power was universally available. This result reflects the efforts made over the last decade to provide squatter settlements with urban services.

This improvement, however, was not concurrent with improvements in the sanitation infrastructure. Although the percentage of households connected to the public wastewater system increased from 1 percent in 1973 to 26 percent in 1991 and to 51 percent in 2000, this percentage still fell short of the percentage for the municipality (88 percent), and was also lower than the percentage of households connected to the public wastewater system in the peripheral ring (79 percent).

The first "myth" about the specificity of space use and households in squatter settlements holds partially true.

Table 17.6: São Paulo Municipality: Household Indicators for Squatter Settlements, Peripheral Ring, and São Paulo Municipality, 2000

Indicator	Squatter Settlements in São Paolo Municipality	Peripheral Ring	São Paulo Municipality
People per household	4.02	3.75	3.50
People per room	1.16	0.94	0.77
People per bedroom	2.91	2.41	2.13
Rooms per household	3.91	4.33	5.54
% of households > 1.5 people/room	19.06%	9.37%	6.58%
% of households > 2 people/room	57.49%	40.08%	30.48%
% of households without bathroom	0.30%	n/a	1.26%
Average # of bathrooms per household	1.07	1.24	1.45
% of households with electric power	99.82%	99.82%	99.84%
% of households with piped water	98.08%	97.30%	98.62%
% of households connected to the wastewater system	51.00%	79.22%	87.84%
% of households with regular garbage collection	80.19%	98.63%	99.19%

Source: Fundação do Instituto Brasileiro de Geografia e Estatística Demographic Census of 1991 and 2000.

Myths About the Squatter Population

The second myth is the idea that a squatter settlement is a place of poverty, the urban territory occupied mainly by the poor, the spatial embodiment of social exclusion, an equivalent of Marcuse's "abandoned city" (1996). The myth sees the squatter population as a specific type: in the somewhat prejudiced popular imagination, the typical squatter is a black, northeastern, unemployed, and criminal individual.

Although squatters are mostly northeastern migrants (70 percent of the migrant squatters are from the northeast), they are not recent migrants. Thus, the trajectory of the squatters is different from what is popularly imagined, that those who come from the northeastern rural area go straight to São Paulo squatter settlements. Squatters have oftentimes lived in rental housing, which is a different experience relative to the squatter settlements in São Paulo. The impossibility of paying the rent or of staying at a relative's place drives them to squatter settlements.

The percentage of employees with formal, registered employment is similar in squatter settlements and in the population of the capital as a whole. This debunks the myth that squatters are unemployed. Above all, they are poor workers: in 1980, many heads of family were industrial workers; in 1993, tertiary employment was prevalent in squatter settlements and outside them. In 1980, the average income of the squatter population over ten years old was equal to two minimum salaries, while in 1991 it was 4.5 minimum salaries in the population at large. Thus, we notice that the population living in squatter settlements is poorer than the average population of the municipality. On the other hand, the average income of the residents of the peripheral ring was 3.34 minimum salaries in 1991. The comparison of the three population groups shows greater poverty among the squatters. However, the average income in squatter settlements has increased in recent decades (Pasternak 2001).

Today, squatter settlements are home not only to the extremely poor, but to many families who used to live in other types of housing, mostly rental housing. Impoverishment and a downward trajectory for lower-middle-class segments have driven new social groups to squatter settlements. In the long term, this might change the traditional profile of squatters: what seemed to be the simple expression of socio-spatial segregation turns into a complex and intricate reality.

The comparison of consumer goods possessed by squatters and non-squatters in the municipality of São Paulo is astonishing. Squatter dwellings were flooded by consumer goods. In addition to basic goods, such as stoves, radios, and refrigerators, color television sets are common. These television sets stand out both in the homes and in the landscape of squatter settlements: they dominate the rooms, and the antennas are part of the typical landscape of the settlement. Proportionately, there are more television sets in squatter settlements in São Paulo than in Brazil as a whole, and the same applies to VCRs. Sound equipment, washing machines, microwave ovens, and even computers can be found quite frequently. Even automobiles are not rare in São Paulo squatter settlements.

Squatters do not live in separate enclaves. They are incorporated into the economic world. They are consumers of new and second-hand industrial products and of services. To build their homes, they buy cement, bricks, pipes, wood, and other material. Their homes are decorated with ready-made purchased furniture, possibly from the more low-end lines sold by retail stores in the city. This population has reduced purchasing power, but is, however, completely integrated into urban life.

Myths About the Homogeneity of Squatter Settlements

The third myth has it that squatter settlements are homogenous spaces, both for sociological analyses and political activity. Obviously, there are great differences in the physical structure: precarious or consolidated squatter settlements, occupied recently or for many years, located on flat or uneven terrain, in the center or the periphery. But the heterogeneity and social diversity inside and between squatter settlements has seldom been studied.

Preteceille and Valladares (2000) challenge this myth in their analysis of the squatter settlements in Rio de Janeiro. They state that most of the poor population of the metropolis lives outside squatter settlements. In São Paulo, different types of metropolitan settlements have also been observed: there were predominantly proletarian squatter settlements, with most dwellers working in the secondary sector; the so-called popular squatter settlements, occupied predominantly by household and unskilled service workers; agricultural squatter settlements, housing mainly farm workers; and even "superior" squatter settlements, places whose residents are often office workers and even higher-class individuals.

Squatter settlements are not a separate social world, contrary to Olavo Bilac.[3] Their spatial proximity to different urban segments gives squatter spaces several socioeconomic profiles. As Valladares (2000, 15) states, "squatter settlements are, on average, poor areas, but they are not evenly so, and they are not the only ones in the agglomeration of Rio de Janeiro which present such social characteristics. They gather neither most of the poor, nor the most destitute of places and, after all, they don't gather only the poor. There, modest social categories can be found, but not poverty-stricken ones, and even medium-stratum categories, which shows that there is a diversified social structure and, undoubtedly, processes of social mobility to be considered."

For São Paulo, these myths partially correspond to the empirical reality. There are specificities both as regards space and the squatter population. But there are also many commonalities between the squatter population and the populations of other urban settlements and life conditions. There is, moreover, a diversity to squatter settlements that often goes overlooked; the integration of these settlements into urban space means that the squatter population cannot be reduced to any one form of work or social level. These settlements are inhabited by workers who, like any metropolitan dweller, produce in a variety of ways and consume a variety of goods as they inhabit and participate in the urban fabric.

Chapter 18

The Education of Urban Dwellers: The Kenyan Experience

Faith Macharia

In any discussion on development in sub-Saharan Africa one must, at the outset, be wary of too much generalization, which can turn simplistic. Africa is a very large continent, and the sub-Saharan region is characterized by an enormous diversity of nation states, peoples, and customs. There are, however, numerous challenges in common, challenges that continue to hinder Africa's development and demand a united front if they are to be overcome. Armed conflict, civil strife, declining economies, and high rates of population growth: all have implications for development.

The African Dream

Each African nation, at the moment of its independence, seemed intimately aware of the relationship between education and development. With the end of colonial rule, political independence was expected to open the gates to development, equity, justice, and material well-being. Newly independent African countries, without exception, loudly declared their commitment to fighting ignorance and disease, to eradicating poverty, and to eliminating inequality and repression. Development was viewed as a process of giving Africans control of their lives again. It was intended to enable people to improve themselves: to keep healthy, to meet their families' basic needs, and to acquire the knowledge and information necessary to make decisions about crucial issues in their own lives and the lives of children. Within this vision, education for all children was identified as a priority of all countries. Some stated their goal of providing compulsory and universal primary education and increased options at other education levels in their initial development plans and manifestos. Such was the optimism characterizing the dawn of independence.

Kenya is among the African countries that has made major strides toward this elusive dream. There is no doubt that significant progress has been made in Kenya, with phenomenal growth in education and training for both rural and urban dwellers. The free primary education (FPE) introduced in Kenya by the current National Rainbow Coalition (NARC) government and the abolition of school fees were important milestones to economic and social development. In particular, it has been established that providing primary education to women hastens a society's development. Kenya's achievements in education have been impressive; adult illiteracy is among the lowest of any country in sub-Saharan Africa.

But despite spending of over 6 percent of gross domestic product (GDP) on education (more than twice the average for low-income countries), primary school enrolment and completion rates declined during the 1990s. This was abruptly reversed in January 2003, when the government introduced free universal primary education and abolished charges. This brought 1.2 million children into school immediately. Significant challenges still remain to ensure that these children complete their education and that the million or so still not in school can be included in the system. Communities in urban slums such as Kibera and others like it are still particularly vulnerable to exclusion and dropping out.

Education for Urban Dwellers in Kenya

Education is widely recognized as key to national development. An increase in access to and quality of education is critical to socioeconomic growth and productivity, increased individual earnings, and, thus, the reduction of poverty and income inequalities. It also contributes significantly to improved health, enhanced democracy, good governance, and effective leadership.

There has been a growing concern among various stakeholders about the status of education in Kenya. The government, parents, nongovernmental organizations, and development partners recognize that although major strides have been made in education in quantitative terms, serious shortcomings remain in Kenya's education system.

Kenya's National Land Policy dates from independence; there has been no clearly defined or codified policy since then. The policy designates all land in Kenya as public, community, or private. This has led to land-related problems such as intertribal/community fights, the mush-rooming of slums, and land grabbing. These factors continue to hinder provision of quality education for urban dwellers in Kenya, and particu-larly for girls and women, who are more vulnerable both in terms of their socioeconomic position and their health situation. In Nairobi alone, the urban poor make up 55 percent of the total population and occupy 5 percent of the total residential land area (Badiane 2008, 7).

Education in urban slums is characterized by low enrollment, high rates of waste due to high drop-out rates, repetition and absenteeism, and low rates of achievement, retention, and completion. Poor perform-ance results from the low quality of education, caused in turn by poor teacher motivation and inadequate infrastructure and learning materi-als. In its *World Development Report*, the World Bank cites various studies that link basic education with the fostering of agricultural innovation and productivity, improving resource management and utilization, pro-moting the use of new technologies, and enhancing the capabilities of people to harness the knowledge they need for their own and their countries' development (World Bank 1997). The Delors Report, *Learn-ing the Treasure Within*, adds yet another dimension of education: learn-ing is no longer an activity merely preparing one for a productive life; it is a requirement throughout life, a continual process for each human being of adding to and adapting one's knowledge, skills, judgment, and capacities for action (Delors 1996). The report identifies four pillars of education: learning to know; learning to do; learning to live together; and learning to be.

Investment in human knowledge, skills, and capacities is and must remain a priority for all nations, especially the poor countries, if their economies are to improve. Education's strong effect on individual pro-ductivity and health makes it an essential part of any effort to increase the well-being of individuals, communities, and, indeed, the world.

The year 2008 marked the first time in history that more than half of the world's population lives in urban areas. "One out of three," accord-ing to the then-executive director of UN-HABITAT, Anna Tibaijuka (2009, website), live "in low-income urban settlements in developing countries." Tibaijuka coined the term *homo urbanus* to describe the swell of slum dwellers, whose worldwide population of 1 billion is projected to double in the next thirteen years. Slums are characterized by "shelter deprivations," a term which denotes lack of water, lack of sanitation, overcrowding, nondurable housing, and a lack of security of tenure (Tibaijuka 2009, website). These informal settlements result from rural-urban migration which has led to an upsurge of slums in urban areas as people have moved from the rural areas in search of a better life and employment (although the forces behind this population shift may vary from city to city; for example, see Pasternak, this volume).

In Nairobi, Kenya, there are five major urban slums: Kibera, Mukuru, Mathare, Korogocho, and Kawangware. Kibera is the largest slum in all of sub-Saharan Africa. According to various estimates, Kibera is home to about 800,000 urban dwellers crowded in an area of about 630 acres (House of Commons 2004).The informal settlements are characterized by mud-walled, corrugated iron–roofed settlements grouped along the railway line for several miles, crowding along the steep narrow mud tracks until Kibera reaches the posh suburbs of Nairobi.

Nonformal Schools

Due to the massive increase in enrollment accompanying recent population growth, not all school-age children were able to be absorbed into the formal system of education. This brought about the introduction of new, nonpublic sponsors of formal education into informal settlements, specifically religious institutions, the private sector, and affluent individuals. This type of education, labeled "nonformal," is defined as "any organized system of learning activity outside the framework of the formal education system." It embraces programs designed to meet both individual objectives and broader national goals. It is not a substitute for formal education but, rather, complements it in order to expand access to education (Gathenya 2004, 9).

Nonformal programs are highly favored by slum dwellers because of the following:

1. They are affordable.
2. They are flexible in their management style.
3. They are accessible to the locals.
4. They have relatively few pupils.

These schools charge a minimal fee but actually accommodate the poorest students without charge. With the introduction of FPE, private/nonformal schools in Kenya experienced a decline in enrollment of about 6,500 pupils, while the public formal schools experienced an increased enrollment of about 3,300 pupils. In Kibera today, there are seventy-six private or nonformal primary and high schools enrolling over 12,000 pupils and five government schools on the periphery of Kibera (Tooley 2005, 28). The schools are run by local entrepreneurs, a third of whom are women. While it is true that nonformal schools' facilities are generally of a lower quality compared to those of the government public schools, we must recognize that, because much of education happens in the interaction between pupils and their teachers, it is not necessarily possible to correlate the quality of education with the quality of education buildings.

It is worth noting that despite having more teachers, the public schools have higher teacher absenteeism than the nonformal schools. Research has also shown that nonformal or private schools in Kibera outperformed the public schools. A comparative study of student performance in science and mathematics found that pupils from private and public schools performed at the same level, yet the nonformal schools served a more disadvantaged population (Tooley 2005, 31).

Challenges Facing Education in Urban Places Toward a Sustainable Future

Kenya has made gradual progress toward the achievement of basic education for all, but challenges remain and require that these efforts be continued and strengthened. Among them are:

1. Kenya must take full advantage of those communities which demonstrate social cohesion, mutual aid, and solidarity, since these capacities can help counter persistent disparities and inequalities in the education system.

2. Kenya must ensure that the expansion of education is accompanied by improvements in education. The system must not only educate more students, it must educate all its students better. This will require teacher training to be improved and the overall status and welfare of teachers to receive greater attention. It also calls for innovative and collaborative efforts in the production of textbooks and other learning materials to improve quality and reduce cost.

3. Information technology is still a largely untapped educational resource. It could be used to address specific issues in education delivery, increasing access and improving student retention/persistence, quality, and achievement. At the tertiary level, Kenya could use technological innovations for efficient, more cost-effective ways of producing, managing, disseminating, and accessing knowledge.

4. With specific reference to girls' and women's education, Kenya needs to sustain the political will to eliminate gender disparities at all levels of education and to strengthen the mechanisms in place for monitoring the implementation of gender equity and equality policies and programs. In addition, Kenya needs to seriously address aspects of its cultural attitudes which continue to hinder the advancement of women. Some traditional cultural practices, negative attitudes, and beliefs continue to hinder the education of children, especially girls. Among these are early or forced marriage, initiation rites, and circumcision.

5. The rising incidence of HIV/AIDS is already eroding the gains

made in education, and it threatens future educational opportunities. Its spread is accelerated by drug abuse, commercial sex trade, unprotected practices among hetero- and homosexual couples and *in utero* mother-to-child transmission (UNAIDS 2009, 9). The death of parents leads to households headed by children who have lost virtually all hope of attaining schooling (Akunga et al. 2000). Resources that could have been used for education are used for caring for the sick as accumulated savings are spent on medication, further impoverishing survivors. Girls are more likely than boys to drop out of school in order to take care of the sick and the young. The most recent UNAIDS study reports that Kenyan women between 15 and 19 years are three times more likely to be infected than their male counterparts, and those in the 20–24-year-old cohort are 5.5 times more likely to be living with HIV than men of the same ages. Further, only a small percentage (12 percent) of those infected with HIV AIDS receive treatment (UNAIDS 2009, 22–25).

6. In urban areas, girls are exposed to sexual harassment and abuse while their rural counterparts suffer from having to walk long distances to school. Both issues contribute to high drop-out rates (Elimu Yetu Coalition 2005). In urban areas, girls are subjected to harassment, rape, and even forced marriage. Such insecurity is rife in slum areas such as Kibera and Mathare, and the situation has been accelerated by illegal sects which operate within the slums. This security situation worsens in civic election years and is connected to political competition and instability. Female pupils are not the only ones affected; many boys and young men have ended up victims of shootings or beatings as a result of criminal activity or because of mistaken identification during police crackdowns.

7. Poor and haphazard planning in major towns such as Nairobi has accelerated the increase of traffic jams and strained the few amenities available (such as water, housing, hospitals). This strain will only escalate, as the population is predicted to double in the next twenty years, and it has sharp implications for the education system in both the near and medium term. Immediate challenges include shortages of teachers, materials, and facilities (classrooms, desks, playgrounds, and workshops). The medium-term problem is one of quality. With classes originally meant for forty children now accommodating up to eighty children, there is real concern that this crowding will negatively impact the quality of teaching. Matters are made worse by the fact that teachers are in short supply, with the national deficit estimated at 31,000. The government is not in a hurry to employ more teachers because of the heavy financial implications that entails. It should be noted that the congestion is more widespread in urban schools while staff shortages are prevalent in rural areas. In Nairobi and other urban centers, schools

are overstaffed with teachers seeking postings because urban areas offer better prospects for social and economic advancement than rural areas.

8. Drug and alcohol abuse also pose significant risks to pupils' educational prospects. Boys are lured by their peers to peddle drugs to get quick money. So-called kiosks near schools in urban areas of Nairobi and Mombasa harbor criminal activities such as sale of illegal drugs, beer, and even *miraa*. These kiosks are places where pupils get something to eat during tea and lunch breaks. They create an opportunity for boys to carry drugs and for men to prey upon young and often unsuspecting girls. As a result, many boys and girls end up dropping out of school. For girls, there are the dangers of unwanted pregnancies, abortions, and STDs; boys are often tempted to drop out and join their peers in earning quick money.

Ongoing Challenges

These practices and attitudes call for a nationwide alert on the status of education for communities in urban slums. Further challenges receive more lengthy treatment below.

Child Labor

Rapid urbanization has increased the demand for domestic child labor, and girls tend to replace their mothers when they come to towns to stay with their fathers, uncles, or brothers. The work burden of girls at home is demanding, leaving girls no time to study. It is not uncommon to see a girl in a primary school, in an informal settlement in Nairobi, being forced to look after her younger brothers and sisters; or to fetch water and withstand the long queues in the evening (Lockheed and Lewis 2007, 2). Demands of this type affect girls' performance and they drop out of school. In Mombasa, girls engage in commercial sex with tourists, and, in some cases, some are married at an early age. Those who continue with education perform poorly due to fatigue.

Inappropriate School Curriculum and Teacher Attitudes

The tendency to stereotype subjects according to gender makes school less attractive to both girls and boys, and produces results that reinforce harmful stereotypes. Girls are thought to dread math and science while boys are believed to dread English, Kiswahili, social studies, and home economics. These disparities appear to be confirmed by national examinations since teachers tend to focus more on those students they assume to be most able. Textbooks portray certain careers as dominated by men or women, and this affects the choice of careers. Inappropriate language also tends to discourage girls and boys in performing better, and certain teaching methods negatively impact education for girls.

Water and Sanitation

Free primary education, though an important step in increasing access to education, has also overstretched physical facilities in public schools both in rural and urban areas. Provision of adequate water and sanitation facilities is essential for effective learning, attracting enrollment (particularly female enrollment) in schools, and for reducing the incidence of water-borne diseases and worm infestation among pupils and students. In Kenya, only 56 percent of schools in the country have access to water and sanitation facilities (UN World Water Assessment Program 2006, 134). Water and sanitation access in Kenyan schools is rated by the Ministry of Education in such a way as to obscure the scope of these problems. When fewer than 40 children share one latrine the accessibility is considered "fair"; 40 to 100 students per latrine is considered "bad"; conditions are deemed "dangerous" only once more than 100 students share a single latrine (Rukunga and Mutethia 2006, website).

This lack of sanitation facilities affects both boys and girls, but it disproportionately affects female enrollment. Many female students miss school during menstruation because schools are without separate toilets, sanitary pads, facilities to dispose pads, and/or water-access. This lack of facilities is made more acute by sexual prejudice. In a school in Kariobangi, toilets were locked for fears of being made dirty; the girls were forced to use the playground or go to nearby places with toilets. Thus the poor sanitation conditions that afflict many urban dwellers greatly hinder the education of girls and women.

The Education of Girls and Women in the Urban Setting

Compelling evidence links education for girls and women with numerous benefits, contributing to the popular view that education is the foundation of development. The World Conference on Education for All, held in 1990 in Jomtien, Thailand, underlined the role of education in ensuring a safer, healthier, more environmentally sound world. The conference also identified education as a crucial contributor to social, economic, and cultural progress, to tolerance, and to the capacity for cooperation, among other benefits.

The education of girls and women is today widely recognized as the most effective development investment a country can make. Girls' education raises economic productivity; reduces fertility rates; lowers infant and maternal mortality; improves the health, nutrition, and well-being of families; and ensures better educational prospects for children. It promotes sound management of environmental resources and is closely associated with the reduction of poverty because it enables women to become productive members of the economy. Education increases democratization of societies by increasing women's participation in community and national affairs. The education of girls and women is of particular significance to urban slums, where economic and social development is grossly constrained by rapid population growth and inadequate development of the human resource base. Women are the foundation of life in urban slums, due to their multiple and critical roles as homemakers, caretakers, workers, producers and managers of food, and managers of environmental resources such as water and fuel. Their education does, therefore, act as a springboard for sustainable development.

In the light of this reality, it is particularly distressing that over 30 million girls in sub-Saharan Africa are missing school. Those who are enrolled in school are frequently so poorly served that, by the end of the fourth year, more than half have dropped out without acquiring functional literacy. The completion rate at the primary school cycle in Kenya, for example, remains at 72.1 percent for girls compared to 80.3 percent for boys. As we go up the education ladder, this gap widens dramatically: the undergraduate student population at the public universities consists of 30 percent females and 70 percent males. The dropout rate at both secondary and tertiary levels is also higher for girls than it is for boys (Republic of Kenya 2005).

Enriching the Knowledge Base

The good news is that Kenya has made progress as a country. In the last two decades, a wealth of knowledge has been generated on the constraints hindering female participation in education and development. Advances have also been made in formulating successful strategies for addressing these constraints. Although within Kenya efforts are still needed to convince some communities of the importance of educating girls and women, concerted efforts are now focused on ensuring that all girls enroll in school and that they persist and complete each cycle of the education system so they can reap full benefits from such education. Several efforts (such as those currently being undertaken by the Forum for African Women Educationists, Kenya Chapter [FAWE Kenya]) are under way to enrich the knowledge base on female participation, to provide models of what needs to be done to increase that participation, and to develop a comprehensive plan to accelerate it (for example, FAWE 2004).

Constraints to Girls' and Women's Education in Urban Places

Among the barriers FAWE Kenya has identified to girls' and women's education are the following: low quality of education, lack of relevance and practical application; hostile learning environment characterized by exploitation of girls' labor and by sexual harassment; lack of female role models; school-management practices that discriminate against girls; policies of exclusion, e.g., of pregnant school girls and adolescent mothers; lack of articulation of policies for the achievement of gender equity; inequitable policies and practices in resource allocation; gender-blind policies in the selection and posting of teachers; and inadequate policies for monitoring gender equity in education. Some of the larger obstacles and structural barriers to female education are discussed below.

1. *Poverty.* In Kenya more than 50 percent of the total population lives on less than a dollar a day. This greatly hinders the parents' ability to meet direct and indirect costs of education—school uniforms, sanitary towels and decent inner wear, school bags, toiletries, learning materials, transportation, lunch, etc. Girls are often the first casualties when education becomes unaffordable and parents have to choose which child continues with education.

2. *Opportunity cost of schooling.* This is higher for girls than for boys because of their multiple roles as household workers and assistants. Late enrollment, absenteeism, and dropping out are closely associated with these roles. In urban places, girls join their mothers selling goods by the roadside and in kiosks in order to supplement family income. This prevents regular school attendance.

3. *Household size.* This determines how many, and which children will be educated. In most instances, urban dwellers in slums have large families with children who are closely spaced. When economic hardship requires that a choice be made of who should go to school, girls often lose.

4. *Socialization.* This is a determinant of who goes to school and for how long. Parental perception of the value of education is often influenced by the parents' own level of education. School is sometimes seen as an alienating force that undermines cultural values. Those holding traditional attitudes toward marriage often take the view that investment in a daughter's education is "watering another man's garden," since the benefits, it is seen, will accrue to another family. Socialization patterns assume girls should be docile, passive, and modest, which disadvantages

girls when they have to share learning facilities and equipment with boys and encourages them to suppress expressions of their own intelligence. These factors not only shape girls' classroom experiences, but influence decision-making about and investment in girls' education.

5. *Gender bias.* Gender bias is evident in the curriculum materials and methodology. Women are portrayed as the image of poverty, giving poverty a feminine face. This occurs because the majority of urban slum dwellers who are actually visible in production activities are women. Their images thus come to be associated with these scenes, further reinforcing the connection between femininity and powerlessness.

The FAWE Kenya Strategy

Forum for African Women Educationalists Kenya (FAWE Kenya) works with partners to ensure implementation of a wide range of support in response to the multiple problems facing girls' and women's education in urban Kenya. Among the strengths of FAWE Kenya are its ability to balance the independence of a nongovernment organization with access to and influence over mainstream education and government policies; its broad network of members who bring together various specialized skills; and its credibility, developed patiently over the last ten years, with government, other NGOs, and funding agencies. In recognition of the crucial role that women play in development, FAWE Kenya identified its overall mission as helping to ensure that women and girls are an integral part of the intellectual and technical resource base needed for the survival and prosperity of the nation. FAWE Kenya works to ensure that gender equity and equality is built into all educational policies; that where gender imbalances in education persist, positive and specific short-term affirmative action is taken to redress them; and that there is continual and rigorous debate on, and review of, all social policies that impinge on education policy. The organization undertakes demonstrative intervention on education to demonstrate what works in improving girls' and women's education.

Promising Interventions and Lessons Learned

Although elite private schools exist in the developing world, there also exist private schools for the very poor population. The fact that the private schools are in the slums does not mean that the performance in these schools is inferior; in fact some of the nonformal or private schools in Kenya outperform the public schools.

Studies on the impact of FPE in Kenya show that there has been an increased enrollment of up to 57 percent in registered private or non-formal schools and public government schools (Guthenya 2004, 5). However, there also exist nonregistered private or nonformal schools for which enrollment data are unavailable. The introduction of government-provided education also had a serious impact on the nonformal schools, in that more than twenty of them in Kibera closed as children left to join the public primary schools (Tooley 2005, 28). These increased numbers in the formal public schools have compromised high-quality education, however, and have led some parents to return their children to private or nonformal schools.

The urban poor have found innovative ways of helping themselves educationally in their very destitute settings by setting up nonformal schools which more flexibly meet the needs of slum dwellers, including defraying the indirect costs (such as school uniforms) that often burden poor parents.

The nonformal schools in the slum of Nairobi, Kenya, are typically mud walls with corrugated iron sheet roofs. These nonformal schools are far from the public eye in the heart of the slums; they are poor structures, often inadequately lit and ventilated. The Kenyan government, however, has recognized their existence, and such schools are now able to access the grants for free primary education through the Ministry of Education in Kenya. These grants are equivalent to those provided for the children in primary schools and are based on the pupil enrollment in the school.

The problems hindering girls' and women's education for urban dwellers are interrelated and hence demand a multifaceted strategy and comprehensive approach. Each set of constraints needs to be matched with corresponding interventions. The enactment of gender-responsive education policies needs to be accompanied by gender-sensitive planners, practitioners, and budgeting, and by the development of gender-responsive indicators for monitoring implementation. The provision of bursaries and other subsidies needs to be complemented by supportive parents and conducive environments, both at home and at school. This calls for successful advocacy programs, gender-sensitization of teachers and curriculum developers, a legal end to early marriage, and flexible school calendars (including multigrade and multishift systems) that take into account the competing priorities for girls' time. All these activities need to be undertaken at the same time because they are complementary. This approach is labeled "the package approach."

No single agency has capacity adequate to address all these constraints. In Kenya, the government alone cannot provide all the support needed to facilitate the achievement of Education for All (EFA) or of gender equity at all levels of the education system. The task at hand demands a combination of partnerships—governments, NGOs, religious organizations, researchers, the media, community leaders, women's organizations, teachers' organizations, development partners, and individuals—to ensure that all the specific constraints are addressed. Different actors contribute according to their area of strength, experience, or expertise. The media is particularly suited for advocacy outreach, while community and religious leaders are credible door-to-door campaigners. The latter are also well placed for identifying the real poor in the case of bursary awards. Women's organizations undertake advocacy and monitoring roles, while teachers' organizations facilitate gender sensitization and the creation of a girl-friendly school environment. It is indeed team work.

The provision of additional resources alone is not adequate. It has to be accompanied by sustained political will, commitment to the achievement of gender equity, supportive policies, and other mechanisms for ensuring the implementation of gender responsive policies. Lack of resources for new programs is no longer an excuse for doing nothing. It is more important to ensure gender mainstreaming within ongoing policies and programs.

General improvements aimed at the education system do not benefit girls alone; improvements that target girls also benefit boys. Girls' empowerment and peer support is an important strategy for improving girls' participation. The creation of gendered clubs provides platforms to share experiences and engage in self-confidence-instilling activities. It is important that boys, too, are sensitized to the importance of girls' education and the fact that they too stand to benefit from it.

Notes

Chapter 1. World Urbanization

1. The author had this exchange with one of the member of the Stiglitz Commission at the Global Agenda Council Meetings, Dubai, UAE, November 2009.

Chapter 2. Human Population Grows Up

This article is based on two prior versions (Cohen 2005, 2009). This revision has been updated with estimates and projections available as of June 2010.

Chapter 3. Measuring and Coping with Urban Growth in Developing Countries

1. UN-HABITAT analysts developed the 350-city Global City Sample from a universe of 4,000 cities with populations over 100,000 in order to track urban-focused Millennium Development Goals.

2. The source for urban growth rates is UN Department of Economic and Social Affairs, *World Urbanization Prospects: The 2003 Revision.* The development indicators come from the UN Demographic and Health Survey, supplemented by UN-generated Population Census Tables where DHS was missing data. Currently, UN-HABITAT has produced one or more development indicators for 119 cities, a sample that will grow to 350 cities in the future.

3. There is a long tradition in development studies to use U5MR as a proxy for poverty in the absence of income data. Another indicator, gender disparities in literacy, is not commonly used to indicate poverty, but it is also a key factor because literacy is one of the most essential survival skills in cities (UNFPA 2007). If a significant portion of women are illiterate, neither they nor their children can benefit from the opportunities offered by cities.

4. The UN-HABITAT analysts first clustered the fifty-two cities into three groups (high, medium, and low development) according to the indicators. High-development cities were those with high levels of infrastructure, low U5MR, and low or no gender literacy gap. Medium-development cities were those that had lower levels of infrastructure coverage, higher U5MR, and greater gender literacy gaps. Low development had even worse indicators. They next divided the sample by population growth rate, with "low" being at or below 2.5 percent per year and "high" above 2.5 percent.

5. Granting that intracity disparities in development are the weakest point of these cities, the authors did not factor this into the analysis because it cuts across

all levels of population growth, high or low. Among the low-growth cities that suffer such inequalities are Ho Chi Minh City, Cairo, Istanbul, and Rio de Janeiro (ACHR 2001; Sutton and Fahmi 2001; Güvenç 1996; Pamuk and Cavallieri 1998).

Chapter 5. Urban Growth and Spatial Development

1. Cities and towns are both urban settlements in the urban system of China. A city (*shi*) is an administrative unit affiliated to and under the leadership of a province (*sheng*), autonomous region (*zizhi qu*) or autonomous state (*zizhi zhou*). A town (*zhen*) is an administrative unit affiliated to and under the leadership of a county (*xian*) or autonomous county (*zizhi xian*) which is normally rural.

2. The informal sector (*fei zhenggui jingji*) refers to individual economic operation and activities, household-based small firms, and other small firms engaging in activities with little legal restriction on their operational scope and with little capital.

Chapter 7. Measuring and Modeling Global Urban Expansion

1. The financial support of the World Bank and the National Science Foundation (SES-0433278) helped to make this research possible. Special thanks are due to Alison Kraley, whose efforts and assistance have been central to this work. Thanks are also due to Solly Angel and Daniel Civco, who collaborated on and served as co-investigators in earlier stages of this research.

Chapter 8. Urban Growth Models

1. These are not the only available examples of operational urban planning models. Other well-known models in use in the U.S. include DRAM/Empal, MEPLAN, What-If, U-Plan, LEAM, Places3, and CommunityViz (U.S. EPA 2000). Urban models in use outside the U.S.—where they are also known as spatial development models—include MEPLAN, TRANUS, and LILT.

2. Different impact models require different levels of spatial resolution. Travel-demand models have traditionally relied on zonal data, whereas air and water pollution models make use of point- or line-level data. Land-cover, habitat, and environmental impact assessment models typically draw on spatially explicitly site-level data, while fiscal impact models typically require community-level data. As locally inaccurate or untested as UGMs can be, it is worth noting that many impact assessment models are even more untested and inaccurate. Coupling an inaccurate UGM or activity allocation model with an inaccurate impact assessment model is not a formula for good planning or decision-making.

3. In terms of parameter accuracy, UGMs are best calibrated for single metropolitan areas using extended time series or change data at the highest level of spatial resolution permitted by the available information. Doing so provides the modeler with some assurance that the model parameters capture longer-term drivers and are not an artifact of any particular spatial aggregation system. In terms of parameter reliability, UGMs are best calibrated across multiple metropolitan areas for select time periods at a common level of spatial resolution.

Doing so provides the modeler with the knowledge that the model parameters capture the essence of urban change across multiple contexts, and are therefore generalizable. The best way to identify accurate and reliable parameters is to "fit" them to the available data. This is best done statistically using some form of least squares or maximum-likelihood procedure. As a second-best alternative, UGM parameters can be identified using Monte Carlo simulation procedures. Once calibrated, model parameters should also be validated. Validation is typically done by applying the model parameters to a different time period, location, or observation sample, and evaluating how well the model predicts the observed outcomes. Biased parameter estimates create bad models and even worse predictions. UGM parameter estimates can be biased because the model is incomplete (meaning that it does not incorporate all the relevant variables), because the unit of analysis is incorrect, because the model structure does not correctly control for interactions between the model variables, because the model variables are incorrectly conceptualized or operationalized, or, in the case of spatially explicit UGMs, because the model does not take into account potential spatial interactions and/or spatial autocorrelation.

4. Unlike CA models, which rely on ad hoc rules and coefficients, SLEUTH's coefficients are calibrated from historical data. This is done through a brute-force Monte Carlo method, where the user indicates a range of values and the model iterates using every possible combination of parameters. For each set of parameters, simulated growth is compared with historical growth using several least-squares regression measures, such as the number of urban pixels, the number of urban cluster edge pixels, the number and size of urban clusters, and other fit statistics, such as spatial match. For each set of parameter values in a Monte Carlo iteration, the model calculates measurements of simulated urban patterns for each control year in the time series. These measurements are then averaged over the set of Monte Carlo iterations and compared to measurements calculated from the actual historic data.

5. Although CA models like SLEUTH have been quite successful at recreating historical patterns of urban development, they have been criticized for their seeming inability to account for processes driving urban change. Recently, advances have been made in developing hybrid CA that can incorporate process-based factors. Webster and Wu (2001), for example, incorporate microeconomic urban theory into a spatially explicit CA to investigate the effects of alternative planning regimes on land-use patterns.

6. Like CUF II, CURLA is calibrated using a nonordinal multinomial logit estimator. Unlike CUF II, CURLA includes both own-site and neighborhood variables. Own-site variables measure the physical, accessibility, and policy characteristics of each site. Neighborhood variables measure similar characteristics for neighboring sites, and are one way of incorporating threshold effects and spatial autocorrelation. Originally calibrated for all of California, the CURLA model tended, when used for forecasting and simulation purposes, to overestimate changes to higher-density categories in high-amenity locations and to underestimate low-density changes.

7. The key difference among CUF variants is whether changes in site status are nominal (i.e., undeveloped to developed) or multicategory—that is, across multiple land uses or densities. CUF models use grid cells as their unit of analysis.

8. This is likely because jobs in California have already decentralized, essentially equalizing urban and suburban job accessibility.

9. We distinguish between total consumption and per capita resource consumption. Urban growth always results in increases in total resource consumption, especially when it is accompanied by rising incomes. Whether it also results in increased per capita resource consumption will depend on whether resources are properly priced.

Chapter 11. Strategic Directions for Local Public Finance in Developing Countries

1. There is a considerable literature on the politics of national-level revenue generation, including Brautigam (2008); Therkildsen (2001); Sabates and Schneider (2003); Schneider (2003); Moore (2004); Addison and Levin (2006); Moore (2007).

2. The material in this section is covered in greater detail in Smoke (2008).

3. There are useful reviews of decentralization and governance from various perspectives, including Tendler (1997); Manor (1998); Schneider (1999); Blair (2000); Crook (2003); Olowu (2003); Wunsch and Olowu (2003); Eaton (2004); Shah and Thompson (2004); O'Neill (2005); Ribot and Larson (2005); Shah (2006b); Bardhan and Mookherjee (2006); Smoke, Gomez, and Peterson (2006); and Cheema and Rondinelli (2007). None of these is particularly focused on revenue issues.

4. The URA is a national mechanism, but the findings have relevance for local governments in Uganda.

5. There is little specific work on participation and revenue generation, but there are a number of recent synthetic reviews of participatory government in general, including Blair (2006); Commins (2006); Platteau (2006); and Manor 2007.

6. An extended version of this discussion is provided in Smoke (2008).

7. Grant-loan linkages are discussed and examples presented in Smoke (1999) and Friere and Petersen (2004).

Chapter 12. Public-Private Partnerships and Urban Governance

1. In Asia particularly, scholars cite the need for a realignment of risks between principal participants (Kumaraswamy and Morris 2002).

2. A number of OECD countries have well-established PPP programs. The United Kingdom's Private Finance Initiative (PFI), begun in 1992, is most well known, but other countries with significant PPP projects include Finland, Germany, Greece, Italy, the Netherlands, Portugal, and Spain (International Monetary Fund 2004).

3. Until 1992, when new regulations were superseded by the Private Finance Initiative, British governments operated under rigid rules inhibiting the involvement of private-sector capital in the financing of public-sector projects (Flinders 2005).

4. See Moore (1994), National Audit Office (1998), Hall (1998), European Transport (1999), Akintoye and Beck (2003).

5. Newman and Verpraet (1999) based their conclusion on an analysis of the relationship between partnership and public policy undertaken through a European research network between 1995 and 1997. The research network examined case studies of "leading" partnerships in economic development aimed at giving big cities a "competitive edge," and covered cities in France

(Lyon, Paris), Germany (Stuttgart), Italy (Rome, Milan, Venice), Spain (Madrid), Britain (London), and the Netherlands.

6. The projects are Highway 407 toll roadway in the northern region of the Greater Toronto Area, the Prince Edward Island Fixed Link bridge across Northumberland Strait, and the redevelopment of Pearson International Airport in two phases, Terminal 3 followed by Terminals 1 and 2; in the latter project, the government was forced to cancel the contract within a year of the project award because issues of compensation for the private consortium could not be resolved through negotiation (Daniels and Trebilcock 1996).

7. They catalog four special challenges: creating and preserving genuinely competitive bidding and rebidding processes; the difficulty of writing complete contingent-claims contracts with long-term contracts; accommodating the risk bearing of large-scale up-front costs; and the financial sensitivity of these projects to changes in the governmental policy environment, which is also exacerbated by the long-term nature of the PPP contract. Drawing on the three case studies, they illustrate how the difference between success and failure, relative to the conventional economic model of infrastructure development and public procurement, resides in the institutional details—the design of the bidding process, the contract negotiation process, and the contract monitoring and enforcement processes. Faulty design, they argue, can "substantially attenuate potential efficiency gains from this particular form of privatization of public sector activities" (Daniels and Trebilcock 1996, 390).

8. When the toll road was put up for sale within two years of completion, the Ontario Province minister of privatization conceded that this high-profile PPP project was a failure. Risk sharing, one researcher concluded, was not present at all: "There was continuing secrecy surrounding the contract, delayed presentation of the toll technology, questions about the tendering process and how tolls would be collected from out-of-province drives and no announcement of the cost of upgrading safety although the government paid for it" (Boase 2000, 89).

9. Flinders, a political scientist at the University of Sheffield with a list of publications on governance, views PPPs as something of a Faustian bargain: the efficiency gains and service improvements come only in some policy areas (building and managing prisons and constructing roads, for example, not hospitals and schools) and typically at the expense of accountability, public control, and the public-service ethos. Rosenau (1999) echoes this position.

10. Daniels and Trebilcock (1996, 408) cite empirical evidence suggesting that with heavy and detailed regulatory oversight of a utility (or other infrastructure project) a private operator is not likely to yield performance notably different from that of a public enterprise.

11. The private partner's ability to secure conventional financing is directly affected by the terms and conditions of these contracting arrangements, many of which are contentious. Ghere (2001) itemizes three in particular: which partner assumes which of the many risks affecting the cost stream; how performance requirements imposed by the public partner affect cash flows; and how operating stipulations, covenants, and monitoring compliance, including environmental protection mandates imposed by other levels of government, are factored into costs over time. Legislative efforts, on the other hand, can confer financing benefits to private contractors, bolstering credit in some areas, for example, extending credit equity (secured loans, loan guarantees, and standby lines of credit) for private toll road construction (445).

12. For a succinct argument on why public administrators have to hone their

political skills (even more than their production management skills), see Ghere (2001, 447–48). Based on their study of the Asian experience with PPP infrastructure projects, Kumaraswamy and Morris (2002) emphasize as well the primacy of political skills.

13. Ghere (2001) uses the patent as a comparative reference for probing the "strategic intricacies" of public-private partnerships. He frames the discussion in terms of game theory, choices that arise in the contexts of interdependence, imperfect information, and chance. His insights have to do with the distinction he makes between procurement management (the traditional view of privatization contracting out) and political collaboration. From that perspective, government is not so much buying services from a competitive market as seeking a time-bound merger with a capitalized partner willing to serve the public interest for a profit.

14. The literature presents other anecdotal examples of failed accountability. For example, Rosenau (1999) cites the situation in which Corrections Corporation of America (CCA) was reported to have "explicitly misinformed" city and state officials about the security risk of inmates housed in a Youngstown-based private prison. Instead of "promptly notifying" officials when five murderers escaped, CCA attempted to cover it up. "If the same event happened in a public prison," she asks, "would accountability dynamics have been different?" She cites accountability problems in policy-level partnerships in the electric service sector as well and instances of failed government responsibility that are not hard to come by. In short, no sector is a priori more accountable or immune from lapses. "Hard evidence is absent," she notes, and "both sides make convincing cases" (20).

Chapter 13. City Building in China

1. *National Eleventh Five-Year Development Plan*, Beijing: National Development Reform Commission, Government of China.

2. Germany is the number one exporter of manufactured goods by value, but China's image as factory of the world is based on its dominance in consumer goods.

3. Megapolitan regions account for the vast majority of China's economic output. It is forecast that by 2020, the three largest megapolitan areas (the Pearl River Delta, anchored by Hong Kong, Shenzhen, and Guangzhou; the lower Yangtze Delta, anchored by Shanghai; and Beijing-Tianjin-Heibei) will account for 65 percent of China's GDP, and 18 percent of its population.

4. For a summary of findings of the first stage of this World Bank research, see Webster, Cai, and Maneepong (2006).

5. In Xi'an, densities in the built-up area decreased slightly, from 13,503 to 13,395 persons per km², between 2000 and 2005 (*China Urban Statistics Yearbooks* 2001, 2006). (Wuhan was the only major urban region where densities increased over the same period, from 21,007 to 22,868 persons per km².)

6. FDI to Xi'an was only $260 million U.S. in 2003; it rose to $500 million U.S. in 2004.

7. The level of income inequality is measured by the Gini coefficient, a number between zero and one, where zero represents equal income distribution and one represents a situation in which only a few households control all the wealth.

8. Rural and urban household income data are defined differently in China. However, disposable income of urban residents approximates net income of

rural households. Urban and rural households are defined according to registration status (*hukou*), not spatial location per se, but rural households are much more likely to be located on the periphery of the city.

9. A large differential between mean and median incomes often indicates a relatively small number of high-income households are pushing the mean up relative to the median.

10. Little housing was constructed during the Cultural Revolution, which ran from 1966 to 1976.

11. Floor area ratio, a regulatory instrument frequently utilized by planning authorities, is the ratio of floor space to development site ground space, including the building's footprint.

12. Tianjin's population will be 90 percent urban in 2020; in 2006 it was 82 percent urban. In this highly urbanized situation, late-stage rural-urban migration will compensate for any new rural dwellers.

13. In China, protected land is essentially current cultivated land rather than land based on agricultural potential, i.e., class 1 agricultural land, the measure usually used in Western countries. However, given that trial and error farming in China over centuries has identified virtually all high-potential agricultural land, and that it is being farmed, there is an approximate congruence between the two definitions.

14. For a detailed explanation of Tianjin's unique transportation characteristics, see Zacharias (2003).

15. The total number of motor vehicles was 1.12 million.

16. Six hundred and fifty kilometers of metro line are planned by 2020, of which two hundred and thirty kilometers would be within the third ring road. Twenty-six kilometers are currently operating.

17. The facility is on the site of the central railroad station, which has been demolished.

18. Only 3.8 km², or 13.3 percent of infill land, is found within the first ring road, while 5.8 km², or 20 percent, is found between the first and second ring road; thus most infill land is found between the second and third ring roads.

19. This estimate is somewhat optimistic, as some of the infill sites identified are currently populated.

20. These detailed plans put forward criteria for (1) local construction character, (2) FARs, (3) height, (4) local road network, and (5) percent green land.

21. *National Eleventh Five-Year Development Plan.*

22. See the website of Alain Bertaud, http://alain-bertaud.com.

Chapter 14. Financing Housing and Urban Services

1. For an earlier review of this topic, see Kim (1997).

2. There is already a large literature on this subject. See Calomiris (2008), Gramlich (2007) Gwinner and Sanders (2008), Jaffee (2009), and Shiller (2008), just to name a few.

3. Malpezzi and Vandell (2002) also suggest a possibility that LIHTC has not increased housing supply substantially, as the new units built with the subsidy substituted for unsubsidized units that would have been built.

4. See Inman (2006) for a detailed discussion of revenue sources.

5. The data for two groups of countries are taken from separate sources and

also cover different time periods. Therefore, caution should be exercised in interpreting them.

6. This subsection draws from Peterson (2002) and Kehew et al. (2005).

Chapter 15. Managing Urban Infrastructure and Services in India

1. Compared to most other developing countries, India uses a more rigorous definition (based on demographic, occupational, and civic criteria) of an urban area; if that definition were to be comparably relaxed, the level of urbanization in the country would be much larger.

2. Even during a period of global economic slowdown, between April 2008 and March 2009 the economy recorded a GDP growth rate of 6.7 percent (Government of India 2009).

3. The population size and total investment correlation estimated from the sixty-three cities' data is 0.814.

4. These commissions could be more effective still by increasing the specificity of their recommendations, justifying them with detailed analyses, and working out the sharing formula by which funds could devolve from state to local bodies.

5. Two more cities of historic and religious importance were later added to bring the number of cities covered to sixty-five.

Chapter 17. Thinking About Urban Services Needs in Fast-Growing Cities

1. "In Latin America, populism has encompassed many forms, but all have shared qualities of being urban-based, multiclass coalitional, hierarchical, cooptive, ad hoc, and nonrevolutionary, led by ebullient (if not charismatic) figures who promised to redress popular grievances and to build social solidarity." Marc Becker, Truman State University. "Terms and Definitions," Latin American History—Resources. www2.truman.edu/~marc/resources/terms.html (accessed on June 4, 2007).

2. Population Count is a summarized count of population between the National Census. It was created in the 1990s, due to the enormous internal migration that makes difficult the use of intra-census estimate.

3. Olavo Bilac wrote, in 1890, a chronicle with the title *Fora da vida* [Outside life], where he describes meeting a washerwoman at the Conceição hill, who hadn't gone down to the center of the city for thirty-four years: "And so materially close to us, on her hill, this creature has been there for thirty-four years so morally separated from us, so actually distant from our lives, as if, pulled back in space and time, she were living in the previous century, in the depths of China." Olavo Bilac, *Vossa Insolência: Crônicas*, ed. Antônio Dimas (São Paulo: Companhia das Letras, 1996).

Bibliography

3iNetwork. 2006. *India Infrastructure Report 2006: Urban Infrastructure*. New Delhi: Oxford University Press.

Abdel-Rahman, Hesham M., and Alex Anas. 2004. "Theories of Systems of Cities." In J. Vernon Henderson and Jacques-Francois Thisse, eds., *Handbook of Regional and Urban Economics*. Vol. 4, *Cities and Geography*. Amsterdam: Elsevier.

ACHR. 2001. "Ho Chi Minh City." Asian Coalition for Housing Rights. http://www.achr.net/sup_vietnam.htm.

Adams, D., and E. H. Hastings. 2001. "Assessing Institutional Relations in Development Partnerships: The Land Development Corporation and the Hong Kong Government Prior to 1997." *Urban Studies* 38 (9): 1473–92.

Addison, Tony, and Jorgen Levin. 2006. *Tax Policy Reform in Developing Countries*. Copenhagen: Ministry of Foreign Affairs.

Agarwala, Ramgopal. 1983. *Price Distortions and Growth in Developing Countries*. World Bank Staff Working Paper No. 575, Washington, D.C.

Ahmad, Etisham, and Vito Tanzi. 2002. *Managing Fiscal Decentralization*. Oxford: Routledge.

Akintoye, A., and M. Beck, eds. 2003. *Public Private Partnerships: Managing Risks and Opportunities*. London: Blackwell.

Akunga, Alice et al. 2000. *The Impact of HIV/AIDS on Education in Kenya and the Potential for Using Education in the Widest Sense for the Prevention and Control of HIV/AIDS: A Government of Kenya and Unicef Kenya Country Office Study*. Nairobi: Government of Kenya.

Alexandrov, A., T. Ivanova, M. Koeva, T. Madzharova, and V. Petrova. 2004. *Application of QuickBird Satellite Imagery in Updating Cadastral Information*. Proceedings of 2004 ISPRS Congress, Istanbul, Turkey.

Alonso, W. 1964. *Location and Land Use: Toward a General Theory of Land Rent*. Cambridge, Mass.: Harvard University Press.

Amis, Philip. 1990. "Key Themes in African Urbanization." In Philip Amis and Peter Lloyd, eds., *Housing Africa's Urban Poor*. International African Institute. Manchester, UK: Manchester University Press.

Angel, Shlomo. 2000. *Housing Policy Matters: A Global Analysis*. Oxford: Oxford University Press.

Angel, Shlomo, Stephen C. Sheppard, and David.L. Civco. *The Dynamics of Global Urban Expansion*. Washington, D.C.: World Bank, 2005. http://siteresources.worldbank.org/Inturbandevelopment/Resources/dynamics_urban_expansion.pdf.

Annez, Patricia Clarke. 2007. "Urban Infrastructure Finance from Private Operators." In George Peterson and Patricia Clarke Annez, eds., *Financing Cities:*

Fiscal Responsibility and Urban Infrastructure in Brazil, China, India, Poland, and South Africa, 284–306. New Delhi: Sage Publications.

Arnott, Richard. 2009. "Housing Policy in Developing Countries: The Importance of the Informal Economy." In Michael Spence, Patricia Annez, and Robert Buckley, eds., *Urbanization and Growth*, 167–96. Washington, D.C.: World Bank.

Asian Development Bank. 2009. *Urban Poverty in India*. New Delhi: Business Standard Books.

Asian Development Bank, International Bank for Reconstruction and Development/World Bank, and Japan Bank for International Cooperation. 2005. *Connecting East Asia: A New Framework for Infrastructure*. Washington, D.C.: International Bank for Reconstruction and Development/World Bank. http://www.adb.org/Projects/Infrastructure-Development/Infrastructure-study.pdf (accessed September 12, 2007).

Association of European Transport. 1999. Financing Infrastructure Proceedings of the European Transport Conference. Cambridge, September.

Audretsch, David B. and Maryann P. Feldman. 2004. "Knowledge Spillovers and the Geography of Innovation." In J. Vernon Henderson and Jacques-François Thisse, eds., *Handbook of Regional and Urban Economics*. Vol. 4, *Cities and Geography*. Amsterdam: Elsevier.

Badami, Madhav G., Geetam Tiwari, and Dinesh Mohan. 2007. "Access and Mobility for the Urban Poor in India." In Aprodicio A. Laquian, Vinod Tewari, and Lisa M Hanley, eds., *The Inclusive City: Infrastructure and Public Services for the Urban Poor in Asia*. Washington, D.C., and Baltimore: Woodrow Wilson Press and Johns Hopkins University Press.

Badiane, Alioune, ed. 2008. *The State of African Cities 2008: A Framework for Addressing Urban Challenges*. Nairobi: UN-HABITAT.

Bahl, R. and J. Martinez-Vazquez. 2003. "Fiscal Federalism and Economic Reform in China." International Studies Program Working Paper No. 03–13. Atlanta: Georgia State University.

Bahl, Roy and Jorge Martinez-Vazquez. 2006. "Sequencing Fiscal Decentralization." *Policy Research Working Paper* No. 3914. Washington, D.C.: World Bank.

Bahl, Roy. 2000. "How to Design a Fiscal Decentralization Program." In Shahid Yusuf, Weiping Wu, and Simon Evenett, eds., *Local Dynamics in an Era of Globalization*. Oxford: Oxford University Press.

Bahl, Roy W. and Johannes Linn. 1992. *Urban Public Finance in Developing Countries*. Oxford: Oxford University Press.

Bahl, Roy and Paul Smoke, eds. 2003. *Restructuring Local Government Finance in Developing Countries: Lessons from South Africa*. Cheltenham, UK: Edward Elgar.

Balk, D. 2006. "Urban Footprints: Detecting the Spatial Extent of Urban Areas and Linking Extents with Population Characteristics." Paper presented at the workshop "Re-thinking the Estimation and Projection of Urban and City Populations," Columbia University, New York.

Balk, D., F. Pozzi, G. Yetman, U. Deichmann, and A. Nelson. 2005. "The Distribution of People and the Dimension of Place: Methodologies to Improve the Global Estimation of Urban Extents." In *Proceedings of the Urban Remote Sensing Conference of the International Society for Photogrammetry and Remote Sensing*. Paris: International Union for the Scientific Study of Population.

Baltrusis, Nelson. 2000. "A Dinâmica do Mercado Imobiliário Informal na Região Metropolitana de São Paulo: Um Estudo de Caso Nas Favelas de Paraisópolis e Nova Conquista." Campinas: Dissertation presented to obtain a Master's Degree, FAU-PUCCAMP.

Banco Nacional De Habitação. 1966. *Texto introdutório.* Vol. 2. Brasília: BNH.

Bank for International Settlements. Committee on the Global Financial System. 2006. "Housing Finance in the Global Financial Market." Basel: CGFS Papers No. 26.

Bardhan, Pranab and Dilip Mookherjee, eds. 2006. *Decentralization and Local Governance in Developing Countries: A Comparative Perspective.* Cambridge, Mass.: MIT Press.

Barro, Robert J. 1991 "Economic Growth in a Cross Section of Countries." *Quarterly Journal of Economics* 106 (2): 407–43.

———. 1997. *Determinants of Economic Growth: A Cross-Country Empirical Study.* Cambridge, Mass.: MIT Press.

Bassett, K., R. Griffiths, and I. Smith. 2002. "Testing Governance: Partnerships, Planning and Conflict in Waterfront Regeneration." *Urban Studies* 39 (10): 1757–75.

Batty, M. 1994. "A Chronicle of Scientific Planning: The Anglo-American Modeling Experience." *Journal of the American Planning Association* 60 (1): 7–16.

———. 2005. "New Developments in Urban Modeling: Simulation, Representation, and Visualization." In Subhrajit Guhathakurta, ed., *Integrated Land Use and Environmental Models: A Survey of Current Applications and Research.* New York: Springer-Verlag.

Batty, Michael and Paul Longley. 1994. *Fractal Cities: A Geometry of Form and Function.* San Diego: Academic Press.

Bazoglu, Nefise. 1998. "Ein Helwan and Al Nahda: Assessment of the Urban Community Development Project in Cairo Metropolitan Area." Evaluation report for UNICEF Cairo Office and the Regional Office for Middle East and North Africa, Amman.

Becker, Kristina Flodman. 2004. "The Informal Economy." SIDA (Swedish International Development Corporation Agency).

Benjamin, John D., Glenn W. Boyle, and C. F. Sirmans. 1990. "Retail Leasing: The Determinants of Shopping Center Rents." *AREUEA Journal* 18 (3): 302–12.

Bertaud, A., D. Webster, and J. Cai, et al. 2007. *Urban Land Use Efficiency in China: Issues and Policy Recommendations.* Washington, D.C.: World Bank.

Bertaud, Alain and Stephen Malpezzi. 2003. "The Spatial Distribution of Population in 48 World Cities: Implications for Transition Economies." World Bank, ECA Region Working Paper, Washington, D.C.

Bertaud, Alain and Bertrand Renaud. 1997. "Socialist Cities Without Land Markets." *Journal of Urban Economics* 41 (1): 137–51.

Berube, Alan and Bruce Katz. 2006. *The State of American Cities.* London: Department of Communities and Local Government.

Bessey, K. Michael. 2002. "Structure and Dynamics in an Urban Landscape: Toward a Multiscale View." *Ecosystems* 5 (4): 360–75.

Birch, Eugenie. 2010. "Istanbul—A Megalopolis That Is Beginning to Work." *Citiwire.* Accessed July 25 at http://citiwire.net/post/2167/.

Birch, Eugenie and Susan Wachter, eds. 2008. *Growing Greener Cities: Urban Sustainability in the Twenty-First Century.* Philadelphia: The University of Pennsylvania Press.

Birch, Eugenie and Susan Wachter, eds. 2006. *Rebuilding Urban Places After Disaster: Lessons from Hurricane Katrina.* Philadelphia: The University of Pennsylvania Press.

Bird, R. M. 1999. "Rethinking Tax Assignment: The Need for Better Sub-National Taxes." Washington, D.C.: World Bank.

————. 2001. "Subnational Revenues: Realities and Prospects." Washington, D.C.: World Bank, World Bank Institute, Fiscal Policy Training Program.

Bird, R. M. and F. Vaillancourt, eds. 1998. *Fiscal Decentralization in Developing Countries.* Cambridge: Cambridge University Press.

Blair, Harry. 2000. "Participation and Power at the Periphery: Democratic Local Governance in Six Countries." *World Development* 28 (1).

————. 2006. "Innovations in Participatory Local Governance." Paper prepared for the 2007 World Public Sector Report, United Nations Department for Economic and Social Development New York.

Block, S. A. 2001. "Does Africa Grow Differently?" *Journal of Development Economics* 65 (2): 443–67.

Boase, J. P. 2000. "Beyond Government? The Appeal of Public-Private Partnerships." *Canadian Public Administration* 43 (1): 75–92.

Bocquier, P. 2005 "World Urbanization Prospects: An Alternative to the UN Model of Projection Compatible with Mobility Transition Theory." *Demographic Research* 12 (9). http://www.iussp.org/Activities/wgc-urb/bocquier.pdf.

Bornstein, R. and Q. Lin. 2000. "Urban Heat Islands and Summertime Convective Thunderstorms in Atlanta: Three Cases Studies." *Atmospheric Environment* 34: 507–16.

Boucher, A., K. C. Seto, and A. G. Journél. 2006. "A Novel Method for Mapping Land Cover Changes: Integrating Time and Space with Geostatistics." *IEEE Transactions on Geoscience and Remote Sensing* 44 (11): 3427–35.

Bovaird, T. 2004. "Public-Private Partnerships: From Contested Concepts to Prevalent Practice." *International Review of Administrative Sciences* 70 (2): 199–215.

Brautigam, Deborah. 2008. "Introduction: Taxation and State-Building in Developing Countries." In Deborah Bräutigam, Odd-Helge Fjeldstad, and Mick Moore, eds., *Taxation and State-Building in Developing Countries: Capacity and Consent.* Cambridge: Cambridge University Press, 1–33.

Bretas, P. R. P. 1996. "Participative Budgeting in Belo Horizonte: Democratization and Citizenship." *Environment and Urbanization* 8 (6): 214–22.

Briffault, R. 1999. "A Government for Our Time? Business Improvement Districts and Urban Governance." *Columbia Law Review* 99 (2): 365–477.

————. 2000. "Public Oversight of Public/Private Partnerships." *Fordham University Law Journal* 28: 1357–1395.

Brock, William A. 1999. "Scaling in Economics: A Reader's Guide." *Industrial and Corporate Change* 8 (3): 409–46.

Brock, William A. and Steve N. Durlauf. 2001. "Growth Economics and Reality." *World Bank Economic Review* 15 (2): 229–72.

Brueckner, J. 1987. "The Structure of Urban Equilibria." In E. Mills, ed., *Handbook of Regional and Urban Economics.* New York: Elsevier.

Brueckner, Jan K. and Hyun-A. Kim. 2001. "Land Markets in the Harris-Todaro Model: A New Factor-Equilibrating Rural-Urban Migration." *Journal of Regional Science* 41 (3): 507–20.

Brueckner, Jan K. and Yves Zenou. 1999. "Harris-Todaro Models with a Land Market." *Regional Science and Urban Economics* 29 (3): 317–39.

Brugman, Jeb. 2010. *Welcome to the Urban Revolution: How Cities Are Changing the World.* New York: Basic Books.

Buckley, Robert M. 2005. "Macro Linkages with Municipal Finance: An Overview." Presentation made to municipal officials in Jaipur, India.

Burchfield, N., H. Overman, D. Puga, and M. Turner. 2006. "Sprawl: A View from Space." *Quarterly Journal of Economics* 121: 587–633.

Burki, Shahid Javed, Guillermo Perry, and William Dillinger. 1999. *Beyond the Center: Decentralizing the State.* Washington, D.C.: World Bank.

Burns, Leland S. and Leo Grebler. 1977. *The Housing of Nations: Advice and Policy in a Comparative Framework.* London: Macmillan.

Buxbaum, J. N. and I. N. Ortiz. 2007. *Protecting the Public Interest: The Role of Long-Term Concession Agreements for Providing Transportation Infrastructure.* USC Keston Institute for Public Finance and Infrastructure Policy. Research Paper 07–02. June. http://www.usc.edu/schools/sppd/keston/research/index.html (accessed September 12, 2007).

Cai, Jianming, Douglas Webster, and Tao Qu. 2006. "Perspective Metropolitan Regions in China: Process, Dynamics and Future." Presentation made at the First Chinese Academy of Science—Arizona State University Workshop on Urban Development and Sustainability, Beijing, December.

Cairncross, Frances. 1997. *The Death of Distance.* Cambridge, Mass.: Harvard Business School Press.

Calomiris, Charles. 2008. "The subprime turmoil: What's old, what's new, and what's next." London: Center for Economic Policy Research. http://voxeu.org/index.php?q=node/1561.

Cambridge Systematics, Inc. 2006. *Background Paper #1—National Perspective: Uses of Tolling and Related Issues.* Washington State Comprehensive Tolling Study, Final Report, Vol. 2. September 20. http://www.estc.wa.gov/Tolling/FR1_WS_TollStudy_Vol2_Paper01.pdf (accessed September 12, 2007).

Cardoso, Adauto Lucio. 2007. "Urbanização De Favelas No Brasil: Revendo A Experiência E Pensando Desafios." Trabalho apresentado no XII Encontro Nacional da Associação Nacional de Pós Graduação e Pesquisa em Planejamento Urbano e Regional, Presented in Belém do Pará, Brazil, May 21–27, 2007.

Carlino, Gerald A. 1987. "Productivity in Cities: Does City Size Matter?" *Federal Reserve Bank of Philadelphia Business Review* (November–December): 3–12.

Census of India. 2001. *General Population Tables, Part II A.* New Delhi: Registrar General of India.

Center for International Earth Science Information Network (CIESIN), Columbia University; International Food Policy Research Institute (IFPRI); The World Bank; and Centro Internacional de Agricultura Tropical (CIAT). 2004. *Global Rural-Urban Mapping Project (GRUMP), Alpha Version: Urban Extents.* Palisades, NY: Socioeconomic Data and Applications Center (SEDAC), Columbia University. Available at http://sedac.ciesin.columbia.edu/gpw.

Chamie, Joseph. 2004. "Too Few Children . . . Too Many Migrants?" *Innovation* 5 (1): 54–55.

Champion, T. 2006. "Where Do We Stand? Lessons from the IUSSP Working Group on Urbanization." Paper presented at the workshop "Re-thinking the Estimation and Projection of Urban and City Populations," Columbia University, New York.

Champion, T., and G. Hugo, eds. 2004. *New Forms of Urbanization: Beyond the Urban-Rural Dichotomy.* Aldershot: Ashgate.

Chan, Kam Wing and Ying Hu. 2003. "Urbanization in China in the 1990s: New Definition, Different Series, and Revised Trends." *China Review* 3 (2): 49–71.

Chandler, Alfred D. 1977. *The Visible Hand: The Managerial Revolution in American Business.* Cambridge, Mass.: Harvard University Press.

Chang, Chun and Yijiang Wang. 1998. "Economic Transition Under a Semi-Federalist Government: The Experience of China." *China Economic Review* 9 (1): 1–23.

Chang, Sen-Dou. 1976. "The Changing System of Chinese Cities." *Annals of the Association of American Geographers* 66 (3): 398–415.

Chapman, Murray and Prothero, R. Mansell. 1983–1984. "Themes on Circulation in the Third World." *International Migration Review* 17 (4): 597–632.

Cheema, G. Shabbir and Dennis Rondinelli, eds. 2007. *Decentralized Governance: Emerging Concepts and Practices.* Washington, D.C.: Brookings Institution.

Chen, Nancy, Paolo Valente, and Hania Zlotnik. 1998. "What Do We Know About Recent Trends in Urbanization?" In Richard E. Bilsborrow, ed., *Migration, Urbanization, and Development: New Directions and Issues.* Norwell, Mass.: Kluwer.

China 2000 County Population Census (CD-ROM). All China Marketing Research Co.

China Daily. 2003. "Measures to Protect Farmers' Land Rights." November 20. http://www.chinadaily.com.cn/english/.

China Mayor Association. 2004. *Chinese City Development Report.* Beijing: Commercial Printing House.

China State Statistical Bureau (CSSB). 1999a. *China Population and Employment Statistical Yearbook 1999.* Beijing: China State Statistical Press.

China State Statistical Bureau (CSSB). 1999b. *Comprehensive Statistical Data and Materials on 50 Years of New China.* Beijing: China State Statistical Press.

China State Statistical Bureau (CSSB). 2007. *China Population and Employment Statistical Yearbook 2007.* Beijing: China State Statistical Press.

China State Statistical Bureau (CSSB). 2008. *China Population and Employment Statistical Yearbook 2008.* Beijing: China State Statistical Press.

Christaller, Walter. 1966. *Central Places in Southern Germany,* trans. Carlisle W. Baskin. Englewood Cliffs, N.J.: Prentice-Hall.

Clarke, K. C. and L. J. Gaydos. 1998. "Loose-Coupling a Cellular Automaton Model and GIS: Long-Term Urban Growth Prediction for San Francisco and Washington/Baltimore." *International Journal of Geographical Information Science* 12 (7): 699–714.

Clarke, K. C., S. Hoppen, and L. Gaydos. 1997. "A Self-Modifying Cellular Automaton Model of Historical Urbanization in the San Francisco Bay Area." *Environment and Planning B: Planning and Design* 24 (2): 247–261.

Cohen, Joel. 1995. *How Many People Can the Earth Support?* New York: Norton.

———. 2005. "Human Population Grows Up." *Scientific American* 293 (3):48–55, September. http://www.scientificamerican.com/article.cfm?id = human-population-grows-up.

———. 2009 "Human Population Grows Up." In *A Pivotal Moment: Population, Justice and the Environmental Challenge,* ed. Laurie Mazur, pp. 27–37. Washington, D.C.: Island Press. http://islandpress.org/bookstore/ details039a.html?prod_id = 1944#toc.

———. 2007. *Educating All Children: A Global Agenda.* Cambridge, Mass.: MIT Press.

Coleman, J. 1968. "Equality of Educational Opportunity." *Equity and Excellence in Education* 6 (5): 19–28.

Collier, Paul and Jan William Gunning. 1999. "Explaining African Economic Performance." *Journal of Economic Literature* 37 (1): 64–111.

Collins, Michael, Eric Belsky, and Karl E. Case. 2004. "Exploring the Welfare Effects of Risk-Based Pricing in the Subprime Mortgage Market," Joint Center for Housing Studies Working Paper BABC 04–08. Cambridge, Mass.: Harvard University Press.

Commins, Stephen. 2006. "Community Participation in Service Delivery and Public Accountability: Advancing the MDGs." Paper prepared for the 2007 World Public Sector Report, United Nations Department for Economic and Social Development, New York.

Costa, Sandra Maria Fonseca da and Diogo Corrêa da Silva. "Novas formas de Urbanização em São José dos Campos: Um Estudo da Dispersão Residencial Urbana." Trabalho apresentado no XII Encontro Nacional da Associação Nacional de Pós Graduação e Pesquisa em Planejamento Urbano e Regional, Presented in Belém do Pará, Brazil, May 21–27, 2007.

Couclelis, H. 1997. "From Cellular Automata to Urban Models: New Principles for Model Development and Implementation." *Environment and Planning B: Planning and Design* 24 (2): 165–174.

CPIN (China Population Information Network). 2003. *China's "Urban Poor."* http://www.cpirc.org.cn/news/rkxw_gn_detail.asp?id=539.

Crook, Richard. 2003. "Decentralization and Poverty Reduction in Africa: The Politics of Local-Central Relations." *Public Administration and Development* 23 (1): 77–88.

Crutzen, P. J. 2004. "New Directions: The Growing Urban Heat and Pollution Island Effect—Impact on Chemistry and Climate." *Atmospheric Environment* 38: 3539–40.

Cui, Gong H. and Laurence Ma. 1999. "Mechanism of the Bottom-Up Urbanization in China." *Acta Geographica Sinica* 54: 106–15.

Cunningham, C. 2006. "House Price Uncertainty, Timing of Development, and Vacant Land Prices: Evidence for Real Options in Seattle." *Journal of Urban Economics* 59: 1–31.

Daley-Harris, Sam. 2009. *State of the Microcredit Summit Campaign Report 2009.* Washington, D.C.: Microcredit Summit Campaign.

Daniels, R. J. and M. J. Trebilcock. 1996. "Private Provision of Public Infrastructure: An Organizational Analysis of the Next Privatization Frontier." *University of Toronto Law Journal* 46 (3): 375–426.

Davis, Morris A. and Francois Ortalo-Magne. 2007. "Amenities as TFP and the Factor of Four." Mimeo, University of Wisconsin, Center for Real Estate.

Davoodi, H. and H. F. Zou. 1998. "Fiscal Decentralization and Economic Growth: A Cross-Country Study." *Journal of Urban Economics* 43 (2): 244–57.

Delors, J. 1996. *Learning the Treasure Within.* Paris: UNESCO.

Desai, Nitin. 1996. "Cultivating an Urban Eco-Society: The United Nations Response." In Takashi Inoguchi, Edward Newman, and Glen Paolet, eds., *Cities and the Environment: New Approaches to Eco-Societies.* Tokyo: United Nations University Publication.

Dietzel, C., M. Herold, J. Hemphill, and K. Clarke. 2005. "Spatio-Temporal Dynamics in California's Central Valley: Empirical Links to Urban Theory." *International Journal of Geographical Information Science* 19 (2): 175–95.

DigitalGlobe Inc. 2003. *QB Imagery Products, Product Guide.*

Dillinger, William. 1988. "Urban Property Taxation in Developing Countries." World Bank, PPR Working Paper No. WPS 41, Washington, D.C.

Dirie, Ilias. 2006. *Municipal Finance: Innovative Resourcing for Municipal Infrastructure and Service Provision.* London: Commonwealth Local Government Forum.

Dixon, P. G. and T. L. Mote. 2003. "Patterns and Causes of Atlanta's Urban Heat Island–Initiated Precipitation." *Journal of Applied Meteorology* 42: 1273–84.

Duranton, G. and D. Puga. 2004. "Micro-Foundations of Urban Agglomeration Economics." In J. V. Henderson, and J. F. Thisse, eds., *Handbook of Regional and Urban Economics.* Amsterdam: Elsevier.

Duranton, Gilles and Diego Puga. 2000. "Diversity and Specialization in Cities: Why, Where and When Does it Matter?" *Urban Studies* 37 (3): 533–55.

Durbin Associates. 2005. *A Study of Innovations in the Funding and Delivery of Transportation Infrastructure Using Tolls.* Final Report of the Pennsylvania House of Representatives Select Committee on Toll Roads." November.

Durlauf, Steven N. 2004. "Neighborhood Effects." In J. Vernon Henderson and Jacques-Francois Thisse, eds., *Handbook of Regional and Urban Economics.* Vol. 4, *Cities and Geography.* Amsterdam: Elsevier.

Eaton, Kent. 2004. *Politics Beyond the Capital: The Design of Subnational Institutions in South America.* Stanford, Calif.: Stanford University Press.

Ebel, Robert. 2003. "Fiscal Decentralization in Developing Countries: Is It Happening? How Do We Know?" In James Alm and Jorge Martinez-Vazquez, eds., *Public Finance in Developing and Transition Countries: Essays in Honor of Richard M. Bird.* Cheltenham, UK: Edward Elgar.

Ebel, Robert and Robert Taliercio. 2005. "Subnational Tax Policy and Administration in Developing Economies." *Tax Notes International* 37 (1): 919–36.

Ebel, Robert and Dana Weist. 2006. *Sequencing Subnational Revenue Decentralization.* Washington, D.C.: World Bank.

Ebel, Robert and Serdar Yilmaz. 2002. "On the Measurement and Impact of Fiscal Decentralization." Policy Research Working Paper No. 2809. Washington, D.C.: World Bank.

Economist. 2006. "China's Next Building Site: Building the Nation: Tianjin: Planning a Rival for Shenzhen and Shanghai." June 24, 47–48.

EIS-Africa. 2002. "Geoinformation Supports Decision-Making in Africa, A Position Paper," EIS-Africa, Pretoria.

Elander, I. 2002. "Partnerships and Urban Governance." *International Social Science Journal* 54 (2): 191–204.

Elimu Yetu Coalition. 2005. "The Challenge of Educating Girls in Kenya." In Sheila Aikman and Elaine Unterhalter, eds., *Beyond Access: Transforming Policy and Practice for Gender Equality in Education.* Oxford: Oxfam Publishing.

Elvidge, C. D., K. E. Baugh, E. A. Kihn, H. W. Kroehl, E. R. Davis. 1997. "Mapping of City Lights Using Dmsp Operational Linescan System Data." *Photogrammetric Engineering and Remote Sensing* 63: 727–34.

Emig S. and Z. Ismail. 1980. *Notes on the Urban Planning of Nairobi.* Copenhagen: Royal Academy of Fine Arts.

Eng, Irene. 1997. "The Rise of Manufacturing Towns: Externally Driven Industrialization and Urban Development in the Pearl River Delta of China." *International Journal of Urban and Regional Research* 21 (4): 554–68.

Engberg, L.A. 2002. "Reviews: Public-Private Partnerships. Theory and Practice in International Perspective." *Public Administration* 80 (3): 601–14.

Enyedi, G. 2003. "The Social Sustainability of Large Cities." International Conference on Social Science and Social Policy in the 21st Century, ISSC, Vienna.

Estache, Antonio. 2004. "A Selected Survey of Recent Economic Literature on Emerging Infrastructure Policy Issues in Developing Countries." Paper prepared for the POVNET Infrastructure Working Group, World Bank, Washington, D.C.

Expert Group on Commercialisation of Infrastructure Projects. 1996. *The India Infrastructure Report: Policy Imperatives for Growth and Welfare.* New Delhi: Ministry of Finance, Government of India.

European Commission (EC), Directorate-General Regional Policy. 2003. *Guidelines for Successful Public-Private Partnerships.* March. http://europa.ed.int/

comm/regional_policy/sources/docgener/guid es/PPPguide.htm (accessed September 6, 2007).
———. 2004. *Resource Book on PPP Case Studies.* June. http://europa.eu.int/comm/regional_policy/sources/docgener/guid es/pppguide.html (accessed September 6, 2007).
Falleti, Tulia. 2005. "A Sequential Theory of Decentralization: Latin American Cases in Comparative Perspective." *American Political Science Review* 99 (3): 327–46.
Farlam, P. 2005. *Working Together: Assessing Public-Private Partnerships in Africa.* Johannesburg: South African Institute of International Affairs. http://www.saiia.org.za/images/upload/PPP-NepadReport-Final9_Feb05.pdf (accessed September 6, 2007).
Farrell, Diana. 2004. "The Hidden Dangers of the Informal Economy." *McKinsey Quarterly* 3 (1): 26–37.
FAWE. 2004. *Review of National Education Policies and Plans for Potential for Scaling Up Good Practices in Girls' Education.* Nairobi: FAWE.
———. n.d. "Building Effective Partnerships for Girls' Education in Africa." Paper prepared for FAWE/ WGFP ministerial consultation, Dakar, Senegal.
Fei, Xiaotung. 1984. "Small Town, Big Problem." In *Compendium 1,* ed. Jiangsu Province Small-Town Research Team. Nanjing: Jiangsu People's Press (in Chinese).
Ferchiou, Ridha. 1982. "The Indirect Effects of New Housing Construction in Developing Countries." *Urban Studies* 19 (2): 167–76.
Ferguson, Bruce. 2008. "Housing Microfinance: Is the Glass Half Empty or Half Full?" *Global Urban Development* 4 (2): 1–19.
Fernandes, Edesio. 2007. "Implementing the Urban Reform Agenda in Brazil." *Environment and Urbanization* 19:2 (April): 177–99.
Fernandez, C., E. Ley, and Mark F. J. Steel. 2001. "Model Uncertainty in Cross-Country Growth." *Journal of Applied Econometrics* 16 (5): 563–76.
Financial Express. 2007. *India's GDP Crosses $1 Trillion,* The Indian Express Group, New Delhi, April 26.
Financial Times. 1998. "Perplexed by Blair's *Je Ne Sais Quoi.*" June 15.
Fischer, Stanley. 2003. "Globalization and Its Challenges." *American Economic Review* 93 (2): 1–30.
Fisher, Lynn and Austin Jaffe. 2003. "Determinants of International Homeownership Rates." *Housing Finance International* (September): 34–42.
Fjeldstad, Odd-Helge. 2001. "Taxation, Coercion and Donors: Local Government Tax Enforcement in Tanzania." *Journal of Modern African Studies* 39 (2): 289–306.
———. 2004. "What's Trust Got to Do with It? Non-Payment of Service Charges in Local Authorities in South Africa." *Journal of Modern African Studies 42* (4): 539–62.
———. 2005. "Entitlement, Affordability or a Matter of Trust? Reflections on the Non-payment of Service Charges in Local Authorities." In Steinar Askvik and Nelleke Bak, eds., *Trust in Public Institutions in South Africa.* Aldershot: Ashgate.
———. 2006. "Corruption in Tax Administration: Lessons from Institutional Reforms in Uganda." In Susan Rose Ackerman, ed., *International Handbook on the Economics of Corruption.* Cheltenham, UK: Edward Elgar.
Fjeldstad, Odd-Helge and Joseph Semboja. 2001. "Why People Pay Taxes: The Case of the Development Levy in Tanzania." *World Development* 29 (12): 2059–74.

Flinders, M. 2005. "The Politics of Public-Private Partnerships." *British Journal of Politics and International Relations* 7 (2): 215–39.

Follain, James R. and Stephen Malpezzi. 1981. "The Flight to the Suburbs: Insight from an Analysis of Central City vs. Suburban Housing Costs." *Journal of Urban Economics* 9 (3): 381–98.

Food and Agriculture Organization. 2009. The Global Information and Early Warning System on Food and Agriculture (GIEWS). *Food Outlook: Global Market Analysis.* Rome: FAO, June 2009. http://www.fao.org/giews/english/fo/index.htm

Foster, Viven and Tito Yepes. 2006. "Is Cost Recovery a Feasible Objective for Water and Electricity? The Latin American Experience." WPS 3943, World Bank, Washington, D.C.

Freestone, R., P. Williams, and A. Bowden. 2006. "Fly Buy Cities: Some Planning Aspects of Airport Privatization in Australia." *Urban Policy and Research* 24 (4): 491–508.

Frieden, B. J. and L. Sagalyn. 1989. *Downtown, Inc.: How American Rebuilds Cities.* Cambridge, Mass.: MIT Press.

Friedman, Ken. 1996. *Restructuring the City: Thoughts on Urban Patterns in the Information Society.* Stockholm: Swedish Institute for Future Studies.

Friere, Mila and John Peterson, eds. 2004. *Subnational Capital Markets in Developing Countries: From Theory to Practice.* Oxford: Oxford University Press.

Fundação do Instituto Brasileiro de Geografia e Estatística (FIBGE). Demographic Census of 1980, 1991, 2000, 2005. Accessed July 27, 2010 at http://www.ibge.gov.br/home/default.php.

Gaspar, Jess and Glaeser, Edward L. 1998. "Information Technology and the Future of Cities." *Journal of Urban Economics* 43 (1): 136–56.

Gathenya, T. Wambui. 2004. "Breaking Boundaries to Achieve Quality Education for All: National Strategies for Mainstreaming Non-Formal Education Innovations in Kenya." ICSEI Conference, Barcelona. Accessed at http://www.icsei.net/fileadmin/ICSEI/user_upload/documents/2005_Gathenya_ing.pdf

Gërxhani, Klarita. 2004. The Informal Sector in Developed and Less Developed Countries: A Literature Survey. *Public Choice* 120 (3–4): 267–300.

Ghere, R. K. 2001. "Probing the Strategic Intricacies of Public-Private Partnership: The Patent as a Comparative Reference." *Public Administration Review* 61 (4): 441–51.

Gilbert, Alan. 1996. "The Latin American Mega City: An Introduction." In A. Gilbert, ed., *The Mega City in Latin America.* Tokyo: United Nations University Press.

Glaeser, Edward L., Jed Kolko, and A. Saiz. 2001. "Consumer City." *Journal of Economic Geography* 1 (1): 27–50.

Gleick, J. 1988. *Chaos: Making a New Science.* London: Cardinal.

Godfrey, Brian J. 1995. "Restructuring and Decentralization in a World City." *Geographical Review* 85 (4): 436–57.

Gokturk, Deniz, Levant Soysal, and Ipek Tureli. 2010. *Orienting Istanbul, Cultural Capital of Europe?* London: Routledge.

Goldstein, D. B. and R. K. Watson. 2002. *Transforming Chinese Buildings.* New York: Natural Resources Defense Council.

Government of India. 2004. *National Municipal Accounts Manual.* New Delhi: Ministry of Urban Development.

———. 2005. Jawaharlal Nehru National Urban Renewal Mission: Overview,

Ministry of Urban Development and Ministry of Urban Employment and Poverty Alleviation, Government of Induia, New Delhi.

———. 2006a. "City Development Plan. The CDPs of the 63 JNNURM Cities." http://jnnurm.nic.in.

———. 2006b. *Towards Faster and More Inclusive Growth: An Approach to the 11th Five Year Plan.* New Delhi: Planning Commission.

———. 2009. *Economic Survey 2008–2009.* New Delhi: Ministry of Finance.

Gramlich, Edward M. 2007. *Subprime Mortgages: America's Latest Boom and Bust.* Washington, D.C.: Urban Institute.

Green, Amanda E. 2005. "Managing Human Resources in a Decentralized Context." In *East Asia Decentralizes: Making Local Government Work.* Washington, D.C.: World Bank.

Grimsey, D. and M. K. Lewis. 2004. *Public Private Partnerships: The Worldwide Revolution in Infrastructure Provision and Project Finance.* Cheltenham, UK: Edward Elgar.

Guvenc, Murat. 1996. *Social and Economic Status of Istanbul Residents.* Ankara: Middle East University.

———. 2010. "Urban Historiography and Spatial Analysis." Paper presented at the 14th Conference of the International History of Planning Society, Istanbul,Turkey, July 12.

Gwin, Carl L. and Seow-Eng Ong. 2004. "Do We Really Understand Home Ownership Rates? An International Study." 2004–053-ECO, Baylor University, Waco, Tex.

Gwinner, Britt and Anthony B. Sanders. 2008. "The Sub Prime Crisis: Implications for Emerging Markets." Washington, D.C.: World Bank Policy Research Working Paper No. 4726.

Hall, J. 1998. "Private Opportunity, Public Benefit?" *Fiscal Studies* 19 (2): 121–40.

Harris J. and M. Todaro. 1970. "Migration, Unemployment and Development: A Two Sector Analysis." *American Economic Review* 60 (1) (March): 126–42.

Harris, Nigel. 1986. *The End of the Third World.* New York: Penguin Books.

Hassler, Oliver. 2006. "Going Up Market to Serve Low Income Groups," presentation at the World Bank Group Conference on Housing Finance in Emerging Countries, Washington, D.C.

Henderson, J. Vernon. 1988. *Urban Development: Theory, Fact and Illusion.* Oxford: Oxford University Press.

HM Treasury. 2003. *PFI: Meeting the Investment Challenge.* July. http://www.hm treasury.gov.uk/documents/enterprise_and_productivity/PFI.cfm (accessed September 6, 2007).

Hoffman, Barak D. and Clark C. Gibson. 2005. "Fiscal Governance and Public Services: Evidence from Tanzania and Zambia." Working paper, Department of Political Science, University of California, San Diego.

House of Commons. International Development Committee. 2004. *Kenya: DFID's Country Assistance Plan 2004–07 and Progress Towards the Millennium Development Goals.* Fourth Report of Session 2003–04. London: House of Commons.

Hsu, S. Philip. 2004. "Deconstructing Decentralization in China: Fiscal Incentive Versus Local Autonomy in Policy Implementation." *Journal of Contemporary China* 13 (40): 567–99.

Huang, Y. and W. A. V. Clark. 2002. "Housing Tenure Choice in Transitional Urban China: A Multilevel Analysis." *Urban Studies* 32 (1): 7–32.

IBAM (Instiuto Brasilerio de Administracão Municpal). 2003. "Belo Horizonte's Legislation on PROFAVELA: A Policy Evaluation." Submitted to UN-HABITAT program "Unpacking Good Legislation and Enabling Policies Series." http://www.worldbank.org/urban/mun_fin/uifpapers/demello.pdf.

IBRD. 1994. *The Human Face of the Urban Environment: A Report to the Development Committee, Environmentally Sustainable Development.* Washington, D.C.: World Bank.

IDRC. 2006. *Linking Environmental Management, Natural Resource Use, and Urban Poverty.* Urban Poverty and Environment (UPE) Program. Ottawa: IDRC.

IHDP. 2005. *Human Dimensions of Global Environmental Change.* Bonn: IHDP.

ILRI (International Livestock Research Institute) and CBS. 2002. *Mapping Poverty in Kenya and Uganda.* Nairobi: ILRI.

Ingram, Gregory K. 1998. "Patterns of Metropolitan Development: What Have We Learned?" *Urban Studies* 35 (7): 1019–35.

Inman, Robert. 2006. "Financing Cities." In Richard J. Arnott and Daniel McMillen P., eds., *A Companion to Urban Economics.* Blackwell: 311–31.

International Monetary Fund. 2004. *Public-Private Partnerships.* Report prepared by the Fiscal Affairs Department in consultation with other departments, the World Bank, and the Inter-American Development Bank. March 12. http://www.imf.org/external/np/fad/2004/pifp/eng/031204.htm (accessed September 12, 2007).

Irwin, E. and N. Bockstael. 2006. "Measuring and Modeling Urban Sprawl: Data, Scale and Spatial Dependencies." Invited paper prepared for the Urban Economics Sessions of the 53rd Annual North American Meetings of the Regional Science Association International, November 16–18, 2006, Toronto, Canada.

Iversen, Vegard, Odd-Helge Fjeldstad, Godfrey Bahiigwa, Frank Ellis, and Robert James. 2006. "Private Tax Collection—Remnant of the Past or a Way Forward? Evidence From Rural Uganda." *Public Administration and Development* 26 (4): 317–28.

Ives, A. R., M. G. Turner, and S. M. Pearson. 1998. "Local Explanations of Landscape Patterns: Can Analytical Approaches Approximate Simulation Models of Spatial Processes?" *Ecosystems* 1: 35–51.

Jaffee, Dwight. 2009. "The U.S. Subprime Mortgage Crisis: Issues Raised and Lessons Learned." In Michael Spence, Patricia Annez, and Robert Buckley, eds., *Urbanization and Growth,* 197–235. Washington, D.C.: World Bank.

Jantz, C., S. Goetz, and M. Shelley. 2003. "Using the SLEUTH Urban Growth Model to Simulate the Impacts of Future Policy Scenarios on Urban Land Use in the Baltimore-Washington Metropolitan Area." *Environment and Planning B: Planning and Design* 31 (2): 251–71.

Jin, H., Y. Qian, and B. Weingast. 1999. "Regional Decentralization and Fiscal Incentives: Federalism, Chinese Style." Working paper, Department of Economics, Stanford University.

Johnson Jr, T. 1987. "Upward Filtering of Housing Stock: A Study of Upward Filtering of Housing Stock as a Consequence of Informal Settlement Upgrading in Developing Countries." *Habitat International* 11 (1): 173–90.

Juul, Kristine. 2006. "Decentralization, Local Taxation and Citizenship in Senegal." *Development and Change* 37 (4): 821–46.

Kahnert, Friedrich. 1987. *Improving Urban Employment and Labor Productivity.* World Bank Discussion Paper No. 10.

Kanbur, R. and Venables A. J. 2005. "Introduction" in Kanbur and Venables. eds., *Spatial Equality and Development.* Oxford: Oxford University Press.

Kasarda, John D. and Crenshaw, Edward M. "Third World Urbanization: Dimensions, Theories, and Determinants." *Annual Review of Sociology* 17 (1991): 467–501.

Kannappan, Subbiah. 1983. Employment Problems and the Urban Labor Market in Developing Nations. Ann Arbor: Division of Research, University of Michigan, Graduate School of Business Administration.

Kannappan, S. 1985. Urban Employment and the Labor Market in Developing Nations. Economic Development and Cultural Change 33 (4): 699–730.

Kaufmann, D., F. Leutier, and M. Mastruzzi. 2005. "Governance and the City: An Empirical Exploration into Global Determinants of Urban Performance." World Bank: Policy Research Working Paper 3712.

Kaufmann, R. K., and K. C. Seto. 2001. "Change Detection, Accuracy, and Bias in a Sequential Analysis of Landsat Imagery of the Pearl River Delta, China: Econometric Techniques." *Agriculture Ecosystems and Environment* 85 (1–3): 95–105.

Kaufmann, R. K., K. C. Seto, A. Schneider, L. Zhou, and Z. Liu. 2007. "Climate Response to Rapid Urban Growth: Evidence of a Human-Induced Precipitation Deficit." *Journal of Climate* 20 (10): 2299–2306.

KCC and BTC. 2008. "Baseline Survey for the Kampala Integrated Environmental Management Project, Bwaise III." Kampala: Kampala City Council and Belgian Technical Cooperation, 81.

Kehew, Robert, Tomoko Matsukawa, and John Petersen. 2005. "Local Financing for Sub-Sovereign Infrastructure in Developing Countries: Case Studies of Innovative Domestic Credit Enhancement Entities and Techniques." Discussion Paper No. 1, Infrastructure, Economics and Finance Department, World Bank, Washington, D.C.

Kenya, Government of. 1981. *Economic Survey 1981.* Nairobi: Central Bureau of Statistics, Ministry of Economic Planning and Development.

Kenya National Bureau of Statistics. 2010. "Nairobi's Population, 1948–2020." Accessed July 27 at http://www.knbs.or.ke/.

Kim, Kyung-Hwan, 1997. "Housing Finance and Urban Infrastructure Finance." *Urban Studies* 34 (10): 1597–1620.

Kim, Kyung-Hwan and Bertrand Renaud. 2009. "The Global House Price Boom and Its Unwinding: An Analysis and a Commentary." *Housing Studies* 24 (1): 7–24.

Kirkby, Richard J. R. 1985. *Urbanization in China: Towns and Country in a Developing Economy 1949–2000 A.D.* London: Croom Helm.

Kjær, Anne Mette. 2004. "Institutional History or Quid-Pro-Quo? Exploring Revenue Collection in Two Ugandan Districts." Paper presented at the American Political Science Association Annual Meetings, Chicago.

———. 2005. "Accountability and the Graduated Tax in Uganda." Prepared for Second Meeting on Fiscal Decentralization. Copenhagen: Kommunernes Landsforening.

Kolko, Jed. 2000. "The Death of Cities? The Death of Distance? Evidence From the Geography of Commercial Internet Usage." In Ingo Vogelsang and Benjamin M. Compaine, eds., *The Internet Upheaval: Raising Questions, Seeking Answers in Communications Policy.* Cambridge, Mass.: MIT Press.

Koppenjan, J. 2005. "The Formation of Public-Private Partnerships: Lessons from Nine Transport Infrastructure Projects in the Netherlands." *Public Administration* 83 (1): 135–57.

Krugman Paul. 1991. "Increasing Returns and Economic Geography." *Journal of Political Economy* 99 (3): 483–99.

———. 1998. "Space: The Final Frontier." *Journal of Economic Perspectives* 12 (2): 161–74.

Kumaraswamy, M. M. and D. A. Morris. 2002. "Build-Operate-Transfer-Type Procurement in Asian Megaprojects." *Journal of Construction Engineering and Management* 128 (2): 93–102.

Ladd, H. 1994. "Spatially Targeted Economic Development Strategies: Do They Work?" *Cityscape: A Journal of Policy Development and Research* 1 (1): 193–218.

Laguian, Aprodicio A., Vinod Tewari, and Lisa M. Hanley, eds. 2007. *The Inclusive City: Infrastructure and Public Services for the Urban Poor in Asia.* Washington, D.C., and Baltimore: Woodrow Wilson Press and Johns Hopkins University Press.

Landis, J. 1994. "The California Urban Futures Model: A New Generation of Metropolitan Simulation Models." *Environment and Planning B: Planning and Design* 21 (4): 399–420.

———. 1995. "Imagining Land Use Futures: Applying the California Urban Futures Model." *Journal of the American Planning Association* 61 (4): 438–57.

———. 2001. "CUF, CUF II, and CURBA: A Family of Spatially-Explicit Urban Growth and Land Use Policy Simulation Models." In Richard Brail and Richard Klosterman, eds., *Planning Support Systems*. Redlands, Calif.: ESRI Press.

Landis, J. and M. Reilly. 2006. "Urbanization Scenarios." In Joel Smith and Robert Mendelsohn, eds., *The Impact of Climate Change on Regional Systems*. New York: Edward Elgar.

Landis, J. and M. Zhang. 1998a. "The Second Generation of the California Urban Futures Model. Part 1: Model Logic and Theory." *Environment and Planning B: Planning and Design* 25 (5): 657–66.

———. 1998b. "The Second Generation of the California Urban Futures Model. Part 2: Specification and Calibration Results of the Land-Use Change Submodel." *Environment and Planning B: Planning and Design* 25 (6): 795–824.

Laquian, Aprodicio A. 2007. "Who Are the Poor, and How Are They Served in Asian Cities?" In Aprodicio A. Laquian, Vinod Tewari, and Lisa M. Hanley, eds., *The Inclusive City, Infrastructure and Public Services for the Urban Poor in Asia*. Washington, D.C., and Baltimore: Woodrow Wilson Press and Johns Hopkins University Press.

Lea, Michael. 2009. "Structure and Evolution of Housing Finance Systems." In Loic Chiquier and Michael Lea, eds., *Housing Finance Policy in Emerging Markets*, 29–47. Washington, D.C.: World Bank.

Le Blanc, David. 2009. "Residential Rental Housing Finance." In Loic Chiquier and Michael Lea, eds., *Housing Finance Policy in Emerging Markets*, 363–94. Washington, D.C.: World Bank,.

Lee, D. 1973. "Requiem for Large Scale Urban Models." *Journal of the American Institute of Planners* 39 (3): 163–78.

Lee, Kyu Sik and Alex Anas. 1989. "Manufacturers' Responses to Infrastructure Deficiencies in Nigeria: Private Alternatives and Policy Options." Washington, D.C.: World Bank, Urban Development Department, INU Discussion Paper No. 50.

Leibenstein, Harvey. 1966. "Allocative Efficiency Versus X-Efficiency." *American Economic Review* 56 (3): 392–415.

Levy, S. M. 1996. *Build, Operate, Transfer.* New York: Wiley.

Lewis, Blane. 2003a. Property tax in Indonesia: Measuring and explaining administrative (under) performance. *Public Administration and Development* 23 (2): 227–39.

———. 2003b. Tax and Charge Creation by Regional Governments Under Fiscal Decentralization: Estimates and Explanations. *Bulletin of Indonesian Economic Studies* 39 (2): 177–92.

———. 2005. Indonesian Local Government Spending, Taxing and Saving: An Explanation of Pre- and Post-Decentralization Fiscal Outcomes." *Asian Economic Journal* 19 (3): 291–317.

———. 2006. Local government: An analysis of administrative cost inefficiency. *Bulletin of Indonesian Economic Studies* 42 (2): 213–33.

Li, Ling-hin. 1999. *Urban Land Reform in China*. Basingstoke, Hampshire: Macmillan.

Li, Z. 2003. "Facilitate Urbanization to Develop the Central Role of Cities." *Management Review* 15 (1): 9–11 (in Chinese).

Liebow, E. 1967. *Tally's Corner: A Study of Negro Streetcorner Men*. Boston: Back Bay Books.

Light, Donald. 2004. "From Migrant Enclaves to Mainstream: Reconceptualizing Informal Economic Behavior." *Theory and Society* 33 (6): 705–37.

Lipton, Michael. 1977. *Why Poor People Stay Poor: Urban Bias in World Development*. London: Temple Smith.

Littlefield, Elizabeth and Richard Rosenberg. 2004. "Microfinance and the Poor: Breaking Down Walls between Microfinance and Formal Finance." *Finance and Development* (June): 38–40.

Litvack, J., J. Ahmad, and R. Bird. 1998. *Rethinking Decentralization in Developing Countries*. Washington, D.C.: World Bank.

Liu, Alan P. L. 1992. "The 'Wenzhou Model' of Development and China's Modernization." *Asian Survey* 32 (8): 696–711.

Liu, Feng. 2006. "Interrupted Development: The Effects of Blighted Neighborhoods and Topographic Barriers on Cities." George Washington University Department of Economics, Washington, D.C.

Liu, Z., and G. Smith. 2006. *China: Building Institutions for Sustainable Urban Transport*. Working Paper No. 4, Transport Sector Unit, World Bank, Washington, D.C.

Lo, C. P. 1987. "Socialist Ideology and Urban Strategies in China." *Urban Geography* 8 (5): 440–458.

Lo, C. P., D. A. Quattrochi, and J. C. Luvall. 1997. "Application of High-Resolution Thermal Infrared Remote Sensing and GIS to Assess the Urban Heat Island Effect." *International Journal of Remote Sensing* 18: 287–304.

Lockheed, Marlaine and Maureen Lewis. 2007. *Inexcusable Absence: Why 60 Million Girls Still Aren't in School and What to Do About It*. Washington, D.C.: Center for Global Development.

Lösch, August. 1954. *The Economics of Location*, trans. William H. Woglom. New Haven: Yale University Press.

Lowry, W. P. 1998. "Urban Effects on Precipitation." *Progress in Physical Geography* 22 (4): 477–520.

Lwasa, S. 1999. "Environmental Crisis in Communities of the Urban Poor in Kampala." OSSREA national workshop, Makerere University, Kampala.

Ma, Laurence J. C., and M. Fan. 1994. "Urbanization from Below: The Growth of Towns in Jiangsu, China." *Urban Studies* 31 (10): 1625–45.

Macedo, Joseli. 2004. "City Profile: Curitiba." *Cities* 21 (6): 537–549.

Macedo, Roberto. 1998. "Brazilian Children and the Economic Crisis: The Evidence from the State of São Paulo." In Giovanni Andrea Cornia, Richard Jolly, and Frances Stewart, eds., *Adjustment with a Human Face*. Oxford: Clarendon Press.

Malpezzi, Stephen. 1990. "Urban Housing and Financial Markets: Some International Comparisons. *Urban Studies* 27 (6): 971–1022.

———. 2001. "Tales from the Real Side: The Implications of Urban Research for Real Estate Finance in Developing and Transition Economies." *Cityscape* 5: 139–73.

———. 2006. "Cross-Country Patterns of Urban Development." In R. Arnott and D. McMillen, eds., *A Companion to Urban Economics*. Malden, Mass.: Blackwell.

———. 2007. "The Supply of Real Estate." Presidential Address to the American Real Estate and Urban Economics Association, Chicago.

Malpezzi, Stephen and Zhenguo Lin. 2000. "Urban Transitions and Endogenous Economic Growth." University of Wisconsin–Madison, Center for Urban Land Economics Research Working Paper.

Malpezzi, Stephen and Stephen K. Mayo. 1997. "Getting Housing Incentives Right: A Case Study of the Effects of Regulation, Taxes and Subsidies on Housing Supply in Malaysia." *Land Economics* 73 (3): 372–91.

Malpezzi, S., K. Seah, J. Shilling. 2004. "Is It What We Do or How We Do It? New Evidence on Agglomeration Economies and Metropolitan Growth." *Real Estate Economics* 32 (2): 265–96.

Malpezzi, Stephen, Stephen K. Mayo, and David J. Gross. 1985. *Housing Demand in Developing Countries*. Washington, D.C.: World Bank.

Malpezzi, Stephen and Kerry Vandell. 2002. "Does the Low-Income Tax-Credit Increase the Supply of Housing?" *Journal of Housing Economics* 11: 360–81.

Mandelbrot, Benoit and Richard L. Hudson. 2004. *The (Mis)behavior of Markets: A Fractal View of Risk, Ruin, and Reward*. New York: Basic Books.

Manor, James. 1998. *The Political Economy of Democratic Decentralization*. Washington, D.C.: World Bank.

———. 2004. "User Committees: A Potentially Damaging Second Wave of Decentralization?" *European Journal of Development Research* 16 (1): 192–213.

———. 2007. "Strategies to Promote Effective Participation." Paper prepared for the 2007 World Public Sector Report, United Nations Department for Economic and Social Development, New York.

Manski, Charles F. 1993. "Identification of Endogenous Social Effects: The Reflection Problem." *Review of Economic Studies* 60 (3): 531–42.

Maps Geosystems. 2004. "Development of PromptInformation GIS Toolkit and Land Parcel Locator." Dubai, UAE.

Marcotullio, Peter J. 2007. "Variations of Urban Environmental Transitions: The experiences of Rapidly Developing Asia-Pacific Cities," in Peter J. Marcotullio and Gordon McGranahan, eds., *Scaling Urban Environmental Challenges*. London: Earthscan.

Marcuse, Peter and Ronald van Kempen, eds. 2000. *Globalizing Cities. A New Spatial Order?* Oxford: Blackwell, pp. 1–27.

Marques, E.C., and R. M. Bichir. 2003. "Public Policies, Political Cleavages, and Urban Space: State Infrastructure Policies in São Paolo." *International Journal of Urban and Regional Research* 27 (4): 811–27.

Martin, Carlos. 2008. "Going to Scale with Housing Microfinance: The Role of Commercial Banks." microREPORT 92, USAID, Washington, D.C.

Matrix Development Consultants. 1993. *Nairobi Informal Settlements: An Inventory.* Nairobi: Matrix Development Consultants.

Masahisa, Fujita, Paul Krugman, Anthony J. Venables. 1999. *The Spatial Economy: Cities, Regions and International Trade.* Cambridge, Mass.: MIT Press.

Matsukawa, Tomoko and Odo Habeck. 2007. "Recent Trends in Risk Mitigation Instruments for Infrastructure Finance." *Gridlines* 20: 1–4.

McCarney, P. M., M. Halfani, and A. Rodriquiez. 1995. "Towards an Understanding of Governance: The Emergence of an Idea and Its Implications for Urban Research in Developing Countries." In R. Stren and J. Bell, eds., *Urban Research in the Developing World.* Vol. 4, *Perspectives on the City.* Toronto: Center for Urban and Community Studies, University of Toronto.

McGee, T. G. 1991. "The Emergence of *Desakota* Regions in Asia: Expanding a Hypothesis." In Norton Ginsburg, Bruce Koppel, and Terrence G. McGee, eds., *The Extended Metropolis: Settlement Transition in Asia.* Honolulu: University of Hawaii Press.

McGee, Terry. 1971. *The Urbanization Process in the Third World: Explorations in Search of a Theory.* London: Bell.

McGranahan, Gordon J. 2007. "Urban Transitions and the Spatial Displacement of Environmental Burdens" in Peter J. Marcotullio and Gordon McGranahan. eds., *Scaling Urban Environmental Challenges.* London: Earthscan.

McGranahan, Gordon, Deborah Balk and Bridget Anderson. "The rising tide: Assessing the risks of climate change to human settlements in low-elevation coastal zones." *Environment and Urbanization* 19 (1):17–37, 2007.

McMillen, Daniel P. 2004. "Employment Densities, Spatial Autocorrelation, and Subcenters in Large Metropolitan Areas." *Journal of Regional Science* 44 (2): 225–44.

Mello, de Luiz. 2005. "Fiscal Responsibility Legislation and Fiscal Adjustment: The Case of Brazilian Local Governments." Presentation at the World Bank's practitioners' conference, "Mobilizing Urban Infrastructure Finance in a Responsible Fiscal Framework," Jaipur, India.

Mesarina, Nino and Christy Stickney. 2007. "Getting to Scale in Housing Microfinance: A Study of ACCIÓN Partners in Latin America." *ACCIÓN Insight* (21): 1–15.

Mills, Edwin S. and Richard Price. 1984. "Metropolitan Suburbanization and Central City Problems." *Journal of Urban Economics* 15 (1): 1–17.

Ministry of Education and Sports (MOES). 2007. *Annual Education Sector Review.* Kampala: MOES.

Ministry of Labour and Social Security (China). 2003. *Skills Training in the Informal Sector in China.* http://www.ilo.org/public/english/employment/infeco/download/china.pdf.

Mohan, Dinesh. 2004. *The Road Ahead: Traffic Injuries and Fatalities in India.* New Delhi: Transportation Research and Injury Prevention Programme, Indian Institute of Technology.

Mohan, Rakesh. 1994. *Understanding the Developing Country Metropolis: Lessons from the City Study of Bogotá and Cali, Colombia.* Oxford: Oxford University Press.

———. 2005. "Managing Metros." *Seminar.* Special volume no. 557 on India.

Molders, N. and M. A. Olson. 2004. "Impact of Urban Effects on Precipitation in High Latitudes." *Journal of Hydrometeorology* 5: 409–29.

Montgomery, M. R. and D. Kim. 2006. "Forecasting City Growth Rates in the Developing World: Illustrative Examples." Paper presented at the workshop "Re-thinking the Estimation and Projection of Urban and City Populations," Columbia University, New York.

Moomaw, Ronald L. 1988. "Agglomeration Economies: Localization or Urbanization?" *Urban Studies* 25 (2): 150–61.

Moore, C. and J. Pierre. 1988. "Partnership or Privatization? The Political Economy of Local Economic Restructuring." *Policy and Politics* 16 (3): 169–73.

Moore, J., ed. 1994. "Private Funding for Roads in the United Kingdom." In *New Ways of Managing Infrastructure Provision*. Paris: Organisation for Economic Cooperation and Development.

Moore, Mick. 2004. "Revenues, State Formation, and the Quality of Governance in Developing Countries." *International Political Science Review* 25 (3): 297–319.

———. "How Does Taxation Affect the Quality of Governance?" *Tax Notes International* 47 (1): 79–98.

Moretti, Enrico. 2004. "Human Capital Externalities in Cities." In J. Vernon Henderson and Jacques-Francois Thisse, eds., *Handbook of Regional and Urban Economics*. Vol. 4, *Cities and Geography*. Amsterdam: Elsevier.

Mukwaya, P. 2001. "Urban Sprawl and Challenges of Public Transportation Services Delivery in Kampala, Uganda." Institute of Geography, Norwegian University of Science and Technology, Trondheim.

———. 2005. "Can City Form Be Harnessed to Reduce Transport Energy Use? Solutions to Greenhouse Gas (GHG) Emissions Problems in Kampala City Region." Working paper, START Fellowships, Kampala.

Murray, S. 2006. *Value for Money? Cautionary Lessons about P3s from British Columbia*. Vancouver, B.C.: Canadian Centre for Policy Alternatives.

Muth, Richard F. 1969. *Cities and Housing*. Chicago: University of Chicago Press.

Mwiria, Kilemi, et al. 2007. *Public and Private Universities in Kenya: New Challenges, Issues and Achievements*. Oxford: James Currey Publishers.

National Audit Office (UK). 1998. *The Private Finance Initiative: The First Four Design, Build, Finance and Operate Roads Contracts*. HC 476. 1997/1998. Executive Summary available at http://nao.org.uk/pn/9798476.htm (accessed September 12, 2007).

National Bureau of Statistics of China. 2000. *China Urban Statistical Yearbook 2001*. Beijing: NBSC, Government of China.

National Bureau of Statistics of China. 2005. *China Urban Statistical Yearbook 2006*. Beijing: NBSC, Government of China.

National Council for Public Private Partnerships. 1998. *Partnerships for Progress: Communication and Understanding . . . The Keys to Success*. Washington, D.C.: NCPPP.

National Development Reform Commission. 2005. *National Eleventh Five Year Development Plan*. Beijing: NDRC, Government of China.

National Environment Management Authority (Uganda). 2000–2001. *State of the Environment Report for Uganda*. Kampala.

———. 2002. *State of the Environment Report*. Kampala.

National Institute of Urban Affairs. 2000. *Indo-USAID Financial Institutions Reforms and Expansion (FIRE-D) Project*. New Delhi: National Institute of Urban Affairs.

———. 2003. *Urban Governance Decentralization in India, A Review*. New Delhi: National Institute of Urban Affairs.

———. 2005a. *Impact of Constitution 74th Amendment Act on the Working of Urban Local Bodies*. New Delhi: National Institute of Urban Affairs.

———. 2005b. *Status of Water Supply, Sanitation and Solid Waste Management in Urban Areas*. New Delhi: National Institute of Urban Affairs.

National Research Council. Panel on Urban Population Dynamics. 2003. *Cities*

Transformed: Demographic Change and Its Implications in the Developing World, ed. M. R. Montgomery, R. Stren, B. Cohen and H. E. Reed, Committee on Population, Division of Behavioral and Social Sciences and Education. Washington, D.C: National Academies Press.

Newman, P. and G. Verpraet. 1999. "The Impacts of Partnerships on Urban Governance: Conclusions from Recent European Research." *Regional Studies* 33 (5): 487–91.

Nieto, Begoña Gutiérrez. 2004. "Private funding of microcredit schemes: Much ado about nothing?" *Development in Practice* 15 (3–4): 490–95.

Norstrand, J. 1994. *Kampala Urban Study Final Report. Structure Plan: Part II*. Kampala: Kampala City Council, 245.

Nyakaana, J., H. Sengendo, and S. Lwasa. "Population, Urban Development and the Environment in Uganda: The Case of Kampala City and Its Environs." PRIPODE Workshop on Urban Population, Development and Environment Dynamics. June 11–13, 2007, Nairobi, Kenya. http://www.cicred.org/Eng/Seminars/Details/Seminars/PDE2007/PDEpapers.htm

Obudho, R. A. 1999. "Urban Development, Natural Planning and Management Strategies," in R. A. Obudho, ed., *Urbanization and Management of Urban Centres in the 21st Century*. Nairobi: Kenya Academy of Sciences.

Obudho, R. A. and J. Peter. 2002. "The Role of Urbanization and Suburbanization Processes in Urban Land Management Practice in East Africa." In O. H. Washington and Volker Kreibich, eds., *Urban Land Management in Africa*. Dortmund: Spring Center.

Oke, T. R. 1976. "City Size and the Urban Heat Island." *Atmospheric Environment* 7: 769–79.

Olowu, Dele. 2003. "Local Institutional and Political Structures and Processes: Recent Experience in Africa." *Public Administration and Development* 23 (1): 41–52.

Olsen, E. O. 1987. "The Demand and Supply of Housing Service: A Critical Survey of the Empirical Literature." In E. S. Mills, ed., *Handbook of Regional and Urban Economics*. Vol. 2. New York: Elsevier Science.

O'Mara, M. P. 2004. *Cities of Knowledge: Cold War Science and the Search for the Next Silicon Valley*. Princeton, N.J.: Princeton University Press.O'Neill, Kathleen. 2005. *Decentralizing the State: Elections, Parties, and Local Power in the Andes*. Cambridge: Cambridge University Press.

Osborne, D. and T. Gabler. 1993. *Reinventing Government: How Entrepreneurial Spirit is Transforming the Public Sector*. New York: Plume.

O'Sullivan, D. 2001. "Exploring Spatial Process Dynamics Using Irregular Cellular Automaton Models." *Geographical Analysis* 33 (1): 17.

Pamuk, Ayse and Fernando Cavallieri. 1998. "Alleviating Urban Poverty in a Global City: New Trends in Upgrading Rio-de-Janeiro's Favelas." *Habitat International* 22 (4): 449–62.

Pasternak, Suzana. 2001. "Desenhando Os Espaços Da Pobreza." São Paolo: Paper presented to Faculty of Architecture and Urban Planning, University of São Paulo.

Pasternak, Suzana and Lucia Bogus. 2006. "Como Anda São Paulo Cadernos Metrópole Número Especial." São Paulo: EDUC.

Pasternak Taschner, Suzana. 1978. "Favelas No Município De São Paulo: Resultados De Pesquisa." In Eva Blay, ed., *A luta pelo espaço*. Petrópolis: Vozes.

———. 1984. "A cidade que virou favela." *Espaço e Debates* 12 (4): 37–65.

Pasternak Taschner, Suzana and Maura Veras. 1990. "Evolução E Mudança Das Favelas Paulistanas." *Espaço e Debates* 31: 52–71.

Pataki, D. E., D. R. Bowling, and J. R. Ehleringer. 2003. "Seasonal Cycle of Carbon Dioxide and Its Isotopic Composition in an Urban Atmosphere: Anthropogenic and Biogenic Effects." *Journal of Geophysical Research* 108: 4735.

Peirce, Neal and Johnson, Curtis. 2008. *Century of the City, No Time to Lose*. New York: The Rockefeller Foundation.

People's Daily. 2002. "Experts Say China's Urbanization Rate Tipped to Rise." July 20.

———. 2004. "China's Rural Migrant Workers Total 99 Million." February 9. http://english.people.com.cn/200402/09/eng20040209_134327.shtml.

Perrot, J. and G. Chatelus, eds. 2000. *Financing of Major Infrastructure and Public Service Projects: Public-Private Partnership*. Paris: Presses Pont et Chausées.

Petersen, John. 2006. *Municipal Funding Arrangements: Global Experience and Lessons Learned*. International Workshop on Strengthening Local Infrastructure Financing. Washington, D.C.: World Bank.

Peterson, George. 2000. "Building Local Credit Institutions." Urban and Local Government Background Paper No. 3, World Bank, Washington, D.C.

———. 2002. *Banks or Bonds? Building a Municipal Credit Market*. Washington, D.C.: Urban Institute.

———. 2007. "Land Leasing and Land Sale as an Infrastructure Financing Option." In George Peterson and Patricia Clarke Annez, eds., *Financing Cities*, 284–306. Thousand Oaks, Calif.: Sage.

Peterson, George and Eliza Muzzini. 2005. "Decentralizing Basic Infrastructure Services." In *East Asia Decentralizes: Making Local Governments Work*. Washington, D.C.: International Bank for Reconstruction and Development/World Bank.

Peterson, George E. and Patricia Clarke Annez, eds. 2007. *Financing Cities*. Thousand Oaks, Calif.: Sage.

Ping, Xin-Qiao and Jie Bai. 2005. "Fiscal decentralization and local public good provision in China." China Center for Economic Research No. E2005.004, Beijing: China Center for Economic Research, Peking University.

Platteau, Jean-Philippe. 2006. "Pitfalls of Participatory Development." Paper prepared for the 2007 World Public Sector Report, United Nations Department for Economic and Social Development New York.

Population Reference Bureau. 2009. *2009 World Population Data Sheet*. Washington, DC: Population Reference Bureau. http://www.prb.org/Publications/Datasheets/2009/2009wpds.aspx.

Potere, D. & A. Schneider. 2007. "A Critical Look at Representations of Urban Areas in Global Maps." *GeoJournal* 69: 55–80.

Potsiou, Chryssy, Yerach Doytsher, Paul Kelly, Rafic Khouri, Robin McLaren and Hartmut Müller. 2010. Royal Institute of Chartered Surveyors. "Rapid Urbanization and Mega Cities: The Need for Spatial Information Management." Paper presented at FIG conference, Copenhagen, January.

Potter, Robert B. and Ashok Kumar. 2004. "A Profile of NOIDA: A New Town in the National Capitol Region of India." Geographical Paper No. 174, University of Reading Department of Geography, Reading, UK.

Preteceille, Edmond and Licia Valladares. 2000. "Favela, Favelas: Unidade Ou Diversidade Da Favela Carioca." In Queiroz Ribeiro and Luis Cesar, eds., *O futuro das metrópoles: desigualdade e governabilidade*. Rio de Janeiro: REVAN/FASE.

Prothero, R. Mansell and Murray Chapman, eds. 2010. *Circulation in Third World Countries*. London: Routledge.

Public Citizen. 2003. *Water for All: Campaigning to Keep Water as a Public Trust.* March. http://www.citizen.org/cmep/Water/ (accessed September 12, 2007).

Pugh, C., ed. 1996. *Sustainability, the Environment and Urbanization.* London: Earthscan.

Quigley, John M. 2007. "Regulation and Property Values in the United States: The High Cost of Monoploy." In Gregory K. Ingram and Yu-Hung Hong, eds., *Land Policies and Their Outcomes.* Cambridge, Mass.: Lincoln Institute of Land Policy.

————. 2008. "Just Suppose: Housing Subsidies for Low-Income Renters." In Nicholas P. Retsinas and Eric S. Belsky, eds., *Revisiting Rental Housing,* 300–318. Washington, D.C.: Brookings.

Rabinovitch, Jonas. 1996. "Innovative Land Use and Public Transport Policy: The Case of Curitiba, Brazil." *Land Use Policy* 13 (1): 51–67

Rappaport, Jordan and Jeffrey D. Sachs. 2003. "The United States as a Coastal Nation." *Journal of Economic Growth* 8 (1): 5–46.

Rauch, James. 1993. "Productivity Gains from Geographic Concentration of Human Capital: Evidence from the Cities." *Journal of Urban Economics* 34 (3): 380–400.

Renaud, Bertrand. 1987. "Another Look at Housing Finance in Developing Countries." *Cities* 4 (1): 28–34.

————. 1995. "The Real Estate Economy and the Design of Russian Housing Reforms, Part II." *Urban Studies* 32 (9): 1437–51.

Republic of Kenya. 2005. *Education Statistical Booklet.* Nairobi: Ministry of Education, Science and Technology.

————. n.d. *National Action Plan on Education for All, 2003–2015.* Nairobi: Ministry of Education, Science and Technology.

Ribot, Jesse and Anne Larson, eds. 2005. *Democratic Decentralization through a Natural Resource Lens.* Oxford: Routledge.

Riitters, K. H., Oneill, R. V., Hunsaker, C. T., Wickham, J. D., Yankee, D. H., Timmins, S. P., Jones, K. B. and Jackson, B. L. 1995. "A Factor-Analysis of Landscape Pattern and Structure Metrics." *Landscape Ecology* 10: 23–39.

Roberts, B. and T. Kanaley, eds. 2006. *Urbanization and Sustainability in Asia: Good Practice Approaches in Urban Region Development.* Manila: Asian Development Bank; Washington, D.C.: Cities Alliance.

Rodden, Jonathan A., Gunnar S. Eskeland, and Jennie Litvack, eds. 2003. *Fiscal Decentralization and the Challenge of Hard Budget Constraint.* Cambridge, Mass.: MIT Press.

Rosenau, P. V. 1999. "Introduction: The Strengths and Weakness of Public-private Policy Partnerships." *American Behavioral Scientist* 43 (1): 10–34.

Rosenthal, S. and W. Strange. 2004. "Evidence on the Nature and Sources of Agglomeration Economies." *Handbook of Regional and Urban Economics* 4: 2119–71.

Rugadya, M. A. 2006. "Situation Analysis Report and Action Plan for Kampala City Council: Kagugube 1 and Mbuya 1 Parishes." In *Cities Without Slums Sub-Regional Programme For Eastern And Southern Africa.* Kampala: Kampala City Council.

Sabates, Ricardo and Aaron Schneider. 2003. "Taxation Perspectives: A Democratic Approach to Public Finance in Developing Countries." IDS Seminar Report. Brighton: Institute of Development Studies, University of Sussex.

Sagalyn, L. B. 1990. "Explaining the Improbable: Local Redevelopment in the

Wake of Federal Cutbacks." *Journal of the American Planning Association* 56 (4): 429–41.

———. 2001. *Times Square Roulette: Remaking the City Icon.* Cambridge, Mass.: MIT Press.

———. 2006. "Meshing Public and Private Roles in the Development Process." In M. Miles, G. Berens, and M. A. Weiss, eds., *Real Estate Development: Principles and Process.* Washington, D.C.: Urban Land Institute.

———. 2007. "Public/Private Development: Lessons from History, Research, and Practice." *Journal of the American Planning Association* 73 (1): 7–22.

Sala-i-Martin, Xavier. 1997. "I Just Ran Two Million Regressions." *American Economic Review* 87 (2): 178–83.

———. 2001. "Comment on 'Growth Economics and Reality,' by William A. Brock and Steven N. Durlauf." *World Bank Economic Review* 15 (2): 277–82.

Sassen, Saskia. 2009. "Cities Today: A New Frontier for Major Developments." *Annals of the American Academy of Political and Social Science* 626 (1) (November): 53–71.

Satterthwaite, David. 1997. "Sustainable Cities or Cities That Contribute to Sustainable Development?" *Urban Studies* 4 (10): 1667–91.

Satterthwaite, David. 2003. "The Links Between Poverty and the Environment in Urban Areas of Africa, Asia, and Latin America." *Annals of the American Academy of Political and Social Science* 590 (November): 73–92.

Saxenian, A. 1996. *Regional Advantage: Culture and Competition in Silicon Valley and Route 128.* Cambridge, Mass.: Harvard University Press.

Scanlon, Kathleen, Jens Lunde, and Christine Whitehead. 2008. "Mortgage Product Innovation in Advanced Economies: More Choice, More Risk." *European Journal of Housing Policy* 8 (2): 109–31.

Schneider, A., K. Seto, and D. Webster. 2005a. "Spatial and Temporal Patterns of Urban Land Use Change in Chengdu, China, Using Remote Sensing and Landscape Metrics." *Environment and Planning: Planning and Design* 32 (3): 323–45.

———. 2005b. "Urban Growth in Chengdu, Western China: Application of Remote Sensing to Assess Planning and Policy Outcomes." *Environment and Planning B* 32 (3): 323–45.

Schneider, Aaron. 1999. "Participatory Governance for Poverty Reduction." *Journal of International Development* 11 (4): 521–34.

———. 2003. "Who Gets What from Whom? The Impact of Decentralization on Tax Capacity and Pro-Poor Policy." IDS Discussion Paper, Institute of Development Studies, University of Sussex Brighton, UK.

Schneider, Aaron and Marcelo Baquero. 2006. "Get What You Want, Give What You Can: Embedded Public Finance in Porto Alegre." IDS Working Paper, Institute of Development Studies, University of Sussex, Brighton, UK.

Scott, Allen J., ed. 2001. *Global City-Regions, Trends, Theory and Policy,* Oxford: Oxford University Press.

Scott, Ian. 1981. *Urban and Spatial Development: The Mexican Case.* Baltimore: Johns Hopkins University Press.

Segal, David. 1976. "Are There Returns to Scale to City Size?" *Review of Economics and Statistics* 58 (3): 339–50.

Segal, David, ed. 1979. *The Economics of Neighborhood.* San Diego: Academic Press.

Seto, K. C. and M. Fragkias. 2005. "Quantifying Spatiotemporal Patterns of Urban Land-Use Change in Four Cities of China with Time Series Landscape Metrics." *Landscape Ecology* 20 (7): 871–88.

Seto, K. C. and R. K. Kaufmann. 2003. "Modeling the Drivers of Urban Land Use Change in the Pearl River Delta, China: Integrating Remote Sensing with Socioeconomic Data." *Land Economics* 79 (1): 106–21.

———. 2005. "Using Logit Models to Classify Land Cover and Land-Cover Change from Landsat Thematic Mapper." *International Journal of Remote Sensing* 26 (3): 563–77.

Seto, K. C. C. E. Woodcock, C. Song, X. Huang, J. Lu, and R. K. Kaufmann. 2002. "Monitoring Land-Use Change in the Pearl River Delta Using Landsat TM." *International Journal of Remote Sensing* 23 (10): 1985–2004.

Seto, K. C., R. K. Kaufmann, and C. E. Woodcock. 2000. "Landsat Reveals China's Farmland Reserves, but They're Vanishing Fast." *Nature* 406: 121.

Shah, Anwar. 1994. "The Reform of Intergovernmental Fiscal Relations in Developing and Emerging Market Economies." Policy Research Working Paper No. 23, World Bank, Washington, D.C. .

———. 2004. "Fiscal Decentralization in Developing and Transition Economies: Progress, Problems, and the Promise." Policy Research Working Paper No. 3282, World Bank, Washington, D.C.

———. 2006a. "A Practitioner's Guide to Intergovernmental Fiscal Transfers." Policy Research Working Paper No. 4039, World Bank, Washington, D.C.

———. 2006b. "Corruption and Decentralized Public Governance." Policy Research Work Paper No. 3824, World Bank, Washington, D.C.

Shah, Anwar and Theresa Thompson. 2004. "Implementing Decentralized Local Governance: A Treacherous Road with Potholes, Detours, and Road Closures." Policy Research Working Paper No. 3353, World Bank, Washington, D.C.

Sheppard, J. M., H. Pierce, and A. J. Negri. 2002. "Rainfall Modification by Major Urban Areas: Observations from Spaceborne Rain Radar on the TRMM Satellite." *Journal of Applied Meteorology* 41: 689–701.

Sheppard, Stephen. 2006. "Infill Versus Outspill: The Microstructure of Urban Expansion." Williams College Working Papers in Economics, Williamstown, Mass.

Shiller, Robert J. 2008. *The Subprime Solution: How Today's Global Financial Crisis Happened, and What to Do About It.* Princeton, N.J.: Princeton University Press.

Siemiatycki, M. 2006. "Implications of Private-Public Partnerships on the Development of Urban Public Transit Infrastructure: The Case of Vancouver, Canada." *Journal of Planning Education and Research* 26: 137–51.

Singh, A. 1989. "Digital Change Detection Techniques Using Remotely-Sensed Data." *International Journal of Remote Sensing* 10 (6): 989–1003.

Sit, Victor F. S. and Chun Yang. 1997. "Foreign-Investment-Induced Exo-Urbanisation in the Pearl River Delta, China." *Urban Studies* 34 (4): 647–77.

Sivaramakrishnan, K. C., A. Kundu, and B. N. Singh. 2005. *Handbook of Urbanization in India: An Analysis of Trends and Processes.* Oxford: Oxford University Press.

Small, C. 2005. "The Global Analysis of Urban Reflectance." *International Journal of Remote Sensing* 26 (4): 661–81.

———. 2006. "A Global Analysis of Urban Reflectance." Paper presented at the workshop "Re-thinking the Estimation and Projection of Urban and City Populations." Columbia University, New York.

Smoke, Paul. 1999. "Improving Infrastructure Finance in Developing Countries through Grant-Loan Linkages." *International Journal of Public Administration* 22 (12): 1561–85.

———. 2001a. "Strategic Fiscal Decentralization in Developing Countries: Learning from Recent Innovations." In Shahid Yusuf, Weiping Wu, and Simon Evenett, eds., *Local Dynamics in an Era of Globalization.* Oxford: Oxford University Press.

———. 2001b. *Fiscal Decentralization in Developing Countries: A Review of Current Concepts and Practice.* Geneva: United Nations Research Institute for Social Development.

———. 2002. "Fiscal Decentralization in East and Southern Africa: A Selective Review of Experience and Thoughts on Moving Forward." Paper prepared for International Monetary Fund Conference on Fiscal Decentralization, Washington, D.C.

———. 2003. "Erosion and Reform from the Center in Kenya." In James Wunsch and Dele Olowu, eds., *Local Governance in Africa: The Challenge of Decentralization.* Boulder, Colo.: Lynne Reinner Publishers.

———. 2004. "Expenditure Assignment Under Indonesia's Decentralization: A Review of Progress and Issues for the Future." In James Alm, Jorge Martinez-Vazquez, and Sri Mulyani Indrawati, eds., *Reforming Intergovernmental Fiscal Relations and the Rebuilding of Indonesia.* Cheltenham, UK: Edward Elgar.

———. 2006. "Fiscal Decentralization Policy in Developing Countries: Bridging Theory and Reality." In Yusuf Bangura and George Larbi, eds., *Public Sector Reform in Developing Countries.* London: Palgrave Macmillan.

———. 2007. "Fiscal Decentralization and Intergovernmental Relations in Developing Countries: Navigating a Viable Path to Reform." In G. Shabbir Cheema and Dennis Rondinelli, eds., *Decentralized Governance: Emerging Concepts and Practice.* Washington, D.C.: Brookings Institution.

———. 2008. "Local Revenues Under Fiscal Decentralization in Developing Countries: Linking Policy Reform, Governance and Capacity." In Gregory Ingram and Yu Hung Hong, eds., *Fiscal Decentralization and Land Policies.* Cambridge, Mass.: Lincoln Institute of Land Policy Press.

Smoke, Paul, Eduardo J. Gomez, and George E. Peterson, eds. 2006. *Decentralization in Asia and Latin America: Towards a Comparative Interdisciplinary Perspective.* Chichester, UK: Edward Elgar.

Smoke, Paul and Blane Lewis. 1996. "Fiscal Decentralization in Indonesia: A New Approach to an Old Idea." *World Development* 24 (8): 1281–99.

Snyder, Karrie Ann. 2004. "Routes to the Informal Economy in New York's East Village: Crisis, Economics, and Identity." *Sociological Perspectives* 47 (2): 215–40.

Spence, Michael, Patricia Clarke Annez, and Robert F. Buckley. 2009. *Urbanization and Growth.* Washington, D.C.: International Bank for Reconstruction.

Spiekermann, K. and M. Wegener. 2000. "Freedom from the Tyranny of Zones: Towards New GIS-Based Models." In A. S. Fotheringham and M. Wegener, eds., *Spatial Models and GIS: New Potential and New Models.* London: Taylor & Francis.

Spillman, Brenda C. 2003. "Changes in Elderly Disability Rates and the Implications for Health Care Utilization and Cost." Urban Institute. Washington, D.C.: Prepared for the Office of the Assistant Secretary for Planning and Evaluation, U.S. Department of Health and Human Services, Office of Disability, Aging and Long-Term Care Policy, Contract HHS-100–97–0010. February 3. http://aspe.hhs.gov/daltcp/reports/hcutlcst.htm.

SSB (State Statistics Bureau). 2003. *China Cities Statistics Yearbook.* Beijing: China Statistics Press.

SSB (State Statistics Bureau). 2004. *China Rural Residents Survey Yearbook*. Beijing: China Statistics Press.

Steffensen, Jesper. 2005. "Introduction to the Principles for Design of Intergovernmental Fiscal Transfer Systems: An International Comparison of Allocation Criteria." Working paper.

———. 2006. "Monitoring and Use of Fiscal Indicators on Local Governance." Paper presented at conference on senior policy, workshop on local governance and pro-poor outcomes in Africa, Kigali, Rwanda.

Steffensen, Jesper and Henrik Larsen. 2005. "Conceptual Basis for Performance-based Grant Systems and Selected International Experiences." Katmandu: UNDP.

Stern, Paul C., Thomas Dietz, Vernon W. Ruttan, Robert H. Socolow, and James L. Sweeney, eds. 1997. *Environmentally Significant Consumption*. Washington, D.C.: National Academy Press.

Stern, Nicholas. 2007. *The Economics of Climate Change: The Stern Review*. Cambridge: Cambridge University Press.

Stiglitz, Joseph E., Amartya Sen, and Jean Paul Fitoussi. 2009. *Report by the Commission on the Measurement of Economic Performance and Social Progress*. September. Accessed at http://www.stiglitz-sen-fitoussi.fr/en/index.htm.

Straunch, D., R. Moeckel, M. Wegener, J. Gräfe, H. Mülhans, G. Rindsfüser, and K. J. Beckman. 2003. "Linking Transport and Land Use Planning: The Microscopic Dynamic Simulation Model ILUMASS." Unpuplished paper. http://www.spiekermann-wegener.de/pub/pdf/ILUMASS_Geodynamics.pdf.

Sutton, K. and F. Fahmi 2001. "Cairo's Urban Growth and Strategic Master Plans in the Light of Egypt's 1996 Population 'Ris' Census Results." *Cities* 18 (3): 135–49.

Tam, C. M., and A. W. T. Leung. 1999. "Risk Management of BOT Projects in Southeastern Asian Countries." *Proceedings of Joint CIB Symposium on Profitable Partnering in Construction Procurement*, 499–507. London: E & FN Spon.

Taylor, M. Z. 2004. "Empirical Evidence Against Varieties of Capitalism's Theory of Technological Innovation." *International Organization* 58 (3): 601–31.

Tendler, Judith. 1997. *Good Government in the Tropics*. Baltimore: Johns Hopkins University Press.

Tereshchenko, I. E., and A. E. Filonov. 2001. "Air Temperature Fluctuations in Guadalajara, Mexico, from 1926 to 1994 in Relation to Urban Growth." *International Journal of Climatology* 21: 483–94.

Ter-Minassian, Teresa. ed. 1997. *Fiscal Federalism in Theory and Practice*. Washington, D.C.: International Monetary Fund.

Tewari, Vinod. 2004. "Municipal Reforms for Sustainable Urban Infrastructure Development in India." Paper presented at the United Nations Asia Pacific Leadership Forum, "Sustainable Development for Cities," Hong Kong.

Tewari Vinod, U Raghupathi, and J H Ansari. 2007. "Improving Housing and Basic Services for the Urban Poor in India." In Laquian, Aprodicio A, Vinod Tewari, and Lisa M Hanley, eds., *The Inclusive City, Infrastructure and Public Services for the Urban Poor in Asia*. Washington and Baltimore: Woodrow Wilson Press and Johns Hopkins University Press.

Therkildsen, Ole. 2001. "Understanding Taxation in Poor African Countries: A Critical Review of Selected Perspectives." *Forum for Development Studies* 28.

Thielen, J., W. Wobrock, A. Gadian, P. G. Mestayer, and J. D. Creutin. 2000. "The Possible Influence of Urban Surfaces on Rainfall Development: A Sensitivity Study in 2D in the Mesogammascale." *Atmospheric Research* 54: 15–39.

Thiessen, Ulrich. 2003. "Fiscal Decentralization and Economic Growth in High Income OECD Countries." *Fiscal Studies* 24 (3): 237–74.

Tibaijuka, Anna. 2009. "Sustainable Urbanisation: Some Critical Issues." Tenth Gandhi Memorial Lecture, University of Nairobi. Accessed at http://www.un habitat.org/content.asp?cid = 6991&catid = 14&typeid = 8&subMenuId = 0

Titman, Sheridan. 1985. "Urban Land Prices Under Uncertainty." *American Economic Review* 75: 505–14.

Topa, Giorgio. 2001. "Social Interactions, Local Spillovers and Unemployment." *Review of Economic Studies* 68 (2): 261–95.

Tooley, James. 2005. "Private Schools for the Poor." *Education Next* (Fall): 22–32.

Uganda Bureau of Statistics. 2002. *Uganda Population and Housing Census.* Entebbe: National Census Office.

———. 2003. *A Report on the Uganda Business Register, 2001/2002.* Entebbe: UBOS.

———. 2009. *Statistical Abstract.* Kampala: UBOS.

UBOS and ILRI. 2004. "Where Are the Poor? Mapping Patterns of Well-Being in Uganda: 1992 and 1999." Nairobi: Uganda Bureau of Statistics, International Livestock Research Institute, 86.

Uganda Investment Authority. 2005. *List of Licensed Industries in Kampala.* Kampala: UIA.

United Nations. *World Urbanization Prospects: The 2005 Revision Population Database.* New York: United Nations, Department of Economic and Social Affairs, Population Division, 2005.

United Nations. 2007a. *World Urbanization Prospects: The 2007 Revision Highlights.* New York: United Nations, Department of Economic and Social Affairs, Population Division.

United Nations. 2007b. *World Urbanization Prospects: The 2007 Revision Database.* New York: United Nations, Department of Economic and Social Affairs, Population Division.

UNAIDS. 2009. *AIDS Epidemic Update.* Geneva: UNAIDS.

UN Centre for Human Settlements. 1996. *Global Report on Human Settlements 1996: An Urbanizing World.* Nairobi: UNCHS.

———. 2001. *State of the World's Cities.* Nairobi: UNCHS.

———. 2003. *Rental Housing: An Essential Option for the Urban Poor in Developing Countries.* Nairobi: UNCHS.

———. 2004. *The State of the World's Cities 2004/2005: Globalization and Urban Culture.* London: Earthscan.

UNDP (United Nations Development Program). 1997. *Urban and Rural Areas, 1950–2030 (1996 Revision).* New York: United Nations.

———. 2005. *Investing in Development: A Practical Plan to Achieve the Millennium Development Goals.* London: Earthscan.

UN Department of Economic and Social Affairs. 2003. *World Urbanization Prospects: The 2003 Revision.* New York: UNDESA, Population Division.

———. 2005. *World Urbanization Prospects: The 2005 Revision.* New York: UNDESA, Population Division.

———. 2007. *State of the World's Population: Unleashing the Potential of Urban Growth.* New York: UNDESA, Population Division.

———. 2008. *World Urbanization Prospects: The 2007 Revision.* Nairobi: Department of Economic and Social Affairs, Population Division.

———. 2010. *World Urbanization Prospects: The 2009 Revision.* New York: UNDESA, Population Division.

UNESCO. 2003. *Gender and Education for All: The Leap to Equality.* EFA Global Monitoring Report 2003–04. Paris: UNESCO.

UNFPA. 2007. *State of the World Population 2007: Unleashing the Potential of Urban Growth.* New York: UNFPA.

———. 2005. *Financing Urban Shelter. Global Report on Human Settlements 2005.* London: Earthscan.

———. 2006. "Movement of Community Based Economic Empowerment: A Model for Bogor's Poverty Reduction." http://www.bestpractices.org.

———. 2007. "Urban Info Data Base, on Cluster B (Qualitative) Indicators." http://www.unhabitat/guo.urbaninfo.

———. 2008. *State of the World's Cities: Harmonious Cities.* London: Earthscan.

———. 2009. *Planning the Sustainable City: Global Report on Human Settlements.* London: Earthscan.

———. 2010. *State of the World's Cities: Bridging the Urban Divide.* Nairobi: UN-HABITAT.

UNICEF. 1998. "Adjustment Policies and Programmes to Protect Children and Other Vulnerable Groups in Ghana." In Giovanni Andrea Cornia, Richard Jolly, and Frances Stewart, eds., *Adjustment with a Human Face.* Oxford: Clarendon Press.

United Nations. 1980. *Patterns of Urban and Rural Population Growth.* Number 68 in Population Studies. New York: United Nations, Department of International Economic and Social Affairs.

United Nations World Commission on Environment and Development. *Our Common Future* (The Brundtland Report). London: Oxford University Press, 1987, p. 43.

United Nations World Water Assessment Program. 2005. *Case Study: Kenya National Water Development Report.* Paris: UNESCO.

United States Census Bureau, International Programs Center, World POPClock Projection, http://www.census.gov/ipc/www/popclockworld.html.

United States Environmental Protection Agency. 2000. *Projecting Land-Use Change: A Summary of Models for Assessing the Effects of Community Growth and Change on Land-Use Patterns.* Cincinnati, Ohio: U.S. Environmental Protection Agency, Office of Research and Development.

USFHWA. (U.S. Department of Transportation, Federal Highway Administration). 2007a. *Case Studies of Transportation Public-Private Partnerships around the World.* Final Report Work Order 05–002. Prepared for the Office of Policy and Governmental Affairs by AECOM Consult Team. July 7. http://www.fhwa.dot.gov/ppp/int_ppp_case_studies_final_report_8-7-07.pdf (accessed September 12, 2007).

———. 2007b. *Case Studies of Transportation Public-Private Partnerships in the United States.* Final Report Work Order 05–002. Prepared for the Office of Policy and Governmental Affairs by AECOM Consult Team. July 7. http://www.fhwa.dot.gov/ppp/us_ppp_case_studies_final_report_8-7-07.pdf (accessed September 12, 2007).

Usman, Syaikhu. 2001. "Indonesia's Decentralization Policy: Initial Experiences and Emerging Problems." SMERU Research Institute Working Paper, London, England.

Valladares, Licia. 2000. "Les Favelas dans la mondialization, les favelas en tant que marche." Colloque Mondialization economique et gouvernement des sociétés. L'Amerique Latine, une laboratoire. Paris: GREIP (Research Group Education and Multilingual Interaction), IRD (International Relief and Development) and the Universities of Paris 1 and 13.

Van Boxmeer, B. and E. Van Beckhoven. 2005. "Public-Private Partnership in Urban Regeneration: A Comparison of Dutch and Spanish PPPs." *European Journal of Housing Policy* 5 (1): 1–16.

Van Ham, H. and J. Koppenjan. 2002. "Building Public-Private Partnerships: Assessing and Managing Risks in Port Development." *Public Management Review* 4 (1): 593–616.

Verkuil, P. R. 2007. *Outsourcing Sovereignty: Why Privatization of Government Functions Threatens Democracy and What We Can Do About It.* New York: Cambridge University Press.

Villa, Miguel and Jorje Rodrigues. 1996. "Demographic Trends in Latin America's Metropolises." In A. Gilbert, ed., *The Mega City in Latin America.* Tokyo: United Nations University Press.

Vining, D. R. 1985. "The Growth of Core Urban Regions in Developing Countries." *Population and Development Review* 11 (3): 495–515.

Vuletin, Guillermo. 2008. "Measuring the Informal Economy in Latin America and the Caribbean" IMF Working Paper. WP/08/012.

Waddell, Paul. 2002. "Urbansim: Modeling Urban Development for Land Use, Transportation and Environmental Planning." *Journal of the American Planning Association* 68 (3): 297–314.

Waddell, Paul, Ellen Loy Schroer, and Maren Outwater. 2001. *Assessment of Model Requirements: Final Report to the Puget Sound Regional Council on Land Use and Travel Demand Forecasting Models.* Seattle: Prepared for Puget Sound Regional Council by University of Washington with Cambridge Systematics, Inc.

Walker, Darren. *Innovations for an Urban World: Catalyzing Urban Solutions.* New York: Rockefeller Foundation, 2007.

Wang, Jixian and Jiang Xu. 2002. "An Unplanned Commercial District in a Fast-Growing City: A Case Study of Shenzhen, China." *Journal of Retailing and Consumer Services* 9 (6): 317–26.

Wang, Liang-huew and Anthony Gar-on Yeh, eds. 1993. *Keep a City Moving: Urban Transport Management in Hong Kong.* Tokyo: Asian Productivity Organization.

Wang, Yaping. 2004. *Urban Poverty, Housing and Social Change in China.* Oxon: Routledge.

Warnock, Veronica Cacdac, and Francis E. Warnock. 2008. "Markets and Housing Finance." *Journal of Housing Economics* 17 (3): 239–51.

Webster, Chris and Fulong Wu. 2001. "Coase, Spatial Pricing and Self-Organising Cities." *Urban Studies* 38 (11): 2037–54.

Webster, D and S. Guhathakurta. 2008. "Urban Land Allocation System, China." Arizona State University, authors' unpublished research.

Webster, D. R., and L. Muller. 2004. "Global Peri-Urbanization." In S. Sassen and P. Marcotullio, eds., *Encyclopedia of Life Support Systems (EOLSS).* Paris: UNESCO.

Webster, D., J. Cai, L. Muller, F. Zhang, T. Qu. 2006. "Qingdao Reclaims Its Past: Revitalization of the Historic Core." Commissioned Report prepared for the Municipal Government of Qingdao and the Shui On Corporation, Shanghai, November.

Webster, Douglas. 2000. *Financing City Building: The Bangkok Case.* Urban Dynamics of East Asia Series, Asia/Pacific Research Center. Stanford: Stanford University.

Webster, Douglas, Jianming Cai, and Chuthatip Maneepong. 2006. *Metropolitan Governance in China, Priorities for Action in the Context of Chinese Urban Dynamics and International Experience.* Washington, D.C.: World Bank.

Wegener, M. 1994. "Operational Urban Models: State of the Art." *Journal of the American Planning Association* 60 (1): 17–29.

———. 1998a. "The IRPUD Model: Overview." http://irpud.raumplanung.uni-dortmund.de/irpud/pro/mod_e.htm.

———. 1998b. "Applied Models of Urban Land Use, Transport and Environment: State-Of-The-Art and Future Developments." In L. Lundqvist, L.-G. Mattsson, and T. J. Kim, eds., *Network Infrastructure and the Urban Environment: Recent Advances in Land Use/Transportation Modeling.* Berlin: Springer Verlag.

Whyte, Martin King and William L. Parish. 1983. *Urban Life in Contemporary China.* Chicago: University of Chicago Press.

Williams, Colin C. 2001. "Beyond the Commodity Economy: The Persistence of Informal Economic Activity in Rural England Beyond the Commodity Economy" *Geografiska Annaler. Series B, Human Geography*, 83 (4): 221–33.

Williamson, Jeffrey G. 1988. "Migration and Urbanization." In Hollis Chenery and T. N. Srinavasan, eds., *Handbook of Development Economics.* Vol. 1. Amsterdam: Elsevier.

Williamson, John. 2004. "A Short History of the Washington Consensus." Paper presented at Conference entitled "From the Washington Consensus Towards a New Global Governance." Barcelona, September 24.

Wilson, William Julius. 1987. *The Truly Disadvantaged: The Inner City, the Underclass and Public Policy.* Chicago: University of Chicago Press.

Woolcock, Michael J. V. 1999. "Learning from Failures in Microfinance: What Unsuccessful Cases Tell Us About How Group-Based Programs Work." *American Journal of Economics and Sociology* 58 (1): 17–42.

Woodcock, C. E. and A. H. Strahler. 1987. "The Factor of Scale in Remote Sensing." *Remote Sensing of Environment* 21: 311–32.

World Bank. 1997. *Revitalizing Universities in Africa: Strategy and Guidelines.* Washington, D.C.: World Bank.

———. 2004. "Fiscal Decentralization Indicators." Decentralization and Sub-National Regional Economics Thematic Group, Washington, D.C.

———. 2005. *East Asia Decentralizes: Making Local Government Work.* Washington, D.C.: World Bank.

———. 2009. *Reshaping Economic Geography: World Development Report.* Washington, D.C.: World Bank.

———. 2010. World Bank Development Indicators. Accessed July 26 at http://data.worldbank.org/indicator.

World Health Organization. 2005. *Make Every Mother and Child Count: The World Health Report.* Geneva: World Health Organization.

———. 2006. *Working Together for Health: The World Health Report.* Geneva: World Health Organization.

World Resources Institute. 1997. *The Urban Environment.* Washington, D.C.: World Resources Institute, the United Nations Environment Program, the United Nations Development Program, and the World Bank.

Wu, Fulong. 1996. "Changes in the Structure of Public Housing Provision in Urban China." *Urban Studies* 33 (9): 1601–27.

Wu, Fulong and Anthony Gar-on Yeh. 1999. "Urban Spatial Structure in a Transitional Economy: The Case of Guangzhou." *Journal of the American Planning Association* 65 (4): 377–94.

Wu, Fulong, Jiang Xu, and Anthony Gar-on Yeh. 2007. *Post-Reform Urban Development in China: State, Market and Space.* London: Routledge.

Wu, Weiping and Shahid Yusuf. 2004. "Shanghai: Remaking China's Future

Global City." In J. Gugler, ed., *World Cities Beyond the West.* Cambridge: Cambridge University Press.

Wunsch, James and Dele Olowu, eds. 2003. *Local Governance in Africa: The Challenge of Decentralization.* Boulder, Colo.: Lynne Reinner Publishers.

Xu, Jiang and Anthony Gar-on Yeh. 2005. "City Repositioning and Competitiveness Building in Regional Development: New Development Strategies of Guangzhou, China." *International Journal of Urban and Regional Research* 29 (2): 283–308.

Xu, Xueqiang. 1984a. "Characteristics of Urbanization in China: Changes and Causes of Urban Population Growth and Distribution." *Asian Geographer* 3 (1): 15–29.

———. 1984b. "Trends and Changes of the Urban System in China." *Third World Planning Review* 6 (1): 47–60.

Xu, Xueqiang and Si-ming Li. 1990. "China's Open Door Policy and Urbanization in the Pearl River Delta." *International Journal Urban and Regional Studies* 14 (1): 49–69.

Yangcheng Evening News. 2007. "Total Population of Shenzhen Exceeds 12 Million, Reaching the City's Capacity." May 11. http://news.163.com/07/0511/17/3E7SHIKF00011229.html.

Yeh, Anthony Gar-on 1985. "Physical Planning of Shenzhen Special Economic Zone." In K.Y. Wong and D. K. Y. Chu, eds., *Modernization in China: The Case of the Shenzhen Special Economic Zone.* Hong Kong: Oxford University Press, 108–30.

Yeh, Anthony Gar-on, and Xia Li. 1999. "Economic Development and Agricultural Land Loss in the Pearl River Delta, China." *Habitat International* 23 (3): 373–390.

Yeh, Anthony Gar-on and Fulong Wu. 1996. "The New Land Development Process and Urban Development in Chinese Cities." *International Journal of Urban and Regional Research* 20 (2): 330–53.

Yeh, Anthony Gar-on, Jiang Xu, and Hong Yi. 2006. "Fourth Wave of Urbanization in China." *City Planning Review* 30 (Supplement): 13–18 (in Chinese).

Yeh, Anthony Gar-on and Xueqiang Xu. 1984. "Provincial Variation of Urbanization and Urban Primacy in China." *Annals of Regional Science* 23 (3): 1–20.

———. 1990a. "Changes in City Size and Regional Distribution 1953–86." In Yin-Wang Kwok, William Parish, and Anthony Gar-on Yeh, eds., *Chinese Urban Reform: What Model Now?* New York: M. E. Sharpe.

———. 1990b. "New Cities in City System Development in China 1953–86." *Asian Geographer* 9 (1): 11–38.

Yusuf, S. and N. Nabeshima. 2006. *Postindustrial East Asian Cities: Innovation for Growth.* Stanford: Stanford University Press.

Zacharias, J. 2003. "The Search for Sustainable Transport in a Developing City: The Case of Tianjin." *IDPR* 25 (3): 283–98.

Zhang, J. Y., W. Dong, L. Wu, J. Wei, P. Chen, and D.Y. Lee. 2005. "Impact of Land Use Changes on Surface Warming in China." *Advances in Atmospheric Sciences* 22 (3): 343–48.

Zhenshan, Y. "Land Use, 1997, Tianjin Municipality, China." Author's analysis using Google Earth imagery for the World Bank.

Zhou L., R. E. Dickinson, Y. Tian, J. Fang, Q. Li, R. K. Kaufmann, C. J. Tucker, and R. B. Myneni. 2004. "Evidence for a Significant Urbanization Effect on Climate in China." *Proceedings of the National Academy of Sciences of the United States of America* 101 (26): 9540–44.

Zhou, M. and J. R. Logan. 1996. "Market Transition and the Commodification of Housing in Urban China." *International Journal of Urban and Regional Research* 20: 400–421.

Zhu, Haibin. 2006. "The Structure of Housing Finance Markets and House Prices in Asia." *BIS Quarterly Review.* 55–69.

Zou, Deci. 1992. "Impacts of Urban Land Lease System on Urban Development." Unpublished paper, China Academy of Urban Planning and Design (in Chinese).

Contributors

Deborah Balk is Professor, School of Public Affairs, Baruch College/ CUNY and Associate Director, CUNY Institute for Demographic Research, City University of New York. She is currently a member of the International Union for the Scientific Study of Population Working Group on Urbanisation and recently completed service on two National Research Council panels.

Nefise Bazoglu, former Chief, Monitoring Systems, UN-HABITAT, is Senior Fellow, Global Urban Development, and an urban development consultant based in Turkey. She received a Ph.D. in demography from Hacettepe Institute of Population Studies (HIPS) and did her postdoctoral studies in the School of Architecture and Urban Planning at the University of California, Los Angeles.

Eugenie L. Birch is Lawrence C. Nussdorf Professor of Urban Research and Education, Department of City and Regional Planning, School of Design, and co-founding Director, Penn Institute for Urban Research, University of Pennsylvania. Her most recent publications are *Urban and Regional Planning Reader* (2009) and *Practice of Local Planning Contemporary Practices and Principles* (2009) (co-edited with Gary Hack, Paul Sedway, and Mitchell Silver).

Joel E. Cohen is the Abby Rockefeller Mauzé Professor of Populations, a joint appointment with Columbia University and the Rockefeller University where he heads the Laboratory on Populations. His publications include *How Many People Can the Earth Support?* (1995), winner of the Olivia Schieffelin Nordberg Award "for excellence in writing in the population sciences," and *Educating All Children: A Global Agenda* (2006).

Kyung-Hwan Kim is a professor of economics at Sogang University, a fellow at the Weimer Graduate School of Advanced Studies in Real Estate and Urban Land Economics, a research fellow at the Centre for Asset Securitisation in Asia of the Sim Kee Boon Institute for Financial

Economics at Singapore Management University, and a scholar at the Institute for Urban Research of the University of Pennsylvania. He has taught at Syracuse University and worked at UN-HABITAT, and he holds a Ph.D. in economics from Princeton University.

John D. Landis is Crossways Professor and Chair, Department of City and Regional Planning, School of Design, University of Pennsylvania. He is currently engaged in a National Science Foundation–funded project that uses GIS to model, forecast, and develop alternative spatial scenarios of U.S. population and employment patterns, and that explores their impact on travel demand through 2050.

Shuaib Lwasa is Project Director, Urban Harvest, Senior Research Scientist, International Potato Center, and Lecturer in Geography, Makerere University. His most recent publications include *Urban Land Markets, Housing Development and Spatial Planning in Sub-Saharan Africa: A Case of Uganda* (2010).

Faith Macharia is National Director, Forum for African Women Educationalists (FAWE), Kenya Chapter, a pan-African organization dedicated to furthering the education of girls and women.

Stephen Malpezzi is the Lorin and Marjorie Thiefenthaler Professor, and Academic Director, James A. Graaskamp Center for Real Estate, School of Business, University of Wisconsin–Madison. As past president of the American Real Estate and Urban Economics Association, Malpezzi has advised on urban policies in Ghana, India, Indonesia, Korea, Mexico, Sweden, the United Kingdom, and the United States.

Mark R. Montgomery is Professor of Economics, State University of New York at Stony Brook and Senior Associate, Poverty, Gender, and Youth Program, Population Council. He has served as co-chair of the U.S. National Academy of Sciences Panel on Urban Population Dynamics and was lead editor of its 2003 report, *Cities Transformed: Demographic Change and Its Implications in the Developing World.*

Wilber K. Ottichilo is Member of Parliament, National Assembly, Republic of Kenya, and former Director General, Regional Centre for Mapping of Resources for Development (RCMRD), Nairobi, Kenya. In these capacities, he has served as the patron and consultant for *the Emuhaya (Kenya) Strategic Development Plan* (2008).

Suzana Pasternak, who holds a bachelor of architecture, an M.Sc. degree, and a Ph.D. in demography and public health, is Professor, Faculty of Architecture and Planning, University of São Paulo, where she teaches courses on urbanization, demography, and housing.

Lynne B. Sagalyn is the Earle W. Kazis and Benjamin Schore Professor of Real Estate, Columbia Business School, and Director, Paul Milstein Center for Real Estate. She is the author of *Times Square Roulette: Remaking the City Icon* (2001), *Cases in Real Estate Finance and Investment Strategy* (1999), and *Downtown, Inc.: How America Rebuilds Cities* (1989) (with Bernard Frieden).

Karen C. Seto is Associate Professor of the Urban Environment, School of Forestry and Environmental Studies, Yale University. Her research focuses land-use dynamics, forecasting urban growth, and examining the environmental consequences of land-use and urban expansion. She is co-chair, Urbanization and Global Environmental Change Project, International Human Dimensions Programme of Global Environmental Change (IHDP).

Stephen Sheppard is the Robert F. White Class of 1952 Professor of Economics at Williams College and Director of the Williams College Center for Creative Community Development (C^3D). He is co-author of *Dynamics of Global Urban Expansion* (2005) with Shlomo Angel and Daniel Civco.

Paul Smoke is Professor of Public Finance and Planning, Director, International Programs and Director of Doctoral Programs, Robert F. Wagner Graduate School of Public Service, New York University. His most recent publication is *Making Decentralization Work: Democracy, Development, and Security* (2010) with Ed Connerly and Kent Eaton.

Vinod Tewari is Chair Professor for National Capital Region Studies, TERI University, New Delhi. In recent years, he has worked closely with the government of India in developing an urban sector reform agenda and evaluating its implementation in some of the states and urban local bodies. His most recent book (co-edited with Aprodicio A. Laguian and Lisa M. Hanley) is *The Inclusive City: Infrastructure and Public Services for the Urban Poor in Asia* (2007).

Susan M. Wachter is Richard Worley Professor of Financial Management, Director, Wharton Geo-Spatial Lab, The Wharton School, and co-founding Director, Penn Institute for Urban Research, University of Pennsylvania. Her most recent publications include *Neighborhood and Life Chances: How Place Matters in Modern America* (2010) (co-edited with Harriet Newburger and Eugenie L. Birch) and *Growing Greener Cities: Urban Sustainability in the Twenty-First Century* (2008) (co-edited with Eugenie L. Birch).

Douglas Webster is Professor, School of Sustainability and Chair, Global Studies Program, School of Politics and Global Studies, Arizona State University, He is also Advisor, the East Asia Urban Division, World Bank. His most recent publication is *Metropolitan Governance in China: Priorities for Action in the Context of Chinese Urban Dynamics and International Experience* (2005) with J. Cai and C. Maneepong.

Anthony G. O. Yeh is Chair Professor and Head, Department of Urban Planning and Design and Director, Centre of Urban Studies and Urban Planning, University of Hong Kong. His most recent publications include *Governance and Planning of Mega-City Regions: An International Comparative Perspective* (2010) (co-edited with Jiang Xu).

Index

Page numbers in italics represent tables and figures in the text.

Acknowledgments

In July 2007, in Italy, the Rockefeller Foundation hosted the month-long Global Urban Summit at its Bellagio Center. The foundation invited the Penn Institute for Urban Research (IUR) to develop a week-long session, "Toward a Twenty-First-Century Urban Agenda," to explore emerging research issues related to twenty-first-century urbanization. The conferees collectively surveyed the state of current knowledge, highlighted gaps, and aimed to set an agenda to guide future research. This volume, *Global Urbanization*, is representative of the attendees' efforts to wrestle with these issues.

This volume would not have been possible without the support and guidance of the Rockefeller Foundation, especially the vision and commitment of its president, Judith Rodin, and its vice president, Darren Walker, which brought this entire enterprise to life. Additional thanks go to Anna Brown, a Rockefeller Foundation senior research associate who was an active participant in the entire planning process. Thanks also to Pilar Palacia, managing director, Bellagio Center, whose gracious and accommodating presence made for a productive conference. Neal Pierce, Curtis Johnson, and Farley Peters of the Citistates Group were accurate and insightful recorders, as their volume, *Century of the City: No Time to Lose* (2008), a summary of the entire conference, testifies.

Penn IUR is indebted to the continued support of its advisory board, the President's Office, and the Provost's Office at the University of Pennsylvania. Their commitment to developing and disseminating the forms of knowledge necessary for sound urban policy makes publications like this possible. The editors of the volume are grateful to the authors, whose rigor and intelligence this book showcases; to Penn IUR staff Kendra Goldbas, Maritza Mercado, Amy Montgomery, Daniel Stout, and Julie Thompson for their hard work and dedication throughout this project; and to Peter Agree and the leadership and staff at Penn Press, particularly development editor Audra Wolfe, whose thoroughness and care helped guide and shape the volume.

The views expressed in this volume are those of the individual authors and not those of our sponsor organizations.